T0397624

Complicit Participation

Complicit Participation

The Liberal Audience for Theater of Racial Justice

CARRIE J. PRESTON

OXFORD
UNIVERSITY PRESS

OXFORD
UNIVERSITY PRESS

Oxford University Press is a department of the University of Oxford.
It furthers the University's objective of excellence in research, scholarship,
and education by publishing worldwide. Oxford is a registered trade mark of
Oxford University Press in the UK and in certain other countries.

Published in the United States of America by Oxford University Press
198 Madison Avenue, New York, NY 10016, United States of America.

© Oxford University Press 2024

All rights reserved. No part of this publication may be reproduced, stored in a retrieval system,
or transmitted, in any form or by any means, without the prior permission in writing of Oxford
University Press, or as expressly permitted by law, by license or under terms agreed with the
appropriate reprographics rights organization. Inquiries concerning reproduction outside the scope
of the above should be sent to the Rights Department, Oxford University Press, at the address above.

You must not circulate this work in any other form and
you must impose this same condition on any acquirer

Library of Congress Cataloging-in-Publication Data
Names: Preston, Carrie J., author.
Title: Complicit participation / Carrie J. Preston.
Description: New York : Oxford University Press, 2024. |
Includes bibliographical references and index.
Identifiers: LCCN 2024009552 | ISBN 9780197693407 (paperback) |
ISBN 9780197693391 (hardback) | ISBN 9780197693414 (epub)
Subjects: LCSH: Theater and society—United States. | Theater audiences—United States. |
Anti-racism—United States. | Racial justice—United States. | Allyship—United States.
Classification: LCC PN2049 .P745 2024 | DDC 792.0973—dc23/eng/20240315
LC record available at https://lccn.loc.gov/2024009552

DOI: 10.1093/9780197693438.001.0001

Contents

Acknowledgments

Theatrical productions are group projects, and so are monographs (the name notwithstanding). I have many collaborators, mentors, and friends to thank. This book was shaped by more than a decade of teaching, lecturing, and learning at the Mellon School of Theater and Performance Research at Harvard, ably directed by Martin Puchner. I first presented material that became the core of this book at seminars and lectures there, and Martin has influenced my career and thinking in countless ways. I am also grateful to other faculty and staff at the Mellon School, especially Rebecca Kastleman, Andrew Sofer, Harvey Young, Shamell Bell, Elizabeth Phillips, and Sheryl Chen. I first connected with Lizzy Cooper Davis and Robert Duffley through the Mellon School, and they offered invaluable interviews about their work on *Notes from the Field* and *The White Card*.

I presented early drafts of Chapter 1 at the New York-New Jersey Modernism Seminar at Rutgers University, the institution of my graduate training and the starting point for all my scholarly work. I received invaluable feedback from the NYNJ Modernism Seminar participants and organizers, Rebecca Walkowitz and Sarah Cole, who have both been professional mentors as well. The lessons of my professors at Rutgers, especially Elin Diamond and Carolyn Williams, are referenced explicitly and implicitly throughout these pages.

My editor at Oxford University Press, Hannah Doyle, patiently guided this project, believed in its potential, and served as a crucial advocate. Essays drawn from this project appeared in *The Drama Review* ("Hissing, Bidding, and Lynching: Participation in Branden Jacobs-Jenkins's *An Octoroon* and the Melodramatics of American Racism"), *Modern Drama* ("Blackfaced at *The Blacks*: Audience Participation in Jean Genet's Lessons on Race and Gender"), and *Modernist Drama as Contemporary Theatre* ("*Shuffle Along* [1921] and the Challenges of Black Modernist Performance on the Contemporary Stage"); my editors for those essays, Richard Schechner, R. Darren Gobert, and Claire Warden, provided incredible suggestions that influenced my entire book.

Among my fantastic colleagues at Boston University (BU), I am particularly grateful for the mentorship of the late John Paul Riquelme, who sadly passed away as I was finishing this project. Christopher Robinson, a remarkable American Sign Language interpreter in the theater, spoke with me about interpreting *The White Card* and became the true hero of my book. The team at Kilachand Honors College has supported me throughout the writing of this book and worked with me to imagine a community that would enable the full and radical participation of all members. I would especially like to thank Associate Directors Joanna Davidson and Linda Doerrer for their "big dreams sessions" and so much more and Kilachand Postdoctoral Associates Danielle Drees, Amanda Fish, Travis Franks, Trent Masiki, Sravanthi Kollu, Can Evren, Clinton Williamson, Talia Shalev, John Bell, Justin Mann, and Stephanie Ahrens. The influence of the BU Faculty Gender & Sexuality Studies Group is evident throughout the book, and I am particularly grateful to Catherine Connell, J. Keith Vincent, Erin Murphy, Susanne Sreedhar, Takeo Rivera, and Karen Warkentin for invaluable discussions. My colleagues at the BU Center on Forced Displacement, especially Muhammad Zaman, Marina Lazetic, and Chrissy Luccini, have contributed to every journey I have taken since 2019. I would also like to thank BU colleagues Robert Chodat, Bonnie Costello, Sanjay Krishnan, Maurice Lee, Elizabeth Loizeaux, Anita Patterson, John T. Matthews, Leland Monk, Ianna Owen, Takeo Rivera, Virginia Sapiro, and Crystal Williams.

My students at Kilachand Honors College have taught me more than I teach them, and I offer them my gratitude. My former student and now colleague, Nicole Rizzo, has helped me think and write better and supported the last phases of writing and manuscript preparation as an editorial assistant. Another former student, Ramona Ostrowski, offered remarkable insights about her work as a dramaturg for *An Octoroon*.

The families of professors have to endure their book projects (not to mention their tendency to lecture), and my own family is amazingly patient. Derek sat beside me through every play I discuss in this book, and his responses always improve my thinking and writing. This book is for my children—Callan, Tristan, and Beckett—with great love and hope that they will participate fully and radically in changing the world.

PART I
THE TROUBLING PLEASURES OF COMPLICIT PARTICIPATION

Introduction

Complicit participation is the prevailing framework through which many white liberals who identify as allies participate in theatrical and other institutional efforts grouped under the rubric of *diversity, equity, and inclusion initiatives*. I identify the emotional power and political limitations of well-intentioned performances of allyship, particularly my own complicit participation in theater of racial justice and other efforts that seek to depict and challenge institutionalized anti-Black racism and white supremacy.[1] As writer and participant, my own white, cisgender persona is all too present in these pages rather than ceding the stage to voices less regularly amplified than mine. While my voice could never overshadow the brilliance of the Black, Indigenous, and People of Color (BIPOC) authors and performers I discuss here, it may fail to engage BIPOC readers, who hardly need yet another book that centers whiteness. I acknowledge this drawback, but I insist on the need for allies themselves to affirm that allyship can be a shallow, even defensive performance that supports rather than dismantles white supremacy.[2] As someone who has made every ally's claim I address (I even moderated the panel of white allies at my institution's "day of collective engagement" following the murder of George Floyd),[3] I need to ask difficult questions about my own complicit participation—and then inspire challenging conversations beyond this book, ones that must ultimately decenter (my own) whiteness.

"You need to write it up," said my professor in graduate school after coincidentally attending the same matinee where I became the audience participant for a controversial 2003 revival of Jean Genet's *The Blacks: A Clown Show* (1959). I felt urgency and kindness in his voice, but I did not know what to write back then about an actor asking me to tap dance, call him "master," and confess my racism, all of which I willingly performed, before he blackened my face with shoe polish. That was when other audience members demanded that he stop the scene. As I detail in the first chapter of this book, my blackface appearance onstage was the most intense theatrical experience I have known in a lifetime of theatergoing. It took me nearly two decades "to write it up," but that experience ultimately launched this book

Complicit Participation. Carrie J. Preston, Oxford University Press. © Oxford University Press 2024.
DOI: 10.1093/9780197693438.003.0001

on audience participation. I argue that participation in theater of racial justice can lead to intense emotional experiences and insight, but it can also assure theatergoers that they are an enlightened audience of allies and good people fighting white supremacy and patriarchy—while enjoying the comfort of their seats in the auditorium and giving up none of their privilege. *Complicit Participation* describes the emotional release of audience participation (much like the ancient concept of catharsis) that can relieve the pressures of white guilt and produce a complacency that does not lead to other necessary forms of activism and engagement. Audiences often applaud *ourselves* for supporting transgressive theater or BIPOC artists with the price of our (often quite expensive) tickets, just as we celebrate ourselves for particularly articulate statements of allyship, while continuing to participate in the benefits of white supremacy. This book identifies the limits and inadequacy of many different performances of solidarity and allyship, with the goal of making liberal audiences less comfortable with their *complicit participation* and more interested in reimagining communities that invite the *full and radical participation* of all.

I.1. Defining Immersion, Realism, and Theater of Racial Justice

Immersion: Following my impromptu blackface performance at *The Blacks* in 2003, there has been a surge in productions of what is called immersive, interactive, or site-specific theater. I first participated in the immersive craze in 2009 with Punchdrunk's *Sleep No More* (2003) when it was co-produced by American Repertory Theatre (A.R.T.) at the spooky Old Lincoln School, an abandoned school in Brookline, Massachusetts. Inspired by Shakespeare's *Macbeth* and the films of Alfred Hitchcock, *Sleep No More* asked the audience to wander through scenes staged in various ornate rooms wearing distinctive white masks. The British Company Punchdrunk claims to have "pioneered a form of theatre in which roaming audiences experience epic storytelling inside sensory theatrical worlds," a form that "disrupts the theatrical norm."[4] *Disruptions* can quickly become *norms*; by 2011, a company calling itself Emursive had formed to bring *Sleep No More* to New York City's McKittrick Hotel (actually a converted Chelsea warehouse). The McKittrick *Sleep No More* continues as "more tourist attraction than dramatic revelation"[5] with ancillary features including a band, speakeasy, and even a family-friendly brunch in the rooftop restaurant, Gallow Green. The restaurant felt theatrical with lush greenery, old books to peruse, and drawers we could open to find photographs and other interesting objects. By emailing the "Private Events Director" for McKittrick, I could book the set of *Sleep No More* and other spaces in the complex, or even the show itself, for private events and corporate parties.[6] Just how pioneering, disruptive, or subversive is this business of immersive theater when it is offered for bookings by corporate parties?

In 2016, the New York theatergoer could attend ten site-specific, participatory plays.[7] Immersive performance has been slower to recover from the COVID-19 pandemic, but audience enthusiasm seems little dampened, and theaters and other cultural venues have begun offering and aggressively advertising participatory opportunities in 2022. *Time Out New York* currently lists "the best immersive theater in New York right now" with "the king of them all, the long-running *Sleep No More*" still in first position.[8] Yelp ranks a list of "the best interactive theater in Boston, Massachusetts."[9] Among Yelp's "Best Tourist Attractions in Boston, Massachusetts,"[10] garnering 4.5 out of 5 stars, is "Boston Tea Party Ships & Museum," where you get to "Storm Aboard the 18th Century sailing vessels" and "take part in the 'Destruction of the Tea'! Throw tea into the very same body of water where the Boston Tea Party took place over 240 years ago."[11] I attended *Immersive Frida Kahlo* in June of 2022 at Boston's Lighthouse Artspace at the Castle, and I realized while departing the massive space where Kahlo's paintings had been projected, that *Immersive Van Gogh* was up next at the venue.[12] Vincent Van Gogh's distinctive sunflowers were printed on handbags, scarves, and t-shirts, alongside replicas of Frida Kahlo's colorful dresses—all available for purchase in the gift shop through which each audience member must pass to reach the exit. Immersive performances are desirable and highly marketable, a feature of rampant consumerism and the experience economy just as much as experimental theater.

The commodification of "theater business" is nothing new, and neither is audience participation.[13] Audiences have *always* been immersed in theatrical environments, and different communities and social classes have been more or less invited to join and find comfort in these spaces. The source material for *Sleep No More*, William Shakespeare's *Macbeth*, invited participation from Elizabethan audiences with scenes designed to appeal to the so-called commoners who would voice their approval and disapproval—sometimes with the volume of rotten food hurled at the stage. Even when sitting still in a darkened auditorium, we watch a performance within an interactive, multisensory environment.

Realism: The notion that theater audiences are not also participants (regardless of their level of activity in the auditorium) is a relatively recent idea, partially shaped by the realistic dramas and well-made plays that emerged in the second half of the nineteenth century. Playwrights such as Henrik Ibsen (1828–1906), often credited with the invention of realism in the theater, departed from (but also drew on) the wildly spectacular and popular melodramas of the nineteenth century that encouraged enthusiastic participation, as I explore in the second part of the book. Theatrical realism can be considered a unique episode in the history of theater, an exception to the general expectation of audience participation. Realistic actors trained (often in variations of the *method* promoted by Konstantin Stanislavski [1863–1938]) to never "break character" slowly built realist theater's imaginary "fourth wall" separating the stage from the auditorium. The wall was built to limit the audience participation that had been common in earlier forms of theater; it was built, like all metaphorical walls, so that it could be broken as an exciting theatrical effect or impactful confrontation with an audience expecting to watch anonymously from behind that "fourth wall" . . . which is famously broken at the conclusion of Jackie Sibblies Drury's Pulitzer Prize–winning play *Fairview* (2019): "*(Keisha steps through the fourth wall. It's as simple as that.)*"[14] *Fairview* initially presents itself as realistic "*comedic family drama*"[15] with Beverly busily preparing a dinner party in honor of her mother's birthday, aided by her doting husband Dayton, and distracted by her challenging sister Jasmine and daughter Keisha, who "*just does Everything that Teenagers Do.*"[16] Act II replays Act I, but this time the family onstage is drowned out by four voices commenting on that *family drama*. They are playing the voices of audience members. We soon realize that they are white spectators, and presumably because the family onstage is Black, they spend most of the Act discussing a question first proposed by Jimbo: "No, but if you could choose to be a different race, what race would you be?"[17] They voice common stereotypes, riven with racism, exoticism, and sexual desire and often articulated with the language used by liberal allies, such as "race is a construct,"[18] "inherited poverty,"[19] and "the rich profit from racism."[20] Mack uses the gender-inclusive term "Latinx" to describe his highly eroticized choice of races: "[You know, like I have this hot, muggy river of uncut sensuality flowing deep down in my soul. So.] Yeah, if I could choose to be a different race, I'd want to be Latinx."[21]

Finally, in *Fairview*'s Act III, the four commentators come onstage to play out their racist and gendered fantasies. Enacting their stereotypes of Black family life, they turn the birthday party into the revelations of Keisha's non-existent teen pregnancy and the imminent foreclosure on the family home because of Dayton's gambling and/or Beverly and/or Jasmine's drug addiction (all are falsely accused; it does not matter which person committed the fictional infraction). They accuse Dayton of developing syphilis after multiple extramarital affairs and turn dinner into a food fight. Keisha steps out of the fight and through the "fourth wall" to ask the audience to stop watching, "to not be here. Or to let me not be here?"[22] She invites the white people to come up onstage and be the spectacle, "To switch for a little while?"[23] That left few audience members in the auditorium, as reviews regularly point out that "the majority of New York theatergoers . . . [are] white."[24] Or as a review/dialogue in *The New York Times* puts it, "My audience seemed to be about ninety percent white. / Mine as well."[25] Keisha's final monologue on fairness and spectatorship, delivered directly to the few BIPOC audience members, presents a vision of everyone as "A Person Trying" who looks out at the "mountains of effort they had built with their trying" and "took in that view."[26] Then they took in the "view" of what others had done with their "trying" to make lives and found it "to be fair."[27] This is the desired, impossible *Fairview* of the play.

Fairview's final scene of audience participation, as white theatergoers processed to the stage, echoed the four fictional audience members who entered and warped the scene in Act III—and who might initially have been misidentified as annoyingly talkative theatergoers (by the increasingly few audience members not already in the know about this feature of the Pulitzer Prize–winning play). Neither theatrical maneuver alone would get *Fairview* categorized as immersive theater because audience members are not moving through an interactive space throughout the play (although as I noted earlier, all theater viewing is multisensory immersion). Acts II and III demand "the typical theatre audience [who] is white and well-heeled" to consider how they are seeing and judging plays that have "a Black cast perform for an audience of white patrons."[28] Sibblies Drury claims that the origins of *Fairview* were in conversations with Director Sara Benson about "why surveillance affects people of color in a deeper way" and how theater can replicate the power dynamics of surveillance.[29] The play questions the idea that audiences are doing racial justice work when they attend theater depicting Black lives. Instead, theatergoers might be telling their own racist narrative, a story that barely "tethers" (in the language of the play's stage directions) to the actions onstage.[30] Sibblies Drury, in giving voice and stage to the racist inner monologues of white audience members, would make it more difficult for any audience member to ignore their inner monologue or the power of their (white) surveillance, but as Sibblies Drury pointed out, "people are having very different reactions in the same audience . . . the reactions don't fall distinctly along color lines. It's not that all people of color are moved by it, and all white people are uncomfortable and angered. It seems much more complex than that."[31] The complexity of audience participation is a major focus of this book.

Fairview treats realism as a theatrical style to be exploded, but realism can also be deployed, with benefits and risks that I describe most fully in Chapter 6, with a focus on Anna Deavere Smith's *Notes from the Field* (2015). In Smith's work, the link to a racist reality and the exposure of the impact of white supremacy on actual living human beings is crucial to advancing the goals of her Pipeline Project battling the school-to-prison pipeline experienced by BIPOC youth. Yet audience participation (outside of the talkback or other audience engagement event) always breaks the so-called *fourth wall* of realist plays, and the productions I consider in this book use the seeming power of that rupture to support the goals of racial justice.

Theater of Racial Justice: Theater of racial justice works to dismantle structural racism and undermine white supremacy. "Theater of racial justice" works better than "Black or BIPOC theater" for my purposes in this book because a play text might offer arguments against racism without being by and about BIPOC people.[32] This is the case with Jean Genet's *The Blacks*, written by a white man about constructions of race under empire, rather than about the experiences of actual people. Of course, productions can only authentically seek to present a politics of racial justice if they also feature BIPOC creators, performers, and/or production staff, which was the case with The Classical Theatre of Harlem's production of *The Blacks* in which I participated. But BIPOC artists have not been central to every production of *The Blacks*, as I detail in the first chapter. For that reason, this book focuses on plays and productions rather than texts and on political positions or arguments rather than representations of BIPOC experiences. Theater of racial justice *seeks* to advance goals and politics, but this intention does not guarantee an impact or effect. Art, and especially live performance, is unpredictable in its impact. The relationship between artists' intent and impact on audiences or readers has long been recognized as fraught; see famous warnings against "the intentional fallacy," or the assumption that literary critics can identify the author's intention and use it to analyze the success of a literary work.[33]

This book argues that theater of racial justice does not always produce antiracist responses from liberal audiences and that white supremacy can coopt productions and other efforts seeking to advance equity and inclusion—producing complicit participation. Theater that advances arguments for racial justice can also include racist elements and traditions in addition to having racist impacts. For example, theater seeking to amplify the impact of audience participation often draws from historical genres and styles—including melodrama, minstrelsy, and Jazz-Age Broadway—partially because they promoted different forms of audience participation and therefore disrupt assumptions. Melodramatic conventions and techniques are particularly prominent in theater of racial justice, as I discuss with reference to Branden Jacobs-Jenkins's *An Octoroon* (2014) based on Dion Boucicault's nineteenth-century melodrama *The Octoroon* (1859) (Part II) and George C. Wolf's *Shuffle Along, or the Making of the Musical Sensation of 1921 and All That Followed* in 2016 (Part III). History itself becomes an incitement to audience participation in Lin-Manuel Miranda's 2015 smash hit *Hamilton* (also Part III). Historical documentation of racial conflict through photographs and other media are the focus of Deavere Smith's *Notes from the Field* and Claudia Rankine's *The White Card* (2016) (see Part IV). Both explore the power of the aggressively realist forms of photography and video to document racial violence as well the dangerous pleasures and seductions of consuming that violence.

I attended each of these plays and participated in them (which is unfortunately not the case with *Fairview* and many other important plays). At *An Octoroon*, I uttered a melodramatic hiss and watched fellow theatergoers seated next to me bid at a staged slave auction. On Broadway, I sang along with the audience and stood up to clap when the star (Audra McDonald or Lin Manuel-Miranda) took the stage. I entered the Ham4Ham lottery to get cheap tickets to Lin Manuel-Miranda's *Hamilton* and commented on the Ham4Ham street performances on YouTube. I participated in talkbacks and audience "buzz groups"—small group post-show discussions—at *Notes from the Field* and *The White Card*. During many productions, I watched (and judged) as other theatergoers left mid-show or slipped out before the talkback. In the autoethnographic sections of this book, I am the complicit participant in theater of racial justice.

I.2. The Complicit Anecdote and Other Notes of Method

While my fifteen minutes onstage at the revival of Jean Genet's *The Blacks* in 2003 inspired the journey of this book, studying Genet's early recognition of the limits of white allyship helped me develop my methods, particularly the tool I call the *complicit anecdote*. In *Prisoner of Love* (posthumously published in 1986), Genet self-consciously used discontinuous anecdotes to tell the story of his engagement with the American Black Panthers in 1970 and Palestinian freedom fighters from late 1970 to 1972. Partially because of the success of *The Blacks* in New York after its premiere in 1961, two Black Panthers met with Genet in Paris on February 25, 1970, and asked him to help in their struggle.[34] Genet refers to the incident as "another example of how my life and my books have been misinterpreted. The Panthers saw me as a rebel."[35] Calling *Prisoner of Love* a "mirror-memoir for me alone," Genet repeatedly describes misgivings about his anecdotal style: "But it's not enough just to write down a few anecdotes."[36] He invites suspicion about the voice he selected for the book, writing, "And like all the other voices my own is faked, and while the reader may guess as much, he can never know what tricks it employs."[37] One of his tricks-of-voice is to turn himself into a child who was "adopted" by the Black Panthers, even referring to one of them, David Hilliard, as a parent figure: "They'd found a waif, but instead of being a child the waif was an old man, and a White. Childish as I was about everything, I was so ignorant of American politics [. . .]."[38] He registers both his ignorance and his privilege as a white European through an anecdote about the pretrial hearing for Bobby Seale in New Haven, where police attempted to separate Genet from the Panthers and seat him in the "places reserved for whites."[39] He managed to sit near his friends, but when police objected to David Hilliard's communications with a lawyer and an altercation ensued, Genet claimed, "I was right beside them. I can't say I said the same things but I did the same thing they did. And what kept me out of prison is simple—it was because I was white, because I am white. For Blacks there is no escape."[40] Genet acknowledged his *white privilege* before it became a clichéd, albeit necessary, act of allies.

Beyond allowing him to avoid harassment and prison, whiteness afforded Genet psychic privileges, as he details in another anecdote. When the Panthers were preparing to leave for a series of events at Stony Brook University, David Hilliard told Genet he would not go because "There are still too many trees." Genet realized,

So for a Black only thirty years old, a tree still didn't mean what it did to a White—a riot of green, with birds and nests and carvings of hearts and names intertwined. Instead it meant a gibbet. . . . And what separates us from Blacks today is not so much the colour of our skin or the type of our hair as the phantom-ridden psyche we never see except when a Black lets fall some joking and to us cryptic phrase.[41]

Genet could enjoy the tree without the trauma of lynching and the "phantom-ridden psyche" it produces.[42] He also enjoyed the protection of his hosts: "The Panthers protected me so well I was never afraid in America—except for them."[43] Genet's presence among the Panthers may have been a burden, although he continued to correspond with them and write in support long after he left the United States. Genet participated in the Black Panther movement while being complicit in white supremacy, and he wrote about his complicit participation through colorful anecdotes—even as he encouraged readers to be suspicious.

Genet's writing about race feels outdated and racist, including his use of terms like "a Black," his erotic attention to the Panthers' physical beauty, and his suggestion that "what separates us [Whites] from Blacks today is not so much the colour of our skin."[44] Yet other moments predict current strategies of white allyship and detail the pitfalls. He shares an anecdote about the inadequacy of the liberal American professors who often sponsored his public appearances with the Panthers. At Stony Brook, the professors were "very relaxed" and gave a "warm welcome," but according to Genet:

They couldn't understand why I didn't try to distance myself from the Panthers by using a less violent rhetoric. I ought to have calmed down the Panther leaders, made them understand. . . . Both cheques were made out to me, though they were given to the Panthers. I was touched by this fine distinction. A blonde lady professor said:

"We have to protest against the shooting down of the Panthers—at the rate things are going it'll be our own sons next."[45]

Liberal professors and students in the audience wanted to support racial justice on their terms and in the ways that made them comfortable, with checks made out to a white man but no "violent rhetoric."[46] The "blonde lady professor" suggests that a primary reason to worry about police violence is that they might murder her "own [white] sons next," as if the racist "shooting down of the Panthers" is not worthy of protest.[47]

As another version of a "blonde lady professor" who has done nothing as useful or courageous as working for the Black Panthers, I find Genet instructive as a model for how to self-consciously use personal anecdotes to analyze and critique the systems of which I am a part, that is, to use complicit anecdotes.[48] I focus on what happened to *me* and the audience members or theater artists I interview as a form of audience participation I can analyze, but also one that is severely limited and certainly not transparent or universal and one that unfortunately keeps white privilege central to the story. I am also a complicit participant and firm believer in the necessity of the "inclusion and diversity case," which I will continue to reference with the acronym that was chosen by the management consulting firm McKinsey & Company for a series of influential reports on the "business case for inclusion and diversity (I&D)."[49] I choose I&D to reference a case and a culture, in part, because it is not the acronym typically used in the academic and theatrical institutions I inhabit. But I also participate in all of the limitations of I&D work, as I served on my institution's first university-wide Diversity and Inclusion task force, interviewed candidates for our first Chief Diversity Officer, and then served on the advisory board for the new Office of Diversity and Inclusion. I started a diversity initiative, which I termed an *invitation to full and radical participation* in the honors college I directed, and I have written both "diversity statements" and those public performances of solidarity that university leaders send out, and sometimes retract, after particularly horrific or publicized instances of racial violence. I intend my engagement with audience participation and I&D work to be an internal critique, offered with compassion, vigilance, and hope for moving beyond comfortable allyship and toward full and radical participation in racial justice.

I.3. The Complicit Audience

Many artists and critics beyond Genet, including many Black writers, have asked one of the central questions of *Complicit Participation*: Can art, particularly participatory, interactive, or immersive theater, impact audiences to such an extent that they will work to challenge white supremacy, patriarchy, heteronormativity, and class privilege—particularly if these injustices benefit them personally? The Black writer Richard Wright described his alarm after he read reviews of his short story collection *Uncle Tom's Children* (1938): "I found that I had written a book which even bankers' daughters could read and weep over and feel good about."[50] These weeping readers (depicted as feminine) are not moved to change themselves, give up their racial and class privilege, or work for justice in the real world; they closed the book *feeling good*, partially because they had their good cry about the suffering depicted in the stories. Wright set out to create a character, Bigger, for his next novel, *Native Son* (1940), that would invoke horror among all readers rather than invite a good cry. And yet James Baldwin argued (with reference to Harriet Beecher Stowe's 1852 antislavery novel *Uncle Tom's Cabin*) that Bigger functions as "Uncle Tom's descendant, flesh of his flesh" by being "exactly opposite" so that he produces "a continuation, a complement of that monstrous legend it was written to destroy."[51] The exchange points to a challenge, even a double-bind, for writers seeking to produce antiracist art: How can they refuse to invoke sentimental and unproductive tears about racism and at the same time avoid horrifying audiences in ways that might reinforce their investments in white supremacy or their fascination with consuming Black suffering? Can a production of live theater effectively limit the range of audience responses to prevent a good cry, racist horror, or pleasure in Black suffering?

Theater artists and critics have detailed some of the necessary conditions for encouraging specific audience responses. Harry Elam, the Black scholar and director (and current college president), wrote in 1986 about audience participation in "socially-committed American theaters" of the 1960s and 1970s, particularly those of LeRoi Jones, who later changed his name to Amiri Baraka, and Luis Valdez.[52] Jones/Baraka "called his actors the 'Spirit House Movers' to emphasize that they were activists before they were artists . . . the actors and the audience shared a common culture, struggle, and purpose to end their oppression."[53] Valdez's performers in the company El Teatro Campesino were all striking farmworkers, so that spectators and performers "were swept up in a unique bond of spiritual and emotional commitment to the righteousness and eventual success of their cause."[54] Valdez claimed, "Audience participation is no cute production trick with us; it is a pre-established, preassumed privilege."[55]

Valdez emphasizes the context and situation of audience participation, which amplifies the importance of context and situation in all theater. When audience participation within a specific community ("with us") is a "preassumed privilege" and feature of the ritual, it is not a "cute," insulting, or shocking "trick."[56] But as Brandi Wilkins Catanese teaches her students, "the liberatory, utopic possibilities of performance do not find a home in every theatre with every play."[57] For her, understanding the "site-specificity" of theater is the only way "to ensure that our efforts to assert African American drama's longstanding contributions to important conversations about privilege and power are as meaningful for and legible to our audiences as we want them to be."[58] The site-specific questions Catanese encourages us to ask are also about audience specificity, the "racial demographics" and visibility of BIPOC members of the relevant institutions and surrounding communities, and what both say "about the construction of race in our immediate environment."[59]

When Catanese turns from the challenges of teaching African American theater to understanding the impact of professional productions on audiences, similar questions emerge. Take, for example, her reading of Suzan-Lori Parks's famous play *Venus* (1996), about the exhibition of nineteenth-century South African woman, Saartjie Baartman, as a sexual curiosity. Baartman was taken from her home, possibly under false pretenses, and displayed throughout Europe as the "Hottentot Venus" in costumes emphasizing her large buttocks. The "show" continued after she died in 1815 because her brain and sexual organs were preserved and displayed at a museum in Paris until 1974. Catanese argues that the play is an attempt to reimagine "the historical subjectivity of a black female performer" by interrogating the construction of race in both the historical record and in performance.[60] For other critics, most notably Jean Young, Parks ignores historical evidence to present Baartman in "a fictitious melodrama" in which she plays a free individual who was "complicit in her own horrific exploitation."[61] Although both Catanese and Harvey Young disagree (in different ways) with Jean Young's scathing critique of *Venus*, they do recognize that her concerns are "legitimate."[62] Harvey Young asks readers:

> Imagine witnessing the performance of *Venus* at the Yale Repertory Theatre. Not only does Yale, as does every collegiate institution of a similar age and prestige, have a fraught relationship with the history of black captivity and the equal treatment of women, but there is also the fact that sitting alongside you are predominantly white patrons who paid significant sums of money to witness the event. This is the bite in Young's critique. She sees the replay of history in the very presence of white audiences paying to see a black female body appear on stage as an exhibit of otherness.[63]

A similar "bite" is present in the plays I discuss in *Complicit Participation*.[64] Like Yale Repertory Theatre, the relatively well-resourced theaters of Boston and New York mostly serve and depend on the patronage of white, liberal audiences. The productions I discuss had the resources to run talkbacks and print detailed programs and audience engagement toolkits, as well as hire dramaturgs, American Sign Language interpreters, and other theater professionals. The theaters have initiated I&D efforts and partially addressed calls, such as that of "We See You, White American Theater," to face white supremacy in US culture and in their own theatrical institutions.[65] They mount productions that call attention to their audiences' privilege, often employing BIPOC artists and offering challenging audience engagement programs. It is crucial to note that, aside from the Classical Theatre of Harlem, which produced Genet's *The Blacks* in 2003, these theaters are not the important and overlooked theaters that serve primarily Black audiences. The ongoing segregation of theaters is one factor in why the institutions of Boston and New York mount remarkable productions that do not change the world.

While researching this book, I had the privilege of sitting in comfortable seats in the relatively thriving theaters of Boston and New York City, cloaked, like most other audience members, in my racial comfort. I also sat with the misogyny and gendered discomfort I have learned to negotiate, as well as my recognition that other genders face far more bigotry. I observed and spoke with other, mostly white, theatergoers who were typically aware of the antiracist content and interactive, participatory strategies of the plays. That is, they chose to go to those productions with some degree of willingness or even enthusiasm for having their racial and gendered comfort disturbed through audience participation. They also managed to afford the ticket prices, dress codes, and transportation costs to get to the theaters. They identified as liberal-to-progressive art enthusiasts and allies who appreciate what they considered *transgressive theater*. I also conducted semi-structured interviews with theater professionals, including dramaturgs, directors, actors, trainers, and interpreters. I examined some of the data that the productions collected through audience surveys, and I considered production notes and stage manager reports. I spent time with production archives and audience engagement toolkits, when available, and became a participant-observer in talkbacks, smaller buzz group discussions, and other para-theatrical events. I would not consider my method to be "audience research" in that I did not systematically conduct and code surveys and interviews. I used many different strategies to answer my questions, including autoethnographic strategies, but the bulk of the chapters that follow are rooted in performance and textual analysis.

Audience participation, even participation in which racial and gendered discomfort is paramount, does not necessarily lead to a refusal to participate in white supremacy. In fact, participation can grease the wheels of white supremacy. My own racial discomfort could produce the feeling that I had done some penance for my privilege or even something more worthwhile. Audience participation sometimes relieved me from a sense of duty to participate in other forms of activism and left me more satisfied with my complicit participation. For this reason, it is important to carefully consider what theater can do, as well as where it fails to accomplish antiracist goals. Ultimately, the various forms of audience participation I explore in this book, both its joys and risks, discomforts and/or pleasures, can teach us about engagement in the I&D efforts of other systems and institutions, including how to resist the worst forms of complicit participation.

I.4. Preview of the Book

Complicit Participation is organized into four parts, each highlighting a form of participation, and seven chapters, each focused on a specific play, with reference to a recent production that I attended. Part I focuses on "The Pleasures of Complicit Participation," largely by analyzing the impact of an actor blackening my face with shoe polish during a production-specific moment of audience participation at the Classical Theatre of Harlem's 2003 revival of Jean Genet's *The Blacks*. As the moment escalated into a fifteen-minute disruption, audience members and other performers protested the scene, partially because of the explosive intersection of racial and gendered politics. While many in the audience, along with me, were uncomfortable in that interlude, Genet cast all spectators in a painful role at *The Blacks*. From the 1950s—when *The Blacks* was the longest-running off-Broadway play of the decade—to the twenty-first century, the play has proven to be surprisingly, alarmingly (at least for performers like Maya Angelou) *popular* with audiences. By placing my own participation in this longer production history, I argue that *The Blacks* exposes one of the reasons we fail to end white supremacy: the pleasure of participating in our own racially inspired humiliation—a pleasure that has drawn audiences to *The Blacks* for over half a century and one that attends many of the plays I analyze in *Complicit Participation*.

Part II, "The Melodramatics of American Racism," turns back to explore the forms of audience participation common in nineteenth-century melodramas and why contemporary writers like Branden Jacobs-Jenkins adapted that genre to engage audiences in the history of American racism: the institution of slavery was intertwined with the popularity of melodramas in the United States, and the American media continues to use melodramatic conventions at it represents racial conflict. Chapter 2, "Dion Boucicault's *The Octoroon* and the Loudly Immersed Audiences of Nineteenth-Century Melodramas," examines an 1859 melodrama that managed to appeal to audiences on both sides of the impassioned debates about the abolition of slavery and on both sides of the Atlantic Ocean. British audiences demanded and ostensibly wrote (with Boucicault's *help,* or so he said) a revised ending, one that used the new technology of photography to solve a racist murder without killing off the titular *octoroon*. This episode of audience participation exceeded the robust involvement standard in melodramas and provides some insight into what engaged audiences can accomplish—as well as how easily their fervent efforts can be used to sell tickets that profit the white producers.

Chapter 3 argues that the melodramatic forms of audience participation required of audiences at Branden Jacobs-Jenkins's 2016 adaptation, *An Octoroon*, broke down the audience's resistance so that theatergoers would comply with subsequent, more egregious demands, including flashing their bid cards at a slave auction and calling for a lynching. *An Octoroon* worked to disrupt our self-congratulatory belief that we are the perfect antiracist audience by guiding us toward uncomfortable racialized forms of participation. Chapter 3, "Hissing, Bidding, and Lynching at Branden Jacobs-Jenkins's *An Octoroon*" also demonstrates that an adamantly antiracist play with robust audience participation risks bolstering both race- and gender-based prejudices in some audience members. The same might be said of the photographic and now cell phone technologies that capture and circulate images of the murders of Black civilians by police officers. While these recordings have the potential to bring powerful perpetrators to justice, social media users also view and post these recordings as part of their complicit participation in a genre that relieves their own guilt and fulfills racist desires to see Black suffering.

Part III, "Dueling on Broadway," considers the forms of participation in contemporary Broadway musicals, particularly those that invoke an

American past with racial and gendered oppressions some audiences would rather forget. As 2016's contentious presidential race played out on different stages, Broadway witnessed an uneven duel for Tony Awards between two plays that claimed to diversify Broadway with new takes on American history, George C. Wolfe's *Shuffle Along, or the Making of the Musical Sensation of 1921 and All That Followed*, and Lin-Manuel Miranda's *Hamilton*. Chapter 4, "*Shuffle Along* . . . the Campaign Trail" argues that Wolfe abandoned *Shuffle Along*'s original book about a corrupt mayoral election in an all-Black town because it was rife with the racial stereotypes, minstrelsy, and blackface performance that allowed it to become one of the most successful and important Broadway shows of the early twentieth century. Wolfe was certainly hoping to avoid the pain and offense that might attend restaging racist performance, but the book needed to be revisited during a heated presidential race that led to the election of real estate mogul and media personality Donald J. Trump. Ultimately, the sanitized version of *Shuffle Along, or The Making Of* . . . implied that contemporary audiences cannot handle the history of racial performance but also fostered the untruth that this history no longer impacts US politics.

Chapter 5, "*Hamilton* ParticiNation in Diversity and Its Discontents," argues that *Hamilton*'s ongoing popularity across the massive divides of American politics identifies some of the limits of the current inclusion and diversity platform. In November 2016, shortly after the *Hamilton* album had gone double platinum (in 2020 it was certified seven times platinum) and "Hamilteens" who knew every word of the musical were using it to narrate their lives, the *Hamilton* cast addressed Vice President-elect Mike Pence after the performance he attended with his family. They expressed their concerns about a racist, anti-immigrant administration, thereby provoking the Twitter-ire of President-elect Trump, whose victory speech touted (much to my surprise) the very same values of inclusion and diversity that the cast was defending. *Hamilton* has been celebrated for bringing diversity to Broadway and to the story of America's founding, but it also clarified the inadequacy of contemporary I&D efforts. The smash hit's most radical gestures were made not on the Broadway stage but in the "Ham4Ham" street performances, which present an image of the full and radical participation that, I argue, can extend diversity and equity efforts beyond their current reach.

The final part of *Complicit Participation* considers that most conventional of audience engagement programs, the theatrical talkback, and American Repertory Theatre's attempts to reframe the talkback as the "Act II" of two

Boston productions, Anna Deavere Smith's *Notes from the Field: Doing Time in Education* (2016) and Claudia Rankine's *The White Card* (2018). Smith's unique form of documentary theater sought not just to *document* the school-to-prison pipeline that pushes BIPOC students out of school and into the carceral system but also to get audiences engaged in stopping the pipeline. Smith attempted to turn theater into a public forum that confronts difficult cultural challenges and demands audiences participate in social change. The second act of *Notes from the Field* consisted of the audience's participation in group discussions led by "Pipeline Facilitators" before they all returned to the theater for a "Coda." My group's facilitator was a teacher in the Boston Public Schools who was leaving education for medical school. Audiences were not supposed to leave their discussions or the play itself without knowing how to "Get Involved," the title of a page in the program that listed organizations working in the areas of education, criminal justice, youth support, or racial and economic justice. Do facilitated discussions break down the barriers that prevent concern from turning into action? This chapter considers facilitated discussions among the range of participatory activities discussed in *Complicit Participation* and evaluates their unpredictable impact, including the possibility that they will fortify audience beliefs that they are being good *activists* by being good *participants* in the talkback.

Many of the same facilitators and facilitator trainers who worked "Act II" of *Notes from the Field* returned for the A.R.T./Arts Emerson co-production of Claudia Rankine's *The White Card* in 2018—despite the psychic burden of Act II, particularly on BIPOC facilitators. In Chapter 7, "Playing *The White Card* with Claudia Rankine," I argue that Rankine's play demonstrates the hypocrisies of those well-intentioned white allies who attempt to undermine white supremacy by, in this case, supporting Black artists who feed white desires for images of Black death. But the play cannot entirely avoid the dramatized circulation of Black death it so provocatively critiques, even as its Act II generated additional suffering. If *The White Card* participates to some degree in that system, it also reminds me that my own book, *Complicit Participation*, traffics in the very same images of Black suffering, as well as diversity and inclusion efforts, and the problematic centering of whiteness—my own whiteness and that of the mostly white, liberal audiences I analyze. My years of working on *Complicit Participation* have taught me most about my own complicity and contradictions so that I can, to borrow the words of the American Sign Language interpreter for *The White Card*, Christopher Robinson, "Be cognizant of the hypocrisy and call it me."[66]

I.5. Terms of Participation

The English language is changing, and the preferred terms for discussing race, gender, and sexuality have evolved quickly. In the years since 2016 when I began drafting this book, scholars have pointed out that the term "slave" reduces human beings to a subhuman category without agency, power, and complexity beyond this classification. Experts in African diaspora and American slavery studies have recommended replacing "slave" and "slavery" with the language of "enslaved people," "enslavers," and "enslavement." Some have recommended BIPOC, a term standing for "Black, Indigenous, and People of Color," as a replacement for "People of Color" because it foregrounds the specific, institutionalized discrimination experienced by Black and Indigenous people in the United States. Yet one poll indicated that BIPOC is viewed less favorably by those the term is meant to include than by those who identify as "white Democrats."[67] Some publications, including *The New York Times*, a main source for theater reviews in this book, settled on the convention of capitalizing "Black" when referencing people and cultures of African origin in the summer of 2020.[68] Writers representing different political commitments are suspicious, as evidenced by the *New York Times*'s own opinion writer John McWhorter, who refuses to capitalize "Black." He does recommend the use of "enslaved person" rather than "slave," but writes that "the capitalization issue is about style and usage, rather than replacing one word with another, and the written rather than the spoken word."[69]

I am writing a book rather than speaking, and I capitalize "Black," but I fully recognize that this decision may mark my book as being of a particular moment and for a particular demographic of readers. I also acknowledge that language choices can perform allyship in ways that might feel shallow. I thought hard about my terms and tried to select those that will be understandable to most readers of my book but also meaningful, words that said what I am seeking to convey. I changed many terms as I revised the manuscript. For example, when I drafted Part II in 2016, I regularly wrote "slave" and "slavery." While revising, I changed "slave" to "enslaved people" when I was referencing historical people, but I maintained "slave" when the term was selected by a playwright to designate fictional characters. This decision is intended to honor and accurately quote the work of art. Some terms, like "sex slave," were exactly what I needed to say, as I intended to invoke the horrors of the widespread practice of raping enslaved people. Similarly, I believe "slavery" accurately designates the historical institution in the United States in a way that "enslavement" does not—or does not yet. As for "BIPOC," I use this new umbrella term in association with the work of diversity, equity, and inclusion, a sector in which the term is commonly used. Otherwise, I attempt to refer to more specific racial categories, as relevant. I recognize that not all my "terms of participation" will please all readers, and I apologize for any real discomfort as I seek to participate in an evolving and imperfect language.

1

Blackfaced at *The Blacks*

Complicit Participation in Jean Genet's Lessons on Race

1.1. Anecdote

On March 18, 2003, during my last semester of graduate school course-work, I took my mother to a matinee performance of the Classical Theatre of Harlem (CTH)'s revival of Jean Genet's *The Blacks: A Clown Show* (1958). I had studied the play in a graduate seminar, and I thought that my blonde mother, who had grown up on a dairy farm in northeastern Michigan and married the farmer next door, would benefit from the lessons about race her daughter had encountered while studying the play. As with so many lessons in graduate school, I could not have articulated what I learned, but I believed it to be important.

Actors greeted us at the Harlem theater, bowed, gave us white flowers, and escorted us to hard white seats next to a ramp protruding from the stage into the auditorium; they called out: "White folk coming! Make way . . ." The curtain opened on a group of eight Black actors dancing a parodic minuet around a catafalque covered with flowers. Five additional actors wearing white masks that did not completely cover their faces played the "Court": a Queen, her Valet, the Judge, a Missionary, and the Governor, all represent-atives and enforcers of Empire. Archibald, a rowdy master of ceremonies, announced, "You are white. And spectators. This evening we shall perform for you . . ."[1] If we were shocked to have our race identified, he reassured us a few moments later:

> But, in order that you may remain comfortably settled in your seats in the presence of the drama that is already unfolding here, in order that you be assured that there is no danger of such a drama's worming its way into your precious lives, we shall even have the decency—a decency learned from you—to make communication impossible.[2]

Complicit Participation. Carrie J. Preston, Oxford University Press. © Oxford University Press 2024. DOI: 10.1093/9780197693438.003.0002

Having read the script, I knew some plot details that many in the audience could hardly be expected to gather from a play that "make[s] communication impossible." The performances on stage, particularly the ceremonial reenactment of the rape and murder of a white woman whose body supposedly rests on the catafalque, serve as mere diversions. There is no body, and the "ceremony" is intended to distract the audience from an offstage drama in which a black revolutionary leader is tried as a traitor to the movement and executed. No amount of study could have prepared me for how that production refused to allow me to "remain comfortably settled" in my seat.

About a third of the way into the play, Village (played by Obie Award–winner J. Kyle Manzay) demanded that I climb up on the ramp that extended from the stage into the audience (see Figure 1.1). He told me to call him "massa," but I failed to mimic his intonation, and his mockery of my "masterrr" delighted the audience. He ordered me to dance and demonstrated a stereotypical minstrel-show shuffle step. I dusted off the time-step variations from two decades of tap dance lessons, surprised at how easily my legs recalled the patterns. The audience applauded hesitantly. Village asked me if I would clutch my purse if a Black man were following me down the street;

Figure 1.1 The Classical Theatre of Harlem presents *The Blacks: A Clown Show* by Jean Genet; directed by Christopher McElroen. Photo by Richard Termine, 2003. Actor/photo IDs: (from left to right) Yusef Miller, Jammie Patton, Ty Jones (foreground, center), Oberon K. A. Adyepong, and Erin Cherry.

I nodded. He asked me if I were racist like President Bush; I said yes. He took the shoeshine box that had been sitting at the foot of the catafalque and told me to shine his shoes. I had never shined my own or anyone else's shoes, so I did a terrible job. But I tried. I participated, complicitly.

On my knees, quite close to the audience, I could feel their discomfort. One woman called out, "Let her go." Another chimed in, "That's enough." I noted that both were Black, and then felt shame for noticing. Village yelled back, "You think she's had enough? Do you care about this white girl?" He grabbed the shoe polish I was holding, dug in with his fingers, and smeared it over my face. The blackening seemed to take a long time, and I remember raising my face to him from my kneeling position, maybe to speed up the process. When he told me to get off the stage, his bravado seemed a little flat.

Back in my seat with my blackened face, I saw that my mother was in tears. One of the women actors brought me a wet cloth, but it just smeared the shoe polish around. Throughout the play, I felt that my blackened face was still very much in the lights spilling over from the stage. When the play was over, audience members gathered around me, asking if I was okay, including the professor who had introduced me to the play and just happened to be in the audience. That was when I started to cry, feeling shame, confusion— not anger, but a prevalent sense that it was wrong for me, "this white girl" as Village put it, to be the recipient of sympathy and comfort after *The Blacks*—a feeling of *wrongness* that remains as I start this book with an anecdote about myself that centers my own whiteness. Several of the women actors came to me from backstage with makeup remover; my professor and mother tried to clean my face. Then Manzay came to the group and said, "That never happened before." "What never happened?" my professor challenged. "I don't know. It just escalated," he replied, appearing genuinely confused and uncomfortable. None of our attempts to remove the shoe polish worked. The train trip home with my shoe-polished face felt interminable.

It took me nearly fifteen years before I could write something about the production. It took finding a review (while I was preparing to teach the play in a seminar) that described the performance I attended, that described me, but did not mention the shoe polish:

> At one point, Village . . . pulled a woman out of the audience and broke character to harangue her for close to fifteen minutes—until she admitted that yes, she did clutch her purse tighter when black men passed by, and yes, this was the same sort of racism that George Bush was currently displaying.[3]

While other reviews and audience reports on the CTH production regularly describe "a white theatergoer" being "called onstage by a black actor and bullied into humiliating obedience,"[4] I did not find evidence that anyone else left the encounter in blackface.[5]

1.2. Genet on the Wounding of White Audiences

It is tempting to turn my anecdote of being blackfaced at *The Blacks* into evidence of the disruptive, unpredictable, transformative possibilities of audience participation in performance and to suggest that interactive theater is a particularly effective form of political engagement. Yet my reading of Genet's *The Blacks* and its recently published "Preface," alongside responses of audience members from both the 1961 New York premiere and CTH revival, will suggest instead that theater has a limited power to inspire action that combats racism. For the "white audience" Genet claims to address, attending productions that depict white privilege and Black suffering can offer the feeling of being "woke" about race, the philanthropic pleasure of supporting progressive art, and the satisfaction of submitting to white guilt. The pleasures of complicit participation do not necessarily encourage action for racial justice.

I opened this book with a personal anecdote and will return to personal experience, aware that my focus on "this white girl" might seem to contradict my desire to disturb white supremacy and critique white allyship. Genet has taught me to write from within the contradictions, limitations, and even perversions of the personal anecdote as a strategy for analyzing racism and audience participation. If he disregards "his individual adventure"—which he contemptuously calls 'the anecdote[,]' " he does so with a persistently anecdotal style.[6] Genet was suspicious of the presumed coherence and authenticity of individual or personal authority. In *The Blacks*, Archibald repeatedly warns the other characters, "Don't start referring to your real life" and "Don't allude to your life."[7] Yet an anecdote precedes *The Blacks*, signed with Genet's initials, J. G., to emphasize its personal nature; first published in the 1958 edition of the play, it offers an account of the origins of the show: "One evening an actor asked me to write a play for an all-black cast. But what exactly is a black? First of all, what's his color? J.G."[8] In the 1960 edition, Genet added a second note (among other revisions) that foregrounds his whiteness and indicates he not only "intended" the play for a "white audience" but worked out a plan for playing to a "symbolic white" in the "unlikely" event that the play would ever be performed for a "black audience":

> This play, written, I repeat, by a white man, is intended for a white audience, but if, which is unlikely, it is ever performed before a black audience, then a white person, male or female, should be invited every evening. The organizer of the show should welcome him formally, dress him in ceremonial costume and lead him to his seat, preferably in the front row of the orchestra. The actors will play for him. A spotlight should be focused upon this symbolic white throughout the performance. J.G.[9]

The curious insertion of "I repeat" before his *first* claim to be "a white man" writing for a "white audience" might gesture toward the fact that these provocative pretexts distill Genet's much longer "Preface to the Blacks," written in 1955 but suppressed, revised, and suppressed again; it was finally printed in 2002 and translated into English in 2010.[10] The "Preface" describes the origins of the play, indicating that the Belgian actor/director Raymond Rouleau invited Genet to write a play for Black actors. Genet believed that Rouleau was primarily interested in using Black actors for personal gain because he "saw in them wonderful stage objects that had, until then, been unexploited in Europe."[11] Yet Genet perversely accepted the commission, explaining, " 'Yes,' I said to myself, 'the Blacks shall play. But they will put on a show that will snub the audience.' "[12] To achieve that goal, Genet required a white audience or at least a "symbolic white."

A play for Black actors written by a white man needed to "snub" or "wound" white audiences, Genet believed, to prevent them—and himself—from participating in

> that moral abjection that involves taking interest magnanimously, with understanding, in the weak; absolving one's conscience; abstaining from any effective action. It means claiming morality and worthy sentiment for oneself, while the people whom one supports must struggle in abject poverty, up to their necks in it, in dishonest compromise. . . . For, all things considered, it is quite pleasant to support the oppressed with words, spoken or scribed, when at the same time we profit from the benefits of the oppressive community, and from the gratitude of the oppressed.[13]

Genet was wary of the satisfaction he might derive and offer to audiences if he attempted to create a theatrical event that seemed to battle racial oppression. The play could relieve spectators' guilt without requiring that they participate in any "effective action" or give up real "benefits." To avoid that problem of theatrical guilt reduction, Genet developed strategies for engaging the audience in ways that trouble and "wound": "Conversely, I had the right to try and wound the Whitess [sic], and through this wound, to introduce doubt. In fact, I think it is necessary that a scandalous act make them question themselves, worry them with regard to this real problem that causes no conflict in their souls."[14] *The Blacks* tries to "wound" and "worry" by exaggerating the audience's fantasies about blackness, calling attention to spectators' race as well as their desire to exoticize and eroticize the actors, deliberately confusing theatergoers about what is happening in the play, and ultimately directly involving an audience member in the action.

Genet confronted theatergoers with the intransigent racism that infuses their own concern for the oppressed, partially by exaggerating and fulfilling their fantasies of Black people. For Genet, these fantasies are represented by the eighteenth-century object that inspired his play, "a music box, on which four liveried clockwork Negroes were bowing before a little princess made of white porcelain."[15] Even as he acknowledged that much had changed since the creation of this colonialist "curio"—that there are now "black scholars, doctors, engineers, that some of them are French citizens, British subjects"—Genet claimed that the bowing figures continue to "represent Africa in that they symbolise the state in which our imagination delights in dragging them."[16] In the first scenes of *The Blacks*, Genet brought those "liveried clockwork Negroes" to life and used them to exaggerate stereotypes of blackness so as to "worry" white audiences. His stage directions indicate that the actors are dancing a minuet as the curtain opens; then *"[t]he Negroes approach the footlights, make a ninety degree turn, and bow ceremoniously to the Court, then to the audience."*[17] As Archibald introduces each of the characters, they bow again, although one figure, ironically named Snow, resists Archibald's directive until he pleads, "I'm asking you madam, to bow—it's a performance."[18] This confrontation is the first of several that indicate the "performance" might fall apart at any moment. But Archibald presses on, explaining why they appear in blackface: "so we—in order to serve you—shall use our beautiful, shiny black make-up. . . . You are white. And spectators. This evening we shall perform for you."[19] To fulfill the white audience's desires to be *served* by Black performers, Archibald suggests it is not enough for the actors to merely *be* Black; they must be *painted*. "But what exactly is a black? First of all, what's his color?" the prefatory note asks. The play refuses to answer those questions directly, but it represents a

Blackness so indeterminate and yet culturally significant as to require black face paint on Black actors.

As *The Blacks* questions the coherence of the racial categories implied by the commission to write a play for an all-Black cast, it also represents whiteness by a mask *"worn in such a way that the audience sees a wide black band all around it, and even the actor's kinky hair."*[20] Genet invokes the idea that Blackness, whiteness, perhaps all racial categories are "just performances," but he does not imagine that such a presentation of race is always progressive or subversive.[21] In fact, he was aware that the association of race with performance could imply, paradoxically, that people of certain "races" are "natural" performers. In the "Preface," Genet claimed that black people are not performers "by nature, but quite the opposite . . . they become actors as soon as they are looked at by Whites."[22] Black actors fully understand that "we"— by which Genet means white audiences—"are only prepared to applaud when they play buffoons, because this is all they represent in our dreams of emasculating an entire race by refusing it the right to reality."[23] In *The Blacks*, Archibald proclaims that since white culture already assumes they are "thieves," "liars[,]"[24] and "performers[,]"[25] "Let Negroes negrify themselves. Let them persist to the point of madness in what they're condemned to be."[26] In other words, the performance of race may be more maddening than liberating. If Village declares that "[t]his ceremony is painful to me[,]"[27] Genet hopes that the exaggerated depiction of racial stereotypes will be likewise painful to audiences.

Using the white Court as a mirror for the audience, the play predicts and models troubling and even offensive responses to the racial caricatures, responses that are typical of imperialist attitudes toward native populations. The Queen says, "I haven't done anything bad, have I? Obviously, my soldiers have sometimes let themselves be carried away in their enthusiasm."[28] The Valet affirms her good intentions: "And I'm warrant of the fact that we have their welfare at heart. I've hailed their beauty in a poem that's become famous."[29] The Valet is the author of imperialist poetry like Rudyard Kipling's "The White Man's Burden" (1899); he also represents exotic fascinations with Africa. When Village metatheatrically describes the flexibility within live performance and his ability to "speed up or draw out my recital and my performance . . . I can sigh more often and more deeply," the Valet encourages him, "Do sigh more often and more deeply, charming black boy!"[30] The Governor responds to the Valet's erotic outburst by demanding that he provide information about "how rubber stands in the stock exchange," that is, by reminding him of Africa's economic purpose in the French empire.[31] When the Valet's accounts of imperial plunder dissolve into the judgment that "[t]hey're exquisitely spontaneous. They have a strange beauty," the Governor deplores his "damned exoticism."[32] But he advocates equally racist and more violent orientations to colonized populations.

The Court models several racist responses to the play's action but fails to offer any antiracist responses—and there may be none for the physical performances Genet scripts. Trisha Jeffrey's choreography for the CTH production integrated jazz and hip-hop dance with minstrel-derived shuffles and parades (see Figure 1.2). Ty Jones, as Archibald, performed back handsprings. If audiences admire this physical virtuosity, they come uncomfortably close to the Valet's exoticism. If they try to avoid appreciating the "charm" and "beauty" of the actors, they are positioned nearer to the Governor's imperialist perspective. If they walk out of the theater (as some did), they fail to confront racial oppression and conflict. Some spectators might not "get" the parodies of racial stereotypes that prance through the play, in which case *The Blacks* might actually reinforce psychic investments in those stereotypes. Spectators who recognize the deep irony in *The Blacks*

Figure 1.2 The Classical Theatre of Harlem presents *The Blacks: A Clown Show* by Jean Genet; directed by Christopher McElroen. Photo by Richard Termine, 2003. Actor/photo IDs: The Company.

and the way it anticipates what the Governor calls "damned exoticism" risk approaching the Missionary's tone of condemnation and superiority: "The dances take place only at night. Each and every one of them is danced for our destruction. . . . Every thicket hides the grave of a missionary . . . (belches)."[33] The audience, at least the white audience, is offered no correct vantage point from which to watch the play.

The Blacks also attempts to snub and wound white audiences by challenging their ability to follow what is happening. Recall the plot summary I provided: The Blacks reenacts the rape and murder of a white woman for the purpose of distracting the "real" audience, not the colluding onstage Court audience, from suspecting that a "real" drama is taking place offstage. There, another group has assembled another court to try a traitor to the revolution. For this plot to work, the trial and execution taking place elsewhere would need to be a secret from the audience.[34] Instead, the character Newport News openly reports on the trial, saying that the "forms of justice" have been applied and "execution followed."[35] The character referenced as The One Who Played the Valet proclaims of the audience, "Thanks to us they've sensed nothing of what's going on elsewhere."[36] But the audience has sensed that something is "going on" offstage from the first of Newport News's two extravagantly flagged exits to attend the offstage trial. During the first exit attempt, Village interferes: "Not that way, you fool. You were told not to come back. You're spoiling everything [. . .] (Exit Newport News, left.)."[37] This stage business with the wrong exit is precisely replicated fourteen pages later, so the audience is cued to notice that Newport News repeatedly tries to go the wrong way.[38] But the text does not indicate where Newport News was initially heading and what he would have been "spoiling." Something seems to be happening offstage right that interests Newport News, but he has been "told" not to go back there. Instead, he is supposed to attend the trial and execution that he would supposedly reach by exiting left.

A clue about the offstage-right action is given in Newport News's line: "While a court was sentencing the one who was just executed, a congress was acclaiming another. He's on his way. He's going off to organize and continue the fight."[39] The last two claims in Newport News's line seem contradictory: Is this new leader "on his way" to the stage? Or is he "going off" somewhere else to "continue the fight"? Other seeming contradictions include suggestions that the murdered white woman was, respectively, someone Village knew and desired—a stranger, a drunk destitute, a barmaid, or a seamstress—all before the catafalque is revealed to be empty.[40] Genet promotes confusion about what is alleged to be really happening onstage and off in the play's various embedded levels: the performances before the Court, the reenactment of the murder, the trial offstage left, and the revolutionary congress offstage right.

None of these comes to a definite conclusion. The trial offstage left supposedly ends in an execution, but it is not marked by the gunshot "noise" Archibald has led the audience to expect.[41] Instead, "[s]parks of fireworks" flash against the black velvet of the set, and then Newport News steps forward to announce, "I wish to inform you . . ." before being interrupted by Village: "Is he dead?"[42] Newport News affirms, "He has paid." But he could not know since he remained onstage after his last entrance rather than going "back to them," as Archibald had ordered.[43] For his part, Archibald describes the trial as a "serious affair. It's no longer a matter of staging a performance" and calls the traitor a "real man."[44] Newport News responds flippantly, "That's very tough. But though we can put on an act in front of them (*pointing to the audience*), we've got to stop acting when we're among ourselves."[45] He implies that Archibald's talk of the "real man" being tried and executed is a form of "acting" among themselves. A "real" traitor might not exist at all.

The fireworks supposedly signaling the execution interrupt the Judge's demand for a "culprit": "We don't care whether it's X, Y, or Z. If a man's a man, a Negro's a Negro, and all we need is two arms, two legs to break, a neck to put into the noose, and our justice is satisfied."[46] The Valet asks about "all due justice," and Newport News assures him that "[n]ot only were the forms of justice applied, but the spirit as well."[47] These forms—along with the cliché about "the form and spirit"—echo European imperialist culture as represented by the Court in *The Blacks*. When the Missionary inquires, "What about the defense?" Newport News responds, "Perfect. Very eloquent. But it was unable to sway the jury. And execution followed almost immediately upon delivery of sentence."[48] The Black revolutionaries replicate the oppressive institutions of white imperialist culture, including its royal and judiciary courts.

The Blacks suggests that any revolution leading to racial role reversals in the absence of cultural renovation is inadequate:

The Queen: And what about your darkies? Your slaves? Where will you get them? . . .

You'll need them, you know . . .

Felicity (*timidly*): You might, perhaps . . . We'll be good negroes . . .

The Queen: Oh no, not on your life! Governesses? Well, maybe . . .

> The Missionary: If absolutely necessary, tutors for your children . . . and even then . . .
> Felicity: It'll be hard, won't it?[49]

Felicity does not imagine a radically new culture, one without racial hierarchies and forms of servitude. She even appears to agree with the Queen that she will need "slaves" if/when she comes to power and deposes the Queen and her Court. The Queen suggests that while the former court will not become the new slaves, they might serve as "Governesses"—just as women of color regularly care for white families.

The lack of cultural renovation is reinforced in the last moments of the play when Village and Virtue attempt to play a new love scene. Virtue complains, "All men are like you: they imitate. Can't you invent something else?"[50] Village and Virtue both want to imagine new ways of loving, but even Virtue can only reverse a love cliché—"At least there's one thing: you won't be able to wind your fingers in my long golden hair"—and they walk back toward the black backdrop, which rises to reveal the entire cast gathered around yet another "*white-draped catafalque*" like the one that had appeared at the opening of the play.[51] With the reprise of a Mozart minuet, the audience might wonder whether the body on the catafalque is another raped and murdered white woman, the traitor who has been executed, the supposed leader who replaced the traitor, or no body whatsoever. Audiences can't know. But it seems clear that the entire "clown show" of Genet's subtitle is set to begin again. He emphasizes an essential feature of theater: something is actually happening onstage, but the relationship between what happens and "reality" is always in question. Genet uses this theatrical paradigm to explore the troubled ontology of race and question the reality of racial categories. In the process, *The Blacks* traffics in racial stereotypes, producing a degree of disorientation, offense, and confusion that invades the safe space of the auditorium, where audiences often expect to sit in relative comfort. Instead, audiences at *The Blacks* are asked to accept being wounded by the exaggerated portrayals of their racism, disruption of their anonymity, confusion about what is and isn't happening, and participation in the theatrical event.

For some audience members, it would be extremely uncomfortable, even a "nightmare," to be dragged onstage during a performance.[52] Yet participatory, immersive, site-specific, or environmental theater, which tends to dissolve the distinction between audience and actor, is all the rage.[53] There was no such dissolving in Genet's *The Blacks* or CTH's production. When Village pulled me out of the audience, I entered a space clearly demarcated as the stage where the actors were self-consciously performing. Given this demarcation, critics of the production (and even a blind peer reviewer for this chapter) have argued that the audience participation in CTH's revival of *The Blacks* was not "faithful" to Genet. I am not interested in the question of faithfulness, and indeed unfaithfulness may be appropriate for a playwright who proclaimed himself "disturbed by the dismal bleakness of a theatre that reflects the visible world too exactly."[54] Genet did not want his theater to faithfully reproduce reality—he did not believe in a singular reality. Nor did he want his theater to faithfully reproduce his own intentions—he was suspicious of his own intentions.

While my participatory moment with Village was not in the script, Genet does require another episode of direct audience participation in a complicated scene of double surrogacy. Village orders one person from the audience to come onstage and hold the knitting of the white woman played by the character Diouf in the reenactment of the rape and murder.[55] This spectator solves the theatrical problem of what to do with a prop when it would interfere with the action, but in the process, she is made an accessory to the crime. Holding the tools of conventional women's work, this audience participant is feminized as a surrogate for Diouf, who is himself serving as a surrogate for the raped and murdered white woman. After this scripted moment of audience participation and my own blackface appearance, the CTH revival inverted the play's general attitude of antagonism toward the audience when the actors welcomed all the "Black" audience members onstage to dance at the end of the play. Una Chaudhuri wrote of that moment, "How do I feel about not being included in the multi-culti version of Blackness that a part of the audience gets to perform toward the end of the play? (*Okay, I know how I feel: like I did during the O.J. thing, when every poll reported the opinions of blacks and whites, leaving the rest of us feeling like chopped liver*)" (emphasis in the original).[56] Chaudhuri, who identifies herself as non-white, did not feel she was included in either the "Blackness" some spectators were invited to perform with the actors onstage or those presumed to be outside that "multi-culti version of Blackness."[57] While audience members were not bullied into participating in the group dance, the pressure to take the stage or uncertainty about being included in its depiction of Blackness haunted the exuberance enjoyed by some audience members. Such are the strains of racial categories and our participation in them.

CTH's final group dance made it clear that, although not what Genet called a "black audience" in his prefatory note, the audience in Harlem was more diverse and racially indeterminate than most I have joined. As the black/white binary has been undermined to a certain extent (as indicated in the acronym BIPOC—Black, Indigenous, People of Color) since Genet wrote the play, the production may have needed to execute a version of Genet's plan for a performance before a "black audience" in order to achieve the racial tension he imagined in 1958. That is, CTH may have needed to designate a "symbolic white," and I served in that role as I received my white flower, was escorted to my seat near the front, and then dressed in the ceremonial costume of blackface. The discomfort, even "wound," of this audience participation added to the discomfort produced by a play that performs racial stereotypes and fantasies, refuses the audience an appropriate or even anonymous place from which to view them, and makes it nearly impossible for the audience to understand what is happening onstage.

1.3. Audience Responses

If *The Blacks* was intended to be an insult and a wound to white audiences, and if disorientation and offense are the desired and correct responses, why has the play been so successful throughout its performance history? *The Blacks* premiered at Paris's Théâtre de Lutèce in October 1959 under the direction of Roger Blin, with a cast drawn partially from Les Griots, the Black theater group that inspired the play. Produced by a native Algerian, Lucie Germain, with sets and costumes by the Algerian designer André Acquart, *The Blacks* encouraged a cultural reckoning on the ravages of European colonialism, particularly in Algeria and Ghana. Some audience members walked out, including the playwright Eugène Ionesco, who reportedly claimed he felt like the only white man in the (mostly white) audience.[58] Yet the Lutèce was packed every night, and the production transferred to Théâtre de la Renaissance for a long run of 169 performances, winning the Grand Prix de la Critique for best play of 1959.[59] Genet's admiration for the production is evident in the published text where he claims, "In Blin's production—and Blin was right . . ."[60] Most of the stage directions Genet includes in the text actually describe Blin's blocking, reflecting their close collaboration on textual revisions and stage design, despite the fact that Genet refused to attend the Paris premiere.[61] Genet saw the first British production, also directed by Blin, at London's Royal Court Theatre in 1961 and wrote, "The staging that you have perfected, I tell you, has given to my play an extraordinary force which from time to time frightens me a bit."[62]

The controversial US premiere filled St. Mark's Playhouse from 1961 to 1964 for a remarkable 1,408 performances, becoming the longest-running, nonmusical, off-Broadway hit of the decade. According to Owen Dodson, a poet, playwright, and leading director in Black theater, "The play is what I call an absolute insult to the white audience. It is a horror, and yet the hordes keep coming on to be insulted."[63] Dodson asked the panelists to comment on his claim during a Howard University symposium on "The Negro Writer in America" that included the playwright and actor Ossie Davis and the novelists John O. Killens and James Baldwin. Davis responded that the white "hordes" came "to be exposed to [hostility] in the safest possible fashion," and part of that safety derived from the play's claim that "the man on top" will always oppress "the man on the bottom," regardless of color.[64] Killens agreed that Genet assures white audiences that "when the blacks come to power they will be just as bad as you are. This let's [sic] the white people a little off the hook."[65] Yet other important Black activists, intellectuals, and artists celebrated the 1961 New York production. James Baldwin, an acquaintance of Genet who became a celebrated writer and leader in the civil rights movement, regularly attended rehearsals and even served as an informal advisor to the director, Gene Frankel.[66] The production boasted a star-making cast, including Roscoe Lee Browne (Archibald), James Earl Jones (Village), Louis Gosset (Newport News), Cicely Tyson (Virtue), and Maya Angelou (Queen) (see Figure 1.3).

In her account of playing the Queen at St. Mark's Playhouse, Maya Angelou remembered reading the play three times before being able to make sense of it, and like Davis and Killens, she concluded:

> Genet suggested that colonialism would crumble from the weight of its ignorance, its arrogance and greed, and that the oppressed would take over the positions of their former masters. They would be no better, no more courageous and no more merciful [. . .] *The Blacks* was a white foreigner's idea of a people he did not understand.[67]

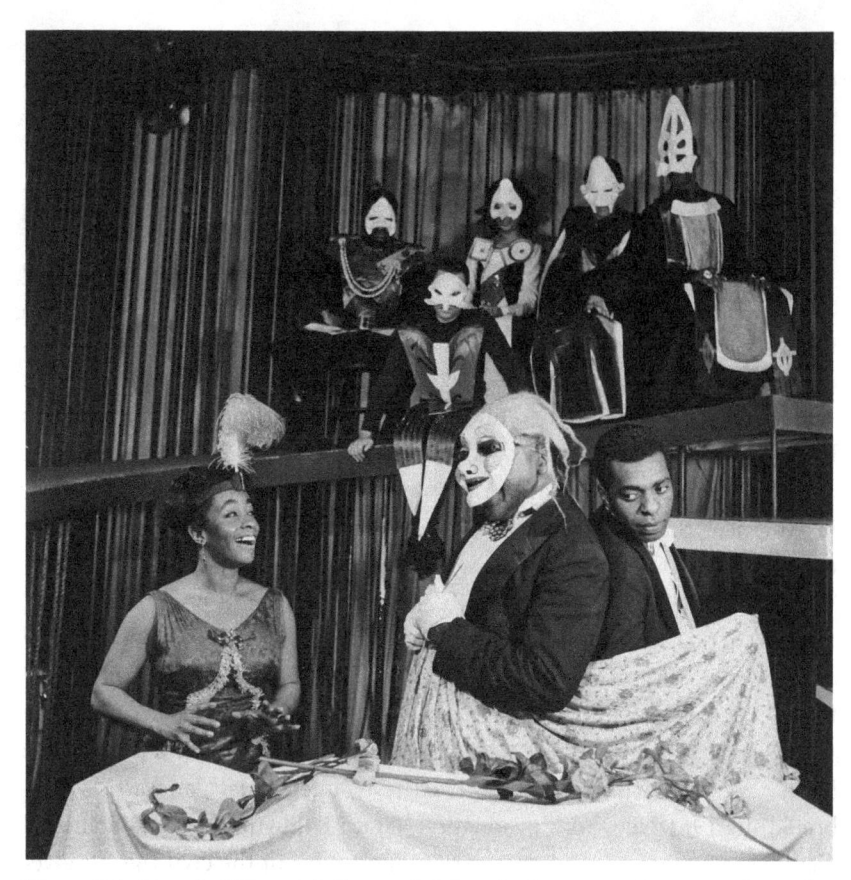

Figure 1.3 Lincoln Kilpatrick (lower right) and other actors in a scene from the stage production *The Blacks*. Photo by Martha Swope. Courtesy of the New York Public Library for the Performing Arts, Billy Rose Theatre Division. (Lincoln Kilpatrick is not listed in the 1961 cast list but joined the cast later. The Court above: J. J. Riley, Charles Gordone, Charles Campbell, Raymond St. Jaques, Lex Monson, and Maya Angelou [not pictured]; Cynthia Belgrave played Bobo, Godfrey M. Cambridge played Diouf [in the mask], and Louis Gosset played Newport News.)

Yet she agreed to play the White Queen after Vusumi Make, a South African freedom fighter and her partner at the time, insisted that the play was a crucial warning against the potential cruelty of Black people. Make told her that "most black revolutionaries, most black radicals, most black activists, do not really want change. They want exchange. This play points to that likelihood. And our people need to face the temptation. You must act in *The Blacks*."[68] Angelou drew on the racist cruelty she had experienced: "I used the White Queen to ridicule mean white women and brutal white men who had too often injured me and mine."[69] Injuries accrued even in her work on the production, when its white producer, Sidney Bernstein, refused to pay her and her friend Ethel Ayer for the music they composed for the play, saying, "You didn't compose anything. You just sat down at the piano and made up something."[70] In fact, Bernstein had previously refused to pay another composer, the jazz percussionist and Black militant Max Roach, who eventually withdrew his music (as his wife, Abbey Lincoln, withdrew from the cast).[71] If Bernstein's remarks about "true" composers reveal his racism, his sexism toward Angelou and Ayer has been intensified by later history: Roach continues to be credited as the composer,[72] and the published text indicates "the music was supervised by Charles Gross" but does not give credit to any of the composers.[73] After asking Bernstein for compensation several times, Angelou, with the support of Make, announced she was leaving the show with a telegram insisting, "She resists the exploitation of herself and her people."[74]

Did Maya Angelou believe she was exploiting herself for white audiences while performing in *The Blacks*? She wrote, "Blacks understood and enjoyed the play, but each night in the theater whites outnumbered my people four to one, and that fact was befuddling."[75] She and the other actors pondered: "If the audience missed the play's obtrusive intent, then the crackers were numbly insensitive. On the other hand, if they understood, and still liked the drama, they were psychically sick, which we suspected anyway."[76] Another possibility materialized in the form of a wealthy and weepy white woman who had seen the play five times in just four weeks (insisting that another woman in her building went twice a week); she told Angelou, "We support you. I mean, we understand what you are saying."[77] When Angelou tried to engage her personally, however, the woman recoiled "and spat out, 'You people. You people.'"[78] Angelou concluded, "She comes to the theater and allows us to curse and berate her, and that's her contribution to our struggle."[79] Is it possible that the white "hordes" were coming to St. Mark's Playhouse to engage in complicit participation at *The Blacks*—to be insulted so that they could cry, sympathize, and seem to support the "struggle" for civil rights, without being inconvenienced by direct action or even personal engagements with Black neighbors?[80]

Norman Mailer, one of the prominent white American writers to celebrate *The Blacks*, gives some insight into the "white hordes" in the audience and what they learned or failed to learn about race and sexuality. In a famous review stretching over two issues of *The Village Voice*, Mailer called the play

> a scourge to liberal ideology, vomitorium for the complacent, Eleanor Roosevelt would be ill, James Wechsler might sweat, Governor Lehman would leave. The play entertains the forbidden nightmare of the liberal: what, dear Lord, if the reactionary is correct, and people *are* horrible. Yet with the same breath, it is revolutionary. Genet's unconcealed glee at the turn of power from the White to the Negro would so charge the paranoia of the reactionary that he might suffer a heart attack.[81]

Like Angelou, Davis, and Killens, Mailer believes the play depicts a reversal of power, one in which newly empowered Blacks would become the oppressors. While Mailer does not claim that *The Blacks* lets white audiences *off the hook*, he suggests that reactionaries might feel bolstered in their racism and that liberals might confront "forbidden" fears about the limitations of their claims for inclusiveness—such as the fact that they might need to include people who "*are* horrible."[82] Mailer's own prejudices are evident when he insists that the actors were good "entertainers" but gave poor line deliveries: "When they chanted in unison, when they danced, when they leaped from platform to platform [. . .] they were first-rate, the play came to life [. . .] But in their dialogue [. . .] they were tense and without individuality."[83] *The Blacks* predicts this criticism, rooted as it is in the stereotype that Black people are natural performers: Archibald proclaims, "They tell us that we're grown-up children. In that case, what's left for us? The theater! We'll play at being reflected in it."[84] The fact that Genet anticipated Mailer's racism in the play (and explicitly argued in his "Preface" against the idea that "Blacks are actors by nature"[85]) did not dissuade Mailer from articulating his stereotypes about Black performers. Mailer's review, along with Angelou's account of the weeping white fan and general suspicion of "psychically sick" audiences, suggests that Genet may have been wounding white audiences but not always teaching them the lessons he intended.

The ease with which audiences could misinterpret Genet's play was just one reason for the criticisms of the Black playwright and activist Lorraine Hansberry. She identified Mailer and Genet's "New Paternalism" and "romantic racism" in a rebuttal of Mailer's review, also published in the *Village Voice*.[86] She appreciated the destructive fury evident in *The Blacks* and in Mailer's response, claiming:

Heaven only knows that men fixed in a posture of consuming outrage because of the spectacle of this world have been [. . .] "the best of men" in all
ages. Genet, Mailer, and [Nelson] Algren are right to be in contempt of the
ghastly hypocrisy of their cultures; artists who are not are, indeed, lesser
artists and lesser men.[87]

While she celebrated their desire to "wound" white audiences and readers,
she claimed they believe that "materially deprived Negroes are, somehow,
the only 'true Negroes'" and that any "desire to escape the grim horrors of
the ghetto" is the "longing of a people to cease being 'themselves' and 'get to
the psychoanalysts as fast as white folks do.'"[88] Hansberry pointed out that
Genet and Mailer were too deeply enmeshed in white bourgeois privilege
to recognize their "romantic" celebration of Black poverty as a strategy for
escaping the cultural stagnation and moral deprivation of their class.

Hansberry wrote back to Genet with her own anticolonial play, *Les Blancs*,
which was never produced in her lifetime but premiered in 1970 with James
Earl Jones playing the lead, Tshembe Matoseh, nine years after he played
Village in *The Blacks*. *Les Blancs* offers a complex, realistic depiction of the
violent struggle for Black liberation centered on a mission hospital in an unnamed African colony.[89] Hansberry believed that Genet's *The Blacks*, with its
indeterminate setting and indecipherable story, treated race as "an abstraction" so as to sidestep the fact that "[t]he problem in the world is the oppression of man by *man*."[90] She agreed with Mailer, Angelou, Davis, and Killens
that *The Blacks* proposes an "elaborate legend" about Black desires to over-
turn white supremacy and then establish a similarly oppressive regime.[91] But
her more fundamental complaint was anchored in her belief that audiences
should be asked to do more than feel guilty; they must

> confront Guilt with a greater imperative: the necessity for action—that
> is, to *do* something about it. The too easy purgation of the Whites—self-
> condemning and self-absolving—the untouched remoteness of the
> Blacks—would be nullified by a drama wherein we were *all* forced to con-
> frontation and awareness.[92]

Genet was wary of trying to use theater to demand that audiences "*do*
something," although he certainly believed in theatrical "confrontation."
Indeed, he worried about the satisfaction his audiences might derive from
imagining that the theater *is* doing something. Fundamentally, Genet

believed neither that theater was a revolt nor that it could incite or support one.[93] He insisted that a Black revolution was necessary, even inevitable, and he did not (as Hansberry claimed) celebrate Black poverty; in his preface, he wrote, "I know that this much abject poverty can only lead to revolt."[94] But he feared that, in addition to fostering the complacency of white audiences, theater might actually hinder community organizing against oppression:

> Despair that is transcended in a work of art can only enable the triumph of a few individuals who, in this way, can break away from the oppressed group of people with no benefit to the group itself, which will only attain salvation by means of effective revolt in the realm of real events.[95]

Genet committed himself to "direct action"[96] on behalf of the American Black Panthers, who invited him to the United States at least partially because of the impact of *The Blacks*.[97] He also worked for the nationalist *fedayeen* of Palestine, although critics have argued that he had little investment in the people for whom he was fighting or hope that they would win.[98] Genet was not against winners per se, but he did oppose the institutions and nations that winners often construct. He claimed, "Listen: the day the Palestinians become an institution, I will no longer be on their side. The day the Palestinians become a nation like other nations, I won't be there anymore."[99] Genet suggested that if the *fedayeen* were to succeed in establishing a Palestinian state, they would reproduce the unjust laws and forms of institutional violence they were fighting:

> Like Algeria and other countries that forgot the revolution in the Arab world, my Palestine thought only of the territory out of which a twenty-second state might be born, bringing with it the law and order expected of a newcomer. But did this revolt, that had been an outlaw for so long, really want a law that would have Europe for its Heaven?[100]

For Genet, revolutionary politics must reject the old repressive institutions and work to invent a new society. He supported revolutions in process but disavowed them if they turned the revolutionary violence he considered necessary into a horrific institutional brutality—a distinction that structures his essay "Violence and Brutality."[101]

At the end of *The Blacks*, the revolutionaries are already establishing brutal neocolonial institutions, including judicial systems that swiftly try and execute supposed traitors. They expect their new society to have an enslaved class. Angelou, Hansberry, and other audiences complained that the play suggested empowered Black people would be as "horrible" as the white rulers if they come to power. But Genet was not focused on what Hansberry called the personal "lust, cruelty, ambition presumed to exist in the blacks."[102] He had already witnessed neocolonial regimes establishing "brutal" institutions and nations, which he understood as a structural problem that, like racism itself, exceeded individual prejudice. *The Blacks* does not offer easy answers for how to avoid institutional brutality, as the curtain is drawn to reveal yet another catafalque and the potential for endless repetition.

The one moment in the play that appears to disrupt the cycle of institutional oppression emerges from the degrading performance of Diouf, who is forced to don a mask and skirt to perform the victim's role in the reenacted rape and murder of a white woman—while an audience member holds the knitting. Diouf is also the most accommodating and liberal character in *The Blacks*; early in the play he pleads, "let me try to come to an understanding with them."[103] His later drag role as the white woman/murder victim results in a social death and exclusion from the Black community of the play but also allows for an alternative way of being in the world. This way avoids both his earlier willingness to accommodate or even forgive white prejudice and his later outcast status, both the violent radicalism of the others and the ironic tone of the entire play. Diouf earnestly claims to be pregnant by Village, who played the rapist in the reenactment, and to have transcended the "cares and concerns" of race and gender: "New relationships come into being along with new things, and these things become necessary," he declares.[104] The only new relation imagined in the play, the only new identity, predicts contemporary ideas of transgender subjectivity and claims that radical novelty will "become necessary." Although Genet was far from optimistic, he did offer the possibility of bringing a new subjectivity into being, which might also provide the foundation for a new institution, even a new state.

1.4. Pleasure and Escalation

The CTH revival of *The Blacks* added additional audience participation beyond the moment Genet scripted because having a spectator hold Diouf's knitting would not be particularly disruptive in the context of contemporary, interactive theater. And so the company needed to invent new ways of wounding and worrying audience members to prevent complacency and the self-satisfied feeling that, in Genet terms, it is "quite pleasant to support the oppressed with words, spoken or scribed."[105] I was appropriately "wounded" by my blackface performance in 2003, but after two decades, I can acknowledge that, along with the wound, I felt a pleasure in the scene that was confusing. Manzay also seemed baffled by the experience. "It just escalated," he said. I believe the escalation occurred because I did not understand the rules of the theatrical moment I was supposed to be playing with Village, which were also the rules and conventions of racial encounter at that time and place. Those rules provided me with three scripts for performance: (1) I could have rushed offstage in embarrassment. (2) I could have played the white racist who refuses to acknowledge my racism. (3) I could have knowingly admitted to racism in the sense that "everyone is racist," while suggesting that I'm more evolved than most for admitting it—the position of complicit participation. Instead, I earnestly claimed my racism and privilege, and my seeming sincerity was crucial to the escalation that surprised Manzay and me. My privilege and relative lack of experience with racial tension, given my roots in a rural, white Midwestern community, enabled my sincerity. I was not, at that time, following a script for liberal apologies for racial oppression; I didn't know the lines back then, although I have certainly learned them since. I complied with each of Village's commands, and because I never broke down in embarrassment or rejected his accusations—never fell into one of the expected roles—he humiliated me until the audience protested.

The audience was most troubled when I was on my knees shining Village's shoes, and he took the shoe polish and lifted my face to blacken it. In that moment we presented the iconography of oral sex. I became a surrogate for the raped and murdered white woman whose body supposedly rests on the catafalque with the shoeshine box underneath, a surrogation both I and the audience sensed at the time. If her identity is inconsistently described, if she seems to be anyone and no one, we should recall that the imaginary threat posed by Black men to white women has had little need for actual victims throughout history.[106] The intersection of racial and gendered oppressions was one reason the women in the audience and actors onstage protested my scene. The encounter had escalated beyond our control as individual actors; it had provoked transgenerational traumas in which complex scripts related to racism and misogyny were operating and colliding, scripts that were also present at the 1961 American premiere, but had become much more visible and ultimately intolerable by 2003.

I would like to believe that the horror invoked by my sexually charged blackface performance at *The Blacks* was productive, but Genet has taught me to be skeptical of the power of theater to intervene in systemic racism or patriarchy. I certainly cannot argue that there was anything *revolutionary* in my inky tears, the sympathy of the audience and cast, or Manzay's confusion about how that encounter escalated. In other words, the production may have achieved Genet's goal of wounding white audiences—even the racially diverse audience that attended CTH's revival. But as was the case with at least some of the white "hordes" attending the 1961 New York premiere, audience members (like me) can experience a relief and even pleasure in being wounded. The wound feels appropriate to the challenge of promoting and participating in a full transformation of race relations, a challenge that Genet explored in *The Blacks* and its preface. He exposed the tendency of white audiences to exoticize Black people and view them as natural entertainers, on stage and off; he exposed the limits of liberal inclusion and the pleasant feeling of supporting "magnanimous causes" without giving up the material benefits of white privilege.[107] *The Blacks* and its popularity with audiences, especially white audiences, provides evidence of the potential pleasure in racially inspired humiliation.

In the past twenty years, I have learned to use the experience of being blackfaced at *The Blacks* to interrogate my students' and my own satisfaction in a liberal multicultural celebration, our frequent but often shallow claiming of various forms of privilege, and our tendency to assume that we are part of a slow but sure march toward a better, less racially divided world. Genet adamantly refused to give answers for the questions he raised, even after he sneaked illegally into American racial politics with the Black Panthers. It may be that we, likewise, need to confront our own complicit participation in racism (along with misogyny and other brutalities) without the comforting illusion of easy answers.

PART II

THE MELODRAMATICS
OF AMERICAN RACISM

Boucicault's and Jacobs-Jenkins's Octoroons

II.1 Introduction to Part II

It was closing night of Company One Theatre's sold-out run of 2016 MacArthur Fellow Branden Jacobs-Jenkins's *An Octoroon* on February 27, 2016.[1] Immediately after a few lucky individuals from the large standby line were seated, Elyas Harris, director of the Theatre's Street Team, took the stage to give the precurtain instructions about turning off cell phones and locating exits. He also announced that the audience was about to see a melodrama that required participation like that of a good nineteenth-century audience, which meant hissing at the villain and cheering for heroes/heroines. His casual dress and tone contrasted sharply with the plush carpets and gilded figurines of the recently renovated Art Deco–style Paramount Performance Center. And that was part of Harris's job, to "counteract *that* atmosphere" and set the "right energy" for a show that would ask the audience to participate in increasingly disconcerting ways.[2] Audience participation in *An Octoroon* was intended to support the goals of Company One's Street Team, "a group of community organizers" hoping to "eliminate Boston's social divides that occur along racial, cultural, economic and geographic lines" by working directly with "Boston neighborhoods, with community groups, on college campuses and in our theatre."[3]

The night I attended, many hissed and cheered as invited, playing the role of an audience from a time when the rules of the theater and its racial and gendered codes were different—but also uncomfortably recognizable to me. The actors found opportunities to remind everyone to comment on the characters, such as when Brandon G. Green modeled a vigorous hiss in his first racist line as the villain M'Closky: "[ssssSSSSSS]See here, you imp! If I catch you and your redskin yonder, poaching in my swamps, I'll cut me a switch and cane the black off of you!"[4] His hiss was both a reminder and a challenge to the audience: *Hiss louder than this!* Contemporary American audiences are taught from a young age that theater is to be watched with quiet respect, which is one reason that immersive theater can *feel* transgressive, even if the audience's participation upholds rather than undermines the dominant culture. The extent of the audience's willingness to break the old rules and comply with Harris's instructions for viewing melodramas would depend on many factors, including the racial, ethnic, gendered, socioeconomic, and generational composition of the audience—all the "social divides" Company One's Street Team hopes to combat.[5] It would depend on group sales, previous knowledge of this play and of Company One, and probably even such mundane variables as the temperature in the theater and the weather outside.

Hissing and cheering were the warmup for a show that would ask the audience to participate in more intense ways, including bidding at a slave auction and cheering for a lynching. The Company One production expanded the audience participation Jacobs-Jenkins scripted to disrupt Boston audiences' (somewhat sanctimonious) tendency to presume they understand the play's humor and message, its parodies and ironies. The presumption of a fairly typical white Boston experimental theatergoer, like myself, is that if I didn't *already* know *An Octoroon*'s specific lessons on race and melodrama, or the tangled histories of American slavery and theater, I would learn them easily; they were already part of my liberal, antiracist worldview. I, along with many white audience members, would admit that I am a member of the racist culture the play challenges, but not that I personally support bigotry. This production would refuse the predominantly white audience that comforting delusion and call attention to their complicit participation in white supremacy.

Jacobs-Jenkins's adaptation of Dion Boucicault's 1859 melodrama *The Octoroon: Or, Life in Louisiana* into *An Octoroon* identifies aspects of racism and audience participation that have not changed since the mid-nineteenth century. The play suggests that contemporary interactive theater often resembles melodrama, minstrelsy, and related forms, a very different perspective from the current obsession with immersive theater as the height of experimental and transformative performance.[6] What kind of work does *An Octoroon*'s hissing and bidding do on a majority white audience? What does it teach its audience about renewed racial tensions and activism evidenced by, for example, the formation of Black Lives Matter and We See You White American Theater, widespread protests of police killings of Black civilians, and demonstrations calling attention to the lack of diversity and equity on American university campuses and in theaters. Despite the success of *An Octoroon*—and partially because of its success—I am concerned about the psychic impact of some interactive, participatory theater on some audiences. For a limited, privileged audience of already-convinced progressives, participation might *feel* transformative but produce no political reevaluation or action. For others, participation might more deeply entrench racist and misogynist attitudes. In between, there is plenty of confusion.

The audience participation in Jacobs-Jenkins's *An Octoroon* becomes clearer, as does the play more generally, after revisiting the forms of melodramatic participation that were part of Boucicault's *The Octoroon* and other nineteenth-century melodramas. Audience participation in theater is not a new phenomenon, although the buzz around immersive theater might suggest otherwise. The lack of audience participation in realist drama after the late nineteenth century was an attempt to reject the incredibly popular melodramas and an exception to the regular participation of audiences throughout theater history. Realism's rules that audiences should sit quietly in the theater have come to dominate conceptions of Euro-American "high" drama so that audiences now assume a figurative "fourth wall" separates the stage from the audience and ignore the fact that it is strange for actors on the stage not to acknowledge the presence of spectators. But, as Jacobs-Jenkins knows, realism's goal of representing the world *as it is* was never the best vehicle for critiquing that world's racism or imagining other worlds. Nor was melodrama perfectly suited to promoting transformative politics, but it developed strategies for involving audiences in political questions. For this reason, melodrama appeals to contemporary playwrights like Jacobs-Jenkins, playwrights deeply engaged with politics who refuse the tendency to offer solutions or answers. Melodramatic audience participation is part of the prehistory of site-specific, immersive, or environmental theater that is more frequently associated with modernist and especially postmodern performance than with the supposedly conservative, sentimental, and even embarrassing genre of melodrama. Much like the minstrel tradition I discuss more thoroughly in Part III, the history of melodrama reveals explicit links between racism and audience participation, the very links Jacobs-Jenkins stages in *An Octoroon*, which is, among other things, a theater history lesson that some audiences might not like learning.

2

Dion Boucicault's *The Octoroon* and the Loudly Immersed Audiences of Nineteenth-Century Melodramas

Branden Jacobs-Jenkins was so fascinated by the largely forgotten dramatist Dion Boucicault that he cast him as "Playwright" in his adaptation of Boucicault's 1859 melodrama *The Octoroon*. "Playwright" offers his biographical details, such as "I brought you people copyrights!," that are at least partially true to Boucicault's mysterious biography.[1] Boucicault argued for "International Copyright" because he was "legally robbed" when works like *The Octoroon* were printed by a "London bookseller" without his permission.[2] He himself was accused of stealing the plot of *The Octoroon* from Mayne Reid's story "The Quadroon"; then the so-called Author of "Whitefriars" came forward to claim that both *The Octoroon* and "The Quadroon" were adapted from his "Masks and Faces" of 1855.[3] Originality is beside the point given that all of these works adapted the common scene in which a girl of mixed-race descent, then called "mulatto/a," is sold to the lecherous man with the highest bid.[4] In fact, Boucicault may have originated the term "octoroon," designating a person thought to be of one-eighth Black ancestry, to distinguish his character from the more common "tragic quadroon." The theme appealed to writers, visual artists, and abolitionists as it represented the horrors of slavery being visited on a lovely, innocent girl who could often pass as white.[5] Her skin color made the argument against slavery more palatable for some white audiences, as it was easier to sympathize with a person who looked more like them. The "tragic mulatto" story also had an erotic appeal, since the trope allowed audiences to imagine how the girl was stripped of her clothes and humanity on the auction block and sold into sexual slavery.

The "tragic mulatto" trope subtly questioned the idea that race is a legible and unchanging category based on skin color because it offered the possibility that someone not considered white at the time might pass as such. Like

Complicit Participation. Carrie J. Preston, Oxford University Press. © Oxford University Press 2024.
DOI: 10.1093/9780197693438.003.0003

other popular writers, Boucicault used the trope to challenge understandings of race in a way that could provoke both erotic interest and sympathy, but, by the end of the play, he closed down the potential subversion and reinstated standard racial hierarchies by killing off the titular "Octoroon." Imagine audience members wiping away their tears at the plight of Boucicault's "octoroon" and proclaiming, "If only the world could be different." At the same time, many spectators were bolstered in their belief that the world could not be different and that they were *good people* for wishing it were. One of Boucicault's innovations was to stage the common story of the "tragic mulatto," including its questions about the visibility of race, in a melodrama, a genre that relies on misrecognition, mistaken identities, and an acting style that emphasizes spectacle and the visual signs of a character's status as hero/heroine, villain, or other stock role. Boucicault's success can be attributed to his ability to use common tropes and generic conventions in provocative ways without tipping into actual subversion—he interested and engaged audiences, offering them the possibility of feeling *and displaying* their great sympathy, without demanding that the world change.

In the premiere of *The Octoroon* at New York's Winter Garden Theater on December 6, 1859, Boucicault, himself, played a variant on a stock character, the Native American Wahnotee (hear "why not he" in the name). Boucicault performed in redface, a more literal "rosy cheeked" performance for an actor celebrated for playing Irish characters, many of whom were depicted as "red in the face" from drinking alcohol.[6] Boucicault maintained his Irish brogue throughout his life, although his Irishness, like much of the rest of his identity, was questionable. He was born in Dublin on December 26th *or* 27th of 1820 *or* 1822, if the obituaries are to be trusted.[7] His last name indicates his father's French extraction, and his first name, according to the character Jacobs-Jenkins based on him, "is actually derived from Dionysus . . . god of harvest and beekeeping, / wine and theatre."[8] *Or*, he may have been named for an Irish physician, Dionysius Lardner, who had a romantic liaison with his mother and supported her after her separation from her husband, leading to speculations that Larder was Boucicault's father.[9] Boucicault's ambiguous Irish-French identity is further complicated by the fact that he made his theatrical career in London and lived in Britain or the United States for most of his life.

Early in his career, Boucicault translated French melodramas to pay his debts, work that may not have fulfilled his literary aspirations but gave him a solid education in melodramatic form.[10] Boucicault's first great success, *London Assurance*, opened at Covent Garden, managed by Charles Matthews, on March 4, 1841, when Boucicault was just twenty-one (or nineteen). After the death of his first wife, Anne Guiot (a French woman with means), on July 9, 1845, he met his second wife, Agnes Robertson, while serving as a "resident hack" for the great actor-manager, Charles Kean, who wanted Boucicault's comedies to help him fund his serious productions of Shakespeare.[11] Robertson was Kean's nineteen-year-old ward and a promising performer, but Kean broke from her and Boucicault after discovering the affair. That scandal precipitated the couple's departure for the United States, where they both found considerable success.

Out of the four hundred plays Boucicault was believed to have written, *The Octoroon; or Life in Louisiana* is the most focused on "American" themes.[12] Boucicault's genius was to identify the most pressing concerns, like slavery, and write about them in a way that would appeal to many potential ticket-buyers on all sides of a cultural debate. He staged the problem of American slavery at a particularly significant moment, just four days after John Brown was executed for his abolitionist rebellion at Harper's Ferry. *The Octoroon* was at least partially conceived five years previously when Boucicault was in New Orleans managing the Gaiety Theatre (1854–1855) and hoping to establish a permanent repertory company with Agnes Robertson as the leading lady.[13] Boucicault studied Southern dialects and speech patterns, spoke with both enslavers and the people they enslaved, and noted rampant prejudice against migrants from northern states, Native Americans, and Scots-Irish immigrants (like himself). He analyzed the spectacle of the slave auction and noted the dramatic and sentimental potential of the so-called fancy-girl auctions of mixed-race women, who were deemed desirable as household servants, rather than "field slaves," and often as erotic objects for their masters.[14] Boucicault demonstrated concern for groups considered racially or ethnically inferior, the poor, and the enslaved quite consistently in his work. While Boucicault chose oppressed groups, including indigenous and enslaved peoples, partially to appeal to the exotic tastes of his audience and capitalize on hot-button issues, his plays also did political and pedagogical work in his time.[15] *The Octoroon* engaged its audience and encouraged some forms of participation and interaction that are specific to melodrama and some that can be generalized to other productions attempting to offer political arguments. Nineteenth-century melodrama is part of the overlooked history of immersive, interactive, or site-specific theater, and theater artists from Jacobs-Jenkins to George C. Wolfe, Lin-Manuel Miranda to Claudia

Rankine, turn back to the participatory conventions of melodrama for their own political theater work.

2.1. Hissing, Cheering, Sympathizing

The hissing and cheering encouraged during Company One's 2016 run of *An Octoroon* was one of the central forms of audience participation in nineteenth-century melodramas. Moments after a character came onstage, audience members judged and responded to the costume, physical characteristics, and other visible signs that indicated who was the gallant hero, evil villain, beautiful ingenue, saucy servant, and other stock characters in melodramas. The hero, for example, strutted with exaggerated masculine strength, whereas the villain slunk onstage as if seeking to hide a moral failing made visible in the body. The heroine was typically the apex of vulnerable femininity, usually dressed beautifully and available for rescue by the hero. Melodramas encouraged audiences to sympathize, often excessively, with the "good" characters and detest, also excessively, the villain. Audiences proclaimed their feelings by hissing and cheering, loudly warning characters of the villain's deceitful plans, and laughing warmly at the saucy servant.

In *The Octoroon*, Boucicault used variants of the stock roles of the melodrama but also created more complicated versions of the character types. The ingenue and titular "octoroon," Zoe, is as good and beautiful but not as "fair" as expected; the villain intelligently critiques the racism and elitism of the culture that marginalizes them both. Boucicault encouraged audiences to sympathize with all characters who are outsiders to "life in Louisiana," as designated by the subtitle of the play. Zoe is the primary magnet for audience sympathy as both the beautiful heroine and the suffering innocent, and Boucicault wrote the role for his wife, Agnes Robertson, who excelled at performing liminal characters like Zoe. Raised with as much privilege as possible for an illegitimate mixed-race daughter of a judge in Louisiana, Zoe is condescendingly ignored by the local aristocrats and adored for her beauty and goodness by all the outsiders. She can pass as white so successfully that she wins the love of George Peyton, heir of the plantation Terrebonne, who has arrived in Louisiana from Paris after the death of Zoe's father/his uncle, Judge Peyton. There is no mention of incest to supplement the obsession with miscegenation that prevents the marriage of the Judge's nephew/heir to his daughter by a quadroon slave.

The opening of the play features enslaved children engaging in typical minstrel show physical comedies such as knocking over breakfast trays and stealing bananas to a soundtrack of Pete's empty threats. The scene also builds anticipation for Zoe's entrance. Salem Scudder tells George:

> Guess that you didn't leave anything female in Europe that can lift an eyelash beside that gal. When she goes along, she just leaves a streak of love behind her. It's a good drink to see her come into the cotton fields—the niggers get fresh on the sight of her. If she ain't worth her weight in sunshine you may take one of my fingers off, and choose which you like.[16]

The irony of Scudder's speech is that Zoe's worth in dollars will soon be weighed in the slave auction, and the fingers of slaves were literally owned and sometimes severed as punishment by their masters. Scudder, the Yankee overseer who squanders the plantation while obsessing over "improvements" and "inventions"—including the camera that figures in the crime scene—is one of the outsiders who loves Zoe. So is George, who is brought up in Paris far from the racial politics of the plantation. He functions as the handsome hero of the melodrama, and his goodness makes him troubled by the condescension with which neighbors like the wealthy Sunnyside and his daughter Dora treat Zoe. But he assumes that it is her illegitimacy, not her race, that prompts their contradictory failure to "notice" or "see Zoe," even as they make observations about her "person" and "manners" that would "offend" a plantation lady.[17]

Jacob M'Closky is the third of the outsiders to enter the opening breakfast scene and fawn over Zoe, although she abhors the erotic interest of the melodrama's villain. Like Scudder, he is a Yankee overseer who mismanaged the plantation, the difference being that he is guilty of malice while Scudder ruins Terrebonne with foolish investments and inventions. M'Closky is marked as Irish by his last name and the "julep" he drinks for breakfast, and early reviews remarked on his status as "a child of Green Erin."[18] M'Closky rails against southern hierarchies and prejudices: "Curse their old families— they cut me—a bilious, conceited, thin lot of dried-up aristocracy. I hate 'em. Just because my grandfather wasn't some broken-down Virginia transplant or stingy old Creole, I ain't fit to sit down to the same meat with them. It makes my blood so hot I feel my heart hiss."[19] His blood is not one-eighth Black like Zoe's, but the racialization of nineteenth-century Irish immigrants meant he was not white enough to be welcome in a southern aristocracy he accurately critiques.[20] He proposes to Zoe, "I am rich, jine [sic] me; I'll set you up grand, and we'll give these first families here our dust, until you'll see their white skins shrivel up with hate and rage; what d'ye say?"[21] Her refusal, "Let me pass," subtly gestures toward her ability to pass as white, which she can do for an outsider like George, but not the others. And she cannot bypass the laws against interracial marriage, which is why M'Closky points out, "I'd marry you if I could, but you know I can't."[22] Even his rival Scudder recognizes M'Closky's love for Zoe as a "sincere feeling."[23] M'Closky's character suggests continuities between American slavery, oppression of Irish immigrants to the United States, and British colonialism in Ireland and elsewhere.[24]

With the character of Wahnotee, the role Boucicault originally performed, the play's critique and sympathy extends to domestic colonization, the genocide of indigenous peoples, and the continued conflict with Mexico over the southern US border, even after the Mexican-American War ended in 1848 (eleven years before the opening of *The Octoroon*). Wahnotee is the fourth outsider to arrive at the breakfast scene and adore Zoe. Sunnyside, the owner of a neighboring plantation, describes him as a "nuisance," asking, "Why don't he return to his nation out West?" M'Closky claims he stays for "thieving and whiskey," but Zoe counters that he loves the enslaved-boy Paul "with the tenderness of a woman. . . . He who can love so well is honest—don't speak ill of poor Wahnotee."[25] Offering a metric for judging others by their capacity to love rather than their race or sex, Zoe presents Wahnotee and Paul as a couple with a complex gender identity and sexuality that is linked to their non-white racial status.

But it is not just love that prevents Wahnotee from "return[ing] to his nation out West";[26] that nation had been occupied as part of the US policy of Native American removal. Early editions of the play identify Wahnotee as "an Indian Chief of the Lepan Tribe," referencing the Apache Lipan tribe of the American Southwest.[27] The Lipan lived in southern Texas and fought on both sides of Texas's battle for independence from Mexico (1835–1836). The Republic of Texas established a treaty that recognized Lipan land rights, but when the US government annexed Texas in 1845, the treaty was broken, and the Lipan were displaced along with many Mexican Americans. The San Saba Treaty of 1851 authorized troops to remove Native Americans from Texas and place them on reservations in the western territories, although most tribal members were actually driven into Mexico.[28] On the same page as a review of *The Octoroon*, *The New York Times* reported that Juan Cortina defeated the

US Rangers sent to crush his five-month occupation of Brownsville, Texas, in protest of Anglo-racism.[29] Paul's claim that Wahnotee "speaks a mash-up of Indian and Mexican" that only he can understand invokes these disputes and connects the experiences of Native Americans, Mexican immigrants, and Black slaves in the United States[30]—and Boucicault's performance in the role for the first audiences added a dash of Irish.

Even without knowing the history of the Lipan or Wahnotee's association with the tribe in early drafts of *The Octoroon*, audiences during Boucicault's period were aware of the forced displacement of Native peoples in the Americas. They were also aware of the "redskin" stereotypes the character Wahnotee invokes when he says "ugh," "rum," and "firewater"—the only English words he speaks in the play to affirm assumptions that Native Americans are less intelligent and more likely to abuse alcohol.[31] Given Wahnotee's limited English language skills, he can be classified as one of the stock characters of melodrama, "the mute," who uses facial expressions and gestures to communicate. "The mute" might seem like an insignificant character to those taught to value the page over the stage, but the role allowed the actor to demonstrate one of the most valued skills in melodrama, the virtuosity of physical expressiveness—which is one reason Boucicault cast himself as Wahnotee.[32] Boucicault's "mash-up" of stereotypes with sympathetic portrayals and melodramatic stock character types was the source of his ability to teach lessons in plays that sold tickets, to do pedagogical work in a popular theater.[33]

Terrebonne is the "good earth" upon which four outsiders with some degree of nonnormative racial and/or gender identities converge to love Zoe and call for the audience's sympathy: Scudder from the north with his foolish inventions and "feminine" tears of love; George from Paris with his European amours and inability to recognize racial laws, M'Closky from Ireland who critiques the prejudices of the southern aristocracy, and Wahnotee from the American Southwest with his limited language skills but ability to love "with the tenderness of a woman."[34]

2.2. Listening In and Aside

Audiences do not have to be hissing, cheering, or vocalizing various other sentiments to be engaged as participants. Sitting and listening is a form of participation, and every theatrical environment is multisensory and immersive. The conventions of melodrama allow actors to engage the audience with a direct address more frequently than other genres; melodramatic speech regularly features soliloquies, in which characters alone onstage vocalize their thoughts and feelings either to themselves or to the audience, and asides, lines that are inaudible to some of the characters but heard by the audience. Soliloquies and asides invite the audience to *listen in* as the recipient or near-recipient of the speech. Both give the audience information that other characters do not know, leading to dramatic irony and the desire to warn characters of a trap waiting for them or encourage them to make a different decision. Soliloquies and asides can deepen the humor as audiences know the joke that is coming, increase the pathos as audiences pity the character who confided in them, or elevate the suspense as audiences predict the theatrical moment to come.

Soliloquies and asides often offer insight into the thoughts or feelings of a character, and thereby help increase the audience's sympathy. In *The Octoroon*, they are used by the villain M'Closky to register his pain over the elitism of the Louisiana upper class and his love for Zoe. He soliloquizes when he deplores the "bilious, conceited, thin lot of dried-up aristocracy," saying, "I'll sweep these Peytons from this section of the country. Their presence keeps alive the reproach against me that I ruined them."[35] As he speaks, he realizes that if the Peytons leave they will take Zoe and admits, "Darn that girl; she makes me quiver when I think of her; she's took [sic] me for all I'm worth."[36] Even when he uses objectifying language, his love of Zoe aligns him with the hero George and other "good guys," making him more sympathetic than most melodramatic villains.

Zoe's asides also register the pain of the prejudice against her but most prominently emphasize her generous, kindhearted character. When Dora, the wealthy heiress from the neighboring plantation, tries to get Zoe to help her woo George so that her fortune might save Terrebonne from debt and auction, Dora says, "If he would only propose to marry me I would accept him, but he don't know that."[37] Moments later, George begins to confess his love for Zoe, whose asides indicate that she misunderstands him and believes he is speaking of Dora:

GEORGE: I can think of nothing but the image that remains face to face with me: so beautiful, so simple, so confiding, that I dare not express the feelings that have grown up so rapidly in my heart.

ZOE: (*aside*) He means Dora.[38]

This comedy of miscommunication quickly turns to pathos as Zoe realizes that George loves her without knowing she is an "octoroon"—and communicates that realization in another aside, "Alas! he does not know, he does not know! and will despise me, spurn me, loathe me, when he learns who, what, he has so loved."[39] Far from despising her, George, upon learning of Zoe's parentage, suggests that they leave the country and find a place where laws will not forbid their marriage. George's declaration helps Zoe recognize her own love for him, but she refuses his proposal declaring that it would hurt Mrs. Peyton: "Will she gladly see you wedded to the child of her husband's slave? [. . .] if I did not crush out my infant love, what would she say to the poor girl on whom she has bestowed so much?"[40]

Zoe's refusal to leave Terrebonne with George is all the more pitiful because an earlier soliloquy, delivered by M'Closky, has revealed that Zoe will soon be auctioned off with the other enslaved people of Terrebonne to pay the debts. Zoe and her family believed that her father, Judge Peyton, had given her freedom, but the papers were not legal. There was a lien on the plantation at the time the Judge signed Zoe's papers, meaning that he was forbidden from changing the value of his property, including his property in people—*including* his daughter by a quadroon mistress. M'Closky's soliloquy clarifies this complex development in the plot, which he discovers while rummaging through the Judge's desk for the papers. He then relates his plan to get to the mailbags before Paul and Wahnotee so as to intercept a letter from a Liverpool creditor that would release Terrebonne from debt and stop the auction—at which M'Closky hopes to buy Zoe. As such soliloquies help the audience keep up with the circumstantial twists of plot that are common in melodramas, they also engage the audience as the recipient of the address and invite their sympathy for characters.

2.3. Applauding and Photographing Poses

Audience participation was encouraged by the tableaux, or living pictures, that regularly punctuated melodramas.[41] Actors posed in these picturesque visual arrangements at the opening (discovery tableaux) and ending (curtain tableaux) of acts in nineteenth-century melodramas, a practice Branden Jacobs-Jenkins would adopt for *An Octoroon*. Boucicault designed a discovery tableau at the opening of Act II that also introduced the new visual technology of photography: "*Scudder, r., Dora, l., George and Paul discovered;*

Dora being photographed by Scudder, who is arranging photographic apparatus, George and Paul looking on at back" [my emphasis].[42] Dora poses for her photograph while Paul watches, as fascinated by the camera as the rest of the nineteenth-century audience.

Photography was first introduced in France in 1839, and when it appeared in *The Octoroon* twenty years later, it would have still been an astonishing new technology for audiences. Cameras at that time produced hazy daguerreotypes and tintypes of subjects who had to sit still (often with their heads in braces) for extended periods of time. Photographers then labored over the plates in dark rooms with various chemical baths.[43] Paul points out that Dora "looks as though she war gwine to have a tooth drawed [sic]" as she tries to hold the pose while Scudder keeps time with his watch.[44] One of the first appearances of a photographic camera onstage, the scene is also remarkable because it produced a photograph of a standard melodramatic pose or tableau. Both photography and acting of the period required the ability to *hold the pose*, a physical challenge that good actors learned to perform without looking like they were undergoing a painful dental procedure.

While the actor's pose did not usually look excruciating, it did not seem natural or realistic either, particularly when it occurred mid-scene. Melodramas stop the action in mid-scene tableaux at crucial junctures in the plot or during very emotional moments. These tableaux function like pictorial versions of asides, in which the actors turn away from the action and toward the audience to strike a pose that visually signals, *we pause here because this moment is important*. Melodramatic posing involved audiences in another manner when it gave them the opportunity to recognize what Martin Meisel coined "realization tableaux," which reproduced familiar images, often illustrations from the novel that was the source for the play.[45] Sometimes a popular novel was adapted for the nineteenth-century stage while it was still being printed, chapter by chapter, in a serial magazine. The play then drew audiences from the excited readers waiting for the next installment to arrive, but with the novel not yet printed, the dramatization was often based on the illustrations hanging in print shop windows—another advertisement for novel, magazine, and melodrama. The actors attempted to *realize* the illustrations in poses that were held to give audiences time to recognize the image and acknowledge a particularly accurate stage realization with exuberant applause.[46] The act of clapping indicated that audience members were part of the in-crowd, aware of the source of the play and the illustration being realized, so clapping was both physical participation in the play and a claim to be part of a community.

The Octoroon was not developed from a novel, but attention from the press, including questions of originality and authorship, indicated how much the melodrama had tapped into the heated issue of slavery.[47] *The New York Times* declared, "Everyone talks about the 'Octoroon,' wonders about the 'Octoroon,' goes to see the 'Octoroon;' and the 'Octoroon' thus becomes, in point of fact, the work of a public mind."[48] In New York, that "public mind" seemed to be turning the play into "a political treatise of great emphasis and significance," although *The New York Times* reviewer found it "perfectly impartial, not to say non-committal" on the question of slavery.[49]

Boucicault's play was hot enough to make possible a form of *realization* related to the melodrama's own media campaign rather than novel illustrations. The play was frequently advertised with illustrations drawn from Act III's poignant scene that forces Zoe onto the auction block. Sunnyside and even Dora bid on her, but M'Closky refuses to give up his plans to buy her as a sex slave. Most of those present at the sale find M'Closky's intentions despicable. But as Pointdexter, the Auctioneer, claims:

> he has the law on his side—we may regret, but we must respect it. Mr. M'Closky has bid twenty-five thousand dollars for the Octoroon. Is there any other bid? For the first time, twenty-five thousand—last time! (*Brings hammer down.*) To Jacob M'Closky, the Octoroon girl, Zoe, twenty-five thousand dollars. (*Tableau.*)[50]

In this moment, George refuses to respect a racist law and brandishes a knife as he rushes at M'Closky (see Figure 2.1). Drawings of this sensational moment show Zoe standing on a table in an elegant white dress, the auctioneer behind her in shadows, with George lunging at M'Closky with the blade but held back by Scudder. An audience of other slaves and planters, including Sunnyside and Dora to the right, mirrors the audience in the auditorium. This sensational scene of a battle between men below the auction block also invoked the common image of an enslaved woman stripped to be sold at auction, which was particularly provocative in the "fancy girl" sales of beautiful, almost-white women like Zoe. Versions of this promotional image appeared in advertisements for the Winter Garden Theatre in 1859, in the *Illustrated London News* (November 30, 1861), and on a poster for the Royal Princess production, among others.[51] Audiences familiar with the widely

SCENE FROM MR. BOUCICAULT'S NEW DRAMA AT THE ADELPHI : THE SLAVE MARKET—SALE OF THE OCTOROON.

Figure 2.1. "Scene from Mr. Boucicault's New Drama at the Adelphi: The Slave Market—Sale of the Octoroon." *The Illustrated London News*, November 30, 1861, p. 561. Courtesy of The Adelphi Theatre Calendar revised, reconstructed, and amplified. Copyright © 2013 and 2016 by Alfred L. Nelson, Gilbert B. Cross, Joseph Donohue. https://www.umass.edu/AdelphiTheatreCalendar/img0 38f.htm.

circulated image would recognize when the actors hit and held this particular pose and acknowledge the achievement with their applause. If the actors looked like they stepped right into the picture, the audience clapped all the more vigorously, while the actors held the pose to keep the applause coming.

Another example of a mid-scene tableau staged at a crucial juncture in the plot occurs when M'Closky murders Paul with Wahnotee's tomahawk to get the letter from Liverpool that will release Terrebonne from debt. The scene is absolutely common in its depiction of a melodramatic villain standing over an innocent victim; a letter that falls into the wrong hands but could solve many plot problems is also standard melodramatic fare. What is remarkable in this scene is that a photograph captures M'Closky's murder pose, and the photograph is discovered later in the play, just when it is needed to solve the crime. Boucicault ingeniously created a murder scene that could (almost) plausibly be captured by early photographic technology. First, Scudder, the Yankee inventor-overseer, had to concoct "a self-developing liquid" with which he prepared several plates while setting up his camera to photograph Dora.[52] Paul convinced Wahnotee, who worried about the camera's gun-like appearance, to take the picture by telling him to raise the apron on the camera, run to a distant tree, and then lower the apron, with promises of rum after the task. Paul sat down on the mailbags to pose for his portrait, and while Wahnotee is gone, M'Closky struck Paul with the tomahawk so that he could steal the letter from the bags. M'Closky then stood still over Paul's body with the letter, allowing the image to be recorded on the photographic plate, as he reads:

> the balance will be paid in full, with interest, in three, six, and nine months—your drafts on Mason Brothers at those dates will be accepted by La Palisse and Compagnie, N. O., so that you may command immediate use of the whole amount at once, if required. Yours, etc., James Brown.' What a find! this infernal letter would have saved all. (*During the reading of the letter, he remains nearly motionless under the focus of the camera.*) But now I guess it will arrive too late—these darned U.S. mails are to blame. The Injun! he must not see me. (*Exits rapidly.*)[53]

Wahnotee returned and, in a scene of expressive gesture characteristic of the melodrama's stock mute character, registered his horror at finding Paul dead and his belief that the camera killed him. Wahnotee smashed the camera with his tomahawk, then "expresses in pantomime grief, sorrow, and fondness, and takes him in his arms to carry him away."[54]

Boucicault provided a realistic justification for the melodrama's typical murder tableau *and* imagined photography and film's future as a documentary force and even as evidence in criminal trials that would ensure justice. When Wahnotee destroyed the camera, the self-developed photograph was miraculously preserved until it was found at the crucial moment as a lynch mob was assembling to avenge the murder. M'Closky accused Wahnotee, who attempted to describe how the camera killed Paul in his "mash up of Spanish and Indian" (that sounded more like the French Boucicault spoke fluently). M'Closky convinced the mob that Wahnotee was confessing, and they screamed, "Lynch him! Lynch him!" Scudder stopped them to demand a standard of justice: "This lynch law is a wild and lawless proceeding."[55] Pete discovered the photographic plate displaying the scene of the murder just in time.[56] Scudder attributed divine attributes to the camera: "[Y]ou thought that no witness saw the deed, that no eye was on you—but there was, Jacob

M'Closky, there was. The eye of the Eternal was on you—the blessed sun in heaven, that, looking down, struck upon this plate the image of the deed. Here you are, in the very attitude of your crime!"[57] God's eye was figured as the camera lens, with the sun as light and developing liquid. The photograph convinced Scudder to abandon his earlier critique of "lynch law" when it threatened Wahnotee and instead present it as part of a "higher power" that intervened to produce evidence of M'Closky's crime. Scudder claimed that lynch law is necessary "in the wilds of the West, where our hatred of crime is measured by the speed of our executions—where necessity is law!"[58] Scudder unleashed the mob on M'Closky, who escaped by setting fire to a waiting steamboat in another remarkable spectacle.

Scudder's exclamation over the plate recovered from the camera, "Here you are, in the very *attitude* of your crime!" [italics, my emphasis] revealed the double meaning of the pose captured in the photograph.[59] "Attitude" now refers to a mental, emotional, or moral state, but in the nineteenth century, it commonly appeared as a theatrical term for a bodily pose that also indicated the mental state of the character.[60] The mental, emotional, or moral state implied in the pose began to take precedence, particularly outside of theatrical conversations, so that *attitude* became a stance of the mind rather than body. M'Closky was photographed in the attitude (pose) of his crime that also revealed his criminal attitude or predilection for crime. The visual technology of photography achieved one of the central impulses of melodrama: to pause bodies in a meaningful and revealing pose that could be analyzed to clarify character and intention. Both melodramatic tableaux and photography present the illusion of a society in which it is possible to discern villains and heroes and their class and racial status by their appearance. Yet, *The Octoroon* staged the danger that character and race *might not be visible* and the octoroon woman might pass as white so effectively that the hero would fall in love with her—all while assuring that the technology of photography would make crime and justice visible.

Melodrama predicted the photographic impulse that would rivet artistic and technological imaginations but also inspire social engineers interested in racial purity and eugenics following the invention of the camera. Boucicault placed this new technology onstage and taught the audiences that flocked to the play about its potential. The early photographic apparatuses, the daguerreotypes and tintypes of the 1840s and 1850s, had begun to generate excitement about photography's aesthetic possibilities, documentary potential, and use in law enforcement and criminology.[61] Belief in the photograph's ability to provide a close-up of not only the face but also the guilt or innocence—even the *soul*—of the subject made photography of great interest to physiognomists, who were trying to prove that physical features reveal personality.[62] It was only a short step from imagining that photographic collections would confirm a "criminal look" to using photography as a way to categorize racial features and confirm racial prejudices and hierarchies.[63] Melodrama was prephotographic, or photography was melodramatic, not only because both depended on the physical ability to hold the pose but also because the promise of visual recognition was crucial to the spectators' interest *and participation* as they applauded and exclaimed their approval.

Melodramas were the great popular entertainment of the nineteenth century, in part, because audiences enjoyed melodramatic forms of participation. They hissed at villains and cheered for heroes, listened to soliloquies and asides as if they were being treated to intimate secrets, participated in dramatic irony—often to the point of warning characters of what was about to happen—and applauded tableaux and living pictures in recognition of a great pose or particularly accurate *realization*. Audiences participated in these and other ways long before the arrival of what is called immersive, participatory, or site-specific theater.

Every audience throughout theater history has had the opportunity to be immersed in a multisensory site and to participate in the performance, even if that participation was primarily active listening. Yet melodrama has been particularly appealing to contemporary playwrights hoping to engage with racial and gender-based oppression. Branden Jacobs-Jenkins not only drew from melodrama's combination of stock characters, music, dance, and punctuated posing to create a political and pedagogical theater; he literally rewrote Boucicault's *The Octoroon* as *An Octoroon*. Company One's 2016 staging ironically, self-consciously adapted melodramatic acting techniques and forms of participation to create a production that encouraged audiences to participate in Boucicault's dramatic reenactments of slave auctions and lynch mobs. My next chapter takes up the meanings of this participation for contemporary audiences who have inherited the legacy of slavery along with photography's potentially justice-promoting, definitely participatory descendants: cell phone video, body cams, and other surveillance technology.

3

Hissing, Bidding, and Lynching at Branden Jacobs-Jenkins's *An Octoroon*

Elyas Harris of Company One Theatre's Street Team told the Boston audience for Branden Jacobs-Jenkins's *An Octoroon* that we were watching a melodrama and needed to hiss and cheer like any good nineteenth-century audience. Harris's pre-show talk was part of the show, designed to get the audience to participate in particular ways during *An Octoroon*—which is not actually a melodrama. The Boston production experimented with different forms, including melodramatic reenactments alongside parodies and lecture-demonstrations about melodramas and theater history. According to the dramaturg Ramona Ostrowski, audiences were so confused about what they were seeing and so many left at intermission that the production team decided to post someone in the lobby holding a sign that read "Talk to me." Ostrowski described her own experience holding the sign: "There were lots of questions. [. . .] Who wrote this? When was it written? How much of the text is old/new? They didn't ask about the plot so much. More about orientation."[1] The audience wanted to talk.

The intermission chat with someone from the creative team about generic confusion and other responses to *An Octoroon* provided an opportunity for audience participation that supplemented the hissing and cheering encouraged by Harris. Of course, leaving at intermission was also a form of complicit participation, a performed disgust at the other modes of participation the production encouraged. Hissing at the villain and cheering for the hero were just the warm-up for a production that went on to ask audiences to participate in more uncomfortable ways, including bidding at a slave auction and cheering for a lynching. The production's goal was to begin with seemingly benign forms of participation, wear down theatergoers' defenses, and then invite them to participate in reenactments of horrific and highly theatrical scenes of racial violence. As my interview with dramaturg Ostrowski revealed, the creative team hoped that many in the audience would be jostled from their assurance that they were on the "good team,"

Complicit Participation. Carrie J. Preston, Oxford University Press. © Oxford University Press 2024.
DOI: 10.1093/9780197693438.003.0004

the "woke" team. They might begin to question their assumptions that they are effectively fighting racism by attending innovative theater of racial justice like *An Octoroon*. But audience participation does not always follow the author or creative team's goals, as my conversations with the artists and theatergoers revealed. Some audience members refused the instruction to hiss and cheer and some left the theater altogether—both still forms of participation. Some felt bolstered in their belief that they are not racist and do not need to participate in *An Octoroon* to prove it, while others felt distress at the racial tension invoked by the play because they experience racism every day of their lives. Some did not understand the ironic displays of racial performance, which might then serve to bolster their racist worldview. Many were confused in ways that an intermission conversation did not clear up. And that confusion was often a very productive, if uncomfortable, form of participation.

3.1. The Prologue to a Boucicault Adaptation

Jacobs-Jenkins's play opens with a performed prologue titled "The Art of Dramatic Composition" (after a Boucicault essay) that introduces a playwright character BJJ (Jacobs-Jenkins's initials). BJJ explains his decision to mount an adaptation of *The Octoroon* with a casual familiarity, even intimacy, that initially bolsters the audience's tendency to believe they are the play's perfect audience: savvy theatergoers ready to tackle the big problems of American racial politics. In Boston, BJJ (played by Brandon Green) took his seat as one of the last audience members admitted—dressed only in his underwear. He delivered his first line from a mid-row seat: "Hi, everyone. I'm a 'black playwright.' Now I don't know what that means, but I'd like to tell you a story . . ."[2] Necks craned to locate the voice, the audience giggled, and there were larger guffaws when BJJ rose from his seat, pushed across the row, came down the aisle, and arrived at the stage, in the full glory of his skivvies. He directly addressed the audience with a story about how his decision to adapt Boucicault's melodrama *The Octoroon* emerged from his sessions with a therapist, but the production faced challenges.

BJJ: But then all the white guys quit. And then I couldn't find any more white guys to play any of the white guy parts, because they felt it was too "melodramatic."[3]

After all the "white guys" quit, BJJ decided to accept his therapist's idea that he, himself, should play the white roles. He double-cast himself as the villain, M'Closky, and as the hero, George. To prepare for those roles, he set up a vanity onstage and, per the stage directions, "violently" put on white-face.[4] (See Figure 3.1.) With this anecdote, Jacobs-Jenkins tempts his audience to take BJJ's account as the true origins of the show. After all, he gave the character his own initials and introduced him as "a black playwright."[5] Then, BJJ declared his whole opening statement a lie: "Just kidding. I don't have a therapist. / I can't afford one."[6] The monologue closes with an account of the (nonexistent?) therapist's interpretation of BJJ's dreams.[7] BJJ (the character) undermined any likelihood that an audience could know the truth about the impetus for the production.

Part of the impetus for the Prologue was a briefly infamous 2010 failed production of Jacobs-Jenkins's *The Octoroon: An Adaptation of* The Octoroon *Based on* The Octoroon, which was slated for P.S. 122 (recently renamed Performance Space New York). This troubled (pre)history is appropriate given that the play, which would become just *An Octoroon*, with *An* indicating *one of many*, is centrally concerned with theater history. The

Figure 3.1 Brandon G. Green as BJJ in *An Octoroon* by Brandon Jacobs-Jenkins, directed by Summer L. Williams. Company One Theatre in partnership with ArtsEmerson, 2016. Photo by Paul Fox.

original director for the 2010 production, Gavin Quinn of the Irish group Pan Pan, left the production twelve days before the premiere, citing artistic differences with Jacobs-Jenkins, who then took over as director. According to an assistant director, Lacy Warner, "The director, the set designer and half the cast quit right before opening night, and if that wasn't bad enough, a leaked email from the male lead—about how much he hated the show—was published in *The Village Voice*."[8] The *Voice* was widely criticized for printing an email that was clearly addressed to the actor's friends, inviting them "to a trainwreck" and claiming, "So now the play has transformed from an engaging piece of contemporary theatre directed by Gavin Quinn to a piece of crap that wouldn't hold a candle to some of the community theater I did in high school, directed by Branden Jacob-Jenkins [sic]."[9] P.S. 122 reframed *The Octoroon: An Adaptation of* The Octoroon *Based on* The Octoroon, to which tickets had already been sold, as a workshop and closed the show to critics. Before this workshop performance, Jacobs-Jenkins "came out and directly addressed the audience about his theatrical anxieties."[10] When he set about revising, he added the prologue, "The Art of Dramatic Composition," which also directly addressed the audience about anxieties and partially recounted the failure of the P.S. 122 production. BJJ uses the Prologue to ironically claim, "I can respect the pussies who pussy out of a project" because they refuse to play a "racist whose racism isn't 'complicated' by some monologue."[11]

The Prologue introduces a second white Playwright character (played by Brooks Reeves in Boston), who also entered through the auditorium in his underwear, visibly intoxicated. He claimed to be Dion Boucicault and proceeded to make fun of BJJ's own "complicated" monologue: " 'You are melodramatic.' (*beat, off BJJ's glaring, again whiny,*) 'Fuck you—meh meh meh.' "[12] The two playwrights exchanged an absurd number of "Fuck you's" (fifty-eight instances are scripted) before BJJ left and turned the stage over to the Playwright/Boucicault's own "complicated" monologue.[13] This very drunk Playwright put on redface for his role as Wahnotee, the Native American character that Boucicault played for the premiere of *The Octoroon* at New York's Winter Garden Theatre in 1859. His preparations are possible only with the help of his Assistant (played by Harsh Gagoomal in Boston), who Jacobs-Jenkins dictates should be "played by an Indigenous American actor/actress, a South Asian actor/actress, or one who can pass as Native American," according to the "Dramatis Personae" in which "Actor ethnicities [are] listed in order of preference."[14] The Assistant then blackened his own face to play the old slave Pete and young slave boy Paul because, as the Playwright explained, it is possible to "use Negroes in your plays now," but shockingly remarked, "you have to pay them . . . 'Course, you still can't find any Indian actors—Hey, where did all the Indians go?"[15] 'Course, Gagoomal, the actor who played the Assistant appeared to be (and was) of Indian descent, so his disgusted glare at his Playwright boss cracked up an audience already piqued by the use of the inaccurate term "Indian" rather than "Native American."[16]

The Prologue is an irreverent riff on racialized performance traditions as the actors literally put on the blackface, redface, and whiteface of melodrama. The targeted performance traditions range from melodrama to the typical made-for-TV movie about a typical "magical negro with PTSD" who is "trying to get out of a generic ghetto with his obese girlfriend who is also pregnant and who also has AIDS from a history of sexual abuse [. . .] which some idiot's going to describe as representative of 'the Black experience in America.'"[17] The continuities in racialized performance since the nineteenth century include the pleasures of feeling "sympathy" (the [nonexistent?] therapist's word) for stereotypical, improbable characters designated as representatives of "the Black experience."[18] The tragic plot of the made-for-TV "Black experience in America" is as familiar now as was the trope of the tragic sale of the beautiful "mulatta" woman to a lecherous bidder for a nineteenth-century American audience, which hissed and cheered to signal their sympathy.[19]

As the contemporary Boston audience hissed, cheered, and played at being a nineteenth-century audience as instructed, they were also performing sympathy and antiracist commitments in more contemporary ways, even before the performance; they purchased their tickets to attend and support a show written by a "black playwright."[20] Or, if they had not heard about Jacobs-Jenkins's identity—which he complicates so effectively in the Prologue—they saw, while buying tickets, Company One's quote of *The New York Times* review: "Hilarious and harrowing . . . The decade's most eloquent theatrical statement on race in America today."[21] Or maybe they read the *Boston Globe's* review claiming that "Jacobs-Jenkins approaches the subject of race from unexpected and provocative angles" or were intrigued by the photograph of Brandon Green as McClosky in whiteface.[22] While theatergoers came to the production with different background knowledge, and a few ended up there with no preparation, most expected the play to be a "statement on race in America today."[23] The Prologue began to challenge its audience's desire to confront racism from its first line: "Hi everyone. I'm a 'black playwright.' (*beat*) Now I don't know what that means . . ."[24]

3.2. Poses and Projections in *An Octoroon*

"The Art of Dramatic Composition: A Prologue" ends with the two play-wright characters in whiteface and redface, while the assistant is in black-face (see Figure 3.2). They are ready to begin "the show," the adaptation of Boucicault's *The Octoroon* . . . or part of it. Jacobs-Jenkins's stage directions call for melodramatic performance techniques; most prominently, the actors pose in tableaux. A failed curtain tableau joke closes Act I. After M'Closky's long soliloquy in which he narrates his discovery that Zoe was not legally freed because of the lien on the estate when the Judge signed her free pa-pers, the stage directions indicate: (*M'CLOSKY stands with his hand extended towards the house. Music. An attempt at a tableau. He holds the tableau for a while before DIDO walks in with a washing bucket and some laundry.*)[25] M'Closky is embarrassed and "frazzled" by his interrupted tab-leau so he leaves, returns minutes later, strikes Dido, and says, "And don't you ever fuckin' sneak up on me like that again, you nigger bitch! (*An actual TABLEAU.*)"[26] The gag of Dido interrupting M'Closky's conventionally

Figure 3.2 Brooks Reeves as Playwright and Harsh Gagoomal as Assistant in *An Octoroon* by Brandon Jacobs-Jenkins, directed by Summer L. Williams. Company One Theatre in partnership with ArtsEmerson, 2016. Photo by Paul Fox.

villainous tableau and his shockingly offensive line call the audience's attention to the tableau feature of melodramatic staging, to the interrupted joke tableau and then "*actual TABLEAU*."[27] This stage direction, like others that reference tableaux, have a somewhat sarcastic tone. After M'Closky kills Paul while the slave boy poses for a photograph, the stage direction reads:

> *To his horror, WAHNOTEE finds him dead, expresses great grief, raises his eyes. They fall upon the camera. He rises with a savage growl, he seizes tomahawk and smashes camera to pieces, then goes to Paul, expresses grief, sorrow, and fondness. Maybe he starts to make a grave—sobbing and digging with his hands? I don't know. In any case, there's a TABLEAUX.*[28]

Jacobs-Jenkins describes the expressive possibilities of the "mute" character, one of the standard character types in melodramas discussed in the previous chapter. He also ridicules the hyperemotional nature of that performance style as he lists emotions and then shrugs, "*I don't know.*" But all that expression would obviously, "*[i]n any case,*" end in a tableau.[29]

The performers in the 2016 Boston production struck the scripted tableaux with great delight and self-consciousness about the acting style they were performing. Company One's dramaturgs and creative team worked extensively with the actors to help them understand the history of melodramatic acting styles and the purpose of the poses they were to perform. The rehearsal and production blog in January shared the team's process: "Though it is hard for us to understand [tableau posing] as a construct today, melodramatic audiences would have found these tableaux not only helpful in understanding the basic plot of a piece, but also as intense, moving pieces of art."[30] Dramaturg Ramona Ostrowski claimed that it was easy for the actors to grasp the acting style "in theory," but they needed more "encouragement" to "push past their natural discomfort with posing."[31] I would suggest that their discomfort was not "natural" but that it stemmed from their training in what Ostrowski referred to as "contemporary" and "classical" acting techniques. Their poses were parodies of tableaux, so that each pose stopped the action not to offer an "intense" expression but to include the audience in a joke about the overblown or overperformed tableaux realizations of nineteenth-century melodramas (see Figure 3.3).

The apex of the joke is Act II's discovery tableau featuring Dora posing for a photograph. Jacobs-Jenkins's version of the scene makes explicit the implicit connections Boucicault draws between melodramatic posing and

Figure 3.3 (From left) Harsh Gagoomal as Paul, Brooks Reeves as Wahnotee, Bridgette Hayes as Dora, Shawna M. James as Zoe, and Brandon G. Green as M'Closky in *An Octoroon* by Brandon Jacobs-Jenkins, directed by Summer L. Williams. Company One Theatre in partnership with ArtsEmerson, 2016. Photo by Paul Fox.

photography. George serves in Jacobs-Jenkins's adaptation as the hero/ love interest *and* the photographer, whereas in Boucicault's *The Octoroon*, the photographer is Scudder, the good but foolish Yankee overseer whose plantation-ruining "improvements" and inventions included a camera with a "self-developing liquid" that produced a photograph without multiple washes in darkrooms—a character Jacobs-Jenkins cut.[32] George, as cameraman, commands, "Now don't move,"[33] while Dora continues to prattle on to Zoe about her attraction to George, who looks at his watch to time the development of the plate (see Figure 3.4). The stage directions repeatedly comment on an "awkward" feeling: "*Dora's smile and pose melt into something so hideous it's hard to look at.*"[34] While the photograph develops, Jacobs-Jenkins pauses the entire stage in a tableau that emphasizes the technical and physical requirements of photography in the 1850s and presents melodramatic posing as a proto-photographic practice: If you were a good melodramatic actor, you should have been proficient at holding the pose for a photographic plate as well.

Figure 3.4 Brandon G. Green as George and Bridgette Hayes as Dora in *An Octoroon* by Brandon Jacobs-Jenkins, directed by Summer L. Williams. Company One Theatre in partnership with ArtsEmerson, 2016. Photo by Paul Fox.

When Jacobs-Jenkins rewrites Act IV's lynch scene on the wharf, his BJJ and Playwright/Boucicault "step forward from the tableau" that occurred in Boucicault's *The Octoroon* and pause the reconstruction/remake to give a lecture on the structure of melodramas.[35] They inform the audience that Act IV is the "most important of all the acts in a melodrama" and will be too "tough" to perform without explanation because, first of all, they need more actors for the lynch mob. Act IV was also difficult to perform because it is supposed to contain the "Sensation Scene," which is intended to "overwhelm your audience's senses to the end of building the truest illusion of reality" while giving them the moral of the play.[36] The Playwright claims, "You basically sort of give your audience the moral, then you overwhelm them with fake destruction."[37] In Jacobs-Jenkins's interpretation, the moral of Boucicault's play is found in George's speech against vigilante justice and lynching and defense of Wahnotee as "a poor, ignorant savage" after he is accused of murdering Paul.[38]

[I]t is against my nature to believe him guilty; and if he be, this isn't the place, nor you the authority to try him. I appeal against your usurped authority;

this lynch law is a wild and lawless proceeding. You call yourselves judges—
you aren't—you're a jury of executioners.[39]

In Boucicault's melodrama, the speech belongs to Scudder, the character
Jacobs-Jenkins cut in order to simplify the plot and consolidate the play's
moral authority and inventiveness in one hero.

As in Boucicault's melodrama, Jacobs-Jenkins's Wahnotee is saved by the
discovery of the self-developed photograph which revealed that M'Closky
killed Paul with the tomahawk to steal the letter that would save the plantation. He stood over Paul's body reading the letter long enough for the camera
to capture the image on the plate. The photographic evidence leads Scudder
(in Boucicault)/George (in Jacobs-Jenkins's version) to contradict the moral
argument against vigilantism he just delivered and encourage the lynching of
M'Closky. The camera and its miraculous, justice-promoting photograph are
part of the "Sensation" of the melodrama's Act IV. But, according to BJJ and
the Playwright, cameras are no longer sensational:

PLAYWRIGHT: You know, it's really hard to describe how this scene works
BJJ: because it actually would have been really exciting to audiences 150 years
    ago—having someone caught by a photograph.
PLAYWRIGHT: They were a novel thing,
BJJ: which is why this whole plot is more or less centered around a camera.
    But photographs to us?
ASSISTANT: Boring.[40]

BJJ and the Playwright claim that to produce a "novelty" comparable to a
photograph for a nineteenth-century audience, one that would give the audience "a sense of having really witnessed something," they would have to
set fire to the entire theater and bring the audience "as close to death as possible" before rescuing spectators one by one.[41] But theater fires are too dangerous and would destroy the play's run, not to mention any chance for new
productions. They considered "sacrificing an animal onstage" but worried
about animal cruelty laws and the irrelevance of such a ritual.

BJJ: Anyway, I figured I'd try something. I hope it isn't too disappointing,
    *Assistant has wheeled out an overhead projector. He projects a lynching
    photograph onto the back wall.*
    Where was—okay, sorry, I lost my place. I'm going to go back:
    They perform the following in the light of the projection.[42]

The Boston production used multiple photographs, each of which foregrounded a mob participating in an actual lynching that took place a century after Boucicault's play, projecting them in a slow sequence as the actors were absolutely still (another tableau). The most troubling of the lynching photographs, for me, focused on the image of a child in the foreground pointing at the mutilated body of the victim but looking directly into the camera. The presence of the crowd was notable in each image, perhaps to suggest connections between the theatrical audience and the lynch mob. The sequence ended with Tyler Shields's photograph of a naked Black man pulling on the rope that hangs someone dressed in a white Ku Klux Klan costume from a tree. The image appears in Sheilds's series titled *Historical Fiction* that seeks to "reflect some of the most traumatic events in America's history" and "portray the perspective of those who witnessed such tragic events rather than those who fell victim to them.[43] As the image faded, BJJ said, "Where was—okay sorry, I lost my place. I'm going back."[44] In the Boston production, this line was performed as meaning that BJJ could not find his place in that reimagined lynch scene with its reversal of victim and perpetrator. BJJ rewound to an earlier moment, transformed into George again, and repeated his statement that "this lynch law is a wild and lawless proceeding," thereby delivering the play's moral twice.[45]

While Boucicault's melodrama featured a lynch mob interrupted by a photograph, the lynching photographs projected in the Boston production of *An Octoroon* depicted events and a kind of mob violence that was not prevalent until after the Civil War ended American slavery. Most states had laws against killing enslaved people, although they were certainly maimed and murdered by enslavers as well as by mobs that called themselves "committees of safety."[46] In 1859, the year Boucicault's *Octoroon* opened, the Supreme Court of Louisiana stated, "Slaves are regarded in our law, both as property and persons."[47] By these laws, M'Closky was guilty of both destruction of property and murder when he killed Paul, whose value was about to be determined in the sale of Terrebonne's *property*. The term "lynch" first emerged in the 1830s, generally associated with a humiliating punishment like whipping/tarring/feathering.[48] Boucicault's scene reflects the mid-nineteenth-century rise in deadly vigilantism in the South and West that targeted Native Americans and Irish American-Yankees as well as enslaved people. So *An Octoroon*'s display of lynching photographs from the civil rights movement was intentionally anachronistic.

As BJJ predicted with his preemptive apology, I found the lynching photographs to be a "disappointing" and deeply troubling version of the "Sensation Scene," which was certainly part of Jacobs-Jenkins's point.[49] The

Assistant set up the overhead projector as if it were a distasteful but obligatory gesture, which was particularly noticeable given that Jacobs-Jenkins
might have chosen the more cinematic technique of projecting the "lynching
photograph" from the back of the auditorium.[50] The onstage presence of the
projector, a relatively obsolete apparatus of visual media, added to the immediacy of the experience and to the sense that the actors, not some offstage
force, were forcing me to see the image. I hoped that each photograph would
be the last, and many in the audience were deeply disturbed by the depiction of torture, dismemberment, and atrocity taken from the perspective
of the triumphant white lynch mob. There was a collective gasp the night
I attended, and this was a typical response.[51]

But Jacobs-Jenkins encouraged a level of audience participation that went
far beyond gasps of shock, horror, and sympathy. The characters ask the audience to join the mob onstage as they shout for a lynching. Jacobs-Jenkins
sets up this participation by turning from the projected photographs back
to Boucicault's plot, where the mob repeatedly calls, "Lynch him!" when
M'Closky demands the execution of Wahnotee. The mob aims the same
phrase at M'Closky after the photograph is recovered showing that he, not
Wahnotee, killed Paul: "Lynch him! Lynch him! Down with him."[52] Jacobs-
Jenkins's version does not have a mob because, as BJJ acknowledges at the
opening of Act IV, "I grossly underestimated the amount of white men
I would actually need here."[53] There is only BJJ, who also plays George and
M'Closky in whiteface, the Playwright who performs Wahnotee in redface,
and the Assistant, as Pete and other slaves in blackface. And rather than
adding their voices to the supposed mob, BJJ and the Playwright force the
overworked and overlooked Assistant to say the crowd's first lynch line alone:

> And the crowd's like,
> (*No one says anything for a second. BJJ and PLAYWRIGHT look at
> ASSISTANT expectantly.*)
> ASSISTANT: "Lynch him!"[54]

He clearly did not want to say it, and I felt sorry for him. When the crowd
was supposed to turn on M'Closky a few moments later, the Assistant
encouraged the audience to participate by gesturing to them as he said:

> ASSISTANT: And everyone's like,
> EVERYONE: (*A loud, harsh, clear whisper.*)
>   Guilty! Lynch him![55]

"Lynch him!" is repeated three times in the script, with the Assistant egging "everyone" on.[56] The absence of the crowd onstage makes the lynch mob lines all the more available and necessary for audience participation.

Many in the Boston audience followed the Assistant's directions, perhaps in sympathy for him, and joined the mob by shouting, "Lynch him!" I could not do it, but I felt tugged in two directions at once: the impulses both to join in the audience community and to assert my difference—even superiority—by refusing to participate. And then I was troubled by my desire to feel superior to the rest of the audience, *as if I knew why they yelled or that my refusal to do so would exonerate me from my own racism.* The notion that theatergoers could perform an enlightened perspective on race was one of the reasons many came to Jacobs-Jenkins's *An Octoroon.* Whether they cried, "Lynch him" or not, they were in fact participating in the mob that extended from the stage into the house, a participating audience that mirrored the mobs in the lynching photographs. While my own problematic desire for moral superiority encouraged my silence, it propelled others to yell out. Such was the case for the reviewer Damon Krometis, who wrote:

> I was living a contradiction. I was on the side of the good, demanding a racist murderer be punished, but I was also a man in those photographs, smiling below the dangling feet of a dead African American. I was joyous over the white character dragged off to "justice," but horrified it was a black actor playing the role.[57]

Krometis associates his contradictory feelings of joy and horror with the fact that he was calling for the lynching of an Irish character played by a Black actor in whiteface who had murdered a slave boy (played by a South Asian or Indian actor in blackface). The production's use of redface, whiteface, and blackface characters undermined the desire to imagine fixed identities associated with "good" or "bad" sides in racial violence. Krometis could not find "the side of the good" when the "racist murderer" was played by a Black actor. Of course, *anyone* can be a "racist murderer."[58] The fiction that an individual's morality is determined by skin color is part of the logic of racism. So is the idea that Black actors must play certain kinds of roles and that a "black playwright" must create certain kinds of roles as well as work toward racial liberation.[59] Such assumptions persist, even after BJJ enters and addresses the entire audience: "Hi, everyone. I'm a 'black playwright.' / (beat) / Now I don't know what that means [. . .]"[60] Jacobs-Jenkins asks a version of Jean Genet's question, "What is a black?"

Jacobs-Jenkins encourages audience participation partially to expose and undermine the "side of the good" that typical progressive audiences imagine they can join. This is certainly uncomfortable, and it can produce a degree of self-consciousness about our desire for *An Octoroon* to confirm and even celebrate our liberal attitudes about race.[61] Krometis claims that the Boston production of *An Octoroon* reaffirmed his belief in theater, particularly what he calls "interactive theatre": "My task as witness to this event was to wrestle with my ever-shifting position, and think about how I could solidify one in real life."[62] For me, the play exposed my desire for solidity, for a clear ethical position, and then repeatedly pulled that moral ground out from under me. The experience was disorienting and demanded personal reflection, but it left me with many questions about what this form of participation might teach its audience.

3.3. Bidding on *An Octoroon*

The audience participation encouraged during Jacobs-Jenkins's version of the slave auction invites similar questions to those provoked by the lynch mob scene. Most importantly, what kind of psychic work does bidding at a staged auction charged with sexual desire do to the participants, others in the audience, and the performance in general? To set the scene: The Terrebonne plantation is so encumbered with debt that the family must sell the enslaved people, including Zoe, because although the Judge signed free papers for his daughter, the lien on Terrebonne at the time he signed prevented him from diminishing the value of the estate. Many in the audience at Boucicault's melodrama in the late 1850s would have known that as a light-skinned woman, Zoe could have been sold at one of the "fancy girl" or "yellow girl" auctions that trafficked in the widespread practice of sexual slavery.[63] These events required certain kinds of performances from the mixed-race women who could be asked to sing, dance, and even remove their clothing for potential buyers to inspect their flesh.[64] While the Boston audience of *An Octoroon* would have been less aware of those practices, M'Closky made it clear that he was bidding on Zoe for the purpose of sexual slavery (see Figure 3.5).

In the stage direction leading up to the scene, Jacobs-Jenkins indicates, "There is either 1 or 99 people playing various bidders. Or maybe there's

Figure 3.5 Brandon G. Green as M'Closky and Shawna M. James as Zoe in *An Octoroon* by Brandon Jacobs-Jenkins, directed by Summer L. Williams. Company One Theatre in partnership with ArtsEmerson, 2016. Photo by Paul Fox.

some clever way to force the audience into doing this."[65] The Boston production distributed approximately twenty bid cards to the audience during each performance.[66] The auctioneer, Lafouche, encouraged the audience to bid through his gestures and showed excitement when bidding wars developed between characters and theatergoers. The more the audience bid, the longer we extended the extremely uncomfortable scene, forcing the auctioneer and other characters to adapt. During one performance, the auction went on for so long that the production team had to discuss strategies for ignoring the bidding and moving the scene forward.[67] During the bidding war over Zoe, the audience might have thought they were, like George, attempting to save her from the fate of becoming M'Closky's sex slave. Even Dora, the wealthy plantation heiress whose desire for George was foiled by his love for Zoe, invaded the male sphere of the auction in an attempt to outbid M'Closky. But however much the audience, George, and Dora might imagine they were trying to save Zoe, they were also imaginatively participating in the sale of human beings and an institution that once defined "slave" by as little as "one drop in eight" of Black blood.[68]

In his review of the production, Damon Krometis claimed that the auction scene challenged the ethical position he had staked while hissing at villains and cheering for heroes—the version of melodramatic participation Elyas Harris encouraged in his introduction to the play in Boston.[69] Krometis felt that during the slave auction:

> we started to lose our place of moral authority by reducing a human life to price tag. [sic] This sensation was unsettling, yet still manageable. Due to the exaggerated acting of the company, the two-dimensionality of the scenic design and the tinny sound of the music, I felt I was still within a theatrical conceit.[70]

Krometis began to experience his participation as *unmanageable* during the lynching scene in Act IV when "the images of lynching destroyed the notion that I had the moral high ground."[71] Like Krometis, I was more disturbed by "Lynch him!" than the bids for Zoe. This seemed to be a common feeling in the audience, judging by the enthusiastic participation in the auction and the reluctance during the lynch trial. These responses warrant particular attention as they expose complex intersections of attitudes about race and gender. The acting was what Krometis called "exaggerated" throughout the play as actors stepped in and out of two-dimensional tableaux and played several different roles, even in the same scene. So, if the "theatrical conceit" was not greatly altered between the auction and lynching scene, the content must have contributed to our different responses.[72] Both scenes reveal the crucial role of the audiences that historically participated in slave sales and lynchings, as well as the theatrical elements of these events as human beings were exhibited to the audience, judged, sometimes forced to dance and sing, and then either sold or tortured and murdered.

Contrasting the two atrocities—sex slavery versus lynching—in an attempt to determine which is worse would be meaningless and even offensive. Yet the Boston production of *An Octoroon* led its audiences into behaviors many considered not just *unmanageable* but deplorable—from hissing and cheering at clearly identified villains and heroes to physically bidding on slaves and a so-called octoroon who was raised as a free person, to demanding a lynching. Dramaturg Ramona Ostrowski described the strategy:

> You can boo because everyone else is booing without wondering why [...] then wave your card without thinking. That is the superficial, easy part.

Hopefully since you've gone that far, when the expectations are shaken up, other expectations might be shaken loose as well.[73]

For Ostrowski, the shake-up primarily happened in Act IV when, she explained, "We are calling for the lynching of a Black body, but we don't realize until we've done it."[74] Through its staging and dramaturgy, the production gradually indoctrinated the audience into participating in more egregious actions and, in the process, suggested that participating in a lynching is worse than participating in a slave auction.

3.4. The Women of *An Octoroon*

Boucicault's *The Octoroon* does not raise the question of whether it is worse to join a lynch mob or bid for a slave woman, but his Zoe is forced to decide whether to become M'Closky's sex slave or commit suicide. She chooses death, despite her desire to live, begging Dido to give her poison: "You can protect me from that man—do let me die without pain."[75] Jacobs-Jenkins's revision suggests that Zoe primarily kills herself not to refuse sexual slavery but to save George the pain of imagining her in that condition. His Zoe delivers Boucicault's plaintive line, "I sat outside his door all night and heard his sighs—his agony—torn from him by my coming fate; and he said, 'I'd rather see her dead than his!' "[76] But, then, Jacobs-Jenkins has her add, "I cried for hours before I rose up with the resolve to end my own life! For his sake!"[77] Not in the Boucicault, this line gives precedence to the feelings of the man who cannot tolerate his beloved belonging (literally) to another man, that is, to jealousy and even male competition. It presents Zoe's suicide as a sacrifice for George's "sake" rather than a refusal to live a life she finds unacceptable to her.[78] Jacobs-Jenkins might have added this line to make explicit the privileging of men's lives and feelings in Boucicault's *The Octoroon*, and in melodramas more generally. But his adaptation does not comment on or confirm this interpretation of his addition.

I am not suggesting that Jacobs-Jenkins ignores the intersections of racism and misogyny; he makes Zoe both the most sympathetic, beautiful, and adored woman onstage as well as the primary example of the horrors of slavery. In this, he follows Boucicault, as well as nineteenth-century abolitionists, who used a white-appearing woman threatened with sex slavery to appeal to those wishing to *rescue* a woman in distress. The strategy indicates a racist bias for lighter skin and an obsession with perceived sexual improprieties and miscegenation over other abuses of slavery—all are aspects of intertwined racism and misogyny. If Jacobs-Jenkins intended to comment on the misogyny implicit in this abolitionist strategy, however, his message is not clear. And that lack of clarity is uncharacteristic in a play that allows the male characters to engage in extensive metatheatrical commentary throughout the Prologue and Act IV's lynching scene. Imagine if Zoe, like BJJ, turned to the audience in an aside that complained about how melodramatic conventions render her a pawn of male desire—and ultimately ask her to take her own life because her beloved would "rather see her dead than his!'"[79] She might insist, *My life is not devoted to his comfort.*

Such a line might have been spoken by the three very funny "slave" women characters Jacobs-Jenkins added to *An Octoroon*—Dido, Minnie, and Grace—but they are not afforded the same privileges of irony and critique as the male characters (see Figure 3.6). Neither they, nor any other women actors, are double cast. All four men play multiple roles that conflict with their apparent race and even species in the case of Br'er Rabbit. According to the list of Dramatis Personae, Minnie, Dido, and Grace should be played by "African-American actresses," while Zoe should be played by "an octoroon actress . . . or actress of color who can pass as an octoroon," and the rich heiress Dora is "played by a white actress, or actress who can pass white" [sic].[80] The addition of the "slave" women characters allows for the Playwright's comment, "You can actually use negroes in your plays now. That's pretty great. You really save on makeup. But can you believe you have to pay them? So we could only afford three negresses."[81] The Playwright implies that Black women actors are cheaper, which is true and fascinating in a production that resulted in performance reports listing the final price of the slaves: "Zoe sold for $26,001.00 tonight," although Pete went for as little as $200, and audience bids could push Zoe's price to $70,000.00.[82] After the Prologue, the scenes Jacobs-Jenkins added to Boucicault's melodrama feature the three "slave" women, who comment on other characters, the plot, and their enslaved status with tremendous energy and humor—in lines that resemble some examples of contemporary African American (vernacular) English in rhythm, pronunciation, and content:

> MINNIE: I know, right? Grace's ass always talking about running away now that Massa dead and I'm like, Bitch, you need to calm your busybody ass down. Haven't she heard these slave catchers got these new dogs nowadays

that can fly and who are trained to fuckin drag yo' ass out of trees and carry you back [...] That kind of naivete is how niggas get kilt.[83]

In contrast, Jacobs-Jenkins's "slave" men characters speak the stereotypical southern dialect Boucicault wrote in the original, following the conventions of the nineteenth-century stage. The upper-class white characters speak the standard English written by Boucicault, despite the fact that white enslavers in New Orleans would have spoken southern dialect "in real life." Jacobs-Jenkins cleverly defends his choice to have the "slave" women characters speak a version of contemporary African American vernacular with a note in the script: "(*I'm just going to say this right now so we can get it over with: I don't know what a real slave sounded like. And neither do you.*)"[84] But Jacobs-Jenkins does not explain why the corresponding men "slaves" speak so differently in his play. While it is true that many in his audience are not aware of how enslaved people spoke, some indication is provided by "Voices from the Days of Slavery," the almost seven hours of recorded interviews held by the Library of Congress and accessible online.[85] Linguists debate the relationship between the speech patterns of enslaved people and some contemporary

Figure 3.6 Obehi Janice and Elle Borders as Minnie and Dido in *An Octoroon* by Brandon Jacobs-Jenkins, directed by Summer L. Williams. Company One Theatre in partnership with ArtsEmerson, 2016. Photo by Paul Fox.

African American vernacular, weighing the relative contributions of the West African languages many enslaved people spoke, regional English dialects, the English spoken by Irish immigrants, and Caribbean Creole English.[86] So African American (vernacular) English is associated with the historical speech of enslaved peoples to some extent, but that does not appear to be Jacobs-Jenkins's point with the dialogue of the three women characters, or so the note about not knowing *"what a real slave sounded like"* would suggest. Another possible message would be that there are Black women who continue to live in horrible, conditions much like enslavement. But again, Jacobs-Jenkins does not clearly establish these continuities with the performances of Dido, Minnie, and Grace.

Instead, these "slave" characters perform a litany of stereotypes including, according to the stage directions, the gossipy, jealous, "super-nice, super-fake"[87] Black women who "act kinda ghetto"[88] and celebrate getting sold to be slaves on a steamboat; they imagine "coasting up and down the river, looking fly, wind whipping at our hair and our slave tunics and shit and we surrounded by all these fine, muscle-y boat niggas who ain't been wit a woman in years."[89] It's all clever, and audiences in Boston certainly appreciated Dido, Minnie, and Grace's scenes with strong laughter. A young Black woman at an audience talkback shared her impression that there were many in the audience who were *"just* laughing" at stereotypical "Black girls."[90] One reviewer associated Dido and Minnie with the popular television show about a women's prison, *Orange Is the New Black*, and particularly the characters Taystee and Poussey; critics often claim that these characters cross from irony into demeaning stereotypes.[91] Jacobs-Jenkins is certainly well acquainted with the stereotypes that bolster racism. His BJJ describes the typical role for a "black guy" in popular theater and entertainment (like *Orange Is the New Black*):

> some football playing illiterate drug-addict magical negro with PTSD and anger management issues who's secretly on the DL but is simultaneously trying to get out of a generic ghetto with his obese girlfriend [. . .] God forbid any actor of color not have to jump at the chance to play an offensive bag of garbage so far from his own life but which some idiot's going to describe as representative of "the Black experience in America."[92]

The passage works by accumulating a litany of familiar stereotypes that expose the ways in which both racists and allies perpetuate such beliefs about

Blacks, partially so that audiences can express their sympathy and feel good about how liberal and antiracist they are. Call it *racial catharsis*—which Jacobs-Jenkins refused to provide to his audience. He might be making a similar point with the women "slave" characters, but they are not afforded the same level of self-conscious critique exhibited by the male characters. The women seem to function as *merely* humor and stereotypes: they don't get to discuss their own perceived identities and "garbage" roles.

In the Boston production, the discrepancy between *An Octoroon*'s treatment of race and gender was reinforced by the audience participation. During Act I, when Dido and Minnie discuss whether they ever had to "fuck" the former "Massa Peyton," Minnie points out, "Naw, he only like lightskinned-ed girls. But Renee, you know, who was fuckin' him all the time, said he had the biggest dick she ever seen?"[93] A man in the audience called out, "Naw girl," perfectly pitched to the characters' speech patterns. That comment from the auditorium made other audience members laugh—laugh at someone mimicking women talking about the institutionalization of rape in slavery. Wasn't he making a joke of it, and was that joke being encouraged by the other forms of audience participation offered by the play?

I do not believe that Jacobs-Jenkins's *An Octoroon* encourages misogyny, but gender and sexuality were not treated with the same irony that so effectively undermined racial identities. Company One's strategy of asking the audience to engage in ever more uncomfortable and disorienting activities, from hissing to bidding on an enslaved person to supporting a lynching, unintentionally taught the audience that participating in a slave auction that will result in sexual slavery is less horrific than participating in a lynch mob. The strategy also highlighted the different presentations of race and gender in the play and in American culture more generally. Take this thought experiment: Instead of adding three enslaved women speaking African American vernacular, what if Jacobs-Jenkins had inserted three comparably stereotypical Black male characters? Their vernacular language would have meant something different at a moment when high-profile police shootings indicate the vulnerability of Black men and their perceived threat to white authorities. Although the Black Lives Matter movement was largely initiated by Black women who identify as queer, their work has been obscured as the cultural response pits #blacklives against #bluelives—masculine power and authority matters in the deadly contest played out on American streets and neighborhoods.[94]

3.5. The Matter of Black Lives: "Shall We Have One Law for the Red-Skin and Another for the White?"

Jacobs-Jenkins's *An Octoroon* teaches important lessons about audience participation in the racial dramas and atrocities of this moment, particularly as they are recorded on digital devices by bystanders and disseminated through social media. BJJ and the Playwright are absolutely wrong when they claim that photographs are "boring" to us now, and that "the kind of justice" represented by the discovery of a photograph that documents the murder of a Black boy by a white overseer is "actually a little dated."[95] Even without dwelling on developments in visual technology like film, video, and digital media, the posed photograph appears to hold a great deal of interest in the age of the "selfie" and the circulation of images on Facebook, Twitter, TikTok, and other social network platforms. Instagram, which launched in 2010 as a free photo and video sharing app that allows users to share images of their lives with followers or friends and comment on the posts of others, is now owned by Facebook and, in June 2021, boasted 1.074 billion users.[96] They clearly do not find photography boring.

"The kind of justice"—or injustice—represented by the circulation of a photograph that documents the murder of a Black boy by a white authority is absolutely relevant, hardly "a little dated."[97] As I began to write this chapter in the summer of 2016, a few months after seeing *An Octoroon* in Boston, cellphone videos recorded the horrifying deaths of two Black men, Alton Sterling and Philando Castile, at the hands of police officers just a day apart (July 5 and 6, 2016). The footage of these and many subsequent murders ignited widespread public protests and demonstrations, often under the rubric of Black Lives Matter, and ultimately played a role in investigations and trials, although recordings have certainly not been considered definitive evidence or proof of "conviction" by "Heaven," to echo *The Octoroon*.[98] I worry that I risk causing offense by associating the recordings of real tragedies like the murders of Sterling and Castile with theatrical conventions. Without diminishing the real suffering of victims and survivors of violence, I hope to point out that long-standing melodramatic conventions organize modes of viewing the recordings of tragedies on social media and modes of participating in the social media event. This is a function of the social media machine, which is a major inheritor of melodramatic conventions alongside TV, film, and cable news, as Branden Jacobs-Jenkins understood when he resurrected Boucicault's *The Octoroon*. I in no way wish to diminish the efforts of courageous survivors and witnesses of police violence who bravely record events and share them with the world.

Philando Castile's death was recorded and live-streamed by his girlfriend Diamond "Lavish" Reynolds on Facebook, a platform that allowed her to document the murder, create live witnesses, and ask for help for herself and her four-year-old daughter—who was in the back seat. The first frame of the excruciating ten-minute recording is troublingly reminiscent of a melodrama's "discovery tableau" as it reveals Officer Jeronimo Yanez, with his gun drawn and pointed at the bloody and groaning Castile. Yanez kept his gun aimed at the dying man for three minutes and thirty-nine seconds, as the police dashcam revealed.[99] Reynolds reported the incident as she filmed with her cell phone, claiming that Officer Yanez asked Castile for his license and registration after pulling him over for a broken taillight in Falcon Heights, Minnesota. Reynolds said, "He [Castile] let the officer know that he had a firearm, and he was reaching for his wallet, and the officer just shot him in his arm."[100] Yanez screamed his response to her, "I told him not to reach for it. I told him to get his hands up." Reynolds calmly responded, "You told him to get his ID, sir, his driver's license." Moments later, Castile was still, and Reynolds began to pray, "Please Jesus don't tell me that he's gone." Facing a panicked police officer with a gun, Reynolds was careful to address him politely and calmly as "Sir." "Yes, I will, Sir, I'll keep my hands where they are." She spoke directly to her Facebook audience after police officers took her phone: "They threw my phone, Facebook." Her daughter retrieved the phone and helped Reynolds continue filming after she was handcuffed.

A vast social media audience for Reynolds's video witnessed the gut-wrenching trauma experienced by mother and child—the first viewers watched in real time as Reynolds narrated, prayed, and wailed, as the police screamed obscenities and barked orders, as the child cried and, in the final moments, comforted her mother. Four million watched the video in the first twenty-four hours after the incident. That number soared to 5.7 million Facebook views in the next two weeks, with countless more as the video circulated in news reports and other media.[101] Viewers joined an audience much larger than the capacity of any theater and participated in the event by circulating the video, posting their responses in their social media accounts, and, in some cases, attending and supporting protests against police violence. Certainly far more of the spectators viewed the recording, sometimes repeatedly, and participated in social media protests than in the in-person, bodily protests or wider social movements—although we often feel that our posts in support, or BLM flags over our profiles, are impactful and satisfying forms of participation. As for Boucicault's ideal of an "eye of the Eternal" or a trial in which "Heaven has answered and convicted you," the recording of Castile's death became evidence for both the prosecution and defense in the trial that acquitted Officer Yanez of manslaughter.

Boucicault predicted a particularly modern "kind of justice" (or lack thereof) as juries and other audiences on social media view recordings of the violent encounters between police officers and Black citizens—and perhaps hope for a *heavenly conviction* rarely born out in a court of law.[102] The first such recording to "go viral" was George Holliday's 1991 footage of the brutal beating of Rodney King by four Los Angeles police officers—all of whom were acquitted.[103] Thirty years later, Holliday's camcorder is as obsolete as Boucicault's photographic plates, and we now record digital clips on cell phones with increasingly sophisticated built-in cameras—then screen them live or post them quickly to social media. Body cams, dash cams, nanny cams, and other electronic surveillance devices are ubiquitous. If Reynolds's recording of the death of Philando Castile was unprecedented in its circulation via social media, there were many earlier incidents. In just the two years prior, 2014–2016, online footage of no less than fourteen Black men or boys killed by police officers has circulated.[104] The police shooting of twelve-year-old Tamir Rice in Cleveland was captured by surveillance cameras on November 22, 2014. Laquan McDonald was shot sixteen times in Chicago on October 20, 2014, as he walked away from police officers, as a dash cam video revealed. The body camera of the police officer who shot Samuel Dubose in Cincinnati on July 19, 2015, captured the incident. Bystanders filmed the police killing of Eric Garner on July 17, 2014, in Staten Island and the arrest of Freddie Gray, who suffered a spinal cord injury in the custody of the Baltimore Police Department and died a week later.

These and many subsequent killings by police have been caught on various bystander and dashboard or body cameras, producing the hope that documentary technology will protect the oppressed and contribute to justice, a democratic potential Boucicault imagined very early in the history of photography. The footage has resulted in much outrage, but few criminal convictions or prison sentences. On-duty police officers fatally shoot roughly 1,000 civilians yearly, resulting in charges for only 104 officers between 2005 and 2019.[105] Derek Chauvin became just the tenth former police officer to face jail time, a sentence he received for murdering George Floyd on May 25, 2020.[106] Prior to his conviction and sentencing to twenty-two-and-a-half years of prison, the murder of George Floyd seemed to follow a very similar pattern to that of Philando Castile. The headline of the initial Minneapolis Police press release on May 25, 2020, read, "Man Dies After Medical Incident During Police Interaction," and the report claimed that during a routine arrest, officers "noted he appeared to be suffering medical distress" and "called for an ambulance. He was transported to Hennepin County Medical Center by ambulance where he died a short time later."[107] The incident might never have been investigated had it not been recorded by bystanders (despite harassment from police at the scene), most notably by a seventeen-year-old high school student, Darnella Frazier. Her cell phone recorded Derek Chauvin kneeling on Floyd's neck for nine minutes and twenty-nine seconds, as Floyd repeatedly cried out in pain, said "I can't breathe," and cried for his mother before he lost consciousness and stopped breathing. Frazier posted the video to Facebook, where it went viral and sparked outrage and widespread protests. Frazier was awarded a Special Citation by the Pulitzer Prizes for "a video that spurred protests against police brutality around the world, highlighting the crucial role of citizens in journalists' quest for truth and justice."[108]

3.6. Conclusion

The lynching photographs projected in Jacobs-Jenkins's *An Octoroon* remind those who care to pay attention that, in a racist society throughout history, the privileged have been able to document atrocity with impunity; the photograph that might have served as evidence of murder was a souvenir for participants in the lynch mob. The spectators in the foreground of the lynching photographs projected at Company One's 2016 production of *An Octoroon* mirror the audience in the theater. The production worked to put its audience in the lynch mob; they had already been hissing at villains and bidding at a slave auction, and they were encouraged to call for the lynching of Wahnotee and then M'Closky. For many, including me, that participation was very disturbing, but what did it teach?

I return again (and again) to the image of the young girl pointing at the mutilated body of the lynching victim in the foreground of that horrific photograph. Consider what such events taught the children who were present at lynchings, but also what participation in the virtual lynch mob of *An Octoroon* might teach children—and the inner child of an adult. I remain concerned about the psychic appetite for racist pleasure that the scene satisfied, even when the spectators thought they were knowingly, ironically participating. I am also concerned that an ironic participation could foster a self-satisfied belief that *I* would never have been part of a lynch mob, under any circumstances, and *I* am not complicit in racism. These divergent risks haunt the forms of participation offered by productions that work to engage the politics of race. In attempting to confront audiences with their own racism, certainly a worthy goal, these plays might unintentionally reinforce racist tendencies in some. And when audiences believe they are too savvy to allow that to happen, the plays might (equally unintentionally) reinforce liberal spectators' beliefs that they are "beyond" the racist logic of their culture. That child in the lynching photograph could have been any of us and should challenge our certainty that we would have never, in any circumstance, found ourselves or people like us in a lynch mob. She challenges me, but does she remain to do so after the image fades?

Jacobs-Jenkins suggests that he arrived at the idea of the lynching photographs because the theater can no longer give us the experience of "witness" because "we can more or less experience anything nowadays."[109] And this is precisely why participatory, interactive, and immersive theater is the rage. Audiences want to feel like they have "really witnessed something" and had an authentic, personal, or live experience when they have access to so much *mediatized witnessing* through TV, film, and social media.[110] Watching yet another clip from the list of unarmed Black people killed by police officers can make us feel desensitized to such violence, while live theater might offer another perspective. As the Assistant says at the very end of Act IV, "Anyway, the whole point of this thing was to make you feel something."[111] I believe the Boston production of *An Octoroon* did make audiences *feel* progressively more uncomfortable with their participation in the play. If it does not also provide answers to the problems of racism, if its pedagogical mission is less pronounced than its affective or sentimental mission, that is appropriate both to Boucicault's melodrama and the melodramatic extremes of contemporary American racism—which was a big part of Jacobs-Jenkins's point in *An Octoroon*. He uses a passage from Boucicault's "The Art of Dramatic Composition" as an epigraph that indicates a primary interest in producing feelings of sympathy through theatrical illusions:

> If such an imitation of human beings, suffering from their fate, be well contrived and executed in all its parts, the spectator is led to feel a particular

sympathy with the artificial joys or sorrows of which he is the witness. This
condition of his mind is called the theatrical illusion. The craft of the drama
is to produce it, and all its concerns conduce to, and depend upon, this
attainment.[112]

Boucicault was so successful at producing his desired "theatrical illusion"
in *The Octoroon* that, when the play opened in London on November 18,
1861, seven months after the outbreak of the US Civil War, the British audience summarily rejected Zoe's suicide. A debate about the ending of the play
raged in the press, and Boucicault defended his tragic conclusion in a letter
"To the Editor of the *Times*": "In the death of the Octoroon lies the moral and
teaching of the whole work. Had this girl been saved, and the Drama brought
to a happy end, the horrors of her position, irremediable from the very nature of the institution of slavery, would subside into the condition of tempo-
rary annoyance."[113] Boucicault eventually succumbed to public opinion, but
not without protesting that the audience's response to Zoe's suicide signaled
that "they had grown indifferent to the feelings, and the happiness and purity
of black women;" he argued that this response represented a huge change
from "the good old days when *Uncle Tom* [from Harriet Beecher Stowe's
Uncle Tom's Cabin of 1852] made all England cry."[114] London audiences
were less satisfied than Americans with a play that avoided making a clear
argument about slavery while using the suffering it caused to provoke sympathy; they recognized they were not getting a true abolitionist drama from
Boucicault. He, with some sarcasm but also a promotional tone that would
bring audiences back to the show yet one more time and increase ticket sales,
announced, "A new last act of the drama, composed by the public and edited
by the author, will be represented this evening. He trusts the audience will accept it as a very grateful tribute to their judgment and taste, which he should
be the last to dispute."[115] The new happy ending allowed George Peyton to
rescue Zoe from death and "in another land Zoe and Peyton will solemnize
a lawful union, and live for the happiness of each other."[116] Could audience
participation be any more influential than when the audience rewrites the
play's conclusion?

Jacobs-Jenkins rewrote Boucicault's melodrama once again and refused to
give his audience a sentimental finale. His Zoe goes off with the poison after
confusing and infuriating Dido by treating her like the "mammy" scripted
by Boucicault, a role Dido reluctantly plays before Minnie enters and
sympathizes with her fury that Zoe had cast her as "mammy" in her suicide

scene. We do not see Zoe take the poison, and that frustrates any audience desire for a tear-jerking ending. As Minnie and Dido's conversation ends the play, the mortgage plot remains unresolved, and the tragic love story between Zoe and George is pushed offstage. In some productions, Br'er Rabbit is the last character on the stage. It's a confusing ending, and Jacobs-Jenkins might be suggesting that if his audiences want a clear lesson on race, a pedagogical theater, they will have to write their own conclusion. Jacobs-Jenkins's work suggests there are no easy answers to the melodramatics of American racism. The audience reaction he hopes to achieve is ambiguous and ambivalent, with confusion as a desired outcome. In an interview, he said, "My dream was always to have an experience where an audience member would turn to another audience member, a stranger, and be like, 'What did we just go through?' And, like, kind of begin to talk."[117] Jacobs-Jenkins's work as produced by Company One certainly gave his audience "an experience."[118] Stranger, I want to talk.

PART III

DUELING ON BROADWAY

III.I. Introduction to Part III

Dueling was in the air in 2016. Fans learned "The Ten Duel Commandments" from Lin-Manuel Miranda's smash hit *Hamilton*, which staged two eighteenth-century duels.[1] Or, since many could not get their hands on *Hamilton* tickets, even if they were able and willing to pay an *average* price of $1,200 per ticket in May 2016, they learned the "Ten Duel Commandments" (the rules and lyrics) on the *Hamilton* soundtrack, which Miranda cleverly posted on YouTube, believing, correctly, that the free music would generate paying fans.[2] Although less deadly than Alexander Hamilton's fatal shootout with Aaron Burr, a contest was brewing between Miranda's *Hamilton* and that other potential Broadway hit (but miss), George C. Wolfe's *Shuffle Along, or the Making of the Musical Sensation of 1921 and All That Followed* (a wordy title that I will abbreviate as *Shuffle Along, or the Making of . . .*). Both staged versions of American history and cast mostly Black, Indigenous, and People of Color (BIPOC) performers. Both played on Broadway during the spring of 2016 while a contentious *political* duel raged between the campaigns of Donald Trump and Hillary Clinton to become the forty-fifth president of the United States. Only *Hamilton* was still playing in November to comment, quite publicly, on Trump's victory and imminent accession to the White House. *Shuffle Along, or the Making of . . .* closed at a loss on July 24, 2016, after just one hundred performances—404 fewer shows than the original *Shuffle Along* had in New York in 1921 before it began touring the country.[3]

Why was the fate of *Hamilton* so very different from *Shuffle Along, or the Making of . . .*? *Hamilton* broke the record for highest weekly gross at $3.26 million, as premium tickets surged to another record-breaking $998 over Thanksgiving week of 2016.[4] The duel between *Hamilton* and *Shuffle Along, or the Making of . . .* reveals the preferred versions of American history and messages about diversity that garner audience participation in the form of purchasing tickets, music, and merchandise—all the conventional forms of participation that are not typically considered part of immersive or participatory theater (although I have argued that theater is *always* an immersive experience). But Broadway requires so much purchasing participation, as *Shuffle Along*'s closure demonstrates, that other paratheatrical opportunities to participate can "make or break" a show. Lin-Manual Miranda was a genius at generating *Hamilton*-related material to circulate on social media, from the soundtrack on YouTube to pre-show street performances before the "Ham4Ham" ticket lottery. These materials enabled potential audiences (not-yet ticketholders) to recite the songs and become fans of the performers—but also to articulate their preferred position in relation to American history and the "inclusion and diversity" platform. Audiences love *Hamilton* because it allows them to applaud the triumphant history of the nation they already know, retold with an emphasis on *inclusion* through casting actors of color who trumpet inclusive one-liners such as "Immigrants: We get the job done!"[5] Less appealing to audiences is the complex and lesser told history of *Shuffle Along, or the Making of*... and of African American performance, which often had to accommodate racist traditions like blackface minstrelsy, among others, that influenced *Hamilton*'s blockbuster style.

4

Shuffle Along . . . the Campaign Trail

Why did George C. Wolfe's much-anticipated *Shuffle Along, or the Making of the Musical Sensation of 1921 and All That Followed* close early and at a loss in the spring of 2016? Its veteran and controversial Broadway producer, Scott Rudin, blamed his decision to close on the upcoming maternity leave of six-time Tony Award–winner Audra McDonald (Lottie Gee), who announced what the press called an "unexpected" pregnancy at the age of forty-five.[1] (See Figure 4.1.) The blame seems misplaced given that McDonald had always planned to take a leave in the summer of 2016 to reprise her role in *Lady Day at Emerson's Bar & Grill* in London—although that leave was planned for three months rather than the six months of the maternity leave.[2] After closing the show, Rudin brought a suit against insurer, Lloyd's of London, for refusing to pay on two policies worth $14.1 million, a Non-Appearance and an Abandonment Policy entitling producers to compensation if a performance had to be canceled due to the "Death, Accident, or Illness" of McDonald.[3] Lloyd's of London claimed that pregnancy is not a death, accident, or illness and that the show did not need to close when it was playing at 101.25 percent capacity during its final week.[4] *Shuffle Along, or the Making of . . .* boasted many other stars in addition to McDonald, including Brian Stokes Mitchell and Billy Porter, Tony Award winners for *Kiss Me, Kate* (1999) and *Kinky Boots* (2013), respectively. And the play was choreographed by the great dancer Savion Glover, winner of a Tony for choreographing *Bring in 'da Noise, Bring in 'da Funk* (1996), also directed by Wolfe. Despite its Tony talent, *Shuffle Along, or the Making of . . .* did not win any of the ten Tony Awards for which it was nominated, partially because the litigious Rudin failed in his bid to have it reclassified as a revival so it would not have to duel with *Hamilton*, winner of eleven of its record-breaking sixteen Tony nominations. After four years of court battles, Rudin and Lloyd's of London finally agreed to "discontinue" the case without public comment in October 2020.[5] By then, *Shuffle Along, or the Making of . . .* was all but forgotten amid the devastation to the performing arts and shuttering of Broadway brought on by the COVID-19 pandemic.

Complicit Participation. Carrie J. Preston, Oxford University Press. © Oxford University Press 2024.
DOI: 10.1093/9780197693438.003.0005

The new *Shuffle Along, or the Making of . . .* was not a revival. Wolfe refused to restage many aspects of the show that perform racist stereotypes, cutting most of the book and the comic sketches, which, like the song-and-dance numbers, were largely derived from the American blackface minstrel traditions.[6] Wolfe united the *making of* trope with the *show within a show* structure to create occasions for the original *Shuffle Along* numbers to appear as rehearsals alongside a story about the artists who created and starred in the musical. The play focused on the break-up of *Shuffle Along*'s artistic team, Noble Sissle, James Hubert "Eubie" Blake, Flournoy E. Miller, and Aubrey Lyles, and their subsequent marginalization from the historical record. Especially in the second act of *Shuffle Along, or the Making of . . .* , this material was presented in a didactic, pathos-filled history lesson that did not garner the great enthusiasm of *Hamilton*'s retelling of the American Revolution. Wolfe's strategy aligns with the goal of remembering Black artists, but it attempts to forget *Shuffle Along*'s roots in the blackface minstrel tradition, which were the foundation for its historical success as well as its ability to offer multiple, even contradictory, political statements and appeal to diverse audiences. Sissle, Blake, Miller, and Lyles adapted the minstrel tradition to break into an entertainment industry controlled by white men,

Figure 4.1 Audra McDonald as Lottie Gee and Brandon Victor Dixon as Eubie Blake in *Shuffle Along, or, the Making of the Musical Sensation of 1921 and All That Followed*, directed by George C. Wolfe. Photo by Julieta Cervantes.

represented in *Shuffle Along, or the Making of . . .* by the potential investor Henry Cort, who demands blackface humor. Ironically, Rudin, a member of the current generation of white producers, closed a play that depicted the challenges faced by Black artists, thereby putting the entire cast and crew out of work, all the while blaming a pregnant woman of color.

There is much to unpack in this mini-drama complete with lawsuits, dueling musicals deeply rooted in American history and commitments to BIPOC performers, and a dash of pregnancy shaming.[7] This chapter will argue that *Shuffle Along or the Making of . . .* did not close early because a star left the show, but because the audience left the theater without feeling like they had participated in an important *inclusion and diversity* (I&D) project and a vision for how they might continue to participate—both of which *Hamilton* offered.[8] *Shuffle Along, or the Making of . . .* reveals the challenges of restaging Black theater on contemporary stages and the related pitfalls in approaches to the racist past and present of the United States. The production hoped to recall Black contributions to musical theater, but only presented select, palatable portions: specific songs and snippets of the book alongside recreations of some of the original costumes, which, as *the making of* portion of the play revealed, were occasionally remnants from other shows. The original choreographer, Lawrence Deas, is never mentioned in Wolfe's production, and Savion Glover did not attempt to offer period choreography, even when, as in the show's famous dance instruction song, "I'm simply full of Jazz," the lyrics literally describe movements that have become classic jazz steps.[9] *Shuffle Along, or the Making of . . .* asks audiences to remember the creators of the 1921 *Shuffle Along* but encourages them to forget many aspects of the play, particularly those that do not fit comfortably into contemporary visions of theater history and I&D platforms. If *Shuffle Along, or the Making of . . .* had staged minstrel song-and-dance numbers commenting, sometimes satirically, on a plot about election fraud, it would almost certainly not have beaten *Hamilton* out of its awards—or even extended its run. But it could have revealed much about the similarities between current and past racist politics, as well as how laudable I&D efforts can inadvertently support white liberal complacency.

4.1. Blackface Minstrelsy and the Making of American Audiences

The 1921 *Shuffle Along* and its 2016 rewrite clarify the challenges of recovering histories of Black performance, particularly as central aspects, like blackface minstrelsy, are not easily absorbed into our preferred stories of progress toward a less racist, more just society. *Shuffle Along, or the Making of...*, like Branden Jacobs-Jenkins's *An Octoroon* and his earlier exploration of the legacy of minstrelsy, *Neighbors* (2010), reveals that American theater's current attempts to interrogate racial constructs often involves a reckoning with minstrel theater as one of the origins of Black performance in the United States. Theater artists like Genet, Wolfe, and Jacobs-Jenkins provocatively resurrect the materials of minstrelsy: the burnt cork, tambo and bones, Black wit, wench dance, and performing, laboring blackened or Black-but-still-blackened body. They also resurrect the minstrel show audience, but they cannot control that audience's responses to finding itself at a minstrel show. Whereas Jacobs-Jenkins and Genet set audiences adrift to deal with blackface performance in ways that might range from horror to pleasure, Wolfe couched blackface performance in a history lesson and worked to ensure that the audience would find it pathetic. Miller (played by Brian Stokes Mitchell) and Lyles (played by Billy Porter) discuss performing in blackface, and Miller, the more practical and compliant of the characters, claims that it is offensive when white actors blacken their faces but Black performers in blackface can be "saucy and subversive."[10] Miller blackens his face onstage and turns toward the audience with an exaggerated, pathos-filled grin. On the evening I attended, the audience responded with audible gasps of horror. Wolfe presented blackface as a sad necessity for the 1921 production that can be explored only for a moment in 2016; the actors do not remain in blackface to perform the great musical numbers of *Shuffle Along, or the Making of...* a choice that keeps the history lesson adamantly separate from the pleasures of the new show. It would have been far more uncomfortable to force the contemporary audience into the place of deriving pleasure from Black actors singing and dancing in blackface.

American theater is deeply rooted in the history of blackface minstrelsy that Wolfe seeks to excavate but also discard in *Shuffle Along, or the Making of...* As evidenced by the original *Shuffle Along*, minstrelsy garnered an ambivalently horrified and fascinated audience for the spectacle of performing racial difference well into the twentieth century. The "Great Migration" of Black Americans from the South to northern cities beginning around 1916 also transported music and dance with roots in slave cultures and minstrelsy.[11] Blues mingled with international musical forms (especially Spanish and French colonial styles) to produce jazz and ragtime, considered core achievements of African American music *and* American music. In fact, jazz and ragtime are so celebrated that their roots in Black culture and minstrelsy are often ignored. Both provided the soundtrack for the Harlem Renaissance, a flowering or renewal of Black arts centered on New York's Harlem neighborhood—which reverberated with the rhythms of *Shuffle Along.*

The music and dance of nineteenth-century blackface minstrelsy and its derivatives, like tap dancing, defined a particular racialized and gendered "Americanness" for national *and* international audiences after 1830. Eric Lott and, more recently, Megan Pugh, have established that nineteenth-century minstrelsy trafficked in deep racial and gendered ambivalence, perhaps most obviously expressed in blackface performance and cross-gender costumes.[12] Minstrel shows appealed to a confounded fascination with the Black (male) body both as a source of entertainment and competition for the American working class. These themes are evident in Robert P. Nevin's early (1867) and influential origin story of minstrelsy, or, as he wrote, "the circumstances— authentic in every particular—under which the first work of the distinct art of Negro Minstrelsy was presented."[13] T. D. Rice, the supposed inventor of blackface minstrelsy, was walking in Cincinnati when he overheard:

> a voice ringing clear and full above the noises of the street, and giving utter-
> ance, in an unmistakable dialect, to the refrain of a song to this effect:
> "Turn about an' wheel about an' do jis so,
> An' ebery time I turn about I jump Jim Crow."
> . . . As a national or 'race' illustration, behind the footlights, might not
> 'Jim Crow' and a black face tickle the fancy of pit and circle, as well as the
> 'Sprig of Shillalah' and a red nose? Out of the suggestion leaped the deter-
> mination; and so it chanced that the casual hearing of a song trolled by a
> negro stage-driver, lolling lazily on the box of his vehicle, gave origin to a
> school of music destined to excel in popularity all others, and to make the
> name of the obscure actor, T.D. Rice, famous.[14]

The story brings Rice, an "obscure actor" with the "merit" of a "proper ap- preciation of his own capacity" (which Nevin views as quite limited), into proximity with the "lolling" stage-driver as singers of the same song, although their labor and prospects are quite different because of their skin color.[15] (See Figure 4.2.) Rice appropriated "Jim Crow" from the "Negro stage-driver" and was launched to fame, while the inspirational singer remains unnamed in this and most other accounts.[16] Rice's apparent appreciation of "Jim Crow"

The Celebrated JIM CROW.

Presented with Nº7 of the WONDER August 5th 1837.

Figure 4.2 Th. D. Rice. The celebrated Jim Crow. Presented with No. 7 of the Wonder, August 5, 1837. Courtesy of Wallach Division Picture Collection, the New York Public Library.

as a "national or 'race' illustration," is compared to the Irish song "Sprig of Shillalah" ["The Sprig of Shillelagh"], which was regularly performed in minstrel shows.[17] Blackface performance is presented in relation to the painted red-nose used to depict the stereotypical drunken stage Irishman, as both would "tickle the fancy" of audiences.[18] Minstrel shows and other cultural forms constructed American whiteness in relation to the status of Irish and Jewish immigrants, and these racialized groups produced most of the blackface performers and audiences for minstrelsy.[19] Minstrelsy allowed those marginalized by race or nationality, gender representation or sexuality, to play with these categories in a way that was couched in humor and fun—and was therefore relatively *safe* for the actors and less threatening to the dominant culture.

According to Nevin's account, Rice was nearing the end of his acting engagement in Cincinnati when he overheard the inspirational stage-driver sing "Jim Crow," so his first opportunity to try out his new act occurred in Pittsburgh. Once again, Rice borrowed or stole from a Black man, literally taking the man's clothes for his costume. Rice's benefactor gets a name in this part of the story, "Cuff," and an occupation; he made his living by letting boys "pitch pennies" into his mouth "and by carrying the trunks of passengers from the steamboats to the hotels."[20]

> Rice, having shaded his own countenance to the "contraband" hue, ordered Cuff to disrobe, and proceeded to invest himself in the cast-off apparel. When the arrangements were complete, the bell rang, and Rice, habited in an old coat forlornly dilapidated, with a pair of shoes composed equally of patches and places for patches on his feet, and wearing a coarse straw hat in a melancholy condition of rent and collapse over a dense black wig of matted moss, waddled into view.[21]

Rice sang his version of the stage-driver's "Jim Crow," and the "effect was electric," eliciting "a thunder of applause."[22] The performance reached a "mirthful" conclusion when Cuff, having learned that a steamboat was arriving and failing to get Rice's attention over the laughter and clapping, ran onstage in "ludicrous undress" to demand his clothes.[23] The white performer triumphed at the expense of the Black man's livelihood and dignity/decency as the act closed with the nude appearance of Cuff, who was described in erotic and racist terms as "an exquisite specimen of his sort."[24] Nevin's account suggests a fascination with Black male bodies and an anxiety about competition with Black labor and artistry.

While the origin stories tend to depict minstrelsy as a "national or 'race' illustration" with deep roots in American racial categories, recent scholarship has called attention to a longer history and the transnational influences on the minstrel show.[25] Accounts of blackface performance in England surface as early as 1377, and English pantomime featured a Black Harlequin character derived from Italian commedia dell'arte and other European traditions of blackface clowning.[26] American blackface minstrelsy, when it arrived in Great Britain in 1836 with T. D. Rice, combined familiar and foreign elements to generate great enthusiasm. American minstrelsy was a "contagion" that crossed international borders, class barriers, and gender lines, as an enthralled, distressed James Kennard, Jr. noted in 1845:

> From the nobility and gentry, down to the lowest chimney-sweep in Great Britain, and from the member of Congress, down to the youngest apprentice or school-boy in America, it was all: "Turn about and wheel about, and do just so, / And every time I turn about I jump Jim Crow."
>
> Even the fair sex did not escape the contagion: the tunes were set to music for the piano-forte, and nearly every young lady in the Union, and the United Kingdom, played and sang, if she did not *jump*, "Jim Crow." . . . [Negroes themselves were not permitted to appear in the theatres, and the houses of the fashionable, but their songs are in the mouths and ears of all.] [insertion in the original][27]

Minstrelsy's racial caricatures had transatlantic appeal, despite the distinct colonial and racial histories of the United States (still six years from the Civil War at the time of Kennard's statement) and Great Britain.[28] Kennard's discussion of the "contagion" of minstrelsy points to its appeal across class and gender lines, although his anxieties about women playing and singing minstrel songs reflects desires to protect the so-called fair sex, which was generally excluded from the public minstrel show.[29]

How did these audiences of different classes, genders, and generations understand the racial identities of minstrel performers in the nineteenth century? Eric Lott claims audiences often mistook blackface performers for Black men, that "in the minds of many, blackface singers and dancers became, simply, 'Negroes.'"[30] I am interested in evidence of a more complicated reception as some audiences considered blackface minstrels to be "Negroes" for the duration of the performance while recognizing that they were white—or became white again—after they left the stage and removed the paint. For these audiences, minstrels danced across racial categories. Promotional materials for the more organized and successful troupes included the tongue-in-cheek claims that the Apollo Minstrels were the "only original Negroes traveling," and Christy's Minstrels were "the very pinks of negro singers."[31] (See Figure 4.3.) If groups of white minstrels were the "only original Negroes," it was partially because they were creating "original" identities, versions of Blackness in which the *pinkness* of the skin that created

Figure 4.3 Music of the original Christy Minstrels (1800–1899). Courtesy of the Jerome Robbins Dance Division, the New York Public Library. Public domain.

them showed through quite intentionally.[32] Audiences for minstrelsy in the nineteenth century enjoyed those performances of race and exhibited a false conscious/self-conscious racial ambivalence that suggests the instability of racial categories.

The notion that a performer could put on blackface and become an "original Negro" provoked laughter, horror, *and pleasure*.[33] Minstrelsy appealed to audiences by staging a hint of racial instability alongside comic stereotypes, generally maintaining the challenge to racial norms at provocative/

entertaining rather than more radical/frightening levels. This is not to say that most audiences in the nineteenth century or today subscribe to what theorists of race call "racial performativity" or "the performative production of race." The phrase refers to the idea that race is not a biological category, not even (or not fully) a cultural construct; instead, it is brought into being through performative speech acts and repeated enactments of identity or selfhood.[34] I am wary of overemphasizing the seemingly radical idea of racial performativity and instability embedded in minstrelsy, when the form more prominently featured racist, comedic appropriations of Black culture that did not overtly fight racism; in fact, the humor and fun may have inured white audiences to racial oppression, making it more normal and tolerable.

Notions of minstrelsy's progressive potential are not new, as indicated by the eminent abolitionist Frederick Douglass, who suggested that Black-blackface minstrels might be "instrumental in removing the prejudice against our race."[35] Douglass's 1948 description of groups like the Christy's Minstrels as the "filthy scum of white society" is regularly cited by scholars and journalists.[36] But a year later, he wrote of "Gavitt's Original Ethiopian Serenaders" with measured enthusiasm, concluding that some of the finer performers "may do much to elevate themselves and their race in popular estimation."[37] For Douglass, the fact that "Gavitt's Original Ethiopian Serenaders" were representing "their [own] race" contributes to their potential elevation (in contrast to the "filthy scum" of white minstrels).[38] Douglass's description of Black blackface minstrelsy leads him to suggest the instability of racial categories:

> The Company is said to be composed entirely of colored people; and it may be so. We observed, however, that they, too had recourse to the burnt cork and lamp black, the better to express their characters, and to produce uniformity of complexion. Their lips, too, were evidently painted, and otherwise exaggerated.[39]

The goal of an impossible "uniformity" of blackness led the performers to blacken their faces and sing in a way that "was but an imitation of white performers, and not even a tolerable representation of the character of colored people."[40] Douglass recognized a double imitation, as minstrels imitate white performers imitating Black culture, which renders race a matter of uncertainty and gossip ("said to be . . . and it may be so").[41] If race, at least in the minstrel show, is an "imitation of an imitation," where is the original to be located?[42] Douglass indicated the possibility that minstrelsy could construct new identities. Mentioning one great singer, Cooper, one great dancer, B. Richardson (in the Virginia Breakdown), and one great player, Davis (the *Bones*), Douglass claimed, "It is something gained when the colored man in any form can appear before a white audience; and we think that even this company, with industry, application, and a proper cultivation of their taste, may yet be instrumental in removing the prejudice against our race."[43] Douglass offered a sophisticated discussion of how Black minstrels could cultivate themselves as well as their audiences through performance.

Douglass's assessment of minstrel performance in the late 1840s was nuanced and complex. He even anticipated contemporary critical theories of "performative identity construction," yet the popular media has used him to vociferously condemn blackface while trying to explain, "Why Ralph Northam, Mark Herring and others darkening their faces is such a big deal" to borrow a subtitle from *USA Today*.[44] Blackface performance was propelled back into the spotlight in January 2019 when Virginia's Democratic Governor Northam faced the circulation of his 1984 medical school yearbook page depicting a photo of a man with face paint standing next to someone wearing a Ku Klux Klan robe.[45] Northam initially acknowledged he was in the photo, and then denied it was him, while admitting to having dressed up as Michael Jackson in blackface. Soon after, Virginia's Democratic attorney general, Mark Herring, revealed that as an undergraduate in 1983, he had put on blackface to costume himself as the rapper Kurtis Blow.[46]

USA Today cites Douglass to argue that "Blackface performances were condemned as offensive from the very beginning":

> In 1848, after watching a blackface act, abolitionist Fredrick Douglass called the performers "the filthy scum of white society" in The North Star newspaper.
>
> Blackface performers, he said, "have stolen from us a complexion denied to them by nature . . . to make money and pander to the corrupt taste of their white fellow-citizens."[47]

The quote is from "The Hutchinson Family—Hunkerism" in which Douglass wrote with great irony of the "miserable dough-face who edits the Cass paper," an editor who found the Christy Minstrels "in harmony with his refined and elegant taste" but deplored the Hutchinson Family singers, claiming their "abolitionism had ruined them."[48] In "Hunkerism," Douglass was far more interested in celebrating the Hutchinson Family than in exploring the complexity of minstrelsy. Yet the line about "the filthy scum of white society," which Douglass was applying to the editor as much as to the Christy Minstrels, is easily quoted out of context in the popular media and used to oversimplify the history of blackface minstrelsy.[49]

As political turmoil shook Virginia, the media failed to discuss the complexity of blackface performance or its use to critique racial constructs by theater artists from Jean Genet to George C. Wolfe and Branden Jacobs-Jenkins. Blackface as it was practiced by performers well into the twentieth century—was a complex phenomenon characterized by bigotry, to be sure, but also by deep ambivalence and even hopes to end racism.[50] Several popular pieces about blackface during the Northam scandal included photographs of the performer Al Jolson (1886–1950). They did not mention that Jolson was a Lithuanian Jewish immigrant and, like many other Jewish and Irish American blackface performers, not considered purely white by many in the first half of the twentieth century. Jolson's blackface performance in *The Jazz Singer* (1927), the first feature-length "talkie," was warmly embraced by the Black press and community; among Black Americans, he was the most popular Hollywood movie star of the late 1920s.[51] Jolson's performances may have been ironically critical of the blackface phenomenon in which he participated.

My point in emphasizing the complexity of blackface performance is not to excuse Governor Northam's racist act of dressing in blackface. I am concerned when the press connects blackface costumes for parties or Halloween to the history of minstrelsy and oversimplifies the performance tradition. There is a danger in ignoring the intricacy and even pleasures of past and current operations of racism. It is all too easy, particularly for white liberals, to call out and condemn individual acts of racism, while ignoring the deeply entrenched systems and institutions that uphold white supremacy. But it is not at all easy to wade into the complexity of American racism and its varied performances.

In February 2019, I was asked by my university's daily news to write a brief "Point of View" piece about the blackface performance tradition and its bearing on the Northam case in Virginia. After the editor initially declared my opinion piece "very good" and shared it with his executive editor, they became, as he wrote, "worried that your words will still be misconstrued and that you'll get considerable pushback on the piece."[52] While grating at his paternalistic tone, I dutifully and quickly revised my piece as he suggested. Even with the revisions, he responded that he could not publish the piece: "We simply can't ignore the fact that there are certain passages here that might be construed as supporting—or not attacking strongly enough—the concept that's under so much fire right now. And that would therefore leave you . . . potentially vulnerable to enormous heat."[53] I should have responded that we are all living in the long burn of white supremacy, and a myopic focus on any particular "fire" of the day can serve as a distraction from the larger struggle against racial oppression. I should have pointed out that the "strong attack" he was demanding might make us feel good about our participation in individual battles but would not help us recognize the insidious complexity of racism or our complicit participation in its operations.[54] Many of us prefer to imagine that everything can be easily classified as either racist or antiracist and that the antiracist position is always obvious and available. As a white writer, it is crucial that I work hard to avoid causing pain when I write about race and be cognizant of the ways my words "might be construed" in different ways. I particularly worry that my discussion of the limits of liberal inclusion and diversity efforts might be construed as an attack on all efforts for racial justice rather than a desire to make them more effective. Yet I also believe I need to be courageous enough to discuss difficult, complex topics on race and refuse to hide behind "white fragility."[55] My "Point of View" was never published in the university's daily.

4.2. *Shuffle Along* (1921) and the Long Burn of Minstrelsy

George C. Wolfe's decision not to restage the most racist elements of the wildly popular *Shuffle Along* of 1921 was motivated less by avoidance than a desire to present a show of racial uplift and history lesson about the creators of the show, while mitigating the risk of distressing audiences, (re)producing racial trauma, or unintentionally supporting audience biases. While I honor the motivation, historical realities were cut alongside the offensive text and performance styles. *Shuffle Along* linked minstrelsy and the modern musical, setting the familiar Black-blackface minstrel acts to the new and exciting music and dance rhythms of the early twentieth century: jazz. Staging racist stereotypes alongside challenges to the limits of Black representation at that time, *Shuffle Along* broke taboos against depicting love between Black characters and Black women's independence from men. Like the minstrel tradition, more generally, *Shuffle Along* staged resistance, ambivalence, and compliance with the racial regime—sometimes all three were operating to different degrees in the same scene with different, even contradictory, interpretations available to subsets of the audience. These racially charged, multilayered meanings were one of the primary legacies *Shuffle Along* adapted from the minstrel show, as well as a key to its success with diverse audiences.

Shuffle Along, as depicted in *the making of* and in most histories (which ignore the choreographer), was the creative product of a fusion of two teams from the mixed-media, interracial vaudeville circuits that had developed out of minstrelsy: the singer-songwriter team of Noble Sissle and James Hubert "Eubie" Blake and the blackface comedy-dance duo, Flournoy E. Miller and Aubrey Lyles.[56] Sissle and Blake were billed as "The Dixie Duo" in the vaudeville circuit, and they were one of the first so-called Negro acts to play without burnt cork blackface, although it was not always easy to avoid "blacking-up," as Blake recalled:

> Some agent had a smart idea for an act for us. We were supposed to shuffle on stage in blackface and patched-up overalls. In the middle of the stage there was a big box with a piano in it. The idea was to look at it as if it were from the moon and I'd say, "What's dat?" and Noble would say, "Dat's a py-anner!" and then we'd do our act.[57]

Sissle and Blake refused to "shuffle" into the "py-anner" from-the-moon act, with its suggestion that Black performers are ignorant yet born with musical ability. Instead, they typically performed in starched and tailored tuxedos, although their music was derived from the minstrel style that had literally trained Blake; his first traveling job was as a buck (tap) dancer for the minstrel show *In Old Kentucky*.[58] Sissle and Blake were recombining these musical influences and producing rags, blues, and jazz for enthusiastic audiences (see Figure 4.4).

Miller and Lyles wore the "blackface and patched-up overalls" that Sissle and Blake rejected, but their approach emphasized the resistance and ambivalence available in minstrelsy.[59] (See Figure 4.5.) They debuted their blackface comic act at Fisk University in Tennessee and took it to Chicago's Mott's Pekin Theatre and then a tour of England before several years on the Keith vaudeville circuit.[60] They were particularly celebrated for tap dances and physical comedy routines, like a famous and much-imitated fight scene that was incorporated directly into *Shuffle Along* as "Jimtown Fisticuffs." Although their brief dramatic sketches filled with small-town humor resembled the

Figure 4.4 Lyricist Noble Sissle and cast members from the musical *Shuffle Along* (ca. 1921). Photo by White Studio ©Schomburg Center for Research in Black Culture, the New York Public Library.

Figure 4.5 Publicity photograph of vaudeville comedy duo Miller and Lyles, looking from behind a door in unidentified comedy routine, between 1909 and 1928. Courtesy of Schomburg Center for Research in Black Culture, the New York Public Library.

narrative scenes typically composing the third act of a minstrel show, they were performing one act in a larger vaudeville show.[61] American vaudeville inherited much from minstrelsy, but along with its dignified French-derived name, it added a rule that there could only be one act featuring Black performers in each show.[62] Therefore, the singer-songwriters Sissle and Blake could not meet the comedians Miller and Lyles in the vaudeville venues they toured. Their collaboration was born when they shared the stage at a 1920

Philadelphia NAACP (National Association for the Advancement of Colored People) fundraiser—a venue suggesting that vaudeville performance, even in blackface, was not universally considered a racist and demeaning entertainment.[63] After another chance encounter in New York, the teams decided to build a full-length show from one of Miller and Lyle's most popular skits, billed as "The Mayor of Jimtown" or "The Mayer of Dixie." *Shuffle Along* developed the skit into the story of a rigged mayoral election in a Black municipality, which may have invoked the festival called Election Day.[64] As early as the 1750s, Black communities elected their own government officials in a parody of the white elections from which they were excluded, wore "white clothing," and marched through town like military regiments.

Shuffle Along's loose plot places the rigged election in Jimtown, where Miller and Lyles play dishonest partners in a grocery store, Steve Jenkins and Sam Peck, who run against each other for mayor (see Figure 4.6). In keeping with their long history of cheating each other in business, the candidates both begin stealing from the store to buy votes and to hire the same detective,

Figure 4.6   Roger Matthews (on balcony) and cast in political campaign scene from the stage production *Shuffle Along* (1921). Photo by White Studio ©Billy Rose Theatre Division, the New York Public Library for the Performing Arts.

Keeneye, to reveal the others' crimes. While developing the book for *Shuffle Along*, the creative team added a romantic love story: The honest candidate, Harry, must win the mayoral race before he can marry his beloved Jessie— so Jessie's father has dictated. Harry loses, Steve is elected mayor, and Sam becomes Chief of Police to enforce laws such as:

STEVE: (Taking pencil into hand) Here's the first law I'm gwine to pass since I've been the Mayor. "Black cats must go." Black c c c c. Say, look here, Sam, how do you spell cat anyhow?

SAM: What do you mean? One of dem jes' plain everyday walkin' 'round cats? . . .

STEVE: Der ain't but six letters in it.[65]

Jimtown citizens complain that the mayor is misusing tax dollars to buy an automobile and hire five gorgeous stenographers who must "slam" [salaam] the mayor when they leave his presence.[66] (See Figure 4.7.) Detective

Figure 4.7 Scene (gentlemen and chorus girls with chapeaus) stage production *Shuffle Along* (1921). Photo by White Studio ©Billy Rose Theatre Division, the New York Public Library for the Performing Arts.

Keeneye, who also happens to be honest Harry's best friend, promises to reveal the election fraud and install Harry as the rightful mayor—which would allow him to marry his beloved Jessie. Audiences never learn how he manages this feat because the final scene is comprised of song-and-dance numbers.

Sissle and Blake's score for *Shuffle Along* featured a mix of songs written to comment on the plot along with music from the team's existing repertory. Most of the critical praise for the production focused on the score. *The New York Times* proclaimed (in the first use of "swing" in connection with music), "The principal asset of 'Shuffle Along,' which arrived at the Sixty-Third Street Music Hall last night with the distinction of being written, composed and played entirely by negroes, is a swinging and infectious score by one Eubie Blake" [sic].[67] This asset aside, the reviewer claimed the play was "extremely crude—in writing, playing and direction," and "none of it is conspicuously native"—by which term the reviewer may have meant "native" to America or to peoples of African descent, but probably just "native" as a racist synonym for "primitive."[68] *Shuffle Along*'s advertisements quoted from celebratory reviews of the music in the *Evening Journal*, which dubbed the play "A breeze of super-jazz blown up from Dixie" and the *Mail*, which claimed, "The principal asset of the new entertainment is the dancing and the jazz numbers."[69]

The score's influence was enduring, and one of the most popular songs would serve as a triumphant campaign song—in yet another story of white appropriation of Black art. Harry S. Truman used, "I'm Just Wild About Harry," to support his successful 1948 presidential campaign, initially without attribution to—perhaps without knowledge of—its Black composers. In the *Shuffle Along* context, this song and "Love Will Find a Way" were considered shocking and dangerous because Jessie's musical declarations of her love for Harry were the first depiction of Black love onstage, such a taboo in 1921 that actors worried they would be booed off the stage (see Figure 4.8). President Truman gave "I'm Just Wild About Harry" a second chance as an election victory song, and the campaign's attention to the song sparked *Shuffle Along*'s failed 1952 rewrite and revival.[70] The "catastrophic failure" of the revival, at least for the veteran drama critic George Jean Nathan, who had seen the original *Shuffle Along* "no less than five times," should not be interpreted as an indication that minstrelsy's long burn had flamed out by 1952.[71] Instead, Nathan suggested that the producers ruined *Shuffle Along* by attempting to bring the show "up-to-date" and instead should "present it exactly as it was in 1921 . . . All the original stuff should be retained." For Nathan this includes

Figure 4.8 "Love Will Find a Way" (1921) by Noble Sissle and Eubie Blake. Sheet music. Courtesy of the Music Division, the New York Public Library. Public domain.

the "spirited old songs," "hot dance number[s]," and even the skits, which he calls "originally comical Negro yokels" and "imbecile Negro humors."[72] The obvious racism in Nathan's phrases indicates that audiences continued to delight in *Shuffle Along*'s minstrel-derived performances from 1921 to 1952. The Black artists and creators were also disappointed by the so-called revival; Eubie Blake complained of the 1952 revival, "They threw my music out of *Shuffle Along*," and he also claimed, "The [new] lyrics and music would have to be equally applicable to white and black audiences."[73] They would also have to be equally available for these audiences to interpret in the ways they preferred, as upholding racism or submitting it to ironical humor.

4.3. Dancing "So Full of Jazz, Jazz, Jazz" with the Dance Instruction Song

The producer's failed campaign to have *Shuffle Along, or The Making of . . . reclassified* as a revival for the purpose of avoiding competition with *Hamilton* for the Tony Awards hinged on how much of the original book and music were restaged in 2016—not the choreography. Recovering and even writing about historical dance performances are difficult, particularly when, as with *Shuffle Along*, the dance often highlighted the skills, idiosyncrasies, and tricks of particular performers. Still, *Shuffle Along* had a choreographer, Lawrence Deas, who was valued by the other creators; Eubie Blake pointed out that just before the Boston tour, the producers "brought in a white dance director named Walter Brooks to give the show 'That Broadway touch.' He got two percent of the production, and Lawrence Deas who had done all the work, was paid off with a small amount of cash and dropped."[74] Deas was also dropped from Wolfe's story of *the making* of *Shuffle Along*, where he does not appear as a character. Deas does not even make it into the "historical pro-gram" that was inserted in the playbill for the 2016 show, which is ahistorical given that the actual programs consulted to produce the insert did, in fact, list "Dances by Lawrence Deas."[75] The omission is also ironic given that the choreography was crucial to the success of the original *Shuffle Along*. Critics celebrated the dancers: "Every sinew in their bodies danced; every tendon in their frames responded to their extreme energy."[76] The great tap soloist Charlie Davis "staggered the audience" with his "sheer speed and endur-ance."[77] Dance has been placed lower in the hierarchy of performance forms that contributed to the musical by most histories, and *Shuffle Along, or the Making of . . .* only amplifies the trend.

Remembering the contributions of Black dancers and choreographers to early twentieth-century art and culture requires more flexible interpretive strategies and a willingness to embrace ambiguity. As a test case, I will use the showstopper "I'm Simply Full of Jazz" sung by Miss Ruth Little (played first by Gertrude Saunders and later by Florence Mills) with the help of the "Jazz Jasmines."[78] The many histories of "jazz" refer primarily to the form of music developed by Black Americans, drawing from slave songs, minstrel shows, blues, and other influences—the most *modern* of musical forms produced in North America.[79] But the "jazz" in these histories does not centrally concern dances like the Charleston or Ballin' the Jack, a move that is sung about and performed in *Shuffle Along*'s "I'm Simply Full of Jazz." Jazz did—and still does—encompass both musical and dance forms, and when Miss Ruth proclaims that she would never get married "Because I'm simply too full of jazz," she references both her song and dance, as well as some jazz spirit we might call spunk or independence.

From one perspective, Miss Ruth offers a proto-feminist argument that the modern *jazzy* girl does not need a man to take care of her. From another, she is a "hazy" and "crazy" young "razz," in line with many stereotypes of silly or mad women.[80] The jazz number offers opportunities for reading a more serious social critique of the institution of marriage and gender roles partially hidden among racial and gendered stereotypes. David Savran argues that a mode of "double reading" must have been available to some audiences, particularly the crowds of enthusiastic Black theatergoers—or they would not have attended *Shuffle Along*, sometimes again and again.[81] The same was true for women, especially Black women, for whom Miss Ruth articulates a rebellious self-sufficiency through a modern jazz song-and-dance derived from minstrelsy, a style rarely performed by women. Minstrelsy was an all-male enterprise until the twentieth century, one that enabled men to dress in drag, play with sexualities, and perform other roles that did not align with the standards of masculinity while using femininity as the brunt of jokes.[82] When Black women took the stage in minstrel-derived styles, they could tap into that resistance and ambivalence while presenting themselves in a manner that was less threatening to white male privilege. Miss Ruth can use a jazz song-and-dance number about jazz to broach ideas that, in another context, might be considered more radical.

Miss Ruth is so "full of jazz, jazz, jazz" that she infects her viewers: "When they see me shake, it makes them shiver, / When I do a break it makes them quiver."[83] Her audience might shake and shiver with erotic desire, pleasure, and/or horror, and they might be infected by her independence and determination not to marry along with her jazz dance. *Shuffle Along's* dance style and choreography were so infectious that the chorus girls were hired by other Broadway musicals to give dance lessons, and the production began offering Wednesday "Special Midnight Matinees" primarily for actors and dancers who could not attend regularly scheduled performances because they were tied up in their own shows.[84] For the audiences who flocked to the 63rd Street Theatre to be infected by *Shuffle Along's* famous jazz dancing, Miss Ruth's "I'm Simply Full of Jazz" provided a dance lesson. The lyrics list the popular jazz dance moves as the music glories in syncopated rhythms, and Ruth with her chorus of Jazz Jasmines demonstrates the moves while singing. This is a dance instruction song, a genre in which the choreography is so crucial to the song that we might say the lyrics are related to dance as a score is to music. Miss Ruth would perform the "shimmie" as she sang about it and demonstrate a "jump way back" or "Boogie Back," "a break," and how to "ball the jack."

'Cause I *kick* like a donkey, *jump way back,*
'Cause I act like a monkey, and *ball the jack,*[85]

This last step was popularized by the song "Ballin the Jack" (1913) written by Jim Burris with music by Chris Smith and made famous by its incorporation into the film *For Me and My Gal* (MGM, 1942), performed by Judy Garland and Gene Kelly.[86] Moves like the "shimmie," "monkey," "break," and "ball the jack" were called *Eccentric dances* that allowed for individual interpretation, and performers used their own musicality and physical ability to stand out from the chorus. The ability to nurture a unique or *eccentric* style, far from the uniformity of, for example, the contemporaneous kick lines and Taylor girls, also reinforced Ruth's message about being too full of jazz for a heteronormative marriage.

This was the great age of dance instruction songs, a moment when American popular culture was established enough to produce international song-and-dance crazes. *Shuffle Along* closed on another dance instruction song, "Baltimore Buzz":

First, you take your Babe and gently hold her,
Then you lay your head upon her shoulder,
Next you walk just like your legs are breaking,

Do a fango like a tango,
Then you start the shimmie to shaking . . .[87]

The dance instruction song was an invitation for audience participation, providing a lesson that would encourage the spectators—if not to jump up and shimmie in the aisles of the auditorium as did the writer F. Scott Fitzgerald at the original *Shuffle Along* in 1921—then to imaginatively join in or dance later with the lyrics to help them remember the moves.[88] Dance instruction songs helped generate and hook audiences before the advent of popular television, when MTV could teach fans the dances stars perform without the help of lyrics. I learned Michael Jackson's moves to "Thriller" (1984) without the benefit of instructions built into the lyrics because I saw him dance on TV. "The Time Warp," from that other Halloween staple *The Rocky Horror Picture Show* (1975), is a dance instruction song that warps back to an earlier period of such dance fads. Boasting a diagram to explain the moves that must be performed when the "blackness" hits the oh-so-bourgeois Brad and Janet, the number features several Black dancers with "Afro" hair styles in the chorus and a minstrel-esque tap dance interlude—performed by a girl in a yellow sequin top hat and tails with a red bowtie—a gesture toward drag.

"The Time Warp" recalls minstrelsy in ways that are insensitive and racist; similarly, much early twentieth-century Black performance *should* make contemporary audiences uncomfortable, regardless of their appeal at the time of their original staging. Rather than forgetting or avoiding this discomfort, we can use it to understand the function of performed racial stereotypes and their similarity to current modes. To be allowed to perform in the usual venues, Black singers and dancers were required to present themselves in the roles accepted by the racist culture of the time. These styles of performance typically drew from the American minstrel tradition, and this is true of *Shuffle Along*'s choreography, book, and music. The fact that jazz music, also influenced by minstrelsy, does not now feel as racist as *Shuffle Along*'s tap dances and skits, partially stems from the fact that music, apart from the lyrics, is less representational and mimetic. The musicians are not forced into recognizably racist movements to the same extent as the actors when they blacken their faces or perform physical humor and "fisticuffs."

The new *Shuffle Along or the Making Of . . .* did not attempt to recover the choreography, use period styles, or even follow the instructions in the dance instruction song "I'm Simply Full of Jazz."[89] A "ball the jack" did not appear in the number, although Adrienne Warren, as Miss Ruth did "shimmie" and "wriggle," while singing the solo parts. The chorus of new Jazz Jasmines did not follow the sequence of "kick like a donkey," then "jump way back," then "the monkey" to the recognizable "ball the jack."[90] Wolfe and the choreographer, Savion Glover, may have felt that these traditional jazz steps were outdated, smacked of racist movements, or would have constrained Glover's choreography—which did feature tap steps that gestured creatively back to the origins of contemporary tap dancing. The decision not to follow the dance instruction songs is most noticeable in "I'm Simply Full of Jazz," as the gap between the lyrics and dance offer a glimpse into the differences in choreography and stage movement from 1921 to 2016. The choice not to recover the movement or even mention choreographic process in *Shuffle Along, or the Making of* . . . may have been partially motivated by commitments to racial justice, but it resulted in the further marginalization of the original choreographer, Lawrence Deas. Ironically, the erasure of Deas replicates the pattern that Eubie Blake had bemoaned when producers brought in a "white dance director" and "Lawrence Deas who had done all the work, was paid off with a small amount of cash and dropped."[91]

4.4. Shuffling toward the White House in 1921 and 2016

What do contemporary critics, artists, and audiences do with a hit created and performed by artists of color that trafficked in racial insult and stereotypes of Black Americans as backward, corrupt, and innately theatrical . . . with a show that allowed Black sweethearts to sing about their love onstage before white audiences, a "taboo," even dangerous act?[92] . . . that began to integrate the theater auditorium by allowing Black audiences nearer to whites?[93] What do we do with the fact that *Shuffle Along* launched the star-studded careers of Josephine Baker, Paul Robeson, and Florence Mills . . . or that the famous writer Langston Hughes referenced *Shuffle Along* as the musical that "symbolized Harlem" and even the reason he enrolled at Columbia University so as to be close to the excitement?[94]

Wolfe claims that we forgot and/or suppressed it: "Something huge happened and then something huge also happened—which was that we don't know anything about it."[95] The company of the new *Shuffle Along, or the Making of* . . . plaintively sings, "They Won't Remember You," but *Shuffle Along* has been remembered, even if its creators are far from household names (then again, not many early twentieth-century musical theater stars are household names). *Shuffle Along* is prominent, even mythic, in musical theater history.[96] Wolfe asks audiences to remember aspects of *Shuffle Along*—particularly to remember the artists who made it and whose careers it made. He did not invite audiences to remember the choreography or the text: "Terrible book, bad book. Everybody knows it's terrible," Wolfe proclaimed when asked about the creative challenges for mounting his 2016 *Shuffle Along, or the Making of . . . .*[97] Audiences were not forced to confront the racial stereotypes the show needed to present in order to make a hit. Wolfe was certainly right to approach this material with care, as depicting racial stereotypes would offend, even traumatize, many contemporary theatergoers and risk supporting racist beliefs in other audiences. The story of the mayoral election and crooked campaign plot is barely present in Wolfe's revision, which instead focuses on romantic intrigue and the conflict that developed between the four creators of *Shuffle Along*; Miller and Lyles were not benefiting from the money that Sissle and Blake were pulling in from the recordings and sheet music, and the writing/acting/dancing team wanted a share of those profits.[98] (See Figure 4.8.) That unprofitable text would have continued to cause trouble if it were included in *the Making Of . . .*, yet refusing to stage it allowed audiences to remember only the fun and palatable parts of the musical and the history of Black performance. Reviewer Kristin Moriah points out that this decision "denied an immersive experience of the original musical sensation and an understanding of what past audiences may have found compelling."[99] If appropriately contextualized in the *making-of* trope, the text could have offered opportunities not only to remember, restage, and confront the history of racism but to comment on contemporary white supremacy.

Wolfe could not have imagined how *Shuffle Along*'s election plot might have resonated with audiences in the spring of 2016 when he decided to abandon the minstrel-derived choreography and story of two crooked candidates, a rigged election, and vote buying after years of unethical business practices. The 2016 US presidential campaign pitted billionaire real-estate mogul and reality TV star–turned Republican Donald Trump against Hillary Clinton, the former First Lady, then New York senator, then Secretary of State for the Democratic administration of President Barack Obama. Trump launched himself into the political spotlight as a supporter of the "birther movement," which claimed that Obama, the United States' first Black president, was born in another country (maybe Kenya, given his father's nationality) and therefore not eligible to be president. Trump continued to push the "birther" lie as a presidential candidate, years after Obama released his birth certificate in 2011.[100] The election of Trump was widely considered a backlash against the Obama presidency and the more inclusive and multicultural society he attempted to promote.[101]

Shuffle Along's story of a crooked campaign exposed by famous detective "Keeneye" was not staged in the months before Donald Trump won the White House. If it had been, audiences might have heard similarities between Sam and Steve's campaign rhetoric and that of the 2016 election:

SAM: . . . What you talkin' 'bout I ain't got no right to be mayors of Jimtown.
STEVE (LOUDLY): It takes brains to be a mayor. You ain't got brains enough to have a decent headache. You jest runnin' against me cost you jealous of me—dat's all you is. Me en' you runnin' a grocery store togeder too. Minute you think I got a chance of gitting elected, you splits the ticket, Dat's what I git fer taking you in the grocery store as my partner. Ought never to have taken you in der in the first place.
(walks to left stage)
SAM (FOLLOWING): Now here listen. Wait a minute. Lemme git you straightened out about dat der grocery store. I put jest as much money in dat store as you did and maybe a lil' more. I dunno.[102]

If such attacks struck audiences as humorously absurd in 1921, they might seem less so today as social media offers new platforms for political insult. In the fall of 2016, Trump tweeted, "Hillary Clinton should have been prosecuted and should be in jail. Instead she is running for president in what looks like a rigged election."[103] He retweeted a meme with the title, "Crooked Hillary—Makes History!," and the image of Clinton's face over a picture of $100 bills next to a Star of David, a symbol of Judaism, emblazoned with the words "Most Corrupt Candidate Ever."[104] While not conducted on Twitter, some of Sam and Steve's banter was performed publicly for the town:

STEVE: Ladies, Genlemenses, folkses and peopleses—When I first entered this race for mayors of Jimtown I had not the least redea—
UNCLE NED: That's language.
STEVE: —that there was a dark horse in the race.
(CHORUS snickers. SAM looks around for a brick.)
STEVE: Surprised I was, I must say ver' much heap surprised I was when I found dat dat dark horse was my own business parter.

TOM: (To SAM): Now say something.

SAM: Well I might be de dark horse but you (pointing to STEVE) ain't gwine never be no black mayor.[105]

By making the understandable decision not to stage this racist banter, *Shuffle Along, or the Making of . . .* did not offer audiences the opportunity to consider the fictional campaign in Jimtown c. 1921 against the one going on outside the theater. Such a comparison might have helped audiences recognize what has and has not changed in American race and gender relations— and politics—in ninety-five years.

Many of the cuts in the 2016 *Shuffle Along, or the Making of . . .* limited the possibility that audiences could find resistant, ironic, or radical messages couched in the more demeaning depictions of race and gender. Multiple readings are available when Uncle Tom and Old Black Joe sing and dance about themselves as "Jimtown electioners" in a number that was not staged in 2016 and that both participated in *and* resisted the "coon songs that had mocked black political ambition since the 1980's."[106] "Uncle Tom and Old Black Joe" was written for the great tapper/choreographer, Charlie Davis, who played Uncle Tom, and another skilled dancer, Bob Williams, who originally played Old Black Joe. The number was most likely a "soft shoe dance, an early form of tap dance from the minstrel stage combining clog and shuffling techniques."[107] The ambivalence and opportunity for multiple readings is built into the character names and the virtuoso dance, particularly as it relates to and undermines the text.[108] Uncle Tom is the title character in Harriet Beecher Stowe's 1852 novel, *Uncle Tom's Cabin*, and while beloved by many abolitionists and sympathizers, the name also became a derogatory term for a subservient, forgiving Black man. Old Black Joe is a stereotypical name and was particularly famous as the title for a popular, nostalgic song by Stephen C. Foster around 1860 in which "Old Black Joe" suggests that it was "better" when slaves worked together in the cotton fields: "Gone are my friends from the cotton fields away."[109] For audiences who knew the song's seeming nostalgia for slavery, the Old Black Joe character would have been deeply ironical performing next to Uncle Tom, especially as the virtuosity of their dancing in jazz and tap styles would have been anything but subservient, unassuming, and nostalgic. Their expert, even ostentatious dancing and the strength of their embodiment put Black artistry center stage in a way that might have alarmed or challenged audiences, without the racist Uncle Tom and Old Black Joe framework in place.

The virtuosity of their dance supports Uncle Tom and Old Black Joe's claims to "have elected every president since '63 / The last one that we elected was old Booker T."[110] Booker T. Washington was an educator, activist, and widely acknowledged leader of the African American community from 1890 until his death in 1915. Although not a president, he advised President Theodore Roosevelt but has been considered too accommodationist by some of the more radical arms of the civil rights movement.[111] Uncle Tom and Old Black Joe's claims about "electing presidents . . . since Booker T" were simultaneously grandiose and bitterly ironic, given the fact that Black Americans lacked access to the polls during national elections, which were far from free and fair. Although the Fourteenth Amendment to the US Constitution gave African Americans the right to full citizenship in 1868, their votes were severely circumscribed until the 1965 Voting Rights Act and beyond. Regardless of how enthusiastically white audiences cheered the skill of the tap dance, they would not ensure the right to vote.

Uncle Tom and Old Black Joe, like the minstrel song-and-dance tradition, were available for ironic or subversive readings, while their self-deprecating humor and stereotypical characterization would have entertained audiences in a nonthreatening way if they did not get the satire. The 1921 *Shuffle Along* used the forms of minstrelsy in an exaggerated manner so as to critique them from within. Of course, these subversive moments were not and are not understood by everyone; as with all satire, audiences must be familiar with the form being critiqued. For some audiences, the racist banter and minstrel song-and-dance merely bolstered racist stereotypes. Contemporary audiences who are less aware of minstrel traditions are even less likely to get the satire, so it makes sense that Wolfe and his creative team abandoned the book. In the one instance when the contemporary performers in *Shuffle Along, or the Making of* . . . donned blackface, the atmosphere was only sad and demeaning. The characters were succumbing to racist demands, and there seemed to be no possibility of using blackface in the provocative and ironical manner that was sometimes achieved by historical minstrelsy and contemporary blackface performance for some performers and audiences.

The 2016 *Shuffle Along, or the Making of* . . . treated contemporary audiences to a sanitized *Shuffle Along*, one with less of the minstrel banter and offensive language that was necessary in 1921 if the show was to succeed with racially mixed audiences, one that did not register the continued failings of American politics (see Figure 4.9). Since audiences were not asked to confront the racist script of *Shuffle Along* or navigate the discomfort of laughing at the humor while being offended, they could celebrate "how far we've come" since 1921 and congratulate themselves on being "woke" enough about race to buy their tickets and help "correct" the historical record by remembering

Figure 4.9 Brandon Victor Dixon as Eubie Blake along with Billy Porter as Aubrey Lyles, Brian Stokes Mitchell as F. E. Miller, and the cast of *Shuffle Along, or, the Making of the Musical Sensation of 1921 and All That Followed*, directed by George C. Wolfe. Photo by Julieta Cervantes.

Shuffle Along—but not its satirical "Jimtown Electioners," "Uncle Tom and Old Black Joe." Some audiences could convince themselves that racism might still be a problem in some places, but the United States is making progress— they might think that the American political system is no longer upholding white supremacy. In fact, Black voters still face unconscionable challenges in accessing polls, and after the 2020 US election, Republican-led states have passed additional measures to disenfranchise minority voters and further curtail the Voting Rights Act, under the guise of stamping out the fraud that, according to Trump, stole the election from him.[112] Trump's false accusations of election fraud stand in stark contrast to the reality of Russian interference in the 2016 election, which emerged during the drawn-out Special Counsel investigation headed by former FBI director Robert Mueller from May 2017 until March 2019. A US federal grand jury indicted thirteen Russians and three Russian businesses for meddling in the US elections to benefit Trump's campaign.[113] The report stopped short of saying that Trump obstructed justice or colluded with Russia, but many are not convinced. Several Keeneyes are still looking into it.

5

Hamilton ParticiNation in Diversity and Its Discontents

After George C. Wolfe's *Shuffle Along, or the Making of the Musical Sensation of 1921 and All That Followed* closed at a loss on July 24, 2016, *Hamilton* went on to win award after award. There was a Grammy, the Pulitzer Prize for Drama, and eleven Tony Awards of its record-breaking sixteen nominations, including Best Musical. Touring companies are now presenting *Hamilton* in cities across the United States, and after it opened in London in December 2017, it broke the record for the most Olivier Award nominations—despite a story about the American Revolution that depicted a campy King George of Great Britain and his wimpy loyalists.[1] *Hamilton* regularly broke its own box office records after it first pulled in the highest weekly gross ever at $3.26 million over Thanksgiving week in 2016, as premium tickets surged to another record-breaking $998.[2]

Thanksgiving 2016 fell the week after Mike Pence, then Republican governor of Indiana, attended *Hamilton* on November 19, just eleven days after the election that put the Trump/Pence ticket in the White House. It is tempting to suggest that the show received a boost after Brandon Victor Dixon, the actor playing Aaron Burr, addressed Pence at curtain call with some pointed remarks about "diverse America," thereby provoking the Twitter-ire of President-elect Trump and the proliferation of hashtags like #BoycottHamilton.[3] But since tickets for the show were sold out for almost a year, there was no immediate boost in the gross, and #BoycottHamilton enthusiasts only needed to restrain themselves from purchasing the secondary market tickets that had swollen to nearly $1,000. When Dixon, still costumed as former vice president Aaron Burr, spoke to future vice president Mike Pence, he asked the audience to record his speech with their phones and post it on social media, thereby expanding the audience into digital space and time.[4] My argument in this chapter is that *Hamilton*'s most "revolutionary" performances take place outside the musical proper for a mix of live and virtual audiences. I will call these para-*Hamilton* performances.

Complicit Participation. Carrie J. Preston, Oxford University Press. © Oxford University Press 2024.
DOI: 10.1093/9780197693438.003.0006

The play itself, by recasting the white "Founding Fathers" of the American Revolution, many of whom held enslaved peoples, with actors of color, provides a message of inclusion and diversity but does not revolutionize cultural conceptions of race, gender, and the so-called American character.

Hamilton adapts and redeploys many familiar genres, including the story of the founding of the United States, plays about presidents and other great figures of conventional histories, and the musical genres of R&B, rap, and Broadway. Revisionary rather than revolutionary, the genius of *Hamilton* is to take forms that audiences already know and love and combine them in ways that indicate commitments to the inclusion and diversity enterprise, which I abbreviate with the acronym I&D when I am referencing what the management consulting firm McKinsey & Company dubbed "The business case for inclusion and diversity (I&D)."[5] *Hamilton* continues to thrive long after *Shuffle Along, Or the Making of . . .* closed at a loss not because it is more radical or challenging but because it tells a familiar story using more familiar and comfortable artistic forms than *Shuffle Along, or the Making of . . . . Hamilton's* I&D message is comforting to a wide range of audiences and assures us we have come a long way since 1776 (and 1921). At the same time, the more radical para-*Hamilton* performances extend audience engagement with the show and allow audiences to participate in somewhat more revolutionary versions of *Hamilton*.

5.1. From Duels over Inclusion and Diversity to Full and Radical Participation

Hamilton's lack of radical content and its ability to offer conventional versions of I&D that appeal across the vast political divides of the Trump era and beyond is evident in Mike Pence's attendance and response. Pence encouraged Fox News's Chris Wallace to go to this "great, great show" and claimed that when audience members booed at his arrival, "I nudged my kids and reminded them, 'That's what freedom sounds like.'"[6] *Hamilton's* depiction of American freedom sounds fantastic in Miranda's eclectic score, which combines rap, R&B, jazz, and traditional Broadway song structures. But as with its inclusive melding of musical and performance styles, *Hamilton* achieves a conciliatory, inclusive vision of the United States that is easy for Pence to endorse alongside political adversaries and fellow *Hamilton* fans, former president Barack Obama and the Trump/Pence opponent in the 2016 election, Hillary Clinton. The play's ability to appeal to audiences with different politics, values, and belief systems is an achievement that should not be ignored, given the divisiveness of most political conversations in our current moment. The I&D project that *Hamilton* advocates has certainly not been achieved across the United States, but it is not a radical or revolutionary project.

Hamilton's core messages about diversity and inclusion were effectively summarized in Brandon Victor Dixon's curtain-call address to Pence, coauthored by Miranda, director Thomas Kail, and producer Jeffrey Seller. To set the scene: As Pence moved to leave the theater, Dixon asked him to stay and listen for a moment. He shushed the booing audience, saying, "There is nothing to boo here, ladies and gentlemen. We are all here sharing a story of love."[7] Then, he encouraged "everybody to pull out their phones and tweet and post because this message is to be spread far and wide." He read the coauthored statement:

> We truly thank you for joining us here at *Hamilton: An American Musical.*
> We really do. We, sir, we are the diverse America who are alarmed and
> anxious that your new administration will not protect us, our planet, our
> children, our parents, or defend us and uphold our inalienable rights, sir.
> But we truly hope that this show has inspired you to uphold our American
> values and to work on behalf of all of us, *all of us.* Again, we truly thank
> you for sharing this show, this wonderful American story told by a diverse
> group of men, women, of different colors, creeds, and orientations.[8]

The audience cheered and proceeded to post their videos "far and wide," as Dixon had encouraged.

Politely and graciously, with two honorific "sirs" sandwiched in the second sentence, Dixon presented the *Hamilton* cast as representatives of "diverse America" who were concerned that "our American values" would be rejected by the administration of Trump and Pence.[9] Trump's campaign slogans from "build the wall [on the US border with Mexico]" to "lock her [Hillary Clinton] up," provided plenty of cause for the alarm Dixon expressed. But the values of diversity and inclusion are not radical or even strictly liberal; they are regularly espoused by both the US Democratic and Republican parties. In fact, ten days before Pence attended *Hamilton*, President-elect Trump began his victory speech with an appeal to those same values and in much the same language. He proclaimed, "I pledge to every citizen of our land that I will be president for all Americans."[10] He referred to the "move-ment"—"not a campaign"—that elected him as "a movement comprised of Americans from all races, religions, backgrounds and beliefs, who want and expect our government to serve the people. And serve the people, it will."[11] Given the similarities between Trump's victory speech and Dixon's curtain-call statement, it might seem surprising that Trump took to Twitter to ex-press his outrage: "Our wonderful future V.P. Mike Pence was harassed last night at the theater by the cast of Hamilton, cameras blazing. This should not happen!"[12] In the second tweet, Trump claimed, "The Theater must always be a safe and special place. The cast of Hamilton was very rude last night to a very good man, Mike Pence. Apologize!"[13] Later that evening, he wrote and quickly deleted: "Very rude and insulting of Hamilton cast member to treat our great future V.P. Mike Pence to a theater lecture. Couldn't even memorize lines!" [Sic]. The following morning, he added, "The cast and producers of Hamilton, which I hear is highly overrated, should immediately apologize to Mike Pence for their terrible behavior."[14]

Future vice president Pence, in contrast, did not demand an apology when he spoke on *Fox News Sunday*:

> I did hear what was said from the stage. And I can tell you I wasn't offended by what was said. I will leave to others whether that was the appropriate venue to say it . . . to watch him [President-elect Trump] bringing together people of diverse views, bringing together people who disagreed with him strongly . . . I just want to reassure every American that in the days ahead I am very confident that they are going to see President-elect Trump be a president for all the people and we embrace that principle.[15]

If both Pence and Trump espouse the same values of inclusion and diver-sity as Dixon and the coauthors of his *Hamilton* statement, why was Trump outraged? It was not the content of the speech that Trump found "rude and insulting," because his victory speech indicated he had learned the language of I&D and the benefits of at least paying lip service to I&D.[16] He appar-ently did not believe that his base who cheered "build the wall" would re-ject being included in a "movement comprised of Americans from all races, religions, backgrounds and beliefs."[17] Trump insisted, and Pence suggested that the "venue" of "Hamiltongate" was the problem: The theater should be "safe and special" not a place of "lecture," according to Trump—who proposed eliminating federal funding for the arts in his first three budget plans.[18] Pence said he "will leave it to others whether that was the appropriate venue to say it," while insisting that there was nothing wrong with "what was said"—nothing wrong with messages celebrating diversity.[19]

The *venue* and full context of Dixon's statement was not simply the *special* place of Broadway but also the annual campaign for Broadway Cares/Equity Fights AIDS, which includes curtain-call speeches encouraging audience members to donate to the Bucket Brigades as they leave the theater. Dixon or one of the other actors would have delivered the Broadway Cares appeal regardless of Pence's presence in the theater, and Dixon did proceed to ask the audience to support Broadway Cares after addressing Pence.[20] This was a particularly poignant gesture given that Javier Muñoz, the actor who played Hamilton that evening (as the understudy for Miranda), is a gay man from Puerto Rico living with HIV.[21] The *Hamilton* team chose to emphasize diversity and inclusion in the statement to Pence, although they might have pointed more directly and contentiously to Pence's previous and damaging record on HIV. While campaigning for congress in 2000, Pence advocated defunding what he called "organizations that celebrate and encourage the types of behaviors that facilitate the spreading of the HIV virus" and supporting "institutions which provide assistance to those seeking to change their sexual behavior."[22] As governor of Indiana, Pence closed down Planned Parenthood, the only resource for HIV testing in southern Indiana, and opposed needle exchange programs, thereby contributing to an outbreak of HIV in the state.[23] By redeploying a Broadway Cares/Equity Fights AIDS curtain-call speech as a statement on diversity and inclusion, the coauthors showed restraint from calling attention to Pence's actions in Indiana.

"We are the diverse America," Dixon said when he introduced the cast of *Hamilton* to Vice President Pence and thanked him "for sharing this show, this wonderful American story told by a diverse group of men, women, of different colors, creeds, and orientations."[24] Dixon's declaration of diversity has become familiar, nearly ubiquitous, in the strategic plans, mission statements, brochures, and slogans of many institutions, from McKinsey's "The business case for inclusion and diversity (I&D)" and beyond.[25] The word "diversity" is deployed to do so much work that it has become a grammatical shapeshifter: We find it in titles like the Diversity Task Force, Office of Diversity and Inclusion, and Chief Diversity Officer. Institutions that have learned to bestow these titles and use this language can increase their rankings. "Diversity" is imagined as a particular kind of aspiration and presumed goal for liberal institutions, as in "*We are working on diversity.*"

Although this common statement is about improving the variety of people composing *the institution*, it actually suggests that there is something about "diversity" itself that needs work. And there is. "Diversity" has become the comfortable word that has replaced more pointed social justice terms like "inequality," "white supremacy," "sexism," "racism," and "power."

"Diversity" is so often paired with "inclusion" that it has become a common phrase and series of acronyms; McKinsey's I&D is less common than D&I or DEI, but the acronyms are a sure sign of mainstreaming and a warning that meaning may be pouring out of the words designated by the letters. I&D, as an institutional mission, is often used to indicate a commitment to hiring people who are underrepresented in that community. But by hiring and *including*, institutions are not necessarily committing to change; their new, more diverse members may be expected to conform and change themselves to be included in the institution as it is.[26] In her study of diversity practitioners in higher education, Sara Ahmed describes diversity statements as "institutional speech acts" or performatives, statements that attempt to do what they say. That is, by claiming their diversity or commitment to diversity, institutions are attempting to *do diversity*—sometimes without doing much of anything else: "The use of diversity as an official description can be a way of maintaining rather than transforming existing organizational values."[27]

I must be clear that despite my concerns about the term "diversity," I am one of the "institutional diversity practitioners" Ahmed studies: I served on our Diversity and Inclusion Task Force, and I am currently a member of the Advisory Board for our Office of Diversity and Inclusion, which was recommended by our Task Force.[28] I created a staff position focused on diversity for the academic unit I directed. I believe it is far preferable to be *working on diversity*, even if that work is often incoherent, frequently stymied, and always incomplete, than to refuse to work on diversity. I also continue to use the term "diversity," despite contradictory and inadequate definitions, as this is the widely accepted and (over)used term. When possible, I avoid phrases like "diverse community," preferring to think and speak of my efforts to build a community that encourages *full and radical participation*. "Full participation (according to Susan Strum et. al.) is an affirmative value focused on creating institutions that enable people, whatever their identity, background, or institutional position, to thrive, realize their capabilities, engage meaningfully in institutional life, and contribute to the flourishing of others.[29] By adding "radical" to "full participation," I acknowledge that participation can also mean tearing apart and recreating institutions, even rewriting our basic

understanding of community, not just including new people in the preex-
isting community. In this sense, *full and radical participation* is the opposite of *complicit participation*, as it demands tearing down the barriers to
another's full participation in the institution, even if those barriers support
your own privilege and comfort. Institutional and community transformation requires more than a brief immersion in theatrical scenes or institutional
I&D statements, performances, and task forces—although those gestures
can provide some momentum. But then we must participate in sustained
and humble work to destroy those obstacles that others have identified as
preventing their full and radical participation.

5.2. Diverse Casting but No Parts for Enslaved People in *Hamilton*

Hamilton's ability to appeal across gaping political chasms is one indication of the fact that I&D has become a widely accepted, even mainstream
value, adopted by companies, universities, theaters, the *Hamilton* team, and
even the former administration of President Trump. While mainstreaming
is an important and valuable step forward, the I&D platform has slipped
further from *full and radical participation* in the process of being widely
accepted—even as racism and white supremacy have shapeshifted into other
forms. *Hamilton*'s casting serves as an example of how mainstream I&D can
be presented as radical disruption when it is far from radical. By casting
Black and Latinx actors in the roles of the "Founding Fathers" Alexander
Hamilton, George Washington, Thomas Jefferson, Aaron Burr, and James
Madison, the production seeks to offer an image of diversity founded on including people of color in the typical story of the American Revolution. Most
critics and audiences have celebrated *Hamilton*'s casting as provocative and
"revolutionary," and a brief but surprisingly well-publicized controversy over
Hamilton's casting call for "nonwhite men and women" would support that
perspective.[30] Actors' Equity Association, the union that represents theater
artists, criticized the casting call, claiming that auditions must be open to anyone, even if specifying the characters' race, gender, age, and other identity
characteristics is common and acceptable.

   Profiles of the battle between *Hamilton* and Actors' Equity over the casting
call appeared in CBS News, *The New York Times*, *Variety*, *Huffington Post*, *The
Guardian*, and the *BBC*, among others. Kate Shindle, the president of Actors'

Equity, claimed that the supposed "firestorm" was actually "a simple disagreement about the language in an employment ad" and went on to advocate for more diversity: "But as rightly celebrated as this musical [*Hamilton*] is, it would be shortsighted to assume that it solves the industry's diversity problem, any more than electing Barack Obama solved America's."[31] The producers of *Hamilton* agreed to change the ad to make it clear that all were welcome to audition while reiterating that, as lead producer Jeffrey Seller articulated, "We will continue to cast the show with the same multicultural diversity that we have employed thus far."[32] The irony of the incident is that all involved were touting diversity as their main goal. Through its president, Kate Shindle, Actors' Equity made sure to claim that *Hamilton* does not fix the lack of diversity in the performing arts. The civil rights attorney Randolph McLaughlin, who claimed that the casting notice violated the New York City Human Rights Law, presented himself as fighting discrimination; and Seller insisted that *Hamilton* would seek "multicultural diversity" in casting, as if anyone were demanding otherwise.[33] The supposed conflict between *Hamilton*, Actors' Equity, and a civil rights attorney became an (occasionally sanctimonious) demand for diversity that nobody was contesting.

Even the right-of-center publication *Observer* used *Hamilton* and Actor's Equity to wade into the competition for the loudest call for more diversity. Following the curtain-call lecture of Vice President-elect Pence in November 2016, *Observer* published an article by Jon Birger pointing to contradictions in the idea that *Hamilton* effectively confronted the Trump-Pence campaign's "harsh language about immigrants" (as *The New York Times* put it).[34] Birger claimed that Actors' Equity will not represent foreign artists with O-I artist visas, much less immigrants without work permits. The union can effectively prevent foreign actors from appearing on Broadway unless "they are an established star or can do something that an American actor can't do."[35] Maria Somma, an Actors' Equity spokesperson, responded to the 2005 banning of a British eleven-year-old from the inescapably racist Broadway blunder, *Tarzan*: "The rules are there to give our own actors the first shot."[36] Birger argues that by ensuring American actors get a "first shot" and refusing membership to immigrants, Actors' Equity comes too close to Trump's slogan, "America first." While it might seem ironical that the "build-a-wall candidate's vice president" loves the Broadway show about immigrants, it is equally inconsistent when "some of the elites quickest to cry xenophobia have already walled themselves off from immigrant competition."[37] While I appreciate Birger's discussion of the xenophobia built into powerful unions, there is a "gotcha" quality to his piece that seems particularly divisive as he proclaims, "Oh how the left rejoiced at the cast of *Hamilton*'s very public upbraiding of Vice President-elect Mike Pence."[38]

As I call attention to elements of *Hamilton* that are less revolutionary than commonly advertised, I do not want to advance another pious, liberal "gotcha," and I have no intention of joining the far-right minority who oppose diversity. Rather, my goal is to identify how white supremacy and patriarchy continue to invade even those cultural works and events, like *Hamilton*, which seek to challenge them. Hoping to challenge anti-immigrant rhetoric, the play attempts to celebrate *Hamilton* as a rags-to-fame immigrant story, whose protagonist high-fives Marquis de Lafayette as they share the line, "Immigrants: We get the job done!"[39] Yet neither was actually an immigrant in the way we use the term today. Lafayette never immigrated to the United States from France (although he was granted posthumous honorary American citizenship in 2002). Hamilton was a citizen of Great Britain moving from British colonies in the Caribbean islands of Nevis, St. Kitts, and St. Croix to another British island port, New York City.[40] As historian Leslie M. Harris points out, Hamilton was one of a tiny number of free migrants, given that 90 percent of all migrants to the Americas on British ships before 1800 were enslaved people or indentured servants.[41] In the Caribbean there were more enslaved people of African descent than people of European descent.[42] When Hamilton became a clerk with the St. Croix office of the New York firm of Beekman and Cruger, he joined a business that supplied plantations with, among other provisions, a yearly shipment of enslaved people from Africa.[43]

Forced migrants from Africa were the majority of immigrants to the Americas during Hamilton's lifetime, but the musical has no roles for enslaved people. Celebrating Hamilton's arrival in New York City in 1772, the cast energetically repeats the line, "In New York you can be a new man."[44] This upward mobility was possible for a free white migrant moving within the British colonies, but certainly not for the enslaved peoples who composed 14.3 percent of the population of New York City.[45] The "greatest city in the world" (according to the musical) contained the largest number of urban enslaved people in the mainland American colonies.[46] When the Schuyler sisters go downtown searching for "a man at work," they would almost certainly have confronted enslaved people at work in hotels, shops, and at the port.[47] An enslaved person might have served Hamilton and his newfound friends their drinks during the tavern song "The Story of Tonight." And yet

Hamilton does not include any enslaved or free people of color as characters. Nor does the musical represent the free people of African descent who fought in the Revolutionary War or the slaves who served military officers from General Washington—who held slaves throughout his lifetime—to Hercules Mulligan—whose slave, Cato, helped him infiltrate the British forces as a tailor-spy. Mulligan raps about his achievements in "The Battle of Yorktown" without mentioning Cato's crucial role.[48]

Only for one brief line does an enslaved person appear on the stage of *Hamilton*, and that is Sally Hemings, who is a part of the historical record because she bore Thomas Jefferson's children and sexual desire (although her children were not recognized by the Thomas Jefferson Foundation until 2000). In his coming-home song, "What'd I Miss?," Jefferson sings, "Sally be a lamb, darlin', won'tcha open it [letter from the president]?"[49] The swing actor who played Hemings in the original cast kicked her leg flirtatiously and danced away with the letter. After recognizing that the scene was demeaning to Hemmings, the cast and creative team revised the choreography to have Hemings turn her back to him to perform the kick while her arms shape a cradle, reminding the audience of the children she bore in slavery; Justice Moore, the performer who danced the role, claimed, "Rather than the playful, romantic energy the previous version had, I'm now playing a person that had no claim over her own life and her own body."[50] The choreographic revision is subtle but significant, and the creative team was seeking to be responsive to criticism of their depictions of slavery when they removed "the white gloves and the pantomimed motions of slaves at work as Jefferson arrives at Monticello."[51] Yet these changes further remove from the stage the fact that slavery was integral to the American Revolutionary period. Jefferson's condescending one-liner with Sally Hemings underscores the fact that *Hamilton* tells the common history of the American Revolution, even in its addition of a few of the twenty-first century's acknowledgments of the personal failings of those *great white men* who remain the focus of the story.

The fact that Jefferson owned enslaved people returns in "Cabinet Battle #1" when Hamilton takes him down as "a slaver":

> A civics lesson from a slaver. Hey neighbor.
> Your debts are paid cuz you don't pay for labor.
> "We plant seeds in the South. We create." Yeah, keep ranting.
> We know who's really doing the planting.[52]

When slavery is mentioned in the lyrics of the musical, it is used to make Hamilton and his friends look good as they are all associated with an anti-slavery position. The fact is that all the so-called Founding Fathers had more ambivalent relationships to the institution of slavery than the musical acknowledges; Alexander Hamilton's birth family and in-laws owned enslaved people.[53] *Hamilton* misses several opportunities to represent the lives of people of color and their significance to the Founding Fathers. While Sally Hemings appears for one line, Aaron Burr's family of color is never mentioned. Burr most likely fathered a daughter, Louisa Charlotte, and son, John Pierre, with a free woman of color, Mary Emmons, who originally worked as a servant for the Burr family, but lived with her children in Philadelphia at the home where Burr stayed while serving in the US Senate between 1791 and 1797.[54] Decades-old rumors about Burr's family were still reported as inconclusive by the *Wall Street Journal* in 2005, so it is possible that Miranda was unaware or unconvinced by the evidence of Burr's relationship to Emmons. *Hamilton's* popularity figures in recent summaries of the evidence about Burr's family of color, evidence that includes letters, genetic tests, and the deed of the house Burr purchased for his probable son John Pierre, a leader in Philadelphia's Underground Railroad.[55]

Hamilton puts Black, Indigenous, People of Color (BIPOC) actors in the standard roles of Founding Fathers but does not acknowledge the fact that enslaved and free people of color were a crucial part of their lives, the American Revolution, and the founding of the United States—a fact that is increasingly being acknowledged by historians intent on correcting the record.[56] *Hamilton* is one example of how the commitment to inclusion and diversity, as by casting actors of color, does not necessarily change larger historical narratives or social and cultural structures. *Hamilton's* casting has been celebrated as "color-blind" but is more accurately called "color-conscious," as Lyra D. Monteiro argues, because the race and ethnicity of the actors were very much considered.[57] The Caribbean childhood of Hamilton was emphasized when the role was originally performed by Lin-Manuel Miranda and his understudy Javier Muñoz, both actors of Puerto Rican descent.[58] The other Founding Fathers, who primarily perform rap and hip-hop styles, were originally played by Black actors. New casts for touring and regional companies present different configurations of diversity, but as of yet, there are no white performers in the roles of the Founding Fathers or BIPOC actors in the role of King George, and none of these casting choices are color-blind or indifferent to race.

What is the impact of these casting choices on audiences? When asked about the casting, students from Bill Coulter's English class at Fort Hamilton High School in southwestern Brooklyn claimed, "It just made me really proud, and feel good about being American. Like I belong here."[59] These feelings of belonging are powerful for BIPOC students, who saw the show with the support of the Theater Development Fund, and many other audiences. For white liberal audience members who could afford *Hamilton*'s tickets and know they belong there, the feel-good atmosphere worries me. How would audiences have felt if slavery were part of the story onstage? How do feelings of *belonging* impact the need to understand historical oppression and fight ongoing racism? Representations of diversity often feel good, but those positive feelings can dull the need for cultural transformations that will topple white supremacy and allow all to thrive and participate fully.

5.2. "I'm Gonna Need a Right-Hand Man (Buck Buck Buck Buck Buck)": *Hamilton*'s Conventional Representations of Gender and Sexuality

In all past and current companies, two *Hamilton* characters have been played by white, male-presenting actors with effeminate bodily and vocal presentations: King George III and the loyalist "Westchester Farmer," Samuel Seabury.[60] Seabury sings his repetitive, melodic warnings to the revolutionaries in upper vocal registers, and Hamilton's friends goad him, "Tear this dude apart."[61] Hamilton steps up to the challenge and raps eighty-three words against Seabury's forty-nine—while mimicking Seabury's rhymes and cadences.

SEABURY: Heed not the rabble	HAMILTON: Yo! He'd have you all
Who scream	unravel at the
Revolution, they	Sound of the screams but the
Have not your	Revolution is comin' The
interests at	Have-nots are gonna
heart.	win this, it's
	Hard to listen to you
	with a straight face.[62]

King George III appears at the end of "Farmer Refuted" to sing the pop-sounding song Miranda describes as "a breakup letter from King George to the colonies."[63] Like Farmer Seabury, King George sings melodically, reaching into high falsetto registers, and with his peals of laughter and non-sense language, the king presents his role as effeminate, infantilized, and silly. The gender codes are clear: *Real men* rap, want to fight in wars, and pursue women rather than colonies.

Hamilton remains surprisingly masculinist. The central story of the musical is the making of Hamilton as a *great man* and the activities that proved his *great manhood* in the Revolutionary period, most prominently the inter-connected acts of fighting wars/duels and pursuing women. Hamilton insists that fighting a war will prove his worth, "God I wish there was a war! / Then we could prove that we're worth more than anyone bargained for."[64] Later, when he meets Eliza, his future wife, he says, "If it takes fighting a war for us to meet, it will have been worth it."[65] His worth as a potential lover and husband is tied to battle. When Hamilton and his hard-drinking, masculine friends in-sist, "I am not throwing away my shot,"[66] they are adopting a term for oppor-tunity that is used in many male-centered contexts, from sports ("I'm gonna take a—/ Shot!"), to sharing alcohol ("Have another—/ Shot!"), to political risk ("If you talk, you're gonna get shot!"), and, albeit implicitly, ejaculation.[67] Hamilton's masculinist heterosexuality is reinforced by his contrast with the Westchester farmer and King George, his bravery in battle, and his "skill with the quill"—an innuendo that connects his writing ability and his sexual per-formance.[68] The link between "quill" or pen and penis has a long history, and heterosexual prowess is an explicit concern a few lines later when Burr, after singing "Ladies! / There are so many to deflower," shares the historical legend that "Martha Washington named her feral tomcat after him [Hamilton]!"[69]

Hamilton's focus on heterosexual conquest is not unusual among musicals or popular entertainment generally, but *Hamilton*'s biography offers opportunities to explore non-normative sexualities and genders that would better support the production's emphasis on I&D. Hamilton and John Laurens were rumored to have been lovers after they met in 1777, and they shared a deep affection with the Marquis de Lafayette. Ron Chernow's bi-ography, *Alexander Hamilton*, which served as Miranda's inspiration and primary source text, points out that historians have "detected homoerotic overtones in their relationship," but "one must tread gingerly" given that men regularly communicated in emotional and intimate language in the eighteenth century.[70] An early editor of Hamilton's letters, probably his son, crossed out words in an effusive April 1779 letter from Hamilton to Laurens and wrote at the top, "I must not publish the whole of this":

> Cold in my professions, warm in friendships, I wish, my dear Laurens, it m[ight] be in my power by action rather than words [to] convince you that I love you. I shall only tell you that till you bade us adieu, I hardly knew the value you had taught my heart to set upon you. Indeed, my friend, it was not well done ... You s[hould] not have taken advantage of my sensibility to ste[al] into my affections without my consent.[71]

In another letter, Hamilton described himself as "like a jealous lover, when I thought you slighted my caresses" because Laurens had not replied to his letters in kind.[72] To suggest, as have some commentators, that Hamilton was bisexual, gay, or queer would be ahistorical, given that these identity categories did not exist at the time.[73] Chernow points out that it would be surprising to find direct evidence of a physical relationship between Hamilton and Laurens, and he concludes, "At the very least, we can say that Hamilton developed something like an adolescent crush on his friend."[74]

After reading excerpts of Hamilton's effusive letters and Chernow's conclusions about Hamilton's "crush" on Laurens, Miranda chose not to explore homoeroticism among the Founding Fathers but to reinforce the typical heteronormative representations.[75] Miranda may have been attempting to avoid the ahistorical gesture of presenting famous Americans as queer—when that identity formation was not available to them—or indulging in more salacious anecdotes—although he did not shy away from Hamilton's confessed affair with Maria Reynolds or his attraction to his sister-in-law, Angelica Schuyler Church, an attraction Chernow describes as "so potent and obvious that many people assumed they were lovers."[76] When Miranda's Burr claims that "Martha Washington named her feral tomcat after him," Hamilton proclaims, "That's true," although Miranda notes in the published script, "This is most likely a tale spread by John Adams later in life. But I like Hamilton owning it. At this point in the story he is at peak cockiness."[77] Miranda decided to demonstrate Hamilton's "cockiness" not through his historically accurate homoerotic attachments with Laurens and other patriots in General Washington's team, but through heterosexual exploits and conventionally masculine traits—although Chernow noted how frequently Hamilton was described as "feminine" by his contemporaries.[78] While

Hamilton emphasizes racial diversity through casting, there is little room for gender or sexual diversity in his pub-going, women-chasing, rap-battling band of revolutionaries.

Representations of femininity in *Hamilton* are more ambivalent. Three women characters appear to be empowered to claim equality with men in their introductory song, "The Schuyler Sisters." They quote Thomas Jefferson's "Declaration of Independence":

ANGELICA: So listen to my declaration:
ELIZA, ANGELICA, PEGGY: "We hold these truths to be self-evident that all
    men are created equal."
ANGELICA: And when I meet Thomas Jefferson,
COMPANY: Unh!
ANGELICA: I'm 'a compel him to include women in the sequel!
WOMEN: Work![79]

The "sequel" referenced might be the Equal Rights Amendment (E.R.A.) to the US Constitution that was proposed a century ago to ensure equality based on sex and passed by Congress in 1972, but never ratified by the required three-quarters of the states. The fact that the equality of women, sexual minorities, and men has never been explicitly protected in the US Constitution gives force to the "declaration" of the Schuyler Sisters.[80] Yet the larger context and staging of the song keeps men and patriarchy firmly in place at the center of the action. The character of Aaron Burr starts the song by describing how the daughters of the rich patriarch Philip Schuyler "Sneak into the city just to watch all the guys at— / Work, work!"[81] The idea that the daughters are searching for men is reinforced in the middle of the song:

ELIZA: Angelica, remind me what we're looking for . . .
ALL MEN: She's lookin' for me!
ANGELICA: Eliza, I'm lookin' for a mind at work.[82]

Burr's reference to "guys at work" is transposed into the near-rhyme "mind at work" by way of the men singing, "She's lookin' for me!"[83] The implicit suggestion is that only men have *minds at work*, perhaps even that only men do *mindful* work. Masculine posturing and heterosexual innuendo are prominently performed when Burr attempts to pick up Angelica with a reference to her "daddy's" money and "fancy heels," which prompts her to deliver her declaration on equality. Despite her incipient feminism, the male gaze remains firmly in place, along with the stereotypes of rich girls "slummin' in the city."[84]

While Angelica and Eliza are undeniably cool characters (Peggy is treated dismissively as a whining daddy's girl who disappears from the play), there are limits to the play's version of feminist history. As Catherine Allgor points out, *Hamilton* neglects the fact that the American Revolution failed to address the institution of "coverture," the subordinate legal status of women.[85] Whereas the institution of slavery was discussed in a Cabinet Battle #3 but then cut from the play, coverture seems to have never made an appearance.[86] Of course, one musical cannot address everything and some topics, songs, and rap battles cannot make the final cut. But it is worth noting that *Hamilton* does not even pass the Bechdel-Wallace test popularized in Alison Bechdel's 1985 comic "The Rule" from *Dykes to Watch Out For*: "I have this rule, see . . . I only go to a movie if it satisfies three basic requirements. One, it has to have at least two women in it . . . who, two, talk to each other about, three, something besides a man."[87] There are two and occasionally three women onstage in *Hamilton*, and they talk to each other, but always about men—usually Hamilton. The Schuyler sisters' supposedly feminist anthem is rooted in stereotypes about rich girls slumming with working-class men. The next two songs featuring the sisters, "Helpless" and "Satisfied," are both about Hamilton. Eliza is alone onstage singing the powerful solo "Burn" about Hamilton's infamous "Reynolds Pamphlet" revealing his affair. The men drink with each other in the tavern, fight in wars, duels, and rap battles, write and debate politics, chase after women . . . whereas the women characters receive or reject their advances and have their babies—even if it is the fathers who sing about those babies in the lovely song "Dear Theodosia." The gender politics, like the racial politics, are not as "revolutionary" as advertised in the musical. But, beyond the musical proper, the actors and audience create other performances inspired by the play—para-*Hamilton* performances—that are far more radical and invite much more audience participation.

5.4. Audience ParticiNation in Para-*Hamilton* Performance

Audience participation in *Hamilton* resembles the more typical involvement of enthusiastic spectators who remain seated and quiet. Or mostly quiet, for the night Pence attended and the afternoon I saw the show in

Boston, audiences stood up and cheered when Hamilton and the Marquis de Lafayette sung their high-fiver, "Immigrants, we get the job done!"[88] Such ovations illustrate my argument in this book that audiences sit in an immersive, multisensory environment with many opportunities to participate, even if they are not asked to come up on stage, hold a character's knitting, boo at villains, bid on enslaved people, or cheer for a lynching. There are many accounts of audiences responding so vocally to *Hamilton* lines that the actors had to pause or even ask for quiet. Audiences typically cheer when, after the opening song breeds anticipation, the character of Hamilton responds to "What's your name man?" with the now-famous answer, "Alexander Hamilton. My name is Alexander Hamilton."[89] Of course, when Miranda was performing the titular role, audiences were also clapping for the famous creator and star of the show.

Hamilton is exceptional in that it has employed digital platforms to extend access to and desire for a stage that might be too far away and far too expensive for many potential audience members. Digital media also enable the creation and circulation of para-*Hamilton* performances that have extended the reach of the musical to such an extent that commentators have referred to "'Hamilton' Nation," "'Hamilton' Inc.," and "the Hamilton Parody Industrial Complex."[90] With #HamFam, #HamilTrash, #EduHam, #Ham4Ham, #Hamilmania, #Hamilween, among other tags, posted by fans with Twitter handles like @pamilton, @ham4fan, and @A(dot)Ham, *Hamilton* Nation is particularly good at turning social media into venues for audience participation.[91] Call it *Hamilton* particiNation, a community for which accessing, sharing, and occasionally creating para-*Hamilton* performances through social media is the founding principle.

Lin-Manuel Miranda gave the first and much-circulated para-*Hamilton* performance even before he knew that he was writing a Broadway musical. Miranda performed the opening song from what was then "The Hamilton Mixtape" at the "White House Evening of Poetry, Music, and the Spoken Word" on May 12, 2009, hosted by President Barack Obama. Since the audience in Washington, DC, that evening was small, the rest of the world heard the way Miranda would rap the name "Alexander Hamilton" through the White House's livestream site or later on YouTube, where, as of this writing, a clip of the performance has been viewed more than 8.8 million times.[92] After the mixtape became the musical, Miranda posted the original cast recording on YouTube, hoping that listeners would like it so much they would buy it. The album reached #1 on the *Billboard* rap chart in 2015 and sold more than three million copies by February 2017—meaning the album went triple plat-inum.[93] Miranda's digital generosity paid off.

Lin-Manuel Miranda has been called a "social media genius" alongside his other abilities to write and perform in hit musicals.[94] He began to cultivate his fan base #HamFam during the mixtape years, and he kept those fans engaged in the project through regular posts on Twitter and Facebook.[95] Miranda maintains a nearly constant digital media presence, typically offering a good morning message on Twitter each day, posting clips of his family and daily life, and sharing musings and bits of creative work.[96] He responds enthusi-astically to fans as he answers their questions and invites their thoughts on his work. He even set up a live video feed backstage at the Richard Rodgers Theater before his performances as Hamilton. Miranda's social media per-sona is a cultivated and diligently maintained role not so different from other roles he creates and performs, and it requires a good deal of time and digital effort. Miranda's fans/social media followers appear to interpret Miranda's media persona as genuine, casual, and authentic and enthusiastically retweet and generate their own posts about *Hamilton* and thereby get to be part of *Hamilton* particiNation.[97]

Miranda's social media followers—that new form of audience—provide publicity for his work and increase ticket sales. His diligent efforts on social media are undoubtedly self-interested and aimed at generating ticket sales, in part, but he and the entire *Hamilton* production team have worked to ex-tend access to *Hamilton* particiNation in ways that do not lead directly to profit. While still in previews at the Richard Rodgers Theater in July of 2015, *Hamilton* established a same-day ticket lottery for $10—the bill bearing a picture of Hamilton—thus a "Hamilton" for *Hamilton* or "Ham4Ham." When seven hundred people showed up for the lottery for twenty-one front-row tickets on the first preview (July 13, 2015), Miranda thanked the crowd with an impromptu speech.[98] For the following preview on Tuesday, July 15, Miranda inaugurated a series of brief performances for hopeful audiences awaiting the $10 ticket lottery two hours before the show. Miranda appeared that afternoon with Jonathan Groff, the actor playing King George III, to perform a rap that recalled their first collaboration on a 2007 music video promoting Miranda's previous Broadway hit, *In the Heights*. Miranda began by welcoming the crowd and marveling at its size, and then continued:

So if you don't win today, please come back and see us again. We're gonna be here. It's fine. Now as a treat for you today, because we have the GroffSauce at our disposal, I thought we would go back to the first time we met . . . Also, if you win tickets to the show, you'll see Groff, but you're not gonna see him rapping. You'll only see him rapping right here, right now.[99]

Miranda pointed to the fact that Groff, as King George III, sings melodic and catchy "pop" tunes rather than the macho raps of the revolutionaries and Founding Fathers. His rap for the lottery crowd was therefore exceptional, live, and immediate, offered only to that audience at that moment in time. Yet Groff's rap is also widely available online, as are the other lottery performances that garnered the name #Ham4Ham, a title that reveals they were created with an eye to their posting on Twitter and YouTube.

#Ham4Ham quickly established conventions as the prototypical genre of para-*Hamilton* performance as well as one of the most radical aspects of the *Hamilton* phenomenon.[100] Miranda and later Groff, or occasionally another performer, typically opened with a welcome and expressions of gratitude for the crowd, then promised that the show would be there a long time and encouraged the crowd to come back and try the lottery again—and again. On July 29, 2015, Miranda opened the #Ham4Ham with a typical explanation of the purpose of the event: "We're doing a little five-minute show so if you don't leave with a ticket you'll leave with a story." While anyone can watch #Ham4Ham online, the "Story of Tonight" or the story of being "In the Room [or sidewalk or street] Where It Happens" (to borrow *Hamilton* song titles) was exclusive to that crowd, that day. Miranda and the other performers repeatedly suggested that they wanted the lottery hopefuls to leave with something, even if they did not win tickets to the show. The events were framed with a spirit of generosity and *good fun*, and the pre-show warm-up style of #Ham4Ham indicated that these performers were not *divas* with elaborate preperformance rituals. One regular attendee at #Ham4Ham pointed out:

> Now, it's easy to look at this and be cynical, if you tend that way, thinking this is all about selling tickets. But . . . the performance is first and foremost for people who haven't bought seats, and very possibly can't get or can't afford tickets any other way. It is an act of generosity by Lin and the company, without a marketing message attached; indeed, it seems more an expression of gratitude to fans than anything else.[101]

#Ham4Ham events were creatively diverse after the standard welcome, but there were three common pursuits: (1) #Ham4Hams shared *Hamilton*ian excitement with other casts and friends, (2) explored Miranda's inspirations, and (3) gave actors opportunities to trade roles. Miranda frequently invited friends to perform, including Billy Porter, who had just finished his Tony Award–winning appearance in *Kinky Boots* and was, at that time, preparing for *Shuffle Along*. Porter sang a Christmas carol for #Ham4Ham on December 9, 2015.[102] #Ham4Ham also featured the casts of *The First Noel*, *On Your Feet*, *Allegiance*, and *Fun Home*, among others. Each of these events served as an advertisement for the performers and their shows, and Miranda's infectious enthusiasm was offered to his social media followers. Miranda jumped up from his position seated on the steps of the Richard Rodgers Theater in great excitement three different times when James Monroe Iglehart, then playing the Genie in *Aladdin*, sang "Make Them Hear You" from *Ragtime* on August 26, 2015.[103] Miranda positioned himself near his own fans by presenting himself as an unabashed fan of other actors and shows.

Miranda's invitations to performers and friends from other shows to join him for #Ham4Hams was one way that he shared his theatrical tastes and inspirations. Another of Miranda's playful ways of highlighting the shows that most influenced him was also a particularly audience-driven version of #Ham4Ham. Miranda would answer any question members of the lottery crowd asked—strictly using lyrics from another production, such as *Les Miserables* (July 18, 2015) or *A Chorus Line* (July 25, 2015).

AUDIENCE QUESTION: What was it like to have [President] Obama come see the show last week. [Audience cheers.]
MIRANDA: (singing from *A Chorus Line*) *And I felt nothing . . .* Just kidding it was awesome.

Through his quotes, citations, and invitations to other artists, Miranda located *Hamilton* within a history of Broadway plays and expressed gratitude for the performances and artists that inspired his work. One artist Miranda identified as a crucial teacher is the legendary composer of Disney musicals, Alan Menken, whose birthday of July 23rd was celebrated at #Ham4Ham. Miranda announced, "The reason I get to stand here today is because I saw *The Little Mermaid* when I was seven years old, and I was never the same again. So can we all sing 'Happy Birthday' to Alan Menken before we do anything, and all of you tweet this to him when you shoot the video?" By encouraging the lottery audience to take a video on their phones and share it with Menken, the singular event of the live singing of "Happy Birthday" on the theater steps became multiplied in different audience-created videos and circulated through social media. Miranda offered a generous and generative opportunity to participate in *Hamilton* nation, even if the lottery participants had not or would never get to see *Hamilton*. The #Ham4Ham events can be considered part of a long history of public street performance, often celebrated for democratically extending access to the theater and for disrupting not only traffic patterns but also social and cultural conventions.[104]

The third common #Ham4Ham show featured actors switching roles, a game that demonstrates the virtuosity of the performer as it challenges stereotypes about which actor and person can play which part. The first #Ham4Ham role switch took place on July 17, 2015, when Daveed Diggs, the skilled rapper who originated the role of Thomas Jefferson took Miranda's part as Hamilton in the "First Cabinet Battle." Miranda claimed, "It gets a little frustrating for Daveed because he has to lose in a rap battle every night. So just for today and just for you guys, playing Hamilton in the first debate will be Daveed Diggs and losing the battle as Thomas Jefferson— yours truly." Miranda emphasized again that #Ham4Ham is a one-time-only event exclusively for the lottery crowd—who will then post the performance on social media. The "Cabinet Battles" ingeniously stage political debates as rap battles with intricate rhythms and rhymes that are abundantly evident in Hamilton's response to Jefferson, who opposed Treasury Secretary Hamilton's plan to establish a national bank and have the federal government assume states' debts:

THOMAS. That was a real nice declaration.
Welcome to the present. We're running a real nation.
Would you like to join us, or stay mellow,
Doin' whatever the hell it is you do in Monticello?
If we assume the debts, the Union gets a new line of credit, a financial diuretic.
How do you not get it? If we're aggressive and competitive
The Union gets a boost. You'd rather give it a sedative?[105]

Rapped at a furious pace with sequenced rhymes and near-rhymes ("credit," "diuretic," "get it," "competitive," "sedative") that require precise articulation, the battles are challenging performances even before the actors traded roles so that Daveed Diggs has an opportunity to "win."

The virtuosity of actors who can take up different parts in the script was also on display at #Ham4Ham on July 27, 2015—the birthday of Thayne

Jasperson, who played the loyalist farmer Samuel Seabury. As a birthday gift, Miranda sang Jasperson's part in "The Farmer Refuted," while Jasperson rapped Hamilton's takedown of Seabury's loyalist arguments.[106] Again, a spirit of generosity is present as the performer who typically "lost" gets to take the winning role. By juggling these parts, the #Ham4Ham event suggests that the winners and losers might not be so clearly distinguishable as *Hamilton*, the musical, often suggests. Coherent positions against the American Revolutionary War existed and other feasible political trajectories were both proposed and possible, but they are drowned out by *Hamilton's* masculinist celebration of battle and revolution. The historian Catherine Allgor imagines an excised number responding to Seabury's argument against "chaos and bloodshed" in "The Farmer Refuted": "The Farmer was right; or, Have you ever heard of Canada?"[107] The United States' northern neighbor followed a gradual political disentanglement from Great Britain that resulted in Canada's independent democratic government with a symbolic affiliation to the United Kingdom.

Several #Ham4Ham events switch gender roles and comment on gender norms that remain firmly entrenched in *Hamilton*, which, as I argue earlier, does not offer revolutionary perspectives on gender and sexuality. The #Ham4Ham performance on July 20, 2015, featured Renée Elise Goldsberry, who originated the role of Angelica Schuyler (and won the 2016 Tony Award for Best Featured Actress in a Musical), rapping "Right-Hand Man" accompanied by the beatboxing of Phillipa Soo, who plays Hamilton's wife, Eliza Schuyler. The performance subtly questioned the cliché of the "right-hand man," as it imagined what it would mean to proclaim that General George Washington needed a *right-hand woman*. Why is there still no concept of the *right-hand woman*? The women characters in *Hamilton* rarely rap, whereas it is the main genre through which men share ideas, demonstrate their intelligence, and claim power, as in the Cabinet Battles. Within the gendered logic of the musical, to sing is feminine or effeminate (in the mouths of the King and Seabury); rap is a masculine genre.

Goldsberry and Soo perform roles written for men with serious intensity in #Ham4Ham events, while *Hamilton's* male actors play *women* with a flippant affectation. On October 25, 2015, the roles of "The Schuyler Sisters" in their introductory song were lip-synched by three King George III's: Brian D'Arcy James (the actor who originated the role at the Public Theater) as Eliza, Jonathan Groff (then reigning king) as Angelica, and Andrew Rannells (a substitute for Groff) as Peggy.[108] All three wore crowns, and all pranced and swung their hips in an imitation of femininity that drew most directly from drag *queen* performance styles—which made their kingly crowns all the more humorous. Groff carried his arms in front of him with bent wrists and a droopy ring finger, while Rannells had a particularly girlish pout as the complaining Peggy. Given that Groff and Rannells are openly gay actors, their performance could appear to exaggerate stereotypes of gayness as well as femininity. Fully achieved masculinity in the #Ham4Ham skit was represented by Daveed Diggs (Marquis de Lafayette/Thomas Jefferson) and Okieriete Onaodowan (Hercules Mulligan/James Madison) who strutted through the performance space in response to Eliza's question (sung by Brian D'Arcy James), "Angelica, remind me what we're looking for . . ." "She's lookin' for me!" Diggs and Onaodowan declared. As the apex of Black masculine confidence, they called attention to the sister kings' whiteness as well as their exaggerated femininity. Another version of Black confidence was represented by Renee Elise Goldsberry (Angelica), who served as emcee and performed Aaron Burr's attempt to pick up Angelica/Groff:

Ah, so you've discussed me.
I'm a trust fund, baby, you can trust me!

While Goldsberry adopted a wide stance and swagger, her portrayal of Burr was no more exaggerated than the strut of Diggs and Onaodowan and less provocative and humorous for the spectators than the stereotypically effeminate King Georges as Schuyler sisters. Women actors can play men's roles seriously, while men can only represent women with exaggerated effeminacy and ridicule.

The discrepancy in audience responses to cross-gendered #Ham4Ham performances can partially be explained by misogyny and taboos against men exhibiting traits conventionally associated with women. Research has long revealed that men receive more pressure about what not to do (negative prescriptive stereotypes) than women, particularly pressure not to exhibit traits, like weakness, that are associated with women.[109] While women are also discouraged from appearing dominant and agentive, they are sanctioned less for behaving *like men* than are men for exhibiting behaviors considered feminine. Of course, there is huge variation in prescriptions based on class, ethnicity, race, and other categories, but women enjoy more opportunity to adopt conventionally masculine self-stylizations than men have to play with femininity.

#Ham4Ham and other para*Hamilton* performances were often more *rev-
olutionary* or radical than the play itself. #Ham4Ham's gender-switching
performances uphold some gender stereotypes but also expose the particularly conservative gender boundaries in the actual musical. #Ham4Ham
indicates some divergent perspectives and positions on the American
Revolution that are not available in *Hamilton*, the musical. #Ham4Ham also
offers a larger range of opportunities for audience participation and engagement on the sidewalk than the opportunities available inside the Richard
Rodgers Theater. While #Ham4Ham is more playful and inclusive, particularly of gender roles and politics, than *Hamilton*, both are examples of
complicit participation. Audiences can enjoy the pleasures of participating
in gestures of allyship, including celebrating a Broadway play framed as a
"revolutionary," without giving up any of their privilege or actually revolting
against white supremacy.

Hamilton particiNation was and continues to be tremendously pleasur-
able. The crowds at #Ham4Ham grew so big that they became a safety risk,
and performers regularly thanked the New York Police officers who provided security and directed traffic on West 46th Street. The audience for
#Ham4Ham was initially defined by its presence at (and hope to win) the
ticket lottery, but encouraged by Miranda and the other performers, audience
members recorded the event on their phones and posted or tweeted widely—
creating a digital audience that could comment, repost, and even recreate
or restage versions of these para*Hamilton* performances. Perhaps inspired
by the energetic response to #HamforHam on social media, the *Hamilton*
team attempted to launch an online lottery in January of 2016. On the first
day, the system crashed under 50,000 entries. The production team fixed that
technology and also began to experiment with digital #Ham4Hams to be
posted on YouTube five minutes before the lottery winners are announced.
The first digital #Ham4Ham was offered on Miranda's birthday, January
16, when Alan Menken reciprocated his earlier "Happy Birthday" serenade
on #Ham4Ham, by singing a series of songs from *The Little Mermaid* with
Miranda.[110]

5.5. Black Mermaid Coda

I conclude this chapter's discussion of audience participation in I&D, race,
and gender with a post *Hamilton* particiNation example: Lin-Manuel

Miranda and Alan Menken's partnership on a live-action remake of *The Little Mermaid*, released in May 2023 after COVID-19 pandemic delays.[111] Miranda's interest in the remake is no surprise given his #Ham4Ham claim, "The reason I get to stand here today is because I saw *The Little Mermaid* when I was seven years old, and I was never the same again." As *Hamilton* continued to tour, the Walt Disney Company announced on July 3, 2019, that the Black singer, Halle Bailey, had been cast as the mermaid Ariel and set off another not-quite debate about race and casting.[112] Supposedly, outraged fans of the red-headed, blue-eyed *animated* mermaid from 1989 made #NotMyAriel trend briefly on Twitter. In fact, there were few followers of the # and many comments that supported Bailey and railed *against* white supremacy; comments opposing the # made it trend. An article in the Black entertainment e-journal, *Shadow and Act*, asked, "Is #NotMyAriel Just Another Russian Troll of Black Twitter?" and gave suggestions about how to identify bots and trolls that amplify messages.[113] Fake accounts are regularly used to sow discord or promote particular political views.[114] There was certainly less of an "uproar over a black Ariel" than Brooke Newman claimed in a *Washington Post* article describing the "white nostalgia" for a fair-skinned, red-headed mermaid cartoon.[115] Newman accurately identified the white supremacist nostalgia that provoked some Tweets in #NotMyAriel, but there were far more comments rejecting those Tweets and performing complicit participation in a social media backlash against racism.

Walt Disney Company has made fortunes on animated "Snow White" princesses awaiting their [equally white] princes. Like many film and media companies, Disney recognizes that films with culturally authentic stories and diverse characters and creative teams make more money at the box office today.[116] Walt Disney Company's commitment to adopting "inclusion standards across Disney General Entertainment and live-action Studio" is articulated as a desire to "Reimagine Tomorrow" and a profit motive: "We believe that forging meaningful connections with our consumers contributes to the growth and viability of the Company, so we purposefully champion a multitude of voices and perspectives."[117] Disney will grow and remain viable with the new demographic of BIPOC children and families interested in raising antiracist children, or at least interested in performing participation in I&D.[118] While I am a supporter and consumer of the enterprise, including the film of *Hamilton* streaming on Disney+, I ask for a more radical transformation of the stories than we see when the same narrative is staged with a more diverse cast and the Black princess sings the same song as the white version.

An image of Ariel's lips puckering up to beg a kiss from Prince Eric was imprinted on my eleven-year-old fantasies, and even now, my mind replays the all-too catchy song "Kiss the Girl," voiced by the Jamaican-accented, reggae-sounding crab, Sebastien (originally played by the Black actor Samuel E. Wright, recast for Daveed Diggs, whose breakout role was as Thomas Jefferson/Marquis de Lafayette in *Hamilton*). Sebastian, one in a series of animal characters cast with Black actors, sings the song to try to set the "moooood" for Prince Eric to kiss Ariel, who has mortgaged her own beautiful voice to the sea witch, Ursula, for a human body and the opportunity to woo the prince.[119] If he does not kiss her within three days, she will become Ursula's voiceless prisoner forever. The point is, Ariel gives up her *voice* to get some shapely legs with which to win the prince. The relevant question is not whether Ariel should be played by a Black or white woman in the remake, but how will that casting choice impact the still-damaging gender representation of silently flirtatious femininity? Do we need another Ariel at all?

PART IV

ACT II OR JUST ANOTHER
TALKBACK?

IV.1. Introduction to Part IV

We are pleased to invite the audience to remain in the theater after tonight's performance for a brief talkback with members of the cast and crew.

I cringe when I hear the talkback announcement right after the reminder to silence your devices and locate the nearest exits. I locate and consider my exit, often planning to make it during the inevitable standing ovation but before the talkback. The talkback announcement suggests that the show is supposed to be addressing a *serious* issue that *needs to be talked about*. And if a show is addressing a serious issue, the standing ovation is almost inevitable because audiences feel they must stand and applaud a theatrical event that tackles topics of race, gender, and ability, also the topics of my final section in *Complicit Participation*, Part IV. The announcement of the dreaded talkback jostles me out of my hushed anticipation of the theatrical event, thrusts me forward to the end of the play, and reminds me of the guilt I will feel if I do not stay for the talkback and the impatience I am likely to experience if I do. I almost always dislike these post-show events. I even dislike them when they have been thoughtfully organized by the theater's outreach team for the class of students I have brought to the theater; I especially hate them when I am running them as the so-called expert invited to facilitate the conversation.

I am not alone in bemoaning talkbacks, even as I am regularly a complicit participant in them. In July of 2017, the Pulitzer Prize–winning playwright David Mamet not only refused to participate but also prohibited talkbacks within two hours of his play; licenses for his productions now threaten a fine of $25,000 per talkback and loss of performance rights.[1] What are these events that Mamet considers so deplorable as to demand a hefty fine? Talkbacks became regular features of theatrical programming in the early 1960s, while other forms of audience participation, aside from clapping, had decreased in the twentieth century.[2] Audiences have always been talking about their experiences in the theater—often vocalizing right through the play, as my discussion of melodramatic hissing and cheering in Part II revealed. But as the popularity of melodrama waned and some theater venues sought to elevate *serious drama* above popular entertainment, new rules for theater etiquette and new stage techniques encouraged spectators to behave in a more subdued manner. Electrical lighting onstage and darkened auditoriums encouraged more hushed audiences.[3] So, too, did realist drama's convention that actors do not acknowledge the existence of audiences, who should watch as if peering through an invisible fourth wall.[4] Animated or angry audiences regularly break these rules, as famously exemplified in the theater riots at the Abbey Theater following the 1907 production of John Millington Synge's *The Playboy of the Western World* or the Parisian audience's raucous disruption at the premiere of the Ballets Russes's *Le Sacre du Printemps* (Vaslav Nijinsky, Igor Stravinsky) in 1913.[5] More often than rioting, theater audiences during the second half of the twentieth century applauded politely and saved their comments for the talkback.

This history of talkbacks suggests that they were invented to provide an outlet for the audience engagement that had been silenced by new rules for theater etiquette, but that was just one factor. A recent *Handbook for Dramaturgy* provides this definition: "Talkbacks are events that connect the audience directly to the artists and when moderated by a dramaturg, can be extremely rich opportunities for increasing your theater's audience and helping them towards a deeper appreciation of your company's work."[6] The statement suggests that dramaturgs can ensure talkbacks function as effective marketing tools to attract audiences and encourage their commitment to the company. Dramaturgs do this by deepening the audience's "appreciation" or understanding, which, the handbook implies, needs to be a bit deeper.[7] Of course, the handbook does not encourage the dramaturg to include these goals while introducing the event. Instead, the handbook instructs the dramaturg to say, "We like to have these direct question-and-answer sessions to give our cast and crew a chance to get direct feedback from the most important people in the theater—the audience—whom we otherwise rarely hear from. It's a chance for us to get to know you and to learn how effective we have been, and how we can serve you better in the future."[8] The aspiring dramaturgs learn to *describe* the event to audiences as an opportunity for the company and artists to learn from them, whereas the handbook's stated purpose is to deepen their understanding and encourage them to buy more tickets. There is a contradiction operating in the definitions and public introductions taught by the dramaturgy handbook, which frames dramaturgy as complicit in duping audiences and encouraging their complicit participation.

The contradictions are part of my problem with talkbacks, and probably among the reasons Mamet forbids them. Talkbacks are presented as follows:

1. *Pedagogical Events* that teach the audience how to appreciate the play and the company—or perhaps theater in general
2. *Promotional Tools* for increasing ticket sales
3. *Audience Focus Groups* that provide opportunities for the artists to learn from the audience and improve their practice
4. *Civic Conversations* that foster personal exploration and honest dialogue about art and community

Of course, several goals can be operating at the same time, and different facilitators, panelists, and participants may bring different intentions to the talkback. But the prevailing structure of theater talkbacks tend to produce *Pedagogical Events*. Many talkbacks position audiences in the role of students as they are moderated by a dramaturg or another member of the artistic team, and the typical panel is filled with other professionals/experts: actors, the director, even the playwright. Sometimes a topic "expert," typically a professor like myself, is invited to moderate the talkback or serve on the panel with the artists. The panelists usually sit in chairs on the stage, in the position of performance and power, a bottle of water beside each seat in recognition of the labor. The moderator asks the audience to stay in the auditorium but move forward to seats closer to the stage, and those of us hanging back or refusing to move forward feel like bad students, squandering their opportunity to learn. If the scholarly and popular writing on talkbacks is any indication, experts and panelists tend to view the audience dismissively, regularly deploring the audience's tendency to ask the actors banal questions such as: "How did you learn all those lines?"[9] If everyone involved dislikes them, why do we keep holding talkbacks?

Promotional Tools: There is evidence to suggest that even if people claim not to like talkbacks, the post-show events increase ticket sales. More studies of audience attitudes about talkbacks are needed—studies that do not primarily recruit subjects from talkbacks, which contributes to a favorable bias as study participants who attend talkbacks are more likely to claim they appreciate the events to which they have committed their time.[10] Research on audiences is more common outside of the United States, but the New York Broadway League demographic questionnaire for the 2010–2011 season introduced a question about talkbacks that revealed audiences claim to be interested enough in talkbacks to deliberately attend the performance when a post-show discussion is offered.[11] Reports from the Wallace Foundation on successful initiatives for audience engagement celebrate the talkback and provide examples of success. Chicago's Steppenwolf Theatre Company responded to a decline in subscriptions by offering a "Public Square" program for audiences that featured talkbacks after every single performance (since 2005); Steppenwolf increased repeat visits to the theater by 61 percent over three years.[12]

Audience Focus Groups: Dramaturgs are framing the talkback as a focus group session if they follow the handbook's recommendation and describe the event as "a chance for us to get to know you and to learn how effective we have been, and how we can serve you better in the future."[13] Presenting the talkback as a focus group on the theatrical event of the evening is a bit disingenuous, because most talkbacks held during the run of a production cannot significantly inform the artists' work. The playwright is rarely present, the plays are already staged, and the performing artists are not authorized to change much at that point. The talkback might influence later productions or future seasons. True audience focus groups are sometimes used during works-in-progress presentations, previews, or Broadway's out-of-town (meaning out-of-New York) trials to gauge audience responses to a play and suggest revisions. Framing a talkback as a focus group might seem inappropriate to theater artists who do not consider audiences as consumers and do not identify *pleasing* the audience or providing a service to be a main goal of their work. The talkbacks I consider here were designed not to please audiences but to make them have difficult conversations about race.

Civic Conversations: Steppenwolf's "Public Square" Program succeeded in cultivating audiences and encouraging them to return to the theater partially by shifting the format of its talkbacks from "Pedagogical Events" to "Civic Conversations." Steppenwolf's research revealed that their audiences understood themselves as " 'lifelong learners' who enjoy pondering new ideas about the human condition."[14] In addition to their nightly talkbacks, they offered other educational events and opportunities to engage with digital content such as podcasts, clips, and blogs. Steppenwolf ensemble members also engaged with audiences online, sharing thoughts about the company's productions and reflecting on the nature of community. As the COVID-19 pandemic shuttered theaters across the world in the spring of 2020, Steppenwolf Education quickly developed their digital materials into a rich set of virtual programs that reached nearly 1,000 people in the first two months.[15] During "Maker May" (2020), every week featured artists "close" to Steppenwolf describing their creative process and providing participants with a "maker challenge," which they then shared during the second workshop of the week.

Many theater companies in addition to Steppenwolf have worked to transform the typical talkback into a civic conversation that does not merely teach but also engages the audience in conversations about the significance of the play and larger questions of humanity and community.[16] In Part IV of this book, I take up two productions and their talkbacks, Anna Deavere Smith's *Notes from the Field: Doing Time in Education*, performed at American Repertory Theater in Cambridge, Massachusetts, in 2016 and Claudia Rankine's *The White Card*, which premiered in 2018 at Boston's Paramount Theater in a co-production by Arts Emerson and the American Repertory Theater. The publicity for both highlighted the opportunities for audience engagement through discussions called, in both cases, "Act II" to indicate that these events were not post-show talkbacks, but crucial parts of the shows. Introduced with a quote by Anna Deavere Smith, "Be more than a spectator," the Act II Initiative is defined by A.R.T. as

> an experiment in disrupting the role of spectator as passive observer. Act II events invite audience members to pursue deeper engagement with productions and highlight the variety of ways that A.R.T. community members continue to create impact in the Boston area and the world.[17]

Note that this description of Act II implies that the theatrical spectator is usually cast in the role of "passive observer," an assumption I have questioned throughout this book by pointing to the current fad of immersive theater and the booing, clapping, occasionally fruit-throwing audiences of nineteenth-century melodramas and earlier forms.[18] A second assumption in the Act II definition is that passive observation is less likely to encourage "deeper engagement" with a performance or subsequent work to "impact" the world outside the theater. Both *Notes from the Field* and *The White Card* promoted "deeper engagement" by asking audiences to confront the insidious operations of racism, interrogate their own position, particularly if they experience white privilege or class privilege, and then work to dismantle white supremacy.[19] The Act IIs of both productions asked audiences to share their own experiences with racial oppression and privilege and how they intersected with the stories told in *Notes from the Field* and *The White Card*. "What are you going to do about this? How can you act?" the facilitators asked, hoping to disturb audience complacency and move them to action.

Did it work? Were audiences prompted to engage more deeply by the Act II conversation and then go out to change the world? Or did they feel like they had done their hard work in the theater and during the—typically uncomfortable—Act II conversations, pat themselves on the back, and return to their usual lives feeling a bit better about themselves? Did Act II prompt activism or even personal reflection, or was it just another talkback and example of complicit participation? The next two chapters consider these questions and the evolution of A.R.T.'s Act II events from *Notes from the Field* to *The White Card*, a development that involved some of the same Boston dramaturgs, facilitators, and Act II team members—as well as the same audience members (like me). While I initially hoped to understand Act II's impact on audiences through interviews and observation, I ultimately realized that qualitative audience research would not answer my question of whether Act II led to action. The motivations for any act are not easily decipherable or even obvious to the actor, and this is particularly true for behavior as complex as activism. (The same is true for trying to assess the impact of college classes; as a professor, I cannot know whether my teaching in the classroom inspires my students to do things in the world, even if they, to my delight, tell me my class motivated them. My delight is part of the problem in that it prompts students to tell me what I want to hear.)

Recognizing that conversations with audiences would tell me only part of the story, I became interested in how the teams that conceived, organized, facilitated, and performed alongside the audience in Act II understood these events in relation to their own art and activism. Taking the Act II title quite literally, I consider Act II in relation to Act I, the play itself, as a singular theatrical event. *Notes from the Field* and *The White Card* have much to teach, but as with each of the pedagogical institutions these plays present— school systems, art museums, police forces, and prisons—their most prominent lessons are not always intended, partially because the institutions are immersed in white supremacy. *Notes from the Field*, *The White Card*, and their Act IIs cannot entirely escape from the systems they attempt to critique, the systems by which racism becomes embedded in educational institutions and the tendency of art and media to turn Black suffering into spectacle. In arguing that the plays and theatrical institutions are complicit, to some extent, in these systems, I do not intend to wag a pious finger at their laudable efforts. Nor do I claim that they ought to have been able to achieve a position outside of white supremacy. Instead, I hope to reveal the infusion of white supremacy through every institution and the insidious, adaptable nature of both racism and I&D platforms. Audiences, despite their own good intentions, are not only spectators of, but also complicit participants in, white supremacy. Recognizing this is perhaps the first small step toward participating differently.

6

Doing Time in Anna Deavere Smith's Act II

The big white T on the program insert stuck out beyond the red program for Anna Deavere Smith's *Notes from the Field: Doing Time in Education* at American Repertory Theater (A.R.T.) in 2016 (see Figure 6.1). As if the inserts were not the most prominent feature of the materials distributed at the theater door, the ushers drew our attention to them by pointing to a map indicating where Discussion Groups were to meet. The ushers deliberately separated couples and groups who attended the play together, so my partner got a card instructing him to meet Discussion Group K in a corner of the theater. He reported that "dread" set in as he realized he was supposed to participate in a Discussion Group and that he was not assigned to my group, saying, "I'm sure most people were dreading it. You don't want to go sit with a bunch of strangers and talk about race." I felt curiosity rather than dread, but I had a researcher's perspective on the Discussion Groups. My conversations with audience members indicated that many people were, in fact, anxious about these Discussion Groups with strangers. Some chose not to participate. Audiences might benefit from those conversations in spite of, or because of, their discomfort—which is certainly differentiated by their race, gender, class, and educational experiences.

As I began studying Smith's *Notes from the Field*, I initially believed the most important question was: Did Act II, and similar programs, tear down the school-to-prison pipeline, a term for the school discipline policies that target Black, Indigenous, People of Color (BIPOC) and poor children with suspensions and expulsions that ultimately push them out of school and into the criminal justice system? Does the potential of this activism outweigh the discomfort and even pain audiences and discussion leaders experienced? I now realize that these questions rest on the presumption that the promotional materials accurately articulate the purpose of Act II as being to "highlight the variety of ways that A.R.T. community members continue to create impact in the Boston area and the world."[1] Or as Anna Deavere Smith explained her goals in an interview: "And these people [the audience] I think have a great potential when we [the performers] have left to network and to

Complicit Participation. Carrie J. Preston, Oxford University Press. © Oxford University Press 2024.
DOI: 10.1093/9780197693438.003.0007

Figure 6.1 Program Insert, "You Are in Discussion Group T." American Repertory Theatre's *Notes from the Field: Doing Time in Education*, created, written, and performed by Anna Deavere Smith at the Loeb Drama Center, Cambridge, MA, August 28, 2016. Courtesy of Carrie J. Preston.

really do the work when we're gone."[2] The notion that the goal of Act II was to get the audience to do something about the school-to-prison pipeline was reinforced by the first question asked during most Act II discussions, variations of which included: "What are you going to do about this / What *can* you do?" and "What is the show asking of me / How can I act?"[3] As I have engaged in further conversations and continued to reflect on the experience,

I have come to the conclusion that Act II did not and never could function primarily as a way to get audience members to *do* something, although it could ask them to *consider* what they were and—especially—*were not* doing. I reframed my central question as: What is the thing being done or performed in Act II?

Act II's *doing* is similar to that of Act I of Smith's *Notes from the Field*. The audience was telling stories about education and racism, stories that demonstrated our limited perspectives and implicit or explicit biases, even as many of us attempted to perform our concern about racial injustice in the school-to-prison pipeline. Our tendency to ramble with our stories led us to sound like many of the monologues in Act I, as we delivered our own *notes from the field*. Together, we were in fact *doing time in education*—specifically in the standard educational format of the small group discussion. That pedagogical exercise made Act II feel quite different from the talkback with experts or artists that is typical of audience engagement programming at many theaters. But Act II was not about direct action or "creat[ing] impact in the Boston area and the world," as A.R.T.'s publicity put it.[4] The audience's role in this performance, like every other theatrical role, was more about *acting* than direct *action*. Act II was an immersive, site-specific performance, and like other examples of immersive audience participation, it carried risks related to audience/participant consent and suffering. These risks were aggravated by the fact that Act II was not advertised as immersive performance to the audience and facilitators. Facilitators had been trained to moderate a conversation, but they became audiences for the bias-riddled monologues of their group members—in a way that mirrored Smith's own artistic process of interviewing and recording people impacted in different ways by the school-to-prison pipeline. I am not suggesting that A.R.T. was attempting to mislead audience members; rather, I am arguing that Act II was a complex experiment and negotiation among the aesthetic goals of Anna Deavere Smith, the programming desired by A.R.T.'s creative team, and the activist commitments of *The Pipeline Project* team. None of them could have known in advance what Act II would turn out to be, or how to accurately manage and market the experience. Some dread and discomfort *are* the appropriate responses to doing time in education and activist theater, and many were offered a valuable learning opportunity. Unfortunately, a good deal of the burden of teaching ended up on the shoulders of BIPOC facilitators and audience members.

6.1. The Pipeline Project: Performing the "Actual"

Anna Deavere Smith remembers the incident that, in 2013, prompted her to initiate *The Pipeline Project*, of which the play *Notes from the Field* is the central work.[5] While filming the television series *Nurse Jackie*, Smith told her castmate, Eve Best, about a student in her native town of Baltimore who was going to jail after urinating in a water cooler at school. Best replied, "Oh, well, whatever happened to mischief," and according to Smith, "That was when it struck me: rich kids get mischief, poor kids get pathologized and incarcerated."[6] Her research led her to the concept of the school-to-prison pipeline, the idea that schools aggressively punish their most vulnerable BIPOC and/or poor students and ultimately push them out of school and into the criminal justice system and eventually prison. The A.R.T. Educational Toolkit revealed striking racial disparities in school discipline: 70 percent of students who are arrested in schools or referred to law enforcement across the United States are Black or Latinx, groups that compose less than 45 percent of public school students.[7] In Boston, Black boys are disciplined at a rate eight times higher than white boys, while Black girls are disciplined eleven times more than white girls.[8] Racism clearly impacts school discipline, and so, too, does the presence of a police officer on school grounds. Schools with an officer on campus had nearly five times the rate of arrests for "disorderly conduct" as schools without the officer—even when studies control for the socioeconomic status of the school.[9]

Evidence of the school-to-prison pipeline was projected into the play by way of an ingenious set created by Riccardo Hernandez. Five panels descended from the ceiling of the Loeb Drama Center at midstage, with five more upstage, enabling projections designed by Elaine McCarthy to present statistics, photographs, film clips, murals, the live video of Smith playing Kevin Moore, the deli worker who recorded police officers beating Freddie Gray, and other footage relevant to the school-to-prison pipeline—all documentary evidence of the research amassed by *The Pipeline Project* team. For some monologues, an onstage videographer (played by Daniel Rattner at A.R.T.) recorded Smith speaking and projected her live onto the screens behind her.[10] (See Figure 6.2.) The audience was confronted with a multimedia performance of evidence that established the reality of the school-to-prison pipeline and its impact on students, families, and all of those who work in and for the intertwined school and prison systems. Anna Deavere Smith's commitment to staging realities is fundamental to her distinctive

Figure 6.2 Anna Deavere Smith and Onstage Assistant Daniel Rattner in American Repertory Theatre's *Notes from the Field: Doing Time in Education*, created, written, and performed by Anna Deavere Smith at the Loeb Drama Center, Cambridge, MA, August 2016. Photo by Evgenia Eliseeva.

performance practice of recording and then presenting monologues by real people, a practice she has been honing for decades. She searches for the personal experiences and voices behind the statistics for each topic she explores in her series of twenty plays she calls *On the Road: A Search for American Character*, of which *Notes from the Field* is the most recent. Smith's artistic practice includes conducting interviews with individuals who hold many different perspectives on a hot-button issue: *Fires in the Mirror* (1992), a finalist for the Pulitzer Prize, examined the riots and racial violence in Crown Heights, Brooklyn after the 1991 incident in which a car in the motorcade of a Hasidic Rabbi swerved out of control, killing a Black child and severely injuring another. The riots after police officers were acquitted for the brutal beating of Rodney King was the focus of Smith's Tony-nominated *Twilight: Los Angeles* (1993).

For *Notes From the Field*, Smith conducted approximately 250 interviews with individuals who bear some relationship to the school-to-prison pipeline in Northern California, Baltimore, Maryland, South Carolina, and Pennsylvania.[11] Smith chose to represent nineteen individuals at

A.R.T. through monologues preceded by "slides with the character's name, their occupation or position, and a title of the piece that follows" projected onto the panels hanging over the stage.[12] According to Smith's "Production Notes," these slides "are essential to the audience's understanding of what they are watching," and they also reinforce the fact that the play presents not fictional characters but real people experiencing the school-to-prison pipeline.[13] Smith constructs her monologues from verbatim selections of the interviews, replicating the intonations, verbal habits, and physical gestures of her subjects. Distinguishing her technique from mimicry or the tradition of performing impressions of others, Smith claims, "People speak of putting themselves into other people's shoes. My way of doing that is to put myself into other people's words."[14] Smith deliberately reveals to the audience her process of shifting between figures and occupying the words of others, as she slowly puts on a hat, scarf, glasses, or a pair of orange waders at the beginning of the monologue. Figure 6.3 shows Smith surrounded by some of the many pairs of shoes she dons to become her character; often as she begins a new monologue, she slowly takes off the pair appropriate to the previous character and puts on the new character's footwear (see Figure 6.3). She might have chosen to use the onstage screens like curtains that would conceal a more thorough change of costume to represent the various individuals she interviewed. Instead, Smith makes the theatrical apparatus and her own artistic practice as obvious and visible as possible to make what she calls American character visible, particularly its intersections with American racism. The changes in her costume and vocal intonations and expressions slowly coalesce into a new figure as she leaves the previous character behind, building a bridge or arc between them. The foundation of that arc is Smith herself, embodying multiple people and perspectives, suggesting she is capacious enough to embrace them all and bring them together.

Notes from the Field opens with a monologue by Sherrilyn Ifill, president of the NAACP Legal Defense and Educational Fund, who emphasizes that instead of investing in education or mental health, the United States invested in prisons, establishing the world's largest system of mass incarceration rather than the world's best school system: "we decided we're going to cut the budget and so we're not investing in education. Yeah. Kinda. We've taken it to the prison system."[15] Smith then explores the pipeline for Native American children through the voice of Taos Proctor, a Yurok Fisherman/former inmate and Abby Abinanti, Chief Judge of the Yurok Tribe in California. Abinanti described how tribal kids are identified as "having behavioral *issues*," which

Figure 6.3 Anna Deavere Smith (surrounded by shoes and other pieces of her onstage costume changes) in American Repertory Theatre's *Notes from the Field: Doing Time in Education*, created, written, and performed by Anna Deavere Smith at the Loeb Drama Center, Cambridge, MA, August 2016. Photo by Evgenia Eliseeva.

leads to suspension, then arrests at school, and ultimately, as with Proctor, incarceration in the California Youth Authority prison.[16] Abinanti pleads, "I get mad at you so I throw you outta school? What is—what is *that?* NO. I get mad at you so we need to come *closer*."[17]

The death of Freddie Gray in police custody in Baltimore is the subject of monologues by Kevin Moore, the videographer of the police beating of Gray, the protestor Allen Bullock, and Jamal Harrison Bryant, the AME pastor who spoke at Gray's funeral on April 27, 2015. The connection between the school-to-prison pipeline and police brutality against Gray and other BIPOC civilians is not stated directly in these monologues, but the connections are easily inferred. As a child, Gray struggled with learning disabilities and behavioral problems, all too common among children who, like Gray, suffer from damaging exposure to lead.[18] He was regularly suspended from school, eventually dropping out altogether, and he was arrested a week after he turned eighteen and incarcerated shortly thereafter (if Gray had a juvenile arrest record, it would not be public).[19] Newsclips and footage of Gray's arrest and death, the trials of the officers, Allen Bullock destroying a Baltimore police car during the protests, and the funeral and sermon by Pastor Jamal Harrison Bryant were projected onto the five panels, adding further documentary evidence to the names and photographs of characters and the statistics about the school-to-prison pipeline.

The section called "The Shakara Story" opened with the cell phone video Niya Kenny took of the violent confrontation between her classmate, identified only as "Shakara," and the Spring Valley High School resource officer, Deputy Ben Fields. When "Shakara" refused to give up her phone and leave the room, the teacher called in Fields. The footage of the incident on October 26, 2015, was projected on the white screens of the set for the audience to witness how Deputy Fields threw "Shakara" and her desk backward, and then dragged the girl across the floor and put her in hand cuffs. For taking the video and protesting the treatment of her classmate, Kenny was also arrested and cuffed, and then, being eighteen years old, taken to an adult detention center in Columbia, South Carolina. As she tells the story, she sat in jail terrified that her mother would be furious at her for not minding her own "business": " 'But he just threw a whole girl across the classroom!' How can you mind your business? Like that's somethin' you need to *make* your business."[20] Kenny's mother understood her protest after seeing footage of the incident, the same footage screened for the audience, played on the local television stations; Kenny's cell phone video of the incident went viral and garnered invitations for her to appear on *Good Morning America* and CNN.[21] The footage was also a major piece of evidence in the case against Deputy Fields, who was relieved of duty for his actions but not charged with criminal civil rights violations. Yet both "Shakara" and Niya Kenny were charged with the crime of "disturbing schools," charges that were later dismissed by the District Solicitor.[22] As with Kevin Moore's footage of the beating of Freddie Gray, cell phone video of police violence against BIPOC people can ignite outrage and widespread protests without leading to criminal charges. For Niya Kenny, the act of *taking the video* and protesting the abuse of her classmate was criminalized by incoherent laws against "disturbing schools."

The idea that cell phone footage—or the threat of a recording—can protect activists, particularly BIPOC protesters, appears again in the penultimate monologue of the play, "Not a Whim Thing to Do." Featuring the artist and activist Bree Newsome, the monologue is introduced with footage of the "actual scene" after Dylann Roof murdered nine parishioners from Mother Emanuel AME Church in Charleston at a prayer meeting on June 17, 2015.[23]

The "cacophony" of newscasters and speakers concludes with video showing protests demanding that the Confederate flag be removed from the South Carolina capitol building.[24] Newsome recalls that when the state "wouldn't even lower the flag to half-staff" after the massacre, activists came together from Black Lives Matter, The Tribe, and environmentalist/Occupy groups to "take it down."[25] As she ascended the flagpole the morning of June 27, 2015, a police supervisor directed two of the officers on the scene to tase her. The white Greenpeace activist who taught her to climb, James Tyson, grabbed the pole and said, "If you electrocute her, you'll have to electrocute me, too."[26] Newsome reflects, "And I think that's when they again became aware that, you know, there are folks standing around with cameras, and, you know, smartphones." The cameras that recorded her ascent may have saved her life, even as they allow audiences at *Notes from the Field* to witness her triumphant descent with the flag into the handcuffs of the police as she recited verses from the Bible.[27]

The projections of slides giving speaker names and locations, statistics, photographs, and videos help Anna Deavere Smith establish the gravity of the school-to-prison pipeline and expand her documentary theater form beyond that of other pieces in her *On the Road: A Search for the American Character* series.[28] Smith has described her technique of performing monologues adapted from interview transcripts as a process of offering "a living document of speech in a moment and time in history."[29] Smith introduces *Notes from the Field* in this vein on the first slide: "The material in this play is composed of verbatim excerpts from interviews conducted by Anna Deavere Smith unless otherwise noted."[30] The "material" of the play includes not only speech but also film, footage, and photographs, the "actual" evidence of the school-to-prison pipeline. The stage directions use the adjective "actual" nine times to introduce the "actual newsclips,"[31] "actual sermon at Freddie Gray's funeral,"[32] "actual footage of the funeral [of Gray],"[33] "actual documentary footage,"[34] "actual cell phone video,"[35] "actual scene," and "actual news."[36] These and other pieces of *actual* evidence are projected across multiple panels with gaps in between, thereby creating a rupture in the image and reinforcing the idea of broken and intertwined educational and carceral systems with a dizzying number of facets (see Figure 6.2). The script's relentless insistence on the *actual* seems to be in tension with the rupture and disruption created by the media barrage, as well as the overt theatricality of Smith's visible costume changes into different characters and the presence of the onstage musician, composer, and bassist Marcus Shelby. The evidence is also projected upon Smith and Shelby's bodies, producing an overwhelming and deeply emotional, often disturbing, layering of images, performance genres, and entrenched problems.

Many in the audience would have found the layered, multimodal performance unfamiliar and felt uncertain of how to respond. The monologue "Handcuffs," added to the play after the A.R.T. production and included in the HBO film, provides one model for how audiences might respond as they observe the emotional reactions of a teacher watching the "Shakara incident" in South Carolina. The scene opens with Sari Muhonen, a Helsinki teacher and teacher educator, watching Deputy Fields wrestle "Shakara" out of her desk on a cellphone. The same video is projected on a screen behind her so that the audience *watches Ms. Muhonen watching.* They see her "making faces, covering her eyes, then peeking out at the video again."[37] She asks, "What is *handcuffed*? (*Listens, shocked.*) Ahh? (*High-pitched sound.*) Nooooooo. That's—that's quite amazing."[38] If the audience were numb to footage of police brutality of Black students, this monologue provided a distanced, international perspective on a phenomenon that, the scene suggests, is distinctly *American.* Ms. Muhonen, teacher of teachers, also teaches the audience that "something went terribly wrong."[39] In Finnish they speak of "pedagogical love" and, she says, "But police officers I don't think is needed anywhere. I have never heard. No. No."[40]

Like Ms. Muhonen, I wanted to cover my eyes and avoid seeing the *actual* footage of "Shakara" being thrown to the ground. My conversations and interviews would indicate that many in the audience were convinced of the school-to-prison pipeline as a system that discriminates against BIPOC children and upholds white supremacy. Many of us felt troubled, complicit, and/or despairing of change. How could we intervene in this system? The videos projected on screens and across the bodies of Smith and Shelby were at some distance from the audience's safe seat in the auditorium. But that relative safety was ripped away in Act II as audience members set off with their discussion group assignments, aided by the maps and "suggested routes" inserted in our programs. The program note from Artistic Director Diane Paulus told us that "By incorporating discussions directly into the performance, this production builds on A.R.T.'s ongoing initiative to place art and audiences in dialogue around the pressing global issues of our time . . . and strengthen our collective capacity for action." The idea is that audiences are unlikely to move from *play* to *action* and more likely to be inspired to act for change by *conversation about the play.* I don't disagree with that idea, and I applaud the goal; but this chapter is not about whether that happened, which would be impossible to determine. The next section is about what *actually* happened in Act II.

6.2. The Act of Act II

As I made my way to meeting point T for Act II, I noticed that some audience members were not planning to participate (see Figure 6.1). They hustled away from the theater building or huddled together, avoiding eye contact with A.R.T. staff and other audience members. A couple I interviewed told me they were aware of Act II when they bought their tickets to *Notes from the Field*, but they claimed, "We went to see Anna Deavere Smith . . . those kinds of discussions are so contrived."[41] Instead of joining their discussion groups, they took a walk across the street to the sunken gardens in Radcliffe Yard. I discussed audience refusals to participate with Elizabeth Cooper Davis, the Act II Facilitator Trainer, who acknowledged there were "all kinds of reasons folks didn't want to participate. . . . There was the impact of ushers randomizing the groups so deliberately so that if there were folks of color, they were separated and usually became the one person of color in the group."[42] Other group members and even facilitators might make racist statements, pretend BIPOC audience members were not present, or, in trying not to ignore them, ask them to educate the white group members or speak for all other people of color. The burden of educating white audiences is heavy, particularly for those who had experienced the school-to-prison pipeline firsthand and may have found the material of the play emotionally taxing. BIPOC theatergoers find themselves in a no-win situation—even in well-intentioned discussion groups.

I do not know how many audience members assigned to group T decided not to join our group at the discussion spot between the theater and Hillard Street. Eighteen of us showed up, with four claiming the chairs and the rest of us standing or sitting on the cement. A young person set out a basket of granola bars and apples, that most teacherly of fruits, and introduced herself as our Act II facilitator. It was then that I noticed every member of the discussion group appeared to be white *except* for the facilitator. The act of offering snacks was a gesture of hospitality intended to build rapport and establish a feeling of community among the group members; to break bread together is meaningful across communities and cultures. But I was uncomfortable that the only BIPOC-appearing woman in the group was also serving the rest of us food. She introduced herself as a recent Harvard graduate and high school science teacher as she passed around lined 5 x 8-inch index cards. She asked us to write down two questions that we would return to and discuss at the end of our twenty-five minutes together: "What is the show asking of me? How can I act?" The question of action was meant to frame the conversation.

Next, our facilitator read a quote from the play, specifically videographer Kevin Moore's comments that Freddie Gray was approached by the police because he had looked them in the eye: "That's how the officers, I guess, wrote the paperwork: That [Freddie] made eye contact. And he looked suspicious. Oh. 'And that gave us probable cause to'. . . do whatever."[43] Our facilitator asked us, "Why is making eye contact a sign of guilt?" She encouraged us to write that question on our card along with an answer. My first thought was, "It's not a sign of guilt." My parents taught me to look authority figures in the eye, as a gesture of respect, not guilt: "Look at me when I'm talking to you." Many of us have repeated a version of this alongside the old adage that if someone did not look you in the eye they were lying or guilty—which, according to researchers, is false.[44] The "rules," true or false, are different for a white girl like me whose family is rooted in a rural, white town in Michigan than for Freddie Gray in Baltimore: Those rules of eye contact are articulated in Smith's performance of selections from the "actual sermon" Reverend Jamal Harrison Bryant gave at Freddie Gray's funeral. He interpreted Gray's gaze at the police as a "revolutionary stance" because Gray "did something that black men were trained to—taught *not* to do. He looked police in the eye."[45] Rev. Bryant continued, "I want to tell this grieving mother, you are not burying a boy, you are burying a grown man. Who knew that one of the principles of being a man is looking somebody in the eye."[46] Based on Rev. Bryant's interpretation, the reason making eye contact is a sign of guilt is that, under white supremacy, Black men are not permitted to claim that they are *men*. To make eye contact and claim manhood while Black is to be guilty in the eyes of the police officers. As I recalled Anna Deavere Smith delivering Rev. Bryant's definition of "being a man," putting his words and intonation in *her* mouth, I thought about drawbacks of insisting on certain forms of masculinity—and thus femininity—particularly for those who refuse normative versions of both.[47] But there was not time to develop those thoughts in our discussion.

When our facilitator asked us to stop writing and share, several Group T members expressed their outrage that a glance was considered "probable cause" for the police to pursue and murder Freddie Gray. One man claimed that the police did not pursue Freddie Gray because of the glance but because he ran away after the glance was exchanged. A woman forcefully told him that the constant police presence in "Black communities" and previous encounters with police made Gray feel unsafe, and given that this episode ended in his death, he was "absolutely right to run." As members of our group munched on apples and granola bars, I felt our distance from the "Black communities" under discussion. The facilitator maintained an inviting, even optimistic expression as she received our comments and occasionally repeated our phrases, such as "eye contact as probable cause . . . constant police presence."

Then the facilitator reminded us of the question she had asked us to write down at the beginning of our twenty-five-minute session: *What is the show asking of me? How can I act?* The first person from our group to respond described not what he would do, but who he thought was to blame for the school-to-prison pipeline: "It's not the teachers or the schools that are the problem here. It's the parents . . ." He adamantly shifted responsibility from the institutions and racist systems to the parents, and his bias was clear, although he never explicitly stated that BIPOC parents are "the problem" for failing to adequately discipline their children or to support hardworking teachers and school administrators. The children caught up in the pipeline might be innocent, he implied, but certainly not their parents. He finished his monologue by pointing out that our facilitator, as a teacher, is "stuck in the thick of it": "What do you think? Are there police officers in your school?" he asked. She paused, and I expected her to refuse to answer and turn the questions back to us. Instead, she told us that she had taken a leave from teaching and was currently studying for the M-CAT and preparing to apply for medical school. Someone blurted out: "But you said you were a teacher." Everyone was quiet for a moment as that news settled over the group. The man who had identified parents as the problem magnanimously offered, "Part of the problem is that we lose all our good teachers because we don't pay them enough." I thought the facilitator had tears in her eyes as Discussion Group T adjourned.

We returned to the theater for the final four monologues in the Coda, which were very powerful, particularly the closing message of forgiveness and redemption in Congressman John Lewis's "Brother":

> And he came in the office and said, "Mr. Lewis, I'm one of the people that beat you on May 9, 1961. I want to apologize." He said, "Will you forgive me?"

> I said, "I forgive you. I accept your apology."
> His son started cryin'. He started cryin'. I started cryin'. . . .
> He called me "brother." And I call him "brother."[48]

Many in the audience were also crying as the onstage bassist, Marcus Shelby, closed with a riff on the spiritual "Amazing Grace." I thought of apologies I have made for my own racist behavior and felt the need to apologize to our Act II facilitator for the pain we had caused and my failure to support her. I regretted that I had not intervened when that member of our group delivered his monologue blaming parents for the school-to-prison pipeline. Beyond my personal culpability, I wondered if my group had behaved in unique ways—or if our experience and conduct were common. Had other groups done better? What would a *good* Act II look and feel like?

I went looking for answers to these questions in conversations with audience members, published reviews, and interviews with Act II staff, as I will discuss in the next section. But first, I want to reflect on the *act* of Act II, what *actually* happened to borrow a word so regularly used by Anna Deavere Smith in the published text of *Notes from the Field*. The process of participation in the event was quite clear:

- The audience was divided into groups of twenty by ushers, who intentionally separated those who came to the theater together.
- Groups were assigned a discussion spot and equipped with snacks, note cards, and pencils.
- Facilitators assigned to each group introduced themselves and then delivered a quote from the play and asked participants to reflect on the quote and person who spoke it.
- Participants were instructed to write thoughts on their note cards and then, after a few minutes of reflection, to share with others in the group.
- Facilitators asked participants to consider what they can do about the school-to-prison pipeline and to write ideas on their note cards.
- Participants were asked to report action items to the group.
- After twenty or twenty-five minutes, Act II was over, groups disbanded, and audience members returned to the theater for the Coda.

The scene that unfolded within this apparatus would be unique to each group, and audience members could choose the degree of their participation. Yet the minimum *act* required to participate in Act II was to sit for twenty-five minutes with the discomfort of being asked to talk with strangers about race, educational discrimination, and white supremacy. The discomfort for many in my group was visibly heightened by the biases articulated by fellow group members and, of course, by the tears of our facilitator. This was not an experience I would soon forget, and that is certainly an indication of the impact of Act II. I worry that racial biases can be consolidated and reinforced when Act II produces an audience for a speaker to expound on, for example, a belief that BIPOC parents are responsible for the school-to-prison pipeline. Given that such comments were not challenged in my group, this individual might have left the group feeling that he was the star of Act II, that he had delivered the most impactful monologue. He *had* delivered a memorable monologue. I worried even more about the facilitator's pain and that this experience would lead her and others in my group to avoid conversations about race and social justice in the future. To the extent that our conversation produced monologues that resembled those that Anna Deavere Smith performed onstage, we were *actually* producing an additional act—Act II for *Notes from the Field*.

6.3. Act II in Review

The idea of Act II as being truly *part of the show* developed during the rehearsal process for Elizabeth Cooper Davis, the Act II Trainer. She told me that she realized, "Act II is the legitimate truly Act II. These are the voices of Act II."[49] Like Davis, I initially assumed that the title of "Act II" was more metaphorical than actual. The promotional materials and program description led me to expect a talkback that was not an optional extension of the audience's time in the theater, but still a talkback: "[Anna Deavere Smith] stops the action of this play in the middle of the show, making room for the audience to talk to each other during a 25-minute facilitated group dialogue."[50] The goal of creating dialogue is commonly articulated in promotional materials for conventional talkbacks. A profile of four different artistic directors from across the United States reveals their agreement that theatrical talkbacks encourage "community engagement and education," allow "the afterlife of the play to exit the theater with each audience member," offer "a safe space for dialogue" and "disagreement," and ask questions such as "What are you, sitting in the audience, going to do in response?"[51] Their language resembles that of Diane Paulus in her Artistic Director's Welcome to

Notes from the Field, which refers to "a second act of facilitated discussions" and claims to "offer the theater as a transformative gathering place, where we can listen, empathize, identify our shared vulnerabilities, and strengthen our collective capacity for action."[52] I imagined Act II as a clever name for an obligatory talkback.

None of the published reviews of *Notes from the Field* treated Act II as an element of the performance. The reviews were largely ambivalent or negative about Act II, although they were overwhelmingly positive in their description of Anna Deavere Smith's performance and the play specifically. The same could be said of a previous version of the play, *The California Chapter*, performed at Berkeley Rep in 2015. Cy Ashley Webb reported of Berkeley Rep's Act II, "I suspect other groups were better than mine—a disproportionately large group whose facilitator apologized for the inability of everyone to hear as he led everyone through a flip chart brainstorming session which engaged some to in [sic] the group to call for revolution and others to pledge to talk to their grandchildren more."[53] Webb points to both logistical difficulties for the Act II enterprise (determining the appropriate size, finding spaces, and ensuring participants can hear) and the challenges of shaping a productive, short conversation with such a diverse group of participants, including revolutionaries, grandparents, revolutionary grandparents, and others.[54]

Cy Musiker described how his facilitator at Berkeley Rep, the poet Dahlak Brathwaite, "asked the audience to accept the challenge implicit in Smith's play, 'to be part of the effort to change (the school-to-prison pipeline)'": "But audience members in our group were less ambitious. One man said, 'To create the society I want to live in, I would be willing to pay higher taxes.' Another said, 'I will vote.'"[55] Musiker registered disappointment in these comments, which do not articulate commitments to participate in radical cultural change; instead, they speak to liberal but relatively minimal efforts to participate in US political life.[56] Liberals tend to believe that everyone should pay taxes appropriate to their earnings and that everyone should have access to the vote and take advantage of that civic responsibility—while protesting efforts by conservative state legislatures that will make voting harder, particularly for BIPOC and working-class voters. Of course, these acts alone do not support liberal political agendas. American taxpayers fund the prison-industrial complex, and voters have elected officials who have actively promoted the school-to-prison pipeline through the "war on drugs" and "zero tolerance" policies—or have been complicit with the pipeline and mass incarceration.[57]

The lukewarm (at best) response to Act II largely persisted when *Notes from the Field* came to A.R.T. in Cambridge, Massachusetts. Patti Hartigan of *The Boston Globe* celebrated Smith's "virtuoso performance" but also warned that "the piece has some gaps and breaks for an earnest yet frustrating audience discussion."[58] Hartigan's language of "audience discussion" resembles the talkback more than the participatory act framework.[59] In a longer review Hartigan placed the Act II effort in relation to earlier A.R.T. engagement projects that, she claims, "did not work":

> The show—which clocks in at almost three hours—breaks in the middle when audience members are sorted into groups to discuss the issues. Smith tried to meld art and community action with the Institute on the Arts and Civic Dialogue, an ambitious gathering of artists and citizens at ART in 1998. The attempts to engage the community did not work then, and this effort, while earnest, feels forced and interrupts the flow of the performance. I was with a group of lovely, engaged theatergoers, but in 25 minutes, I didn't even learn their names. This is a case where the art speaks for itself, and the discussion is better later.[60]

Hartigan implies that "art" does not easily "meld" with "community action" but that "the art speaks for itself"—presumably saying *something* of impact and power. "The discussion" might very well be "better later," as Hartigan suggests, but what if the discussion never happens?[61] What if audience members have their good cry (or equivalent) at the theater, and partially because that emotional release eases them, they never return to the discussion?

This was the question Anna Deavere Smith asked Jeremy Goodwin of the *Boston Globe*: "[As a nation] we're always talking about this conversation on race we're going to have. But when do we have it? We never have it."[62] Goodwin compares Smith's Act II to talkbacks, pointing out that "[t]heater companies have increasingly seized on the talkback as a value-add for ticket-buyers in an increasingly crowded entertainment marketplace." He expressed his disappointment with the questions usually asked during talkbacks, especially the one about "how the actors remember all their lines," and then asks, "But what if the talkback were truly part of the show itself, and not an epilogue?"[63] In this interview, Smith does not frame Act II as "part of the show" of *Notes from the Field*, but more of a break or pause; she claims, "I stop the play in the middle. I come out and say: You know what, this is all

I know. I know a lot of you come to the theater for a takeaway—I don't believe in that," Smith says. "Now show what you got."[64] In my group, and those of Musiker and Hartigan, what we "got" was "earnest" but complacent and sometimes bigoted—and painful for the facilitator.

How did the facilitators understand their role in Act II? The "Notes from the Field Act II Facilitator Application" did not encourage applicants to think of themselves as performers in a part of the show. Applicants were asked to describe their experience with facilitation, their interest in the project, and their ideas about "facilitating transformative conversations."[65] According to Elizabeth Cooper Davis, the facilitator trainer, her team selected applicants who had some "relationship" with the school-to-prison pipeline and experience leading difficult conversations; they came from a wide range of backgrounds, including education, social work, and criminal justice or prison work. Some were teachers, and some were parents. "We were not looking for actors," Davis claimed, while admitting that, upon further reflection, "There was a sense of casting, [that] they *were* part of the show."[66] My fascinating conversation with Davis helped me understand the journey that brought my facilitator, a former teacher/future doctor, to her position in front of Discussion Group T—and ultimately to tears.

The Act II staff, including Davis and the Act II Manager, Kayhan Irani, were hired not by A.R.T. but by Anna Deavere Smith and the Pipeline Project specifically for the 2016 A.R.T. Production.[67] The Act II staff worked with Anna Deavere Smith for approximately three weeks to write the job descriptions, review applications, and hire facilitators.[68] The forty-nine facilitators were asked to commit to seven to twelve shows, attend a weekend training session just before tech week, and be present a half hour before and after the performance. They received $20 per show. Their training mirrored actor-training techniques with warm-ups, cool-downs, and a scene study process. Davis claimed, "The crux of the training was folks running through the script of Act II with others who would pretend to be participants."[69] The Act II "script" included an opening text and a closing text that were intended to be the same across groups, although Davis acknowledged that "folks started playing with it." The quotes used in each discussion group (like Kevin Moore's comment "[t]hat [Freddie Gray] made eye contact") were selected at random during a pre-show circle from a group of quotes previously chosen by the team.[70] Davis reflected, "That was part of the routine: share, warm-up, pick their quotes."[71] The selection of quotes added a chance element into the facilitator script, and of course, the conversation with the audience could never be scripted. Much was left to chance, even before the facilitators started changing the opening and closing texts to fit their needs or facilitation style.

The process of choosing quotes to guide the conversation may have preexisted A.R.T.—at least it was part of the process described by SK Kerastas, one of the facilitators for Berkeley Rep's Act II. Kerastas opened the discussion with a quote from the first monologue of the play worked into a larger question: "Okay, so in the first act of Anna's play, there are multiple references to the urgency of this moment. From Sherrilyn Ifill's opening monologue to the ever-present clock on stage—did anyone catch that? So, let's use this sense of urgency as a jumping off point to brainstorm. This is the moment for what?"[72] The question led a white man to make a "well-intentioned" comment with "racist impact" that "those drugs are what's destroying the black and brown communities"—a comment much like the monologue blaming parents for the school-to-prison pipeline that I witnessed in Group T at A.R.T.[73] This man had learned the liberal tendency both to refer to "black and brown communities" and to focus on an external factor, *drugs*, rather than inherent features like race. And yet he was not ready to claim that this was a moment for him to act, to refuse his white privilege, to learn about how the "war on drugs" had contributed to the school-to-prison pipeline and mass incarceration of BIPOC people, or even to listen to other members of his group. Without discussing why the comment had "racist impact," Kerastas pointed out how challenging it was for facilitators to determine how to respond to such "well-intentioned" comments, although Anna Deavere Smith had offered some guidelines: "As facilitators, we have been told to embrace a spirit of what Anna calls 'radical hospitality.' It is this idea from Jacques Derrida of saying yes first to every opinion, every perspective, every person that comes to these circles."[74]

Kerastas paraphrases Derrida's suggestion, "Let us say yes *to who or what turns up*, before any determination, before any anticipation, before any *identification*."[75] The statement appears near the opening of Derrida's philosophical text, "Step of Hospitality / No Hospitality" or "*Pas d'hospitalité*" in the original French, which plays on the homonym *pas* as *step* and as part of the French negative participle *ne . . . pas*. In keeping with the dual meaning of the title, Derrida goes on to describe a conflict ("insoluble antinomy") between "*The* law of unlimited hospitality" and the laws of "rights and duties," of property, ownership, and citizenship.[76] Derrida would not be surprised that

Kerastas found "radical hospitality" to be an impossible rule for a facilitated Act II conversation on the school-to-prison pipeline:

> But in quick, pivotal moments like this one, radical hospitality can be complicated. If I welcome and affirm this comment, I comply with a racist sentiment, which gives a clear message to the rest of the group about my values, the values of the show, and more directly, their safety in the space. If I name the racist assumptions in this comment and shut it down, the man feels ostracized and communication ends. If I do what I want to do, which is address the comment head on, reframe it, break down the imbedded assumptions, and work together to restructure the sentiment to honor the person's intentions without the racist impact, it would use all of the twenty-five minutes we have together.[77]

Kerastas cannot both "say yes" to the comment with its "racist assumptions" and offer a radical hospitality to those whom the comment marginalizes and offends. Attempting to chart a middle course between "saying yes first to every opinion," on the one hand, and, on the other, a lengthy unpacking that would have taken the entire twenty-five minutes [if not more], Kerastas asked the group "not to make generalizations or assumptions about other communities of people. Especially about black and brown communities."[78] Kerastas seems to have felt that the approach *worked* in the sense that the man did not appear to be humiliated or silenced, and the group could continue the discussion in another direction. But Kerastas recognized that another facilitator would have made a different choice, and that any choice is compromised and risky. Maybe the entire discussion *should* have been devoted to the man's comment about "those drugs" that are "destroying the black and brown communities"; maybe he and others never understood the "racist assumptions" in the comment because Kerastas did not do the unpacking that another context and longer discussion might have allowed.

Kerastas's account of facilitating at Berkeley Rep's *Notes from the Field: The California Chapter* ends abruptly after describing "an older black woman" who demanded that Kerastas "change the question" from the one about individual action that is central to the Act II enterprise: "Can we let go of this *moment-thinking* and talk about systemic coalition-building?" The woman was recording frustration with how the singular acts of donating, volunteering, and even mentorship—acts that might be inspired by an emotional experience at the theater and that might even have been part of the ideal response to Act II for some facilitators, usually addressed the "symptoms" rather than the broader "systems."[79] But there was only a "moment" to discuss the symptoms *and the systems* during Act II. I interpret the abrupt conclusion to Kerastas's essay as a performance of the fact that the Act II session had to be cut off after a quick twenty to twenty-five minutes and an acknowledgment that the discussion would necessarily fail to get beyond "*moment-thinking*" in that amount of time.[80]

Elizabeth Cooper Davis was aware of Kerastas's description of facilitating Act II conversations at Berkeley and encouraged me to read it to understand the challenges faced by facilitators before and during the A.R.T. production. According to Davis, the basic quandary of how the facilitators were to respond to biased statements remained unresolved through the A.R.T. production; she pointed out:

> There was no clarity in advance about whose framework we were using: Does the facilitator have an opinion? If disputes come up, is the facilitator's goal to resolve them? If someone says something racist, is the facilitator supposed to call them on it?[81]

During the year between the Berkeley Rep and A.R.T. productions, these questions were not resolved for Davis or the facilitators she trained. Perhaps Anna Deavere Smith did not intend to resolve them or else failed to communicate her conclusions to the Pipeline and Act II staff. Perhaps Smith was honoring the contradictions at the heart of a law of "radical hospitality" or the fact that we cannot be fully hospitable to all people at the same time while following the laws that ensure individual rights.[82] Derrida cites foundational myths and parables as evidence of this impossibility, including the biblical story of Lot (Genesis 19), who offered his "virgin" daughters as sexual prey for the men of Sodom in order to protect his guests. Extending hospitality to guests, in this infamous story, required an intolerable sacrifice of family.[83]

Not surprisingly, the facilitators suffered under the impossible demands of hospitality, white supremacy, and the lack of clarity about their role. According to Davis, "The facilitators were going through a lot. . . . There was a lot of crying." I asked if she thought Act II was successful, and she said immediately that she had "mixed feelings."[84] For Davis, the challenge was "how to marry a theater process with a dialogic process or a social justice process."[85] In the end, Anna Deavere Smith seems to have privileged the theater process by asking the facilitators to perform an impossible "radical hospitality" and then making space, *saying yes*, to the performance that resulted.[86] Davis arrived at a similar conclusion, saying that although "it wasn't clear in advance" or to every facilitator, she ultimately decided, "We aren't commenting. We aren't correcting. This is what I heard. It's part of the show. But some folks hadn't heard [that]."[87] If the voices that emerged in the facilitated conversation were actually the monologues of Act II, the facilitators and audiences were all performing roles, all *part of the show*. The audience was creating the same kinds of monologues Smith performed onstage: that is, monologues rooted in our distinct perspectives on and experiences with the school-to-prison pipelines, monologues shaped by our biases and privileges. Rather than using "the theater as a convening place to examine the crisis together," as advertised in the program insert, audiences were often performing their biases and limited vision. In the Act II performance that resulted, the facilitators took on the role of Anna Deavere Smith as interviewer and receiver of monologues, although facilitators did not then perform them. Audience members remained the voices of their own monologues, but facilitators still accepted the burden of prompting and receiving the monologues, albeit without Smith's decades-long training and development of an interviewing and performance technique. Davis believed that Anna Deavere Smith "was more interested in the monologues, in the voices that surfaced, and less interested in the facilitator's experience or perspective of the work."[88]

Whether Act II went poorly or well is partially an indication of the group's ability to talk about race; it was also a barometer of the perspectives of the community, as represented by that random group of theatergoers. There is much to learn, to be sure, from a derailed discussion, distressed participants, or a tearful facilitator. Yet it is possible that a terrible experience could do more harm than good for some of the facilitators and participants—even as other participants were learning or being motivated to direct action. Some participants might leave Act II feeling *less* willing to talk about race or engage with art and activism. Others might be fortified in their biases, performed before a welcoming, hospitable group and seemingly affirmed by that group. Some might be more moved by the theater of Act II's monologues and the response of the facilitator than by Act I or the Coda, performed by Anna Deavere Smith. The aesthetic or theatrical purpose of Act II might not always align easily with the social justice mission that was more regularly evident in the promotional materials for *Notes from the Field*. This does not diminish the fact that *Notes from the Field* was attempting to do work for racial justice and invite the audience to participate in that mission through Act II.

I do not know if members of our discussion group or any discussion group at *Notes from the Field* were prompted by Act II to work with any of the organizations tackling the school-to-prison pipeline that were listed in the program. Many of us were forced to articulate our relationship to that pipeline, and several of us performed our privilege and bias in ways that might have been instructive to others and even ourselves. I do not believe that it is impossible to align an aesthetic or theatrical mission with a social justice mission, but I do think there are risks and challenges. In this production, Act II tipped more toward a theatrical event, the *actual* Act II of the show, than a social justice event. I classify Act II as twenty-five minutes of immersive theater, bookended by an adamantly documentary form, and advertised as activism. We, in the audience, were asked to *do some time in education*, as were our facilitators. There were many possibilities for learning, but the lessons were not always those that Anna Deavere Smith, A.R.T., or the Pipeline Project Team anticipated. Audience participation in immersive theater of racial justice is unpredictable, volatile, and often, *complicit* in hurting BIPOC participants and facilitators.

Coda: The History of Act II

Elizabeth Cooper Davis believed that the Act II title and framework emerged from Anna Deavere Smith's work, but Robert Duffley, Editor and Assistant Dramaturg of American Repertory Theater, claimed that A.R.T. was working with "different models" for talkbacks in parallel with Smith.[89] Duffley described the Act II initiative and *Notes from the Field*'s use of Act II as a "convergent development."[90] He pointed out that A.R.T. held an event called Act III in 2014 after *Witness Uganda*, a musical by Matt Gould and Griffin Matthews, two years before *Notes from the Field* came to A.R.T. and a year before Smith staged it at Berkeley Rep.[91] *Witness Uganda*'s Act III was billed as a traditional post-show discussion:

> Join Matt Gould, Griffin Matthews, and members of the cast for "Act III," a twenty-minute post-show discussion that will be held after each performance. On select dates, cast members will be joined by the following experts and scholars, who will reflect on the themes of the show and discuss their own research and work: Diane Paulus, A.R.T. Artistic Director and *Witness Uganda* director; Susan Bissell, Chief of Child Protection,

Programme Division, UNICEF; Susan Cook, Executive Director of the Committee on African Studies at Harvard University [. . .][92]

A.R.T. held an "Act II" consisting of "discussions with activists, artists, medical professionals, and scholars" after Eve Ensler's *In the Body of the World* in May 2016, a few months before Anna Deavere Smith brought *Notes* to A.R.T.[93] The performance history clarifies that Smith and A.R.T. were, in fact, developing similar efforts to engage audiences and invite their reflective participation, which then merged in A.R.T.'s *Notes from the Field*. But it was Smith who first reframed Act II as different from a typical post-show conversation, as a call for audience activism in Berkeley Rep's 2015 *Notes from the Field: Doing Time in Education, The California Chapter*, with an "act two [that] . . . involves you! Anna invites the audience to engage in facilitated reflections and be active agents of change."[94] The emphasis in the promotional materials, reviews, and job announcements related to Act II all supported my assumption that these were audience engagement events or talkbacks attempting to promote future activism and social justice work. I was reading Act II as a metaphor when the literal reading was more apt. The audience was *actually* performing Act II, and like any performance, it was not guaranteed to go well.

When Smith took *Notes from the Field* from Boston to New York and eventually to HBO on film, Act II was abandoned. According to Davis, the venue in New York, Second Stage, did not have the resources or the tradition of engaging with the community that A.R.T. has built with its Boston/Cambridge audiences.[95] A.R.T. has continued to develop its audience engagement programming under the title of Act II while making adjustments to the format that mitigate the negative impact on audiences and facilitators. This is especially clear in the play I consider next, the A.R.T./Arts Emerson production of Claudia Rankine's *The White Card* (2018). In mitigating the pain of the audience and facilitators, the new Act II returned to the familiar terrain of the talkback offering theatergoers a platform to feel like we faced racism and responded correctly, a platform that left most of us more secure in our complicit participation.

7

Playing *The White Card* with
Claudia Rankine

Claudia Rankine's *The White Card* (published 2019) takes a classic theatrical scenario, the dinner party disaster, and uses it to highlight the consumption and manipulation of Black suffering and trauma by those who are well-intentioned and often well-resourced, including some Black artists, athletes, and activists.[1] The play also uses tableaux vivant or living pictures, that spectacular technique of nineteenth-century melodrama (see Chapter 2), to connect contemporary white supremacy with American slavery and its documentation through theatrical and photographic forms. *The White Card*'s two scenes both end with provocative tableaux that position current violence against Black people within the long history of racism in the United States. I begin this chapter with an examination of the tableaux to clarify my central claim that *The White Card* cannot avoid contributing to the phenomenon the play documents so well—the aesthetic presentation of Black suffering. It participates in the phenomenon, even as it reveals that the interest in depictions of Black suffering and death by liberal elites is yet another manifestation of white supremacy. *The White Card* uses tragedies experienced by Black Americans for the purpose of educating audiences about racism and white privilege but also to offer charged emotional, aesthetic, and cathartic experiences to audiences. The Act II talkback asked audiences to stay in the theater for a conversation about race, a conversation that gave audiences the opportunity to share, process, and perform their outrage at atrocity and their frustration with the more subtle forms of racism displayed by the well-intentioned white characters. Can *The White Card*'s Act II, or any participatory event, move an audience from outrage to action? Some audiences might be encouraged to engage in active work on themselves that disrupts their complicit participation, and some might engage in activism in the world beyond the theater. Others feel more certain of their own liberal good intentions, and many fortify their psychic investments in associations of Blackness with violent death and crime.

Complicit Participation. Carrie J. Preston, Oxford University Press. © Oxford University Press 2024.
DOI: 10.1093/9780197693438.003.0008

7.1. Tableaux of Black Suffering

The White Card introduces wealthy entrepreneurs and collectors Charles and Virginia Spencer who, supported by their legacy art dealer, Eric Schmidt, and goaded by their twenty-year-old activist son, Alex, invite the Black photographer Charlotte Cummings to dinner in their Manhattan apartment (see Figure 7.1). Flanked by pieces of their art collection, including Robert Rauschenberg's *White Painting* (1951) hung on blindingly white walls and Robert Longo's *Untitled (Ferguson Police, August 13, 2014)* visible in Figure 7.1, the Spencers attempt to convince Charlotte of their commitment to buying art "with an emphasis on racial injustice."[2] They present her with a life-size sculpture of an autopsy diagram titled "An Anatomy of a Death," showing the bullet-ridden body of Michael Brown, killed by police in Ferguson, Missouri, on August 9, 2014. As the dinner party erodes into racial and gendered conflict, Charlotte lies down on the autopsy piece, "filling in for the missing body," in a curtain tableau, a pose that ends the scene or act.[3] (See Figure 7.2.) The hosts are so taken with their own battles that they do not immediately notice Charlotte's pose, but finally face her with incomprehension

Figure 7.1 Patricia Kalember, Jim Poulos, Daniel Gerroll, and Karen Pittman in American Repertory Theater's world premiere production of *The White Card* at ArtsEmerson. Photo by Gretjen Helene/A Priori Photography.

Figure 7.2 Colton Ryan, Patricia Kalember, Karen Pittman, Jim Poulos, and Daniel Gerroll in American Repertory Theater's world premiere production of *The White Card* at ArtsEmerson. Photo by Gretjen Helene/A Priori Photography.

and shock. For me, watching the play on March 31, 2018, this was not the most shocking placement of bodies in relation to and *as* art on the stage.

I give the *most shocking card* to the tableau Charlotte stages with an unwitting Charles a year after the disastrous dinner party, a tableau that Charlotte photographs in the final seconds of the play. To set the scene: Charles visits her studio to demand why she ultimately refused to sell him her series of tableaux photographic reenactments of tragedies like the massacre at Emanuel African Methodist Episcopal Church where white supremacist, Dylann Roof, killed nine worshippers at a prayer service. Charlotte donated that series to a Harlem Museum and began a new one, *Exhibit C*, featuring extreme close-ups of white skin. At the end of the confrontation, Charles realizes that *Exhibit C* was composed of his own white skin, removes his shirt with his back to Charlotte, and says, "Charlotte, you can shoot me now."[4] Charlotte quickly places her camera on a tripod, ties her smock around her checkered dress like an apron, removes her shoes, steps onto a wooden crate, and binds her hands with Charles's scarf. When Charles, seemingly alarmed by the silence, turns around, she snaps a photograph that was immediately projected on the white walls of the Robert J. Orchard Stage, invoking the familiar iconography of an enslaved woman on the auction block, arms bound and raised in supplication to a white man (see Figure 7.3). Charlotte's tableau with the sculpture of Michael Brown's autopsy suggested the vulnerability of Black Americans to bullets and other violence, while the closing pose on the auction block connects this violence to the long history of slavery and its aftermath in the United States.

In between the tableau of Charlotte stretched out on the outline of Michael Brown's body and Charlotte on the auction block, *The White Card* develops a withering critique of liberal desires to consume Black suffering and death—as art, as news, even as inspiration for activism. Charlotte pointedly asks Charles, "Are you shopping for more black death?"[5] (See Figure 7.2.) But Charlotte had not realized that she, herself, was engaged in a project "to portray black suffering as art" until Charles told her at the dinner party that her work was "no different" than the autopsy sculpture of Michael Brown's body that he had purchased for her.[6] His misunderstanding of her art and mode of supporting/consuming it helped her realize she was, "Completely misguided. I mean I was making my work but I didn't understand what the desire for it was all about. There I was handing over black death spectacle."[7]

Figure 7.3 Daniel Gerroll and Karen Pittman in American Repertory Theater's world premiere production of *The White Card* at ArtsEmerson. Photo by Gretjen Helene/A Priori Photography.

The A.R.T./Arts Emerson premiere of *The White Card* also produces "black death spectacle," with its set functioning like a theatrical gallery for images like the autopsy sculpture of Michael Brown's body and other works of art, media, and photography that depict suffering. *The White Card* design team, led by projection designer Peter Nigrini, made ingenious use of the all-white walls to project works of art being discussed, including Robert Longo's painting depicting the police response to the riots following the shooting of Michael Brown, *Untitled (Ferguson Police, August 18, 2014)* (2014), which the Spencers owned and displayed in their apartment and the audience saw projected to the length of the wall behind them.[8] (See Figure 7.1.) Projections also featured Glenn Ligon's *Hands* (from the 1995 Million Man March),[9] Jean-Michel Basquiat's *Defacement: The Death of Michael Stewart* (1983), depicting the graffiti artist being beaten by New York police officers for "defacing" public property with his art,[10] Gilles Peress's *AFRICA. Rwanda. Kabgayi* (April 1994) showing the site of a massacre,[11] and Kerry James Marshall's *Heirlooms and Accessories* (2002), which enclosed the faces of women watching a lynching in lockets like those that are frequently passed down as heirlooms and worn as accessories—although this version features women who were accessories and witnesses to racial violence and murder.[12] All of these works of art are printed in Rankine's text of *The White Card*, published by Graywolf Press in 2019.

Rankine includes many stories of violence against Black peoples alongside the images. Charlotte recites, "Michael Brown, Freddie Gray, Eric Garner, Sandra Bland, Trayvon Martin, Philando Castile . . ." all people of color killed in police custody, and although the murders were often captured on camera, there were no convictions.[13] Charlestown, the site of the prayer meeting massacre in 2015 and the subject of Charlotte's new series, and Charlottesville, where the white nationalist "Unite the Right" rally was held in 2017, are mentioned repeatedly (on pages 35, 36, 72, 75, 76, 83, and 85): "Charleston, Charlottesville, that's what I know. Our history. The present," says Charlotte.[14] Given the auditory similarity to Charles and Charlotte, the play links the two characters with the two city names ubiquitously.[15] *The White Card* graphically describes the 1998 murder of James Byrd Jr. without naming him: "On the news came the report that white supremacists dragged a black man to his death in Texas. A lynching by car. They tied him to a bumper and dragged him until his head and various limbs detached from the trunk of his body."[16] Charlotte and Charles discuss Dana Schutz's painting *Open Casket* (2016), which references fourteen-year-old Emmett Till's mutilated face in the "open casket" his mother demanded after Till was lynched in Mississippi in 1955.[17] Schutz's work sparked controversy during its American premiere at the Whitney Biennial in New York, when the Black artist Parker Bright stood in front of the painting in a shirt that protested "Black Death Spectacle."[18] Charlotte uses Bright's phrase to describe what she realized about her own work following the dinner party when Charles claimed her series on the Charleston massacre was "no different" than the autopsy sculpture of Michael Brown.[19]

In claiming that *The White Card* actually supplies its audience with the "black death spectacle" the play critiques, I am not suggesting that the play is "no different" than the autopsy sculpture marking the bullet wounds on an outline of Brown's body.[20] *The White Card*'s Charlotte turns her camera away from images of Black suffering and death and onto unexamined whiteness— literally white skin in extreme close-up (see Figure 7.3). Yet Black suffering still occupied so much of the stage at the Paramount Center, in the tableaux, paintings, photographs, and stories of Black deaths. In the attempt to focus on whiteness and examine white mobility, whiteness kept slipping away or hiding behind other images, like the white walls under the projections of injured and murdered Black bodies. For some audiences, the inability to maintain a focus on whiteness might have made visible the pervasiveness of white supremacy. For others, the images of suffering might have fulfilled their desire to witness "black death spectacle" and *feel* like they are part of a movement against racism without having to do any real work *on* themselves or *for* social justice.[21] For me, the elusiveness of whiteness in *The White Card* helped me realize that this book needed to focus on the limits of white allies as consumers of Black death spectacle at theater of racial justice.

Charlotte suggests the grim possibility that images of death and torture might bolster racism in her rebuttal to Charles's repeated insistence that art will offer a "moral imagination" and "catapult us out of here."[22] Artists like Charlotte, according to Charles, "can imagine beyond what is."[23] Charles's commitment to the moral and political influence of art has a long but controversial history in aesthetic and philosophical thought. Charlotte realized that her photographs of the massacre of Black worshippers in Charleston were allowing Charles to buy images of dead African Americans, which he wanted because, as she put it "the black body is in a state you're comfortable with."[24] In this "state," Blackness has been "reduced to suffering" and whiteness is invisible and ignored.[25] The question can be reframed in the context of *The White Card* as a work of art: In its display of artworks, tableaux, and stories of Black suffering, does the play also provide images of Black bodies in a state that makes the audience comfortable? Is it possible for *The White Card* to avoid being part of the phenomenon it critiques? Can the play, by foregrounding these questions in self-conscious and metatheatrical techniques, control how the images of Black death impact the audience? Can (white) audience members be made aware of their own psychic desires for Black death?

7.2. "People" . . . People Like Me?

Rankine and the entire Arts Emerson/A.R.T. creative team for *The White Card*'s world premiere in Boston worked to dislodge the audience's habits of reception and encourage them to recognize how they usually receive images of Black suffering in art and other media. One of their primary methods was to change the seating, thereby shifting the perceptual framework and encouraging audiences to see themselves in the characters and in other spectators watching those characters. Audience members were disoriented from the beginning as they were ushered through a dimly lit hallway and into the blindingly bright, all-white set designed by Riccardo Hernandez. A white rectangle was erected on the Robert J. Orchard Stage of the Paramount Center with stadium seating running along the two long sides. Expecting the typical entrance into a suitably hushed and darkened theater, we instead found ourselves positioned as spectators at a sporting event, seated across from each other, literally facing off above a diminutive white stage, and listening to the distinctive sounds of a tennis match: the pop of the ball, whoosh of the swinging racket, and squeak of tennis shoes on the court. As the play opens, we watched Serena and Venus Williams's match at the 2017 Australian Open projected on the white walls of the theater alongside the characters. The scene takes place in March 2017, a month after the match, and Charles Spencer, Virginia Spencer, and Eric (re)watch and discuss Serena's victory over her sister to win her twenty-third Grand Slam. The audience watched the match *alongside* the characters, looking at the same images projected on walls and listening to the same sounds. From our fully lit stadium seats, we also watched each other watching. We were invited to consider the multiple levels of spectatorship and different ways of watching and how we are like and unlike the characters and other audience members.

The opening banter between Charles and Virginia Spencer and their art dealer Eric, about tennis, race, and gender, introduces the characters as wealthy white liberals who want to fight racism but are willfully blind to their own positions within white supremacy and patriarchy. Virginia, engrossed in the Australian Open tournament, asks if Charles and Eric can tell Serena was eight weeks pregnant at the time of the match. Eric notes that critics suggested her pregnancy might have given her an "unfair advantage": "I read she got some hormonal rush from the pregnancy."[26] Virginia counters, "Now, that's insane. I spent my first trimester between the bathroom and the sofa. Why are men so challenged by the Williams sisters?"[27] Eric is defensive: "I don't have a problem . . ."[28] But Charles interrupts to say that Virginia "means" not Eric, but the president of the Russian tennis federation who referred to the "Williams brothers."[29] Virginia is attesting to the intersection of racism and misogyny faced by Serena and Venus Williams, while the men strategically claim outrage as they position themselves outside the problem.[30] Racism and misogyny exist *out there*, but these characters insist that *they* are not complicit. Responding to West Virginian Pamela Taylor's description of former First Lady Michelle Obama as an "ape in high heels," Eric, who had managed not to be aware of the insult, says, "A woman? Wow. People. Jesus."[31] In the next sentence, he moves on to strategizing how to get Charlotte to sell her art to Charles and Virginia. The racist and sexist "people" are obviously other "people," in Eric's view.[32]

This is just the first of *The White Card*'s many exchanges that reveal the depth of the characters' biases and invite the audience to consider if they are the kind of "people" they see on the stage in front of them.[33] The men profess liberal awareness of injustice without recognizing their own complicity, but Virginia also exhibits deep racial prejudice. As she watches the replay of the 2017 Australian Open match between the Williams sisters, Virginia repeatedly proclaims that Serena is "a beauty" and "stunning," and her pleasure in the athletic performance smacks of racialized voyeurism.[34] She habitually describes Black women and children as "beautiful."[35] In fact, Charlotte asks after Virginia describes yet another "beautiful woman": "By 'beautiful,' do you mean *black*?"[36] Virginia affirms, "She was black but she was beautiful," the grammar, "but," suggesting that Virginia feels beauty and blackness are not a common combination, in spite of her habits of speech.[37] Virginia's microaggressions are painfully obvious as she struggles to pronounce the name of that "fabulous Black author," Ta-Nehisi Coates ("Ta Taa . . .") and then mistitled his 2015 book as "*The World between Us*."[38] "*Between the World and Me*," Charlotte lobbed back, perhaps noting that the mistitled book was prominently displayed on Virginia's coffee table. Claiming, "The phrase 'I can't breathe' will never detach itself from Freddie Garner," Virginia detaches first names and conflates Eric Garner (who died after NYPD officer, Daniel Pantaleo, put him in a chokehold) and Freddie Gray (who died from a spinal injury sustained while in police custody in Baltimore).[39] Virginia professes a commitment to battling racial injustice, but her attention to that work is spotty, and she has little understanding of her own position within white supremacy. She supports the Williams sisters as "stunning" tennis players, while casting Serena in a story about how she "matured" enough to end her boycott of Indian Wells, where she had been subjected to "racial slurs" in 2001.[40] Charlotte points out the problem with this definition of maturity: "Objecting to racism means you're childish?"[41] Virginia owns the right books about racism but fails to learn their titles or authors, leading us to wonder if she displays rather than reads them. She wants to connect with "all those mothers who lost their sons" to police brutality and refuses to accept that she might not be able to know or fully understand "what black people are feeling."[42] She asks repeatedly, "What kinds of feelings am I not having?"[43]

I initially found Charles to be more serious and nuanced than Virginia in his understanding of racism—although this difference followed gendered stereotypes as performed by the actors. That is, Virginia exhibited a silliness in the production I saw that was partially conveyed in stereotypically feminine affectations and enforced by Charles:

VIRGINIA: We were just TiVoing the Australian Open when you arrived.
CHARLES: Ginny doesn't do real time! Bad for the stress lines.[44]

Although Charles suggests his wife finds live tennis too stressful and is overly concerned about her appearance, he presents himself as strong and very serious in his commitment to artists who depict Black suffering. As he describes his collection, "Not all the artists are African American, but all the work considers the violence against them."[45] He wants to buy Charlotte's work for his collection, although she challenges his belief in the influence of art on the "political conversation," saying, "I'm realistic. The work's not on the street, it's in the galleries."[46] When she leaves the stage to serve herself from the "informal" buffet (the Black maid having been given the night off, for obvious reasons), Charles tells Eric that he wants to support Charlotte's career, even give her a million dollars for a new studio and appoint her to the board for his foundation. Charles proclaims that she would fill "that hole there" in the board, and Eric states the obvious: the "hole" is "the diversity issue."[47] Charles and Eric exemplify the I&D response of many institutions to systemic racism and exclusion: *Just appoint more people of color*, as if that necessary first step would absolve the institutions of further efforts, much less radical transformation.

Charles and Virginia's son, Alex, is crucial to revealing the contradictions in his parents, but especially his father who had been successfully navigating the tensions of the dinner up to Alex's arrival—late and straight from a protest of the "Muslim ban" by executive order of then president Donald Trump.[48] Whereas Virginia described herself as "infuriated" that some Black Lives Matter (BLM) members had said "they need allies not masters" and protested Alex's participation, Charles presented himself as understanding: "Perhaps anyone who would be alienated by such comments is not a very useful ally."[49] Charles seemed to approve of Charlotte's points that Black students were "expressing anxiety about white benevolence"[50] and the "long history of white savior rhetoric" and supported Alex's attempts to articulate his understanding of his relationship to the mission of BLM.[51] Yet this son, like so many sons, knows the precise locations of his father's weak spots, including "the Ohio Reformatory for Women." Alex announced to Charlotte that part of Charles's fortune was made by building private for-profit prisons, which demonstrate even more racial disparities than the US mass incarceration system as a whole.

The US Department of Justice (DOJ) began contracting with privately operated prisons, like those built by Charles, to accommodate the dramatic 800 percent increase in the incarcerated population between 1980 and 2013. By that date, approximately 15 percent of its prison population or 30,000 inmates were incarcerated in private prisons.[52] Private prison populations are disproportionately non-white and face a lack of adequate health care, fewer educational and employment opportunities, more severe forms of discipline, and greater probability of abuse when compared to those incarcerated in state and federal prisons.[53] As they cut back on services, private prison companies make sure they do not accept "expensive" inmates through federal contracts containing health stipulations and limits on the age of prisoners as well as lower security levels—contractual arrangements that also contribute to racial disparities.[54] Private prisons pay correctional officers and staff less than counterparts in state and federal prisons, and they employ more racial minorities and women, who must accept the low wages of private prisons because discrimination limits their employment opportunities elsewhere.[55]

White supremacy and misogyny impact those wearing the badges and those in the striped suits throughout the prison system, but especially in private prisons.

The DOJ is well aware of the problem. Following a 2016 DOJ review of inadequate conditions in private prisons, the administration of President Barack Obama announced the initiative to phase out federal contracts with private prison companies and provide greater oversight in the interim as contracts expire. Deputy Attorney General Sally Q. Yates wrote a public memo claiming, "[Private prisons] do not provide the same level of correctional services, programs, and resources; they do not save substantially on costs; [. . .] they do not maintain the same level of safety and security."[56] Despite such damning criticism from the DOJ's own leadership, the Trump administration immediately revoked the DOJ initiative to end the use of private prisons after taking office in 2017; the Trump administration began requesting bids from private companies again, awarding the GEO Group a $110 million contract to build the administration's first new immigrant detention center in April 2017.[57] The Trump administration's policies on incarceration and immigration greatly benefit private prison companies, and they return the financial favor: the GEO Group donated $250,000 to Trump's inaugural committee and moved its 2017 annual conference to a Trump-owned resort in Boca Raton.[58]

Charles's company is not, according to him, supporting Trump in any way: "If this administration's base is solidly white men spewing racist rhetoric, it's not us."[59] But he points out that because he is running a "public company" he must "answer to its shareholders" and cannot make "unilateral decisions."[60] Charles acknowledges that he is "well aware that mass incarceration is an important issue for black communities. It might be *the* issue."[61] Charlotte assumes, "You say that, but it really doesn't touch your life" before Virginia reveals a very personal connection to mass incarceration: "Charles let our son Tim go to prison. He could have used some of those connections of his . . . but he wouldn't."[62] Their eldest son was a commodities trader with a heroin addiction and, according to Alex, "a contradiction to the principles of my father's foundation," so Charles did not attempt to keep him out of prison.[63] In the aftermath of these revelations of professional hypocrisy and personal suffering, everyone tries to salvage the evening with dessert wine, hazelnut cake, and a return to art—that is, to buying and displaying art, an enterprise that, in this case, depends on the profits Charles's company rakes in from mass incarceration.

Of course, the audience had been positioned within the realm of art, its purchase and sale, from the beginning of the show. Although we had not bought autopsy sculptures or other visual representations of Black death, we had purchased our tickets for the theater art we were consuming, an event that dramatically displayed and discussed images of Black suffering. Most of the audience would consider our support of the arts to be very different from that of Charles, who hypocritically uses the proceeds of private prisons to purchase art about the suffering of Black Americans as his way of contributing to their liberation. Yet those of us participating in American capitalism—which, I would venture to say, was most of us able to purchase tickets for *The White Card* (I paid $95)—might ask ourselves Charlotte's question about capitalism and the private prison business: "How do you reconcile yourself to a system that has targeted minorities for profit?"[64] But the fact that few of us are actually building private prisons gave us the proverbial *easy out*. In another version of *The White Card*, Charles could have made his Black-art-supporting fortune in a technology company, a startup, even social media, and such a character probably would have felt compromised but not fatally so. Charles's egregious hypocrisy as he builds a fortune in private prisons limits the ability of many theatergoers to identify with him.

The production design, with its never-darkened stadium seating, forced audience members to watch tennis and the other matchups in *The White Card's* Scene 1 alongside the characters and to watch each other watching the play. We were being encouraged to consider the ways we are similar to the characters, to see their contradictions, hypocrisy, and racism and then recognize these elements in ourselves. It might have been possible for some to see themselves in Virginia's foibles, as she forgot the names of "fabulous"[65] Black authors and victims of police brutality,[66] but she was portrayed as silly. Charles's character initially had more gravity, but he turned into a caricature of hypocrisy. Reviewer Bill Marx felt that "it is far too easy for white audience members to dismiss this crew; these sad cartoon figures wear the dramaturgical equivalent of 'kick me' signs on their backs."[67] I actually do not think that the characters are "cartoons" if that suggests *people* are not like this.[68] They are often worse, as the play documents with reference to actual racial insults like calling Michelle Obama an "ape in high heels."[69] Although it might have been possible for audiences to recognize themselves in the characters with some different choices in the text and performance, it was too easy for us to despise rather than identify with them. Some spectators might have congratulated themselves for supporting a play that, according to advertising materials, "unpacks the insidious ways in which racism manifests itself in everyday situations."[70] Some might have felt brave and woke rather than called to wake up.

7.3. Staying for Act II and the White Card on Your Seat

"In difficult conversations about race, how do we stay in the room?" American Repertory Theater's Artistic Director Diane Paulus claimed in her "Director's Welcome" that this question was the origin of *The White Card*. It is also the question that challenged the audience to stay after the play for Act II, and almost everyone on Saturday, March 31, 2018, stayed in the room. Elizabeth Cooper Davis, the Facilitator Trainer for *Notes from the Field* and one of the facilitators for *The White Card*, acknowledged that people might decide not to stay for various reasons, and she remembered that people of color "would come and say, 'I'm glad you're doing this. I'm out.'"[71] She suggested those who face racism daily might choose to protect themselves from difficult conversations about race, especially if they are one of the only BIPOC members in the conversation. Davis noted that Act II for *The White Card* was intentionally structured quite differently from *Notes from the Field*'s Act II in 2016, partially because of the trauma that was experienced by some facilitators and people of color.[72] The concern that *Notes from the Field*'s discussion groups "may have done more harm than good," as Davis put it, led to the redesign of *The White Card*'s Act II as a twenty-minute "conversation about race" held in the theater after every performance and facilitated by "cross-racial pairs": "There was a sense that both [races] need to be at the front of the space facilitating conversations"—and perhaps that being the lone moderator was too painful.[73] Davis claimed that Stacy Blank Beard, who had led one of *Notes from the Field*'s full-audience Act IIs, suggested using smaller "buzz groups" for *The White Card*, followed by a group report to the entire audience.[74]

Our facilitators for the March 31, 2018, Act II asked us two questions: "What in *The White Card* did you connect with?" and "What was difficult for you?" They instructed us to establish our own buzz groups of about four audience members who had not come with us and gave us eight minutes to share our answers—which was certainly not long enough for my group—or anyone else's. My buzz group of four white adults did not get through the first question about "what we connected with," although the three who spoke were impassioned and compelling as they discussed how they related to elements of the play. Two described their relationships with family members who exhibited racial bias and prejudice, and one in our group confessed to fears of saying or doing "the wrong thing" as reasons she avoids conversations about race. A soft-spoken man stated that we will do "the wrong thing" but "We need to work on our racism daily, the way you brush and floss your teeth." His simile emphasizes personal transformation rather than community work or activism, but he also suggests that transformation requires ongoing effort and we will *all* be healthier if we fight racism. The unique health risks faced by Black people were articulated quite differently in a buzz group that included the eight-year-old daughter of the actor playing Charlotte, Karen Pittman. The young girl told the white adults in her group, "I connected with the fact that Black people are in danger." Pittman's daughter and thirteen-year-old son had been seated in front of us through the play and were in a buzz group with my partner. Shortly after the daughter spoke, Pittman came from backstage and asked if the children wanted to stay and talk more. They did not. Pittman politely thanked the buzz group for including her children and left.

Davis felt that the buzz groups were generally a positive step in the development of Act II, one that clarified the mission of the talkback enterprise. She observed:

> There were buzz groups that went well and groups that were awful for various reasons. I remember one in particular where there was a husband and wife team; he was an Emerson alum and lawyer and then there was a white mother and daughter who were on a college tour. Everyone was sharing as we were asked to do. Not in an intense way. One of the prompts was: What is the hardest part for you? The mother said, "The hardest part for me is this part." But she was really appreciative of it. . . . The show brought up some discomfort for her. She saw herself in the woman, Virginia.[75]

After the buzz groups discussed the two (or one, in my case) questions for eight minutes, the facilitators asked volunteers to present their small-group discussions to the entire audience. This exercise of "reporting out," often called "think, pair, share," is absolutely standard for small-group work in classrooms. With so little time for both the buzz groups and reports, I thought a lot about who was taking up the time for the conversation. I was relieved that the first speaker to the full audience was a Black man, who responded to Charles's line claiming that Charlotte cannot tell him what it means to be white. He pointed out that Black people know "a lot about whiteness" because they are "looking at whites all the time in order to survive." Another audience member pointed out that Charles had not learned anything about whiteness by the end; in taking off his shirt, he was trying to occupy even more space and to "one-up" Charlotte by "helping" her with Exhibit C in a way that performed his beneficence. A third audience member spoke of the "exhaustion" Black people feel at being asked to repeatedly teach about racism, often by well-intentioned white people. It occurred to me that this production, the facilitated discussion, buzz groups, and report-out activity were all doing that exhausting work of teaching, too—of trying to teach us all about whiteness.

The audience member who took up the most space in Act II was a white man who spoke compellingly about the exclusion and prejudice he experiences as a Deaf person, including at that matinee on Saturday, March 31, 2018, which was the only show offering American Sign Language (ASL)-English interpretation in the run of *The White Card*. He had been seated in the wrong place in the theater so he could not see the two interpreters, and it had not been possible for him to trade seats—the reasons were not clear to me—but he felt the production had failed to offer appropriate accommodations to him. Theaters have struggled to determine where to place the ASL-English interpreters so that they will not "detract" from the show or "distract" the hearing audiences or actors (attitudes that further marginalize Deaf audience members who can usually only see one show of a production).[76] Interpreters are typically placed at the side of the stage, and Deaf audiences are seated in a segregated space in front of them, sometimes the worst and sometimes the best and most expensive seats. Theatrical companies and individual productions have faced controversies over whether to charge Deaf patrons the full price ticket for the best seats.

The White Card's unique stadium-like stage configuration made placement of the interpreters even more difficult than usual, explained Christopher Robinson, one of the ASL-English interpreters for *The White Card*: "There was a suggestion that we might be downstage in the first row across from the Deaf audience, with backs to the larger audience—very accessible to Deaf audiences, but possibly distracting to others."[77] Instead, Robinson and his co-interpreter, Shari Coon, were positioned at the back corner of the bleachers, directly behind me, as it turned out. Deaf audience members looked way up at the interpreters, then down to the stage, and then craned their necks back up. Their attention was divided, and Robinson pointed to additional "losses for the Deaf audience" in that two interpreters were representing five characters onstage, with a slight time lag, so it would be difficult to determine which lines belonged to the various characters.[78] The Deaf members of the audience were less likely to experience such divided forms of attention during the profound tableaux of *The White Card*: Charlotte's body stretched out on the autopsy sculpture at the end of the dinner party and then her pose as a slave woman before a shirtless Charles at the end of the play. These meaningful but wordless tableaux underscore the fact that for all the talk of the play, the visual elements of acting, staging, and posing are crucial to the meaning of the play—and are available without interpretation to (sighted) Deaf audiences.

As I invoke the tableaux poses of *The White Card*, I am wary of seeming to imply that there is a deeper, privileged truth in physical, gestural communication in the theater, which, of course, excludes visually impaired audiences. Gestures and poses have a conventional function, much like language, and have worked differently in various historical genres, like melodrama, with their prescriptions for how actors use their bodies—which again invoke racial constructs. Notions of race depend largely (but inaccurately) on the visual markers of skin color. The audience member who was seated in the wrong place to see the interpreters described how he was struggling to understand his white and male privilege (depending on supposedly visible characteristics) and his marginalization as a person whose Deafness is not always visible but who experiences prejudice from hearing people of all races. Deaf people who use ASL as their primary means of communication often resist the idea of Deafness as a disability and consider themselves members of a largely invisible minority linguistic group—among other communities. Deaf Communities of Color face multiple, intersecting forms of discrimination.

When Deaf audiences have the opportunity to attend ASL-interpreted theater, traditional talkbacks are rarely scheduled on those days, partially because interpretation is expensive for cash-strapped theater institutions. But, for *The White Card*'s Act II, a team of ASL-English interpreters entered the theater, one for each buzz group so that Deaf and hearing audiences could communicate with each other rather than being segregated into separate groups. This was a huge commitment on the part of Arts Emerson and A.R.T., and Robinson gave Act II "two thumbs up," saying, "I wish I had more thumbs." One thumb was for the fact that Deaf audience members were included in a forum to which they rarely have access.[79] Deaf audience members have few opportunities to discuss theater publicly or even casually talk about the performance with non-Deaf audiences during intermission or after the show. Robinson's second "thumb up" was for the way the Deaf community and the interpreters helped train the rest of the audience to have difficult conversations about race. He acknowledged that "people need training" to have those conversations, and the buzz groups he participated in with other hearing audiences were "created in a bubble . . . they were going to atrophy right back into the [racist] behaviors."[80] Yet, when he interpreted Act II for a mix of Deaf and hearing audience members, the conversations were much better. He believed that the interpreters served as de-facto facilitators and trainers for the small buzz groups, pushing them forward toward more productive conversation. He also credited the marginalization experienced by the Deaf community and the grammar of ASL for improving those buzz groups. In the buzz groups without interpreters, "people rarely spoke about themselves" and used "distancing pronouns," but the grammar of ASL does not allow for these strategies.[81] ASL requires its users to "start with the first person." Robinson claimed, "They [ASL sentences] all start with, 'I heard, or I read, or that happened to me,'" and this language helped buzz groups get to a "different space in that short amount of time."[82]

The brief twenty-minute time limit for Act II's buzz group discussions and report-out exercise contributed to Bill Marx's negative review of the production:

> What of any substance can be said in such a short time? This is an exercise in risk-adverse branding ("Art Ignites Empathy"), a chance to involve university students in the staging, and an opportunity to convince skeptical foundations, mainstream media, politicians, and fat cat donors that art can make something happen, at least for their images.[83]

I find Act II, for both *The White Card* and *Notes from the Field*, far from risk-averse in the sense that Act II can fail, have no impact on audiences, or cause pain and even trauma for facilitators and audience members alike. I also believe "that art can make something happen," although it is not always the intended *thing*, and sometimes has a lot to do with the circumstance of attending the theater on the one day the production provided ASL-English interpreters and invited the Deaf community.[84] While I agree with Marx that not much "of any substance" can be said in a twenty-minute facilitated discussion, it is important to acknowledge that Act II was part of a longer community-engagement effort for *The White Card*.[85] Arts Emerson had worked to embed conversations about Rankine's work in the larger Boston community over a period of years. Shortly after she published *Citizen: An American Lyric*, Rankine was selected to be Emerson's 2015 Fresh Sound artist-in-residence. Her analysis of racial injustice in Boston during that time led Arts Emerson to commission the play that became *The White Card*.

In the winter of 2018, while the play was in production, the *Citizen* Read Project was launched as "a series of dynamic events co-produced by ArtsEmerson and American Repertory Theater to activate a public dialogue on race and identity in America."[86] Boston area residents could sign up to participate as individuals, with preestablished groups such as book clubs and college courses, or as part of organizations like the City of Boston Arts and Culture Office. The multistep project involved (1) reading Claudia Rankine's *Citizen: An American Lyric* (2014) in January and February 2018; (2) participating in a discussion of *Citizen* and racism in Boston and beyond facilitated by the *Citizen* Read Project team; (3) attending the public dialogue, "Citizen Speak: A Conversation with Claudia Rankine" held on March 4, 2018, and moderated by collaborator and dramaturg P. Carl;[87] and (4) attending a "Citizen Read" designated performance of *The White Card*. In devising the project, P. Carl articulated the goal of having 1,000 people in the Boston area read and discuss *Citizen*. The project exceeded that goal, with more than 1,300 Boston area residents and eighty different groups participating in an extended multipart project—very different from the one-off Act II of *Notes from the Field*.

For Elizabeth Cooper Davis, the *Citizen* Read Project should be understood "in the context of Arts Emerson's engagement work in general and their commitment to being citizens of the city and facilitating ongoing conversations."[88] She found *Citizen* Read's focus on local engagement to be different from and "somewhat more successful" than Anna Deavere Smith's touring project and concern for the aesthetic implications of *Notes from the Field*'s Act II:

> My perspective is that the goal [of Act II in *Notes*] was to disrupt spectatorship to further Anna's decades long experiment with the search for the American character and what does it mean . . . and how the arts can be part of that work. And I think she had, and we had, hopes for it being a springboard for ongoing conversation long after [*Notes from the Field:*] *The Pipeline Project* had left. But, it's different when you don't have to leave.[89]

Davis stayed. After working as a facilitator-trainer for *Notes*, she continued to engage with the Boston theater community's efforts to use art in work for racial justice. She served as a facilitator for *The White Card* and *Citizen* Read, a small group of committed individuals who, she said, conceived of themselves as part of "a social justice team and mission." Davis contrasted that experience with the larger group of facilitators for *Notes*, all of whom had applied for the role and were "cast" based on their relationship to the school-to-prison pipeline and were "part of the show" to some extent.[90]

The *Citizen* Read Project was not *part of the show*—not a version of Act II. The facilitators, always working in pairs to mitigate the potential for harm, used a script, but it was a script that combined the techniques and features of the book club discussion with the institutional workshop on inclusion and diversity.[91] Both the book club and diversity workshop are more likely to be successful when the participants are part of a group with a solid foundation, and Davis identified the relationships between group members as a crucial feature supporting the success of the *Citizen* Read Program. With more than eighty organizations participating in the program, many of the conversations, in fact all of the discussions Davis facilitated, were with preestablished groups.[92] Facilitators who worked with randomly combined individuals who signed up for *Citizen* Read found the experience more challenging; it is difficult to get groups of strangers to talk about race. But the "pre-existing groups had a reason to participate," Davis pointed out, "They had identified this as something that would serve their goals."[93] They committed to reading *Citizen*, engaging in the facilitated discussion, attending the *Citizen* Speak dialogue with Rankine and P. Carl, going to *The White Card*, and participating in Act II during one of the designated *Citizen* Read performances.

But this did not include the matinee on March 31, 2018, when ASL-English interpreters were provided. Nor could Deaf audiences participate in the *Citizen* Read discussions or the *Citizen* Speak dialogue, and this marginalization from the ongoing engagement project of *Citizen* Read is just one of many examples of how opportunities for discussions of racism, prejudice, and normativity are not accessible to the Deaf community. Christopher Robinson celebrated that the production made *one* performance of *The White Card* accessible to Deaf audiences (albeit with a risk of whiplash from looking up at him and the other interpreter and back down to the stage) and particularly that a team of interpreters was deployed so that Deaf audiences could participate in the Act II buzz groups.[94] Such opportunities are all too rare. I asked Robinson if he perceived a contradiction in the fact that *The White Card* called attention to racial injustice while perpetuating the exclusion of people who use ASL to communicate. "Be cognizant of the hypocrisy and call it me," Robinson said.[95]

The White Card intends to teach the audience that they should look at themselves the next time they witness racist acts, say, the arrest of two Black customers in a Philadelphia Starbucks (April 2018)[96] or a woman calling the police to claim, "There's an African American man threatening my life," after he asked her to follow the rules in Manhattan's Central Park and leash her dog (May 2020).[97] Robinson believes that *The White Card* demands, "Turn that camera around and focus it on all the other people in Starbucks, all the people still sitting, on the baristas still behind the counter. Turn the camera around and see me."[98] Robinson discussed the contradictions he experiences within himself as a hearing Black man fluent in ASL and working as an interpreter: "My career depends on the Deafness of others."[99] He connected with Charlotte's realization in *The White Card* that she was trafficking in "black death spectacle" with photographs that recreate scenes of racist murder.[100] Charlotte realizes the ethical complexity of being an artist building a career and livelihood out of aestheticizing Black death. Her art and her career depended on these atrocities, and her representation of them was the reason Charles was interested in her work.

7.4. Conclusion

The White Card points to the sinister implications of making art from atrocity but also participates in that phenomenon. The constant barrage of images, media, and stories about Black suffering, crime, poverty, and murder might promote sympathy in some audiences and racism in others as it replicates common stereotypes of Black people as criminals and/or victims. The result is a widespread psychic investment in these tropes and stereotypes, and even if unintentionally, *The White Card* adds dramatic material to that investment. The artworks depicting Black death were projected on the white walls of the theater as they were discussed in the play or literally laid down on the stage as an autopsy sculpture. The published version of the text includes reproductions of six of these images. Between the two scenes of the play, Boston audiences viewed a media collage of stories related to the mass shooting at Marjory Stoneman Douglas High School on February 14,

2018, and Black athletes taking a knee during the national anthem to protest racism. We heard Fox News's Laura Ingraham telling basketball star LeBron James to "shut up and dribble" on February 16, 2018. All of these clips reveal racism and might help audiences combat white supremacy, but as Charlotte asks of forcing Germans to view photographs of Nazi concentration camps, "Did it ever occur to you it could have the opposite effect? All those bodies could have fed their anti-Semitism."[101] Audiences at *The White Card* probably did not feed their racism with the play, but the images and stories of Black death may have fed their unconscious investment in stereotypes and their understanding of themselves as *good people* supporting theater of racial justice.

Coda

"Be cognizant of the hypocrisy and call it me," Christopher Robinson said, reflecting on how his job as an American Sign Language (ASL)-English interpreter in the theater—always in the wrong spot for someone—depended on Deaf audiences.[1] My job in this book also depends on theater that depicts Black suffering, and my career is likely to be advanced by its publication. I am adding to the barrage of "black death spectacle" by writing a book that discusses not only theatrical works that emphasize Black pain but also associates them with events of racist violence and murder.[2] I repeatedly watched the recording of the murder of Philando Castile as I wrote the conclusion of Chapter 3, becoming some of the hundreds of thousands of Facebook views I mention there. In my chapter on Jean Genet's *The Blacks*, I described my own experience of having my face blackened—and that happened during a moment of audience participation that escalated beyond the comfort of the audience and actors, partially because I was so complicit, complying with each task and readily admitting my racism. Throughout the book I critically examine, but also thereby center, my own position as a white ally who is complicit in every empty or self-congratulatory gesture of allyship that I identify when discussing the limits of the ally framework. I critiqued the shortcomings of the diversity and inclusion project in Lin-Manuel Miranda's *Hamilton*, while participating in many institutional diversity initiatives (I&D) that are typically better advertised than executed. I participated in the Act II discussions and could have contributed to the pain of the facilitators or frustration of fellow audience members. I wanted to cover my eyes when *Notes from the Field* and *The White Card* projected clips of the media's spectacular treatment of racial violence, and I carried home the program's insert listing organizations that battle the school-to-prison pipeline—but never volunteered with any of those organizations.

"Turn that camera around. . . . Be cognizant of the hypocrisy and call it me," and then, Robinson said, "Get back to work."[3] A huge danger of recognizing our complicity and the limitations of the I&D project is that we might refuse to do the necessary work to learn from those deficiencies and work toward

Complicit Participation. Carrie J. Preston, Oxford University Press. © Oxford University Press 2024.
DOI: 10.1093/9780197693438.003.0009

full and radical participation. At the end of *The White Card*'s Act II, after the buzz groups and full group discussion the facilitators gave us a bit more work. They reminded us that we had received a literal *white card* on our chairs, and they invited us to share further comments and post them on the boards outside the theater. I wrote: "To what extent are we in the audience doing exactly what Rankine was critiquing—finding pleasure in and even profiting from 'black death spectacle'"?[4] I headed home with my program indicating that the projections of art and atrocity in the A.R.T./ArtsEmerson production were made possible by corporate donors including JetBlue Airways and the foundations of companies like Liberty Mutual (which was listed in the top ten unethical insurance companies by the American Association for Justice).[5] A.R.T., ArtsEmerson, and other theaters accept compromised funding to mount productions like *The White Card*, which critiques Charles's foundation because it is bankrolled by the private prison industry. This is not to suggest that any of us in the theater were not compromised. The A.R.T. and ArtsEmerson programs also featured ads for a Coldwell Banker Residential Brokerage selling, at *The White Card*, a $15,000,000 "Greek Revival with carriage house" and, at *Notes from the Field*, a $4,7875,000 house in Cambridge, Massachusetts, with the claim of "Building Community One Home at a Time." The ads, prominently placed on the back covers, would suggest that theatergoers are a *market* for these properties and communities, and we certainly are the *audience* for them. I acknowledge one more time that I am a complicit participant in theater for racial justice and institutional performances of activism. I hope that this book encourages more honest acknowledgments of the limits of complicit white allyship, but far from abandoning the effort to dismantle white supremacy, I call it *me* and get back to work.

Notes

Introduction

1. I use the term "theater of racial justice" rather than "Black theater," which tends to designate plays by and about Black people—that is, plays that focus on representations rather than political positions. For an important discussion of the history of definitions of Black theater and of the complexity of defining this theater, see Harvey Young's introduction and special issue on teaching Black plays: Harvey Young, "Introduction: Black Plays," *Theatre Topics* 19, no. 1 (2009): xiii–xviii.
2. See Beth Hinderliter and Noelle Chaddock, "A Rejection of White Feminist Cisgender Allyship: Centering Intersectionality," in *Antagonizing White Feminism: Intersectionality's Critique of Women's Studies and the Academy*, ed. Noelle Chaddock and Beth Hinderliter (Lanham, MD: Lexington Books, 2020), 137–145. While acknowledging that "good has occurred under the banner of allyship," they argue that allyship must be replaced with "co-conspiracy," defined as a "space of shared consequences and a willing loss of social, financial and human capitol alongside white cisgender privilege" (142). To avoid the secrecy and exclusion of the term "conspiracy," I argue for a model of full and radical participation in this book.
3. "A Day of Collective Engagement: Racism and Antiracism, Our Realities and Our Roles," Boston University, accessed September 24, 2022, https://www.bu.edu/provost/diversity/collective-engagement-info/.
4. Felix Barrett, "Punchdrunk About," Punchdrunk, accessed July 30, 2021, https://www.punchdrunk.com/about-us/. Felix Barrett is also Artistic Director at Punchdrunk.
5. Mallika Rao, "'The Dutchman' Solves the Biggest Problem with Immersive Theater," *The Huffington Post*, last modified November 27, 2013, accessed May 16, 2016, https://www.huffpost.com/entry/dutchman-immersive-theater_n_4340779.
6. Email message to author, June 15, 2021, 4:34 pm. The "Private Events Director" wrote, "Is there a particular space you have in mind? Both our wonderful speakeasy 'The Club Car,' and our magical rooftop 'Gallow Green,' are separate from the set of Sleep No More. It is also possible to host a private event within the set of the show either before or after a performance OR the show is available for private groups."
7. Sarah Lyall, "Starring Me! A Surreal Dive into Immersive Theater," *The New York Times*, January 7, 2016, accessed May 16, 2016, https://www.nytimes.com/2016/01/08/theater/starring-me-a-surreal-dive-into-immersive-theater.html?partner=IFTTT.
8. Adam Feldman, "The Best Immersive Theater in New York Right Now," *Time Out*, March 30, 2022, accessed June 1, 2022, https://www.timeout.com/newyork/theater/immersive-theater-in-nyc.

9. Yelp, "Best Interactive Theater in Boston, Massachusetts," accessed June 1, 2022, https://www.yelp.com/search?find_desc=interactive+theater&find_loc=Boston%2C+%20MA.

10. Yelp, "Best Interactive."

11. Historic Tours of America, "Boston Tea Party Ships & Museum, December 16, 1773: A Revolutionary Experience," Boston Tea Party Ships & Museum: #1 Best Patriotic Attraction, accessed June 1, 2022, https://www.bostonteapartyship.com.

12. LighthouseImmersive, "Immersive Frida Kahlo: Her Life. Her Love. Her Art," Immersive Frida Kahlo Boston: The Immersive Art Experience, accessed August 14, 2022, https://www.immersive-frida.com/boston/.

13. Elinor Fuchs pointed to the emergence of "a new kind of theater that mimics in its deep structures of presentation and reception the fundamental culture of contemporary capitalism" (Elinor Fuchs, "Theater as Shopping," *Theater* 24, no. 1 [1993]: 20).

14. Jackie Sibblies Drury, *Fairview: A Play* (New York: Theatre Communications Group, 2019), 102. Adrienne Kennedy's *Funnyhouse of a Negro* (1964) drops new "fourth walls" on the stage for the character of Sarah to break through.

15. Drury, *Fairview*, 4.

16. Drury, *Fairview*, 15.

17. Drury, *Fairview*, 32.

18. Drury, *Fairview*, 33.

19. Drury, *Fairview*, 53.

20. Drury, *Fairview*, 56.

21. Drury, *Fairview*, 41.

22. Drury, *Fairview*, 100.

23. Drury, *Fairview*, 102.

24. Ben Brantley, "Review: Theater as Sabotage in the Dazzling 'Fairview,' " *The New York Times*, June 17, 2018, accessed July 7, 2022, https://www.nytimes.com/2018/06/17/theater/review-theater-as-sabotage-in-the-dazzling-fairview.html.

25. Jesse Green and Salamishah Tillet, " 'Fairview': Watching a Play in Black and White," *The New York Times*, August 7, 2019, accessed July 7, 2022, https://www.nytimes.com/2019/08/07/theater/fairview-ending-debate.html.

26. Drury, *Fairview*, 105–106.

27. Drury, *Fairview*, 105–106.

28. Diep Tran, "Jackie Sibblies Drury: Thinking and Feeling," *American Theatre*, May 29, 2019, accessed July 7, 2022, https://www.americantheatre.org/2019/05/29/jackie-sibblies-drury-thinking-and-feeling/.

29. Michel Martin, "The Pulitzer-Winning Play 'Fairview' Is About Being Watched While Black," NPR, last modified July 14, 2019, accessed July 7, 2022, https://www.npr.org/2019/07/14/739057321/the-pulitzer-winning-play-fairview-is-about-being-watched-while-black.

30. Drury, *Fairview*, 57.

31. Martin, "The Pulitzer-Winning Play."

32. "Theater of racial justice" is preferable to the term "antiracist theater" because "antiracism" suggests an overly simplistic binary between antiracist and racist productions

(although scholars like Ibram X. Kendi certainly do not advocate this simplistic use). See Ibram X. Kendi, *How to Be an Antiracist* (New York, One World, 2019). The term "antiracist theater" also suggests a given production can universally—and for all audiences—accomplish clear antiracist goals and do real work to dismantle structural racism. When I use the term "antiracist" in this book, I refer to antiracist positions, arguments, or claims rather than antiracism as an accomplishment.

33. See W. K. Wimsatt, Jr and M. C. Beardsley's "The Intentional Fallacy," *The Sewanee Review* 54, no. 3 (1946): 468–488.
34. Edmund White, *Genet: A Biography* (New York: Knopf, 1993), 522.
35. Jean Genet, *Prisoner of Love*, trans. Barbara Bray (n.p.: Wesleyan University Press, 1992), 149.
36. Genet, *Prisoner of Love*, 331, 262.
37. Genet, *Prisoner of Love*, 27.
38. Genet, *Prisoner of Love*, 83.
39. White, *Genet: A Biography*, 533.
40. White, *Genet: A Biography*, 534.
41. Genet, *Prisoner of Love*, 46.
42. Genet, *Prisoner of Love*, 46.
43. Genet, *Prisoner of Love*, 83.
44. Genet, *Prisoner of Love*, 46.
45. Genet, *Prisoner of Love*, 46–47.
46. Genet, *Prisoner of Love*, 46–47.
47. Genet, *Prisoner of Love*, 46–47.
48. Genet, *Prisoner of Love*, 46–47.
49. Sundiatu Dixon-Fyle et al., *Diversity Wins: How Inclusion Matters*, May 19, 2020, accessed August 6, 2022, https://www.mckinsey.com/featured-insights/diversity-and-inclusion/diversity-wins-how-inclusion-matters.
50. Richard Wright, *Native Son and How 'Bigger' Was Born* (New York: HarperCollins, 1993), 531.
51. James Baldwin, "Everybody's Protest Novel," in *Notes of a Native Son*, by James Baldwin (Boston, MA: Beacon Press, 1984), 22, previously published in *Notes of a Native Son* (n.p., 1955).
52. Harry J. Elam, Jr., "Ritual Theory and Political Theatre: *Quinta Temporada* and *Slave Ship*," *Theatre Journal* 38, no. 4 (1986): 463.
53. Elam, Jr., "Ritual Theory," 471.
54. Elam, Jr., "Ritual Theory," 470–471.
55. Elam, Jr., "Ritual Theory," 463.
56. Elam, Jr., "Ritual Theory," 463.
57. Brandi Wilkins Catanese, "Teaching *A Day of Absence* 'at [Your] Own Risk,'" *Theatre Topics* 19, no. 1 (2009): 29.
58. Catanese, "Teaching," 36.
59. Catanese, "Teaching," 36.
60. Brandi Wilkins Catanese, "Transgressing Tradition: Suzan-Lori Parks and Black Performance (as) Theory," in *The Problem of the Color[blind]: Racial Transgression*

and the Politics of Black Performance (Ann Arbor: University of Michigan Press, 2012), 112–142.

61. Jean Young, "The Re-Objectification and Re-Commodification of Saartjie Baartman in Suzan-Lori Parks's *Venus*," *African American Review* 31, no. 4 (1997): 699.

62. Catanese, "Transgressing Tradition," 137.

63. Harvey Young, *Embodying Black Experience: Stillness, Critical Memory, and the Black Body* (Ann Arbor: University of Michigan Press, 2010), 132.

64. Young, *Embodying Black Experience*, 132.

65. "We See You, White American Theater," Statement—We See you W.A.T., last modified June 8, 2020, accessed July 20, 2022, https://www.weseeyouwat.com/ statement. Signatories to the movement's original statement, "Dear White American Theater," include Lin-Manuel Miranda, whose work is addressed in Chapter 5 of this book. See "We See You," Statement—We See You W.A.T.

66. Christopher Robinson, interview by the author, Boston University, April 18, 2018.

67. Amy Harmon writes, "In a national poll conducted by Ipsos for *The New York Times*, more than twice as many white Democrats said they felt 'very favorably' toward 'BIPOC' as Americans who identify as any of the nonwhite racial categories it encompasses." Amy Harmon, "BIPOC of POC? Equity or Equality? The Debate over Language on the Left," *The New York Times*, November 1, 2021, accessed July 5, 2020, https://www.nytimes.com/2021/11/01/us/terminology-language-politics.html.

68. Nancy Colman, "Why We're Capitalizing Black," *The New York Times*, July 5, 2020, accessed August 3, 2022, https://www.nytimes.com/2020/07/05/insider/capitalized-black.html.

69. John McWhorter, "Capitalizing 'Black' Isn't Wrong. But It Isn't That Helpful Either," *The New York Times*, March 4, 2022, accessed August 3, 2022, https://www.nytimes.com/2022/03/04/opinion/capitalizing-black.html.

Chapter 1

1. Jean Genet, *The Blacks: A Clown Show*, trans. Bernard Frechtman (n.p.: Grove Press, 1960), 10.

2. Genet, *The Blacks*, 12.

3. Jenny Sandman, "A *CurtainUp* Review, *The Blacks: A Clown Show*," review of *The Blacks: A Clown Show*, Classical Theatre of Harlem, New York, NY, United States, The Internet Theater Magazine of Reviews, Features, Annotated Listings, accessed August 9, 2021, http://www.curtainup.com/blacks.html.

4. Bruce Weber, "Race Peers Out of Masks," review of *The Blacks: A Clown Show*, *The New York Times*, February 13, 2003, Theatre, accessed August 9, 2021, http://www.nytimes.com/2003/02/13/arts/theater/13CLOW.html.

5. See also Una Chaudhuri, "Close Encounters: My *Blacks* Story," *Hunter On-line Theater Review*, accessed August 9, 2021, http://www.hotreview.org/articles/myblacksstory.htm.

6. Jean-Paul Sartre, *Saint Genet: Actor and Martyr*, trans. Bernard Frechtman (n.p.: Pantheon Books, 1963), 5. Sartre's famous biography repeatedly emphasizes Genet's "contempt for anecdote" as "[o]ne of Genet's most constant traits, which was evident even in his conversation" (302; see also 312, 317, 398, 524).

7. Genet, *The Blacks*, 35, 38.

8. Genet, *The Blacks*, 3.

9. Genet, *The Blacks*, 4.

10. For a discussion of the textual history, see Brian Gordon Kennelly, "*En dire trop sur les Noirs?* Contextualizing Genet's Preface to *Les Nègres*," *Journal of Arts and Humanities* 3, no. 11 (2014): 51–66.

11. Jean Genet, "Preface to *The Blacks*," trans. Clare Finburgh, preface to *The Politics of Jean Genet's Late Theatre: Spaces of Revolution*, by Carl Lavery (n.p.: Manchester University Press, 2010), 228.

12. Genet, "Preface to *The Blacks*," preface, 228.

13. Genet, "Preface to *The Blacks*," preface, 230.

14. Genet, "Preface to *The Blacks*," preface, 230.

15. Genet, "Preface to *The Blacks*," preface, 230.

16. Genet, "Preface to *The Blacks*," preface, 231.

17. Genet, *The Blacks*, 9.

18. Genet, *The Blacks*, 10.

19. Genet, *The Blacks*, 10.

20. Genet, *The Blacks*, 8.

21. The application of Judith Butler's idea of "performative gender construction" to racial identity categories has been considered in literary and cultural theory and legal studies—sometimes with the implication that performative racial construction is subversive or liberatory. For the foundational works, see Louis F. Mirón and Jonathon Xavier Inda, "Race as a Kind of Speech Act," *Cultural Studies: A Research Volume* 5 (2000): 85–107; Nadine Ehlers, "Passing Phantasms/Sanctioning Performatives: (Re)Reading White Masculinity in Rhinelander v. Rhinelander," *Studies in Law, Politics, and Society* 27 (2003): 63–91; and John L. Jackson, Jr., *Harlemworld: Doing Race and Class in Contemporary America* (n.p.: Oxford University Press, 2001).

22. Genet, "Preface to *The Blacks*," preface, 232.

23. Genet, "Preface to *The Blacks*," preface, 232.

24. Genet, *The Blacks*, 14.

25. Genet, *The Blacks*, 39.

26. Genet, *The Blacks*, 52. In contrast to Archibald's suggestion of being condemned to performance, Black writers such as Zora Neale Hurston have viewed Black performance as a source of empowerment. Her "Characteristics of Negro Expression" opens with the claim, "The Negro's universal mimicry is not so much a thing in itself as an evidence of something that permeates his entire self. And that thing is drama." Zora Neale Hurston, "Characteristics of Negro Expression," in *The Negro: An Anthology*, ed. Nancy Cunard (London: Wishart, 1934), 39–46, 39.

27. Genet, *The Blacks*, 38.

212 NOTES

28. Genet, *The Blacks*, 95.

29. Genet, *The Blacks*, 95.

30. Genet, *The Blacks*, 18.

31. Genet, *The Blacks*, 19.

32. Genet, *The Blacks*, 19.

33. Genet, *The Blacks*, 94.

34. Derek F. Connon, "Confused? You Will Be: Genet's *Les Nègres* and the Art of Upsetting the Audience," *French Studies* 50, no. 4 (1996): 429.

35. Genet, *The Blacks*, 111.

36. Genet, *The Blacks*, 112.

37. Genet, *The Blacks*, 16.

38. A seeming translation error adds to an [English] reader's confusion. The Frechtman translation states that, after Newport News is stopped by Village, he continues to exit in the same way he started: he "*is about to leave by the left wing, but Village stops him.*" After Village delivers his line, the stage direction states, "*Exit Newport News, left*" (Genet, *The Blacks*, 16). The original French compels the character to switch directions after the interruption: "*Ville de Saint-Nazaire s'incline et va pour sortir vers la droite, mais Village intervient . . . Ville de Saint-Nazaire sort à gauche*" (see Jean Genet, "*Les Nègres: clownerie* [The Blacks: A Clown Show]," in *Théâtre complet*, ed. Michel Corvin and Albert Dichy [n.p.: Gallimard, 2002], 483). See also the endnote in *Théâtre complet*: "Ville de Saint-Nazaire sort toujours à gauche" (1218, n. 15) and the Appendices, including textual revisions and fragments.

39. Genet, *The Blacks*, 111–112. Connon suggests that "the off-right action, which must now be taken to be the 'real' action rather than the off-left action, has the additional threat of being unspecified" (see Connon, "Confused? You Will," 432). The event offstage right remains more of a secret than the supposed trial offstage left. Even if Newport News's hint is quite specific, this other action is easy to miss because there are so many onstage plays within plays and offstage happenings, none of which is convincingly "real."

40. Connon, "Confused? You Will," 433–434.

41. Genet, *The Blacks*, 81.

42. Genet, *The Blacks*, 109–110.

43. Genet, *The Blacks*, 82.

44. Genet, *The Blacks*, 81–82.

45. Genet, *The Blacks*, 82.

46. Genet, *The Blacks*, 109.

47. Genet, *The Blacks*, 111.

48. Genet, *The Blacks*, 111.

49. Genet, *The Blacks*, 107.

50. Genet, *The Blacks*, 128.

51. Genet, *The Blacks*, 128.

52. Elaine Scarry described audience participation as her "own particular nightmare" during her lecture "Consent and the Body in Theatre" at the Mellon School of Theater and Performance Research at Harvard University, June 6, 2017.

53. Gordon Cox, "Air Raids, Ghosts and Escape Rooms: Inside New York's Immersive Theater Boom," *Variety*, July 27, 2017, accessed August 9, 2021, http://variety.com/2017/legit/news/immersive-theater-off- broadway-1202506336/.

54. Jean Genet and Bernard Frechtman, "A Note on Theatre," *Tulane Drama Review* 7, no. 3 (1963): 38.

55. Genet, *The Blacks*, 69–73.

56. Chaudhuri, "Close Encounters," *Hunter On-line Theater Review*.

57. Chaudhuri, "Close Encounters," *Hunter On-line Theater Review*.

58. Edmund White, *Genet: A Biography* (n.p.: Knopf, 1993), 428.

59. White, *Genet: A Biography*, 433–434.

60. Genet, *The Blacks*, 54, n. 3.

61. White, *Genet: A Biography*, 433.

62. Quoted in White, *Genet: A Biography*, 438.

63. Quoted in "The Negro Writer in America: A Symposium," *Negro Digest*, June 1963, 63.

64. Quoted in "The Negro," 63.

65. Quoted in "The Negro," 63–64.

66. Cheryl Higashida, "To Be(come) Young, Gay, and Black: Lorraine Hansberry's Existentialist Routes to Anticolonialism," *American Quarterly* 60, no. 4 (2008): 902; Maya Angelou, *The Heart of a Woman* (n.p.: Random House, 1981), 180.

67. Angelou, *The Heart*, 172–173. Angelou seems to associate *The Blacks* with Black Americans, but Genet's context was more directly French colonialism in Algeria and the Algerian War for Independence (1954–1962).

68. Angelou, *The Heart*, 175.

69. Angelou, *The Heart*, 179.

70. Angelou, *The Heart*, 195.

71. Angelou, *The Heart*, 181.

72. Higashida, "To Be(come)," 902.

73. Genet, *The Blacks*, 5.

74. Angelou, *The Heart*, 197.

75. Angelou, *The Heart*, 183.

76. Angelou, *The Heart*, 183.

77. Angelou, *The Heart*, 184.

78. Angelou, *The Heart*, 185.

79. Angelou, *The Heart*, 185.

80. Killens references white "hordes" in "The Negro," 63; Angelou, *The Heart*, 185.

81. Norman Mailer, "Theatre: The Blacks (Cont.)," *The Village Voice*, May 18, 1961, 14 (emphasis in the original).

82. Norman Mailer, "Theatre: The Blacks (Cont.)," *The Village Voice*, May 18, 1961, 14 (emphasis in the original).

83. Mailer, "Theatre: The Blacks," 14.

84. Genet, *The Blacks*, 38.

85. Genet, "Preface to *The Blacks*," preface, 232.

86. Lorraine Hansberry, "Genet, Mailer, and The New Paternalism," *The Village Voice*, June 1, 1961, 10.

87. Hansberry, "Genet, Mailer," 15.

88. Hansberry, "Genet, Mailer," 10.

89. See Lorraine Hansberry, *Les Blancs* in *The Collected Last Plays: Les Blancs, The Drinking Gourd, What Use Are Flowers*, edited, with critical backgrounds, by Robert Nemiroff (New York: New American Library, 1983), 37–139.

   Hansberry's earlier play, *The Sign in Sidney Brustein's Window* (1964), also had a connection to *The Blacks* in that the titular character was partially based on the version of liberal intellectualism Hansberry found in Sidney Bernstein, producer of the 1961 American premiere of *The Blacks*.

90. Hansberry is quoted by Robert Nemiroff in "A Critical Background" to *Les Blancs* in *Collected Last Plays*, 27–35, 32 (emphasis in the original). For an alternative perspective, see Frieda Ekotto's defense of Genet's abstraction in Frieda Ekotto, *Race and Sex across the French Atlantic: The Color of Black in Literary, Philosophical, and Theater Discourse* (n.p.: Lexington Books, 2011), 7–8.

91. Hansberry, "Genet, Mailer," 42.

92. Hansberry is quoted by Robert Nemiroff in "A Critical Background" to *Les Blancs* in *Collected Last Plays*, 27–35, 32 (emphasis in the original).

93. The detachment of theater from revolution was a primary theme of his earlier play *The Balcony*.

94. Genet, "Preface to *The Blacks*," preface, 233.

95. Genet, "Preface to *The Blacks*," preface, 234.

96. Genet, "Preface to *The Blacks*," preface, 229.

97. White, *Genet: A Biography*, 521–540.

98. See Mara De Gennaro, "What Remains of Jean Genet?" *The Yale Journal of Criticism* 16, no. 1 (2003): 195. De Gennaro writes: "Again and again in Genet's writing on revolution, it is the abstract concepts of rebellion and upheaval that loom large, and not any commitment to (or even faith in the possibility of) improving the lot of particular oppressed factions . . ." (195).

99. Rüdiger Wischenbart and Layla Shahid Barrada, "Interview with Rüdiger Wischenbart and Layla Shahid Barrada," in *The Declared Enemy: Texts and Interviews*, by Jean Genet (n.p.: Stanford University Press, 2004), 244.

100. Jean Genet, *Prisoner of Love*, trans. Barbara Bray (n.p.: Wesleyan University Press, 1992), 373.

101. See Jean Genet, "Violence and Brutality," in *The Declared Enemy: Texts and Interviews* (n.p.: Stanford University Press, 2004), 171–177.

102. Hansberry is quoted by Robert Nemiroff in "A Critical Background" to *Les Blancs* in *Collected Last Plays*, 27–35, 32.

103. Genet, *The Blacks*, 30.

104. Genet, *The Blacks*, 90.

105. Genet, "Preface to *The Blacks*," preface, 230.

106. This old tool in the racist kit was trotted out again by Dylann Roof, the white supremacist who opened fire at Emanuel African Methodist Episcopal Church in Charleston on June 17, 2015, killing nine people at a prayer circle.

107. Genet, "Preface to *The Blacks*," preface, 230.

Part II

1. *An Octoroon*, directed by Summer L. Williams, written by Branden Jacobs-Jenkins, produced by Company One and ArtsEmerson, Paramount Center, Boston, January 29–February 27, 2016.
2. Ramona Ostrowski, Dramaturg for Company One, interview by the author, Boston, MA, August 25, 2016. I am grateful for Ostrowski's informative interview.
3. Call for Applications by Company One, "C1 Street Team Member," September 23, 2015, accessed February 18, 2024, https://companyone.org/wp-content/uploads/2015/01/StreetTeamMember.pdf
4. Branden Jacobs-Jenkins, *An Octoroon* (New York: Dramatists Play Service, 2015), 23.
5. Call for Applications by Company One, "C1 Street."
6. Josephine Machon claims that in immersive theater, "The active decision-making and sensual involvement that is required [. . .] can be transformative on a number of levels; from the playful way in which a participant influences the shape of the event or physiologically, via the engagement of sensory awareness, to the radically transformative; transforming an individual psychologically or ideologically" (see Josephine Machon, *Immersive Theatres: Intimacy and Immediacy in Contemporary Performance* [Basingstoke: Palgrave Macmillan, 2013], 280). Jacobs-Jenkins's *An Octoroon* is not fully immersive, but it is on Machon's "scale of immersivity" in that the active vocal and physical audience participation influenced the tone and duration of some scenes (see Machon, *Immersive Theatres*, 93).

Chapter 2

1. Jacobs-Jenkins, *An Octoroon*, 14.
2. Dion Boucicault, "International Copyright," *The Musical World*, November 9, 1867, 758.
3. Dion Boucicault, "Suum Cuique, The Octoroon," *The Athenaeum*, December 7, 1861, 764–765. "Masks and Faces" was printed in the *London Journal* and *New York Tribune*.
4. For a discussion of Henry Ward Beecher's very theatrical mock slave auctions of young biracial girls and his fascinating disagreement with Boucicault about the danger of the theater, see Lisa Merrill's " 'May she read liberty in your eyes?' Beecher, Boucicault and the Representation and Display of Antebellum Women's Racially Indeterminate Bodies," *Journal of Dramatic Theory and Criticism* 26, no. 2 (2012): 127–144.
5. Emily Clark's *The Strange History of the American Quadroon: Free Women of Color in the Revolutionary Atlantic World* (Chapel Hill: University of North Carolina Press, 2013) explores the myths surrounding the tragic mulatto, the quadroon, and *plaçage* as they were linked to New Orleans and warns against trusting those myths as an accurate history of nineteenth-century mixed-race women's lives.
6. Acclaimed roles included Myles na Coppaleen in *The Colleen Bawn* (1860), Shaun the Post in *Arrah na Pogue* (1864), and Conn in *The Shaughraun* (*The Vagabond*) (1874).

7. Andrew Parkin, "Introduction," in *Selected Plays of Dion Boucicault*, by Dion Boucicault (Gerrards Cross, Buckinghamshire: Colin Smythe, 1987), 8. See also "Dion Boucicault Dead; Pneumonia Suddenly Ends a Wonderful Career. Career of the Most Conspicuous English Dramatist of the Nineteenth Century—His Plays," *The New York Times*, September 19, 1890, 5.

8. Jacobs-Jenkins, *An Octoroon*, 15.

9. Parkin, "Introduction," 8.

10. Parkin, "Introduction," 10.

11. Parkin, "Introduction," 11.

12. Four hundred is the number of plays cited in "Dion Boucicault Dead," 5.

13. Joseph Roach, *Cities of the Dead: Circum-Atlantic Performance* (New York: Columbia University Press, 1996), 217.

14. Roach, *Cities of the Dead*, 215.

15. Questions about genuine political engagement are prevalent in critical discussions of Boucicault and melodrama more generally. In their survey of "Melodramatic Slaves," *Modern Drama* 55, no. 4 (2012): 459–475, Dana Van Kooy and Jeffrey N. Cox note that melodramas and the antislavery movement arose in the same period and that slavery is a perfectly spectacular and sentimental subject for melodramas. Slavery provides the spectacle of bodies categorized by color and made to suffer, often in horrific scenes of torture. Kooy and Cox argue that melodramas like *The Octoroon* used the drama of slavery without encouraging abolitionist efforts. The form of melodrama rejects "emancipatory moves" because it reaffirms patriarchal and white supremacist orders in the end (see Kooy and Cox, "Melodramatic Slaves," 462). Joseph Roach suggests that the political engagement of Boucicault's "humble melodrama" is related to larger geohistorical phenomenon: "Two axes, one running north and south, the other east and west, intersect in Boucicault's play, as they once did in Louisiana: the former axis conjoins the river systems of the Mississippi basin with the Caribbean; the latter follows the path of national expansion conceived by Anglo-Americans as preordained" (see Roach, *Cities of the Dead*, 180).

16. Dion Boucicault, *Selected Plays of Dion Boucicault*, comp. and ed. Andrew Parkin (Gerrads Cross, Buckinghamshire: Colin Smythe, 1987), 139.

17. Boucicault, *Selected Plays*, 140–141.

18. "The Octoroon," *The New York Times*, December 15, 1859, 4.

19. Boucicault, *Selected Plays*, 145.

20. See Richard Dyer, *White: Essays on Race and Culture* (New York: Routledge, 1997), 52–56.

21. Boucicault, *Selected Plays*, 146.

22. Boucicault, *Selected Plays*, 146.

23. Boucicault, *Selected Plays*, 148.

24. For a similar claim, see Katy L. Chiles, "Blackened Irish and Brownfaced Amerindians: Constructions of American Whiteness in Dion Boucicault's *The Octoroon*." *Nineteenth Century Theatre and Film* 31, no. 2 (2004): 28–50.

25. Boucicault, *Selected Plays*, 143.

26. Boucicault, *Selected Plays*, 143.

27. Kathy L. Chiles, "Blackened Irish and Brownfaced Amerindians: Constructions of American Whiteness in Dion Boucicault's *The Octoroon*," *Nineteenth Century Theatre and Film* 31, no. 2 (2004): 36.

28. Nancy McGown Minor, *Turning Adversity to Advantage: The History of the Lipan Apaches of Texas and Northern Mexico, 1700–1900* (Lanham, MD: University Press of America, 2009), 159–163. McGown Minor titled the chapter on this period "Facing the Reservation: The Fourth Crisis Point in Lipan History, 1852–60."

29. "The Octoroon," *The New York Times*, December 15, 1859, 4.

30. Boucicault, *Selected Plays*, 143.

31. Boucicault, *Selected Plays*, 145, 155.

32. In his foundational study *The Melodramatic Imagination* (New Haven, CT: Yale University Press, 1976), Peter Brooks writes, "The mute role is in fact a virtuoso role . . . a role that demands of the actor a deployment of all his dramatic powers to convey meaning. As such, it is a special case, a hyperbolic instance, of a more extensive recourse to muteness in melodrama" (see Peter Brooks, *The Melodramatic Imagination Balzac, Henry James, Melodrama, and the Mode of Excess* [New Haven, CT: Yale University Press, 1976], 61). For the idea of Wahnotee as a mute character and much of my understanding of *The Octoroon*, I am grateful to Carolyn Williams whose graduate seminar on Victorian Theater and Theatricality introduced me to melodrama.

33. Boucicault, *Selected Plays*, 143.

34. Boucicault, *Selected Plays*, 143.

35. Boucicault, *Selected Plays*, 145.

36. Boucicault, *Selected Plays*, 145.

37. Boucicault, *Selected Plays*, 152.

38. Boucicault, *Selected Plays*, 152.

39. Boucicault, *Selected Plays*, 153.

40. Boucicault, *Selected Plays*, 154.

41. In the classic work *Realizations: Narrative, Pictorial, and Theatrical Arts in Nineteenth-Century England* (Princeton, NJ: Princeton University Press, 1983), Martin Meisel writes, "The fullest expression of a pictorial dramaturgy [in nineteenth-century theater] is the tableau, where the actors strike an expressive stance in a legible symbolic configuration that crystallizes a stage of the narrative as a situation, or summarizes and punctuates it" (see Martin Meisel, *Realizations: Narrative, Pictorial, and Theatrical Arts in Nineteenth-Century England* [Princeton, NJ: Princeton University Press, 1983], 45).

42. *Selected Plays of Dion Boucicault* does not include the typical stage directions, so here I cite from Dion Boucicault, "The Octoroon. A Play, in Four Acts," in *Dicks' London Acting Edition of Standard English Plays and Comic Dramas* (New York: De Witt House, 1859), accessed June 17, 2022, http://www2.latech.edu/~bmagee/louisiana_anthology/texts/boucicault/boucicault--octaroon.html.

43. Harley Erdman, "Caught in the 'Eye of the Eternal': Justice, Race, and the Camera, from 'The Octoroon' to Rodney King," *Theatre Journal* 45, no. 3 (1993): 337–338, https://doi.org/10.2307/3208358.

44. Boucicault, *Selected Plays*, 150.
45. Martin Meisel, *Realizations: Narrative, Pictorial, and Theatrical Arts in Nineteenth-Century England* (Princeton, NJ: Princeton University Press, 1983). J. B. Buckstone's melodrama *Jack Sheppard* (1839) was freely adapted from William Harrison Ainsworth's novel, but it closely followed George Cruikshank's illustrations, and the stage directions reference these images at least fourteen times as models for tableaux, set designs, and costumes (see Meisel, *Realizations: Narrative*, 247).
46. Meisel quotes an unidentified review of a dramatization of Charles Dickens's *Barnaby Rudge* from 1841 that describes the audience's very audible recognition of the pose: "It is scarcely necessary to detail a plot which is so well known and generally admired as Dickens's last novel, bearing this title, the tale being fully borne out in the drama here presented, in the most perfect and attractive manner, by a series of *tableaux vivans*, [sic] copied from the illustrations of the tale; these *tableaux* were the admiration of the audience, who testified their delight by the most enthusiastic applause" (see Meisel, *Realizations: Narrative*, 251).
47. On the question of authorship, see Dion Boucicault, "Suum Cuique, The Octoroon," *The Athenaeum*, December 7, 1861, 764–765.
48. "The Octoroon," 4.
49. "The Octoroon," 4.
50. Boucicault, *Selected Plays*, 169.
51. Alfred L. Nelson, Gilbert B. Cross, and Joseph Donohue, eds., "The Adelphi Theatre Calendar," The Adelphi Theatre Project: Graphics, Image for The Octoroon; or, Life in Louisiana, accessed June 17, 2022, https://www.umass.edu/AdelphiTheatreCalendar/img038c.htm; "Princess's Theatre—Posters—Theatre Posters, 1870–1900," National Library of Scotland, accessed June 17, 2022, http://digital.nls.uk/theatre-posters-1870-1900/pageturner.cfm?id=74561470.
52. Boucicault, *Selected Plays*, 150.
53. Boucicault, *Selected Plays*, 156.
54. Boucicault, *Selected Plays*, 156.
55. Boucicault, *Selected Plays*, 172.
56. Boucicault, *Selected Plays*, 173.
57. Boucicault, *Selected Plays*, 173.
58. Boucicault, *Selected Plays*, 173.
59. Boucicault, *Selected Plays*, 173.
60. For an analysis of the "attitude" and its relationship to group tableaux and other posed performances, see Carrie Preston, *Modernism's Mythic Pose: Gender, Genre, Solo Performance* (New York: Oxford University Press, 2011).
61. Erdman, "Caught in the 'Eye of the Eternal,'" 339–340.
62. Erdman, "Caught in the 'Eye of the Eternal,'" 343.
63. See Shawn Michelle Smith's *Photography on the Color Line: W.E.B. Dubois, Race and Visual Culture* (Durham, NC: Duke University Press, 2004), for a discussion of the role of photography in the construction of racist caricatures and scientific typologies. Smith analyzes the phenomena of criminal mugshots and lynching photographs as well as the antiracist uses of photography developed by W. E. B. DuBois. See also Amos Morris-Reich's *Race and Photography: Racial Photography as Scientific*

Evidence, 1876–1980 (Chicago: University of Chicago Press, 2016), for an analysis of photography's contributions to the so-called science of race, with close attention to the German and Jewish contexts.

Chapter 3

1. Ostrowski, interview by the author.
2. Jacobs-Jenkins, *An Octoroon*, 7.
3. Jacobs-Jenkins, *An Octoroon*, 8.
4. Jacobs-Jenkins, *An Octoroon*, 9.
5. Jacobs-Jenkins, *An Octoroon*, 7.
6. Jacobs-Jenkins, *An Octoroon*, 9.
7. Jacobs-Jenkins, *An Octoroon*, 9.
8. Lacy Warner, "An Octoroon: Reflections on a Play about Race, Performance, and the Performance of Race," *Brooklyn*, March 30, 2015, accessed June 17 2022, https://www.bkmag.com/2015/03/30/an-octoroon-reflections-on-a-play-about-race-performance-and-the-performance-of-race/.
9. *Village Voice* contributor, "Disgruntled Cast Member Issues Invite to P.S.122's Troubled Octoroon," *The Village Voice*, June 18, 2010, accessed June 17, 2022, https://www.villagevoice.com/2010/06/18/disgruntled-cast-member-issues-invite-to-p-s-122s-troubled-octoroon/. See the preview by Alexis Soloski, "Branden Jacobs-Jenkins Tries to Revive *The Octoroon*," *The Village Voice*, June 15, 2010, accessed August 14, 2022, https://www.villagevoice.com/2010/06/15/branden-jacobs-jenkins-tries-to-revive-the-octoroon/.
10. Warner, "An Octoroon."
11. Jacobs-Jenkins, *An Octoroon*, 9–10.
12. Jacobs-Jenkins, *An Octoroon*, 12.
13. Jacobs-Jenkins, *An Octoroon*, 9–10.
14. Jacobs-Jenkins, *An Octoroon*, 4.
15. Jacobs-Jenkins, *An Octoroon*, 15.
16. "Hi I'm Harsh," Harsh J. Gagoomal, accessed August 14, 2022, https://www.hiimharsh.com/about.
17. Jacobs-Jenkins, *An Octoroon*, 9–10.
18. Jacobs-Jenkins, *An Octoroon*, 9–10.
19. Jacobs-Jenkins, *An Octoroon*, 9–10. See Emily Clark, *The Strange History of the American Quadroon: Free Women of Color in the Revolutionary Atlantic World* (Chapel Hill: University of North Carolina Press, 2013) on myths of nineteenth-century mixed-race women. For a similar argument about the continuities of melodramas of race, see Linda Williams, *Playing the Race Card: Melodramas of Black and White from Uncle Tom to O.J. Simpson* (Princeton, NJ: Princeton University Press, 2002).
20. Jacobs-Jenkins, *An Octoroon*, 7.
21. Company One—Boston Theatre, "An Octoroon," An Octoroon at C1 Theatre, accessed June 17, 2022, https://companyone.org/production/an-octoroon-play/.

22. Don Aucoin, "A Revealing Mashup of the Present, Past in 'An Octoroon,'" *Boston Globe*, February 2, 2016, accessed June 17 2022, https://www.bostonglobe.com/arts/theater-dance/2016/02/02/revealing-mashup-present-and-past-octoroon/shVXIsO eWLiRg51XBzEBnM/ story.html.

23. Company One—Boston Theatre, "An Octoroon."

24. Jacobs-Jenkins, *An Octoroon*, 7.

25. Jacobs-Jenkins, *An Octoroon*, 26.

26. Jacobs-Jenkins, *An Octoroon*, 27.

27. Jacobs-Jenkins, *An Octoroon*, 27.

28. Jacobs-Jenkins, *An Octoroon*, 33.

29. Jacobs-Jenkins, *An Octoroon*, 33.

30. C1Dramaturgs, "Tableaux," *An Octoroon: A Rehearsal and Production Blog of Company One Theatre* (blog), entry posted January 14, 2016, accessed September 19, 2016, https://octorooncl.wordpress.com/2016/01/14/tableaux/. Another blog post reveals that they studied melodramatic poses in silent film for inspiration. See C1Dramaturgs, "Melodramatic Poses in Silent Films," *An Octoroon: A Rehearsal and Production Blog of Company One Theatre* (blog), entry posted January 22, 2016, accessed September 19, 2016, https://octorooncl.wordpress.com/2016/01/22/melod ramatic-poses-in-silent-film/.

31. Ostrowski, interview by the author.

32. Boucicault, *Selected Plays*, 150.

33. Jacobs-Jenkins, *An Octoroon*, 28.

34. Jacobs-Jenkins, *An Octoroon*, 28.

35. Jacobs-Jenkins, *An Octoroon*, 47.

36. Jacobs-Jenkins, *An Octoroon*, 47.

37. Jacobs-Jenkins, *An Octoroon*, 48.

38. Boucicault, *Selected Plays*, 172.

39. Boucicault, *Selected Plays*, 172; Jacobs-Jenkins, *An Octoroon*, 51.

40. Jacobs-Jenkins, *An Octoroon*, 50.

41. Jacobs-Jenkins, *An Octoroon*, 50.

42. Jacobs-Jenkins, *An Octoroon*, 51.

43. Shields's 2015 *Historical Fiction* series, including "Lynching," was exhibited at the Andrew Weiss Gallery. See Lilly Workneh, "This Striking Image of a Black Man Hanging a Klansman Shows a Different Side of America's Racist History," last modified May 19, 2015, accessed August 18, 2017, https://www.huffpost.com/entry/tyler-shields-lynching-photo_n_7310806.html.

44. Jacobs-Jenkins, *An Octoroon*, 51.

45. Jacobs-Jenkins, *An Octoroon*, 51.

46. Manfred Berg, *Popular Justice: A History of Lynching in America* (Lanham, MD: Rowman & Littlefield, 2011), 39–41.

47. A. N. Ogden, *Reports of Cases Argued and Determined in the Supreme Court of Louisiana, Vol. 14: For the Year 1859* (New Orleans: Office of the Price Current, 1860), 907.

48. The etymology of the term "lynch" is uncertain, but historians often link it to Colonel Charles Lynch of Virginia who established extralegal courts aimed at fighting

crime and loyalist activities during the American Revolution. See Berg, *Popular Justice*, 3. One of the first histories of lynching cited by historians is James Elbert Cutler's *Lynch-Law: An Investigation into the History of Lynching in the United States* (New York: Negro Universities Press, 1969).

49. Jacobs-Jenkins, *An Octoroon*, 47.
50. Jacobs-Jenkins, *An Octoroon*, 51.
51. Performance reports and my discussions with the dramaturg Ramona Ostrowski and other audience members revealed that, as Ostrowski claimed, "You could hear them catch their breath, their stomach drop. And they were silent for the rest of the show." Ostrowski, interview by the author.
52. Boucicault, *Selected Plays*, 171–174.
53. Jacobs-Jenkins, *An Octoroon*, 47.
54. Jacobs-Jenkins, *An Octoroon*, 48–49.
55. Jacobs-Jenkins, *An Octoroon*, 52.
56. Jacobs-Jenkins, *An Octoroon*, 52.
57. Damon Krometis, "The Dissonance of An Octoroon," editorial, HowlRound Theatre Commons, last modified April 17, 2016, accessed April 18, 2016, https://howlround.com/dissonance-octoroon.
58. Krometis, "The Dissonance," editorial, HowlRound Theatre Commons.
59. Jacobs-Jenkins, *An Octoroon*, 7.
60. Jacobs-Jenkins, *An Octoroon*, 7.
61. Krometis, "The Dissonance," editorial, HowlRound Theatre Commons.
62. Krometis, "The Dissonance," editorial, HowlRound Theatre Commons.
63. Roach, *Cities of the Dead*, 216–217.
64. Tiya Miles describes the sexualization of enslaved girls and women on the auction block in *All That She Carried: The Journey of Ashley's Sack, a Black Family Keepsake* (New York: Random, 2022), 184–189. See also Roach, *Cities of the Dead*, 216–217.
65. Jacobs-Jenkins, *An Octoroon*, 43.
66. Ostrowski, interview by the author.
67. Ostrowski, interview by the author.
68. Jacobs-Jenkins, *An Octoroon*, 31.
69. Krometis, "The Dissonance," editorial, HowlRound Theatre Commons.
70. Krometis, "The Dissonance," editorial, HowlRound Theatre Commons.
71. Krometis, "The Dissonance," editorial, HowlRound Theatre Commons.
72. Krometis, "The Dissonance," editorial, HowlRound Theatre Commons.
73. Ostrowski, interview by the author.
74. Ostrowski, interview by the author.
75. Boucicault, *Selected Plays*, 177.
76. Boucicault, *Selected Plays*, 177; Jacobs-Jenkins, *An Octoroon*, 56.
77. Jacobs-Jenkins, *An Octoroon*, 56.
78. Jacobs-Jenkins, *An Octoroon*, 56.
79. Boucicault, *Selected Plays*, 177; Jacobs-Jenkins, *An Octoroon*, 56.
80. Jacobs-Jenkins, *An Octoroon*, 4.
81. Jacobs-Jenkins, *An Octoroon*, 15.

82. Ostrowski quoted from performance reports, interview by the author.

83. Jacobs-Jenkins, *An Octoroon*, 19.

84. Jacobs-Jenkins, *An Octoroon*, 17.

85. "Congress.gov, "Voices from the Days of Slavery: Freed People Tell Their Stories," Library of Congress, accessed August 18, 2016, https://www.loc.gov/collections/voi ces-remembering-slavery/about-this-collection/.

86. For a clarifying and accessible source, see Walt Wolfram and Benjamin Torbert, "When Worlds Collide: The Linguistic Legacy of the African Slave Trade," PBS, accessed August 18, 2016, https://www.pbs.org/speak/seatosea/americanvarieties/ AAVE/worldscollide/#worlds. See also John Baugh, *Out of the Mouths of Slaves: African American Language and Educational Malpractice* (Austin: University of Texas Press, 1999); John R. Rickford and Russell J. Rickford, *Spoken Soul: The Story of Black English* (Hoboken, NJ: Wiley Press, 2000); Walt Wolfram, "The Sociolinguistic Construction of African American Language," in *The Oxford Handbook on African American Language*, ed. Sonja L. Lanehart (Oxford: Oxford University Press, 2015), 338–352; Walt Wolfram and Erik R. Thomas, *The Development of African American English* (Malden, MA: Blackwell, 2002).

87. Jacobs-Jenkins, *An Octoroon*, 19.

88. Jacobs-Jenkins, *An Octoroon*, 41.

89. Jacobs-Jenkins, *An Octoroon*, 42.

90. Ostrowski, interview by the author.

91. Holly L. Derr, "Branden Jacobs-Jenkins' *An Octoroon*," editorial, HowlRound Theatre Commons, last modified March 26, 2015, accessed August 18, 2016, https:// howlround.com/branden-jacobs-jenkins-octoroon.

92. Jacobs-Jenkins, *An Octoroon*, 9–10.

93. Jacobs-Jenkins, *An Octoroon*, 18.

94. See Cathy J. Cohen, "From Combahee to Black Lives Matter: Black Queer Politics, Yesterday, Today and Tomorrow," lecture presented at the Seventh Annual Eve Kosofsky Sedgwick Memorial Lecture in Gender and Sexuality Studies, Boston University, October 25, 2016, accessed February 5, 2017, https://www.bu.edu/hono ringeve/cohen/.

95. Jacobs-Jenkins, *An Octoroon*, 50.

96. Salman Aslam, "Instagram by the Numbers: Stats, Demographics & Fun Facts," *Omnicore* (blog), entry posted February 27, 2022, https://www.omnicoreagency. com/instagram-statistics/.

97. Jacobs-Jenkins, *An Octoroon*, 50.

98. Jacobs-Jenkins, *An Octoroon*, 51.

99. Police Activity, "Police Dashcam Footage of Philando Castile Fatal Shooting," YouTube, June 20, 2017, accessed June 26 2022, www.youtube.com/watch?v=PMKc Wz5nNoM.

100. The original post was taken down after over a million of views, but the footage is widely available. The first three minutes and two seconds are posted by McClatchy, "Girlfriend Live Streams on Facebook after Philando Castile Shot by Officer in Minnesota," *The Kansas City Star*, February 7, 2018, accessed August 11, 2022, https:// www.kansascity.com/news/local/crime/article103161887.html. Yousur Al-Hlou,

"Philando Castile, Diamond Reynolds, and a Nightmare Caught on Video," *The New York Times*, June 23, 2017, accessed August 11, 2022, https://www.nytimes.com/video/us/100000005181340/philando-castile-diamond-reynolds-and-a-nightmare-caught-on-video.html.

101. Claire Wardle, "How Did News Organisations Handle the Philando Castile Facebook Live Video?," *First Draft*, August 6, 2016, accessed June 25, 2018, https://medium.com/1st-draft/how-did-news-organisations-handle-the-philando-castile-facebook-live-video-549ff9a1da36.

102. Jacobs-Jenkins, *An Octoroon*, 50.

103. See Harley Erdman, "Caught in the 'Eye of the Eternal': Justice, Race, and the Camera, from 'The Octoroon' to Rodney King," *Theatre Journal* 45, no. 3 (1993): 333–348, https://doi.org/10.2307/3208358.

104. Jason Harrison, Eric Garner, John Crawford III, Kajieme Powell, twelve-year-old Tamir Rice, Jerame Reid, Charly Keunang, Phillip White, Walter Scott, Laquan McDonald, Christian Taylor, Samuel Dubose, Freddie Gray, and Walter L. Scott were all killed by police or died from their injuries in custody. For links to these graphic videos, see Damien Cave and Rochelle Oliver, "The Raw Videos That Have Sparked Outrage over Police Treatment of Blacks," *The New York Times*, July 7, 2016, accessed August 1, 2016, http://www.nytimes.com/interactive/2015/07/30/us/police-videos-race.html?r=0. See also Jaeah Lee and A. J. Vicens, "Here Are 13 Killings by Police Captured on Video in the Past Year," *Mother Jones*, May 20, 2015, accessed July 31, 2016, https://www.motherjones.com/politics/2015/05/police-shootings-caught-on-tape-video/.

105. Bowling Green State University Police Integrity Research Group, *On-Duty Shootings: Police Officers Charged with Murder or Manslaughter, 2005–2019*, by Philip M. Stinson, Sr. and Chloe A. Wentzlof, research brief no. 9, 2019, accessed June 18, 2022, https://www.bgsu.edu/ content/dam/BGSU/health-and-human-services/document/Criminal-Justice-Program/policeintegritylostresearch/-9-On-Duty-Shootings-Police-Officers-Charged-with-Murder-or-Manslaughter.pdf.

106. Bill Hutchinson, "Why Derek Chauvin's Sentencing Is a Rarity for the US Legal System," *ABC News*, June 25, 2021, accessed June 18, 2022, https://abc7news.com/why-derek-chauvins-sentencing-will-be-rarity-for-the-us-legal-system/10831170/.

107. Eric Levenson, "How Minneapolis Police First Described the Murder of George Floyd and What We Know Now," *CNN*, April 21, 2021, accessed June 18, 2022, https://www.cnn.com/2021/04/21/us/minneapolis-police-george-floyd-death/index.html.

108. The Pulitzer Prizes—Columbia University, "The 2021 Pulitzer Prize Winner in Special Citations and Awards: Darnella Frazier," The Pulitzer Prizes, accessed June 18, 2022, https://www.pulitzer.org/winners/darnella-frazier.

109. Jacobs-Jenkins, *An Octoroon*, 50.

110. Jacobs-Jenkins, *An Octoroon*, 50.

111. Jacobs-Jenkins, *An Octoroon*, 54.

112. Jacobs-Jenkins, *An Octoroon*, 5.

113. Dion Boucicault, "To the Editor of the *Times*," *The Times* (London), November 20, 1861, 5.

114. Anonymous, "Happy Endings," *The Saturday Review*, December 21, 1861, 633.

115. John A. Degen, "How to End 'The Octoroon,'" *Educational Theatre Journal* 27, no. 2 (1975): 172.

116. Degen, "How to End 'The Octoroon,'" 176.

117. Margaret Gray, "Spotlight Shines Brighter on 'Appropriate' Playwright Branden Jacobs-Jenkins," *Los Angeles Times*, September 24, 2015.

118. Gray, "Spotlight Shines."

Part III

1. Joanne B. Freeman points out that Hamilton was involved in no less than *ten* affairs of honor over the course of his life, although the others were negotiated without violence (see Joanne B. Freeman, "'Can We Get Back to Politics? Please?': Hamilton's Missing Politics in *Hamilton*," in *Historians on Hamilton: How a Blockbuster Musical is Restaging America's Past*, ed. Renee C. Romano and Claire Bond Potter [New Brunswick, NJ: Rutgers University Press, 2018], 53–54).

2. Jesse Lawrence, "'Hamilton' Is Broadway's Most Expensive Show—Ever," *The Daily Beast*, last modified May 3, 2016, accessed August 3, 2022, https://www.thedailybe ast.com/hamilton-is-broadways-most-expensive-showever?ref=scroll. See also Renee C. Romano and Claire Bond Potter, "Introduction: History Is Happening in Manhattan," introduction to *Historians on Hamilton: How a Blockbuster Musical Is Restaging America's Past*, ed. Renee C. Romano and Claire Bond Potter (New Brunswick, NJ: Rutgers University Press, 2018), 4.

3. Michael Paulsen, "'Shuffle Along' Decides It Can't Go on without Audra McDonald," *The New York Times*, June 23, 2016, accessed August, 3, 2022, https://www.nytimes. com/2016/06/24/theater/shuffle-along-decides-it-cant-go-on-without-audra-mcdonald.html.

4. Lee Seymour, "Thanksgiving Breaks Many Broadway Records, 'Hamilton' Takes Highest Gross in History," *Forbes*, November 28, 2016, accessed August 3, 2022, https://www.forbes.com/sites/leeseymour/2016/11/28/thanksgiving-breaks-all-broadway-records-hamilton-takes-highest-gross-in-history/#7f95f36d5b2a. See also Michael Paulson and David Gelles, "'Hamilton' Inc.: The Path to a Billion-Dollar Broadway Show," *The New York Times*, June 8, 2016, accessed August 3, 2022, https://www.nytimes.com/2016/06/12/theater/hamilton-inc-the-path-to-a-bill ion-dollar-show.html.

5. Miranda reports that he never expected that the audience's uproarious response to this line would drown out the next few: "So we added two bars just to absorb the reaction. Cheer still drowned 'em out. So we added four bars. Then it felt like we were asking for applause, and they delivered, and it was even worse. We went back to two bars and it is what it is. Why does it get such a delighted response? Because it's true." Lin-Manuel Miranda and Jeremy McCarter, *Hamilton: The Revolution: Being the Complete Libretto of the Broadway Musical, with a True Account of Its Creation, and Concise Remarks on Hip-Hop, the Power of Stories, and the New America* (New York: Grand Central Publishing, 2016), 121.

Chapter 4

1. Michael Paulsen, "'Shuffle Along' Decides It Can't Go on without Audra McDonald."

2. Rudin claimed, "The need for Audra to take a prolonged and unexpected hiatus from the show has determined the unfortunate inevitability of our running at a loss for significantly longer than the show can responsibly absorb." See Michael Paulson, "Decision to Close 'Shuffle Along' Is Debated along Broadway," *The New York Times*, June 24, 2016, accessed August 3, 2022, https://www.nytimes.com/2016/06/25/thea ter/decision-to-close-shuffle-along-is-debated-along-broadway.html.

3. Marissa Saravis, "Shuffle Along Down to the Courthouse: Broadway Producers Argue Actor's Pregnancy Is an Accident Worth $14 Million," *Fordham: Intellectual Property, Media & Entertainment Law Journal*, November 19, 2018, accessed August 3, 2022, http://www.fordhamiplj.org/2018/11/19/shuffle-along-down-to-the-cou rthouse-broadway-producers-argue-actors-pregnancy-is-an-accident-worth-14-million/.

4. Marc Hershberg, "Audra McDonald Stars in New Lawsuit," *Forbes*, November 14, 2016, accessed August 3, 2022, https://www.forbes.com/sites/marchershberg/2016/ 11/14/audra-mcdonald-stars-in-new-lawsuit/#374562ea54c2.

5. Michael Paulson, "'Shuffle Along' and Insurer Drop Pregnancy-Prompted Lawsuit," *The New York Times*, October 21, 2020, accessed August 3, 2022, https://www.nyti mes.com/2020/10/21/theater/shuffle-along-audra-mcdonald-insurer-pregnancy-lawsuit.html.

6. John Jeremiah Sullivan, "'Shuffle Along' and the Lost History of Black Performance in America," *The New York Times Magazine*, March 24, 2016, accessed August 3, 2022, https://www.nytimes.com/2016/03/27/magazine/shuffle-along-and-the-painful-hist ory-of-black-performance-in-america.html?emc=edit_th_20160327&nl=todayshe adlines&nlid=39002302&_r=1.

7. Joanna Dee Das reads the incident as an "ugly and gendered battle over a woman's body" that is in keeping with the lack of attention to dance, choreography, and women dancers in the production. See Joanna Dee Das, "Choreographic Ghosts: Dance and the Revival of *Shuffle Along*," *Dance Research Journal* 51, no. 3 (2019): 93.

8. I adopt I&D from a 2020 McKinsey report on the value of "inclusion and diversity" to reference a widespread cultural effort that is typically abbreviated differently in the theatrical and academic institutions I inhabit. See Sundiatu Dixon-Fyle et al., *Diversity Wins: How Inclusion Matters*, May 19, 2020, accessed August 6, 2022, https:// www.mckinsey.com/featured-insights/diversity-and-inclusion/diversity-wins-how-inclusion-matters.

9. See Dee Das, "Choreographic Ghosts."

10. Soraya Nadia McDonald, "On Broadway: There Is No 'Hamilton' without 'Shuffle Along,'" The Undefeated, last modified June 11, 2016, accessed August 3, 2022, https:// theundefeated.com/features/hamilton-shuffle-along-2016-tonys/.

11. For more detail on this history, see Meghan Pugh's "The Cakewalk, America's First National Dance," in *America Dancing: From the Cakewalk to the Moonwalk* (New Haven, CT: Yale University Press, 2015), 10–28, in addition to the monograph as a whole.

12. Eric Lott, *Love & Theft: Blackface Minstrelsy and the American Working Class* (New York: Oxford University Press, 1993). Megan Pugh argues that the cakewalk is "America's first national dance," a provocative and well-considered choice, but "firsts" are almost always problematic, especially when they exclude the art and culture of Native Americans or "first nations" peoples. See Pugh, *America Dancing*, 10.

13. Robert P. Nevin, "Stephen C. Foster and Negro Minstrelsy," *Atlantic Monthly* 20, no. 121 (1867): 610.

14. Nevin, "Stephen C. Foster," 608–609.

15. Nevin, "Stephen C. Foster," 608.

16. Nevin, "Stephen C. Foster," 608.

17. "Shillelagh" is the Irish word for an oak club associated with St. Patrick, and most versions of the song include a note of Irish nationalism; throughout the 1860s the Christy Minstrels sang "The Bonny Green Flag" to the tune of "Sprig of Shillelagh." See Robert Nowatzki, "Paddy Jumps Jim Crow: Irish-Americans and Blackface Minstrelsy," *Éire-Ireland* 41, no. 3&4 (2006): 178. Listen to the tune posted by the *Irish Traditional Music Archive* (Dublin, 2018). See "Sprig of Shillelagh; Untitled," MP3 audio, 02:55, *Irish Traditional Music Archive*, posted by Peter Wyper, 2018, accessed August 4, 2022, https://www.itma.ie/digital-library/sound/cid-232155. See also Nevin, "Stephen C. Foster," 608.

18. Nevin, "Stephen C. Foster," 608.

19. The extent to which Irish Americans used minstrel shows to pursue racist agendas and establish their own whiteness is debated. See Noel Ignatiev, *How the Irish Became White* (New York: Routledge, 1995), and Kevin Kenny, *The American Irish: A History* (New York: Routledge, 2016).

20. Nevin, "Stephen C. Foster," 609.

21. Nevin, "Stephen C. Foster," 609.

22. Nevin, "Stephen C. Foster," 609.

23. Nevin, "Stephen C. Foster," 610.

24. Nevin, "Stephen C. Foster," 609.

25. Nevin, "Stephen C. Foster," 608–609.

26. Robert Nowatzki's *Representing African Americans in Transatlantic Abolitionism and Blackface Minstrelsy* (Baton Rouge: Louisiana State University, 2010) argues that "despite the claims of nineteenth-century American cultural critics that minstrelsy was indigenous to the United States, blackface performance was not originally American." (See Robert Nowatzki, *Representing African Americans in Transatlantic Abolitionism and Blackface Minstrelsy* [Baton Rouge: Louisiana State University, 2010], 71). I certainly agree that all performance forms borrow, adapt, and appropriate from previous and "foreign" cultural productions, but it is also important to recognize that the nineteenth-century American minstrel show emerged from a particular historical moment and reflected the specific racial, gendered, and class-based anxieties of the United States.

27. Lott, *Love & Theft*, 59. See also James K. Kennard, Jr. "Who Are Our National Poets?" *Knickerbocker* 26, no. 4 (1845): 332–333.

28. Nowatzki, *Representing*, 71–76.

29. Lott, *Love & Theft*, 59. See also Kennard, Jr. "Who Are," 332–333.

30. Lott, *Love & Theft*, 20.

31. Lott, *Love & Theft*, 20.

32. Lott, *Love & Theft*, 20.

33. Lott, *Love & Theft*, 20.

34. There is rich literature considering the application of Judith Butler's idea of "performative gender construction" to racial identity categories. See Judith Butler, *Gender Trouble: Feminism and the Subversion of Identity* (New York: Routledge, 1999). Foundational works on racial performativity include the following: Louis F. Mirón and Jonathon Xavier Inda, "Race as a Kind of Speech Act," *Cultural Studies: A Research Annual* 5 (2000): 85–107; Nadine Ehlers, "Passing Phantasms/Sanctioning Performatives: (Re)Reading White Masculinity in Rhinelander v. Rhinelander," *Studies in Law, Politics, and Society* 27 (2003): 63–91; Nadine Ehlers, "'Black Is' and 'Black Ain't': Performative Revisions of Racial 'Crisis,'" *Culture, Theory & Critique* 47, no. 2 (2006): 149–163; John L. Jackson Jr., *Harlemworld: Doing Race and Class in Contemporary America* (New York: Oxford University Press, 2001). See especially John L. Jackson Jr., "White Harlem: Toward the Performative Limits of Blackness," in *Harlemworld: Doing Race and Class in Contemporary America* (New York: Oxford University Press, 2001).

35. Frederick Douglass, "Gavitt's Original Ethiopian Serenaders," in *The Life and Writings of Frederick Douglass*, ed. Philip S. Foner (New York: International Publishers, 1950–75), 1:142, previously published in *The North Star*, June 29, 1849.

36. Frederick Douglas, "The Hutchinson Family—Hunkerism," in *Uncle Tom's Cabin and American Culture*, ed. Stephan Railton and The University of Virginia (Charlottesville, VA: Stephen Railton; Institute for Advanced Technology in the Humanities; Electronic Text Center, 2005), previously published in *The North Star*, October 27, 1848, accessed August 4, 2022, http://utc.iath.virginia.edu/minstrel/miar03bt.html.

37. Douglass, "Gavitt's Original," in *The Life*, 1:142.

38. Douglass, "Gavitt's Original," in *The Life*, 1:142.

39. Douglass, "Gavitt's Original," in *The Life*, 1:141.

40. Douglass, "Gavitt's Original," in *The Life*, 1:141.

41. Douglass, "Gavitt's Original," in *The Life*, 1:141.

42. See Judith Butler, "Imitation and Gender Insubordination," in *Literary Theory: An Anthology*, ed. Julie Rivkin and Michael Ryan (Malden, MA: Blackwell, 2004), 722–730. "If heterosexuality is an impossible imitation of itself, an imitation that performatively constitutes itself as the original then the imitative parody of 'heterosexuality'—when and where it exists in gay cultures—is always and only an imitation of an imitation, a copy of a copy, for which there is no original." (See Judith Butler, "Imitation and Gender Insubordination," in *Literary Theory: An Anthology*, ed. Julie Rivkin and Michael Ryan [Malden, MA: Blackwell, 2004], 723–724.)

43. Douglass, "Gavitt's Original," in *The Life*, 1:142.

44. Jesse J. Holland, "Blackface, Explained: Why Ralph Northam, Mark Herring and Others Darkening Their Faces Is Such a Big Deal," *USA Today*, February 6, 2019, accessed August 4, 2022, https://www.usatoday.com/story/news/nation/2019/

02/06/blackface-offensive-why-explaining-ralph-northam-mark-herring/279 0475002/.

45. John Eligon, "Yearbook Pages at Northam's Medical School Recorded Both Memories and Prejudices," *The New York Times*, February 5, 2019, accessed August 4, 2022, https://www.nytimes.com/2019/02/05/us/northam-yearbook.html?mod ule=inline.

46. Jonathan Martin and Alan Blinder, "Second Virginia Democrat Says He Wore Blackface, Throwing Party into Turmoil," *The New York Times*, February 6, 2019, accessed March 19, 2019, https://www.nytimes.com/2019/02/06/us/politics/virgi nia-blackface-mark-herring.html?emc=edit_cn_20190207&emc=edit_cn_20190 209&nl=politics&nl=politics&nlid=39002302amp&te=1&te=1.

47. Holland, "Blackface, explained." See also Annika Neklason, "Blackface Was Never Harmless," *The Atlantic*, February 16, 2019, accessed August 4, 2022, https://www. theatlantic.com/entertainment/archive/2019/02/legacy-blackface-ralph-northam-didnt-understand/582733/.

48. Douglass, "The Hutchinson Family," in *Uncle Tom's*.

49. Holland, "Blackface, Explained."

50. See also Daphne A. Brooks, *Bodies in Dissent: Spectacular Performances of Race and Freedom, 1850–1910* (Durham, NC: Duke University Press, 2006).

51. Charles Musser, "Why Did Negroes Love Al Jolson and *The Jazz Singer*? Melodrama, Blackface and Cosmopolitan Theatrical Culture," *Film History: An International Journal* 23, no. 2 (2011): 196–222.

52. Email message to author, February 12, 2019, 2:57 pm.

53. Email message to author, February 12, 2019, 2:57 pm.

54. Email message to author, February 12, 2019, 2:57 pm.

55. See Robin DiAngelo, *White Fragility: Why It's So Hard for White People to Talk About Racism* (Boston: Beacon Press, 2018).

56. See Jean Stearns and Marshall Stearns, *Jazz Dance: The Story of American Vernacular Dance* (New York: Da Capo Press, 1968, 1994); Allen Woll, *Black Musical Theatre from Coontown to Dreamgirls* (Baton Rouge: Louisiana State University Press, 1989); David Krasner, *A Beautiful Pageant: African American Theatre, Drama, and Performance in the Harlem Renaissance, 1910–1927* (New York: Palgrave Macmillan, 2002).

57. Robert Kimball and William Bolcom, *Reminiscing with Noble Sissle and Eubie Blake* (New York: Cooper Square Press, 1973), 80.

58. Kimball and Bolcom, *Reminiscing with*, 43.

59. See David S. Thompson, "Shuffling Roles: Alterations and Audiences in *Shuffle Along*," in *Theatre Symposium, Vol. 20: Gods and Groundlings*, 97–108 (Tuscaloosa: University of Alabama Press, 2012). Thompson points out that "while their look may have been typical, even stereotypical, their materials set them apart. Miller and Lyles developed several routines that could easily be interpreted as either submissive or subversive, depending on the audience." (See David S. Thompson, "Shuffling Roles: Alterations and Audiences in Shuffle Along," in *Theatre Symposium, Vol. 20: Gods and Groundlings* [Tuscaloosa: University of Alabama Press, 2012], 100.)

60. Kimball and Bolcom, *Reminiscing with*, 86.

61. Kimball and Bolcom, *Reminiscing with*, 86.

62. Kimball and Bolcom, *Reminiscing with*, 86.

63. Brian D. Valencia, "Musical of the Month: Shuffle Along," *NYPL Blog*, entry posted February 10, 2012, accessed August 4, 2022, https://www.nypl.org/blog/2012/02/10/musical-month-shuffle-along.

64. See Lott, *Love & Theft*, for a description of the minstrel show's tripartite structure (6) and for an account of the black festival called "Election Day" (48). Scholars have overlooked this influence on *Shuffle Along*'s plot.

65. Noble Sissle et al., *Shuffle Along*, ed. Lyn Schenbeck and Lawrence Schenbeck, *Music of the United States of America; Recent Researches in American Music* 29; 85 (Middleton, WI: A-R Editions, 2018), 312.

66. Sissle et al., *Shuffle Along*, 313.

67. "'Shuffle Along' Premiere: Negro Production Opens at Sixty Third Street," *The New York Times*, May 23, 1921, 20.

68. "'Shuffle Along' Premiere: Negro Production Opens at Sixty Third Street," *The New York Times*, May 23, 1921, 20.

69. Kimball and Bolcom, *Reminiscing with*, 94.

70. Kimball and Bolcom, *Reminiscing with*, 232–233.

71. George Jean Nathan, "The Lesson of Another Failure," in *Reminiscing with Noble Sissle and Eubie Blake*, ed. Robert Kimball and William Bolcom (New York: Cooper Square Press, 1973), 235, previously published in *New York Journal-American*, May 25, 1952.

72. Nathan, "The Lesson," in *Reminiscing with*, 235.

73. Kimball and Bolcom, *Reminiscing with*, 232, 38.

74. Dee Das, "Choreographic Ghosts," 87.

75. Dee Das, "Choreographic Ghosts," 85.

76. Alan Dale, "'Shuffle Along' Full of Pep and Real Melody," in *Reminiscing with Noble Sissle and Eubie Blake*, ed. Robert Kimball and William Bolcom (New York: Cooper Square Press, 1973), 99, previously published in *New York Journal-American*.

77. David Savran, *Highbrow/Lowdown: Theater, Jazz, and the Making of the New Middle Class* (Ann Arbor: University of Michigan Press, 2009), 74.

78. Sissle et al., *Shuffle Along*, 106.

79. See Alfred Appel, *Jazz Modernism: From Ellington and Armstrong to Matisse and Joyce* (New Haven, CT: Yale University Press, 2004); Charles A. Riley, *Free as Gods: How the Jazz Age Reinvented Modernism* (Lebanon, NH: University Press of New England, 2017).

80. Sissle et al., *Shuffle Along*, 129–130.

81. See Savran, *Highbrow/Lowdown*. Focusing on the number "Bandana Days," Savran argues, "The piece can be interpreted as it was on opening night by Alan Dale as a simple, 'jolly' 'darky' 'musical comedy' performed by actors who 'reveled in their work.' Or it can be seen, as it doubtlessly was by many African Americans in the audience, as an ironic reinvention of a racist formula that freely appropriates and satirizes the conventions of both minstrelsy and musical comedy" (see Savran, *Highbrow/Lowdown*, 75).

82. Lott claims, "Most of them [minstrel performers] were minor, apolitical theatrical men of the northern artisanate who pursued a newly available bourgeois dream of freedom and play by paradoxically coding themselves as 'black.' Marginalized by temperament, by habit (often alcoholism), by ethnicity, even by sexual orientation, these artists immersed themselves in 'blackness' to indulge their felt sense of difference" (see Lott, *Love & Theft*, 53).

83. Sissle et al., *Shuffle Along*, 131, 110.

84. Kimball and Bolcom, *Reminiscing with*, 95.

85. Sissle et al., *Shuffle Along*, 126–127.

86. The number from the film is available on YouTube. See "Judy Garland & Gene Kelly—Ballin' the Jack," video, 02:51, YouTube, posted by Ohujapaksu, June 26, 2013, accessed August 4, 2022, https://video.search.yahoo.com/yhs/search?fr=yhs-Lkry-SF01&hsimp=yhs-SF01&hspart=Lkry&p=ballin+the+jack+famous+performance#id=1&vid=886739ef47a340dc32bc9148be028e34&action=click.

87. Sissle et al., *Shuffle Along*, 381–383.

88. Critic George Jean Nathan recounts in his pan of the 1952 revival of *Shuffle Along* that the 1921 original "set Scott Fitzgerald to dancing in the aisle with one of the girl ushers" (see Nathan, "The Lesson of," in *Reminiscing with*, 235).

89. A clip of Adrienne Warren's Tony-nominated performance is available on YouTube. See "I'm Simply Filled with Jazz," audio, 02:44, YouTube, posted by Marco Dog, December 18, 2016, accessed August 6, 2022, https://www.youtube.com/watch?v=C0kZleE4dh8.

90. Sissle et al., *Shuffle Along*, 126–127.

91. Dee Das, "Choreographic Ghosts," 87.

92. Charles McNulty, "How 'Shuffle Along' Director George C. Wolfe Brought Back the 1921 Show That Changed Broadway Forever," *The Los Angeles Times*, April 25, 2016, accessed August 6, 2022, http://www.latimes.com/entertainment/arts/theater/la-et-cm-george-wolfe-20160425-column.html.

93. Thompson, "Shuffling Roles," in *Theatre Symposium*, 97–108. *Shuffle Along* is often credited as having desegregated the Broadway audience, but David S. Thompson points to "caveats": "Whereas blacks had customarily been restricted to the balcony, the critic for *Variety* noted with apparent surprise that 'colored patrons were noticed as far front as the fifth row' on opening night. In fact, ticketing remained decidedly restricted. Two-thirds of the orchestra seating was available to whites only. *Variety* reassured its readers that 'the two races are rarely intermingled'" (see Thompson, "Suffling Roles," in *Theatre Symposium*, 25).

94. Savran, *Highbrow/Lowdown*, 72.

95. McNulty, "How 'Shuffle Along.'"

96. See Jean Stearns and Marshall Stearns, *Jazz Dance: The Story of American Vernacular Dance* (New York: Da Capo Press, 1968, 1994); Allen Woll, *Black Musical Theatre from Coontown to Dreamgirls* (Baton Rouge: Louisiana State University Press, 1989); David Krasner, *A Beautiful Pageant: African American Theatre, Drama, and Performance in the Harlem Renaissance, 1910–1927* (New York: Palgrave Macmillan, 2002).

97. Sullivan, "'Shuffle Along.'"

98. Sullivan, "'Shuffle Along.'"

99. Kristin Moriah, "Shuffle and Repeat: A Review of George C. Wolfe's *Shuffle Along*," *American Quarterly* 69, no. 1 (March 2017): 184.

100. Andrew Prokop, "Trump Fanned a Conspiracy about Obama's Birthplace for Years. Now He Pretends Clinton Started It," *Vox*, last modified September 16, 2016, accessed September 16, 2019, https://www.vox.com/2016/9/16/12938066/donald-trump-obama-birth-certificate-birther.

101. Obama was not always successful at inclusion; he was roundly criticized and dubbed "deporter in chief" for the precipitous rise in the number of deportations during his presidency, although the increase was partially related to a redefinition of the term "deportation." See Anna O. Law, "Lies, Damned Lies, and Obama's Deportation Statistics," *The Washington Post*, April 21, 2014, accessed August 6, 2022, https://www.washingtonpost.com/news/monkey-cage/wp/2014/04/21/lies-damned-lies-and-obamas-deportation-statistics/?utm_term= .5c8032788763cage/wp/2014/04/21/lies-damned-lies-and-obamas-deportation-statistics/?utm_term= .69609d240108.

102. Sissle et al., *Shuffle Along*, 170.

103. 7:23 a.m. October 15, 2016.

104. Anthony Smith, "Donald Trump's Star of David Hillary Clinton Meme Was Created by White Supremacists," *Mic*, last modified July 3, 2016, accessed September 16, 2019, https://www.mic.com/articles/147711/donald-trump-s-star-of-david-hillary-clinton-meme-was-created-by-white-supremacists.

105. Sissle et al., *Shuffle Along*, 170–171.

106. Sissle et al., *Shuffle Along*, lxxii.

107. Sissle et al., *Shuffle Along*, lxxii.

108. Lyn Schenbeck and Lawrence Schenbeck note, "The lyrics were undoubtedly 'read' in various ways and 'seen' variously as well, depending on the performers' visual presentation" (Sissle et al., *Shuffle Along*, lxxii).

109. Robert B. Waltz, ed., "Old Black Joe," *The Minnesota Heritage Songbook*, accessed August 6, 2022, https://mnheritagesongbook.net/the-songs/addition-song-without-recordings/old-black-joe/.

110. Sissle et al., *Shuffle Along*, 183–184.

111. Schenbeck and Schenbeck claim, "Many whites respected Washington's achievements as well, so a reference to him in the show, even in a comic number, may not have registered as racist humor" (Sissle et al., *Shuffle Along*, lxxii).

112. Amy Gardner, Kate Rabinowitz, and Harry Stevens, "How GOP-Backed Voting Measures Could Create Hurdles for Tens of Millions of Voters," *The Washington Post*, March 11, 2021, accessed August 6, 2022, https://www.washingtonpost.com/politics/interactive/2021/voting-restrictions-republicans-states/.

113. Matt Apuzzo and Sharon LaFraniere, "13 Russians Indicted as Mueller Reveals Effort to Aid Trump Campaign," *The New York Times*, February 16, 2018, accessed August 6, 2022, https://www.nytimes.com/2018/02/16/us/politics/russians-indicted-mueller-election-interference.html.

Chapter 5

1. Rhian Daly, "'Hamilton' Just Broke Another Record," NME, last modified March 6, 2018, accessed August 6, 2022, https://www.nme.com/news/hamilton-just-broke-another-record-2255970.
2. Seymour, "Thanksgiving Breaks," *Forbes*. In the last week of December in 2018, *Hamilton* grossed over $4 million. See Michael Paulson, "'Hamilton Leads a Record-Breaking Holiday Week on Broadway," *The New York Times*, January 2, 2019, accessed August 6, 2022, https://www.nytimes.com/2019/01/02/theater/broadway-grosses-hamilton-record.html.
3. Christopher Mele and Patrick Healy, "'Hamilton' Had Some Unscripted Lines for Pence. Trump Wasn't Happy," *The New York Times*, November 19, 2016, accessed March 10, 2019, https://www.nytimes.com/2016/11/19/us/mike-pence-hamil ton.html.
4. Mele and Healy, "'Hamilton' Had."
5. "The business case for inclusion and diversity (I&D)" was influentially articulated by McKinsey & Company in a series of reports; I use McKinsey's acronym, in part, because my institutions tend to use DEI (diversity, equity, and inclusion) or D&I (diversity and inclusion). I&D therefore allows me to reference the "case" for diversity and its benefits for institutions in terms of capital and cultural capital, while differentiating I&D somewhat from the work in which I participate and regularly find full of challenges and limitations yet absolutely necessary. See Sundiatu Dixon-Fyle et al., *Diversity Wins: How Inclusion Matters*, May 19, 2020, accessed August 6, 2022, https://www.mckinsey.com/featured-insights/diversity-and-inclusion/diversity-wins-how-inclusion-matters.
6. Fox 13 News, "Mike Pence on Being Booed at 'Hamilton' Showing: 'That's What Freedom Sounds Like," Fox 13: Salt Lake City, last modified November 20, 2016, accessed August 6, 2022, https://www.fox13now.com/2016/11/20/mike-pence-on-being-booed-at-hamilton-showing-thats-what-freedom-sounds-like/.
7. Mele and Healy, "'Hamilton' Had."
8. Mele and Healy, "'Hamilton' Had."
9. Mele and Healy, "'Hamilton' Had."
10. NPR Staff, "Trump's 2016 Victory Speech, Annotated 1 Year Later," NPR, last modified November 7, 2017, accessed August 6, 2022, https://www.npr.org/2017/11/07/561597910/trumps-2016-victory-speech-annotated-1-year-later.
11. NPR Staff, "Trump's 2016," NPR.
12. Mele and Healy, "'Hamilton' Had." The tweets from @realDonaldTrump were posted on November 19, 2016 at 8:48 am and 8:56 am. See Donald Trump (@realDonaldTrump), "Our wonderful future V.P. Mike Pence was harassed last night at the theater by the cast of Hamilton, cameras blazing. This should not happen!," Twitter, November 19, 2016, 8:48 a.m.
13. Donald Trump (@realDonaldTrump), "The Theater must always be a safe and special place. The cast of Hamilton was very rude last night to a very good man, Mike Pence. Apologize!," Twitter, November 19, 2016, 8:56 a.m.

14. Jayme Deerwester, "Social Media Explodes over 'Hamilton'/Trump Duel," *USA Today*, November 19, 2016; updated November 20, 2016, accessed August 6, 2022, https://www.usatoday.com/story/life/theater/2016/11/19/social-media-explodes-over-hamiltontrump-duel/94129798/.

15. CNN Wire, "Pence: 'I Wasn't Offended' by Message of 'Hamilton' Cast," Fox 17: West Michigan, last modified November 20, 2016, accessed August 6, 2022, https://www.fox17online.com/2016/11/20/pence-i-wasnt-offended-by-message-of-hamilton-cast.

16. Deerwester, "Social Media Explodes."

17. NPR Staff, "Trump's 2016," NPR.

18. CNN Wire, "Pence"; Trump, "The Theater," Twitter; Peggy McGlone, "For Third Year in a Row, Trump's Budget Plan Eliminates Arts, Public TV and Library Funding," *The Washington Post*, March 18, 2019, accessed August 6, 2022, https://www.washingtonpost.com/lifestyle/style/for-third-year-in-a-row-trumps-budget-plan-eliminates-arts-public-tv-and-library-funding/2019/03/18/e946db9a-49a2-11e9-9663-00ac73f49662_story.html.

19. CNN Wire, "Pence."

20. Brian Eugenio Herrera, "Looking at *Hamilton* from Inside the Broadway Bubble," in *Historians on Hamilton: How a Blockbuster Musical Is Restaging America's Past*, ed. Renee C. Romano and Claire Bond Potter (New Brunswick, NJ: Rutgers University Press, 2018), 222–248.

21. Mathew Rodriguez, "HIV Needs to Be Part of the Conversation When We Talk about Mike Pence and 'Hamilton,'" Mic, last modified November 22, 2016, accessed August 6, 2022, https://www.mic.com/articles/160080/hiv-needs-to-be-a-part-of-the-conversation-when-we-talk-about-mike-pence-and-hamilton.

22. "The Pence Agenda for the 107th Congress: A Guide to Renewing the American Dream," Mike Pence for Congress, accessed August 6, 2022, http://web.archive.org/web/20010519165033fw_/http://cybertext.net/pence/issues.html.

23. Steven W. Thrasher, "Mike Pence Is Still to Blame for an HIV Outbreak in Indiana—but for New Reasons," *The Nation*, October 4, 2018, accessed August 6, 2022, https://www.thenation.com/article/archive/mike-pence-is-still-to-blame-for-an-hiv-outbreak-in-indiana-but-for-new-reasons/.

24. Mele and Healy, "'Hamilton' Had." While Dixon discouraged the audience from booing and encouraged them to record and post his statement, he read scripted lines.

25. Dixon-Fyle et al., *Diversity Wins*.

26. Sara Ahmed, *On Being Included: Racism and Diversity in Institutional Life* (Durham, NC: Duke University Press, 2012), 52–53.

27. Ahmed, *On Being Included*, 57.

28. Ahmed, *On Being Included*, 57.

29. See Susan Strum, Time Eatman, John Saltmarsh, and Adam Bush's catalyst paper "Full Participation: Building the Architecture for Diversity and Community Engagement in Higher Education," September 2011, accessed September 12, 2022, https://surface.syr.edu/cgi/viewcontent.cgi?article=1001&context=ia. They argue, "Full participation is an affirmative value focused on creating institutions that enable

people, whatever their identity, background, or institutional position, to thrive, realize their capabilities, engage meaningfully in institutional life, and contribute to the
flourishing of others (Strum 2006, 2010). This concept offers a holistic set of goals
that focus attention on (1) the institutional conditions that enable people in different roles to flourish, and (2) the questions designed to mobilize change at the multiple levels and leverage points where change is needed (3)" (Susan Strum et al., *Full
Participation: Building the Architecture for Diversity and Community Engagement
in Higher Education*, 2011, accessed September 12, 2022, https://surface.syr.edu/
cgi/viewcontent.cgi?article=1001&context=ia). See also Susan Strum, "Activating
Systemic Change Toward Full Participation: The Pivotal Role of Mission-Driven
Institutional Intermediaries," *Saint Louis Law Journal* 54 (2010): 1117–1137.

30. See Michael Paulson, "'Hamilton' Producers Will Change Job Posting, but Not
Commitment to Diverse Casting," *The New York Times*, March 30, 2016, accessed
August 6, 2022, https://www.nytimes.com/2016/03/31/arts/union-criticizes-hamil
ton-casting-call-seeking-nonwhite-actors.html.

31. Kate Shindle, "'Hamilton' Casting Controversy Spotlights the Importance of
Diversity," *Variety*, April 5, 2016, accessed August 6, 2022, https://variety.com/2016/
legit/opinion/hamilton-diversity-casting-actors-equity-guest-column-1201745244/.

32. Quoted in Paulson, "'Hamilton' Producers Will Change Job Posting."

33. Quoted in Paulson, "'Hamilton' Producers Will Change Job Posting."

34. Jon Birger, "'Hamilton' Cast Lectures VP-Elect While Barring Immigrant Actors from
Broadway Roles: Pence-Scolding Musical Star Needs a Lesson on AEA Immigrant
Policy," *The Observer*, November 25, 2016, accessed August 6, 2022, https://observer.
com/2016/11/hamilton-cast-lectures-vp-elect-while-barring-immigrant-actors-
from-broadway-roles/. See Mele and Healy, "'Hamilton' Had."

35. Birger, "'Hamilton' Cast Lectures."

36. Andrew Gans, "The U.K. Evening Times Reports That 11-Year-Old Sam Angell, Who
Had Successfully Auditioned to Play the Role of Boy Tarzan in the Upcoming Disney
Musical *Tarzan*, May Not Be Permitted to Do Do Because He Is Not an American
Citizen," *Playbill*, October 14, 2005, accessed August 6, 2022, http://www.playbill.
com/article/report-actors-equity-blocks-angell-from-broadway-tarzan-com-128612.

37. Birger, "'Hamilton' Cast Lectures."

38. Birger, "'Hamilton' Cast Lectures."

39. Miranda and McCarter, *Hamilton: The Revolution*, 121.

40. Leslie M. Harris, "The Greatest City in the World? Slavery in New York in the Age
of Hamilton," in *Historians on Hamilton: How a Blockbuster Musical Is Restaging
America's Past*, ed. Renee C. Romano and Claire Bond Potter (New Brunswick,
NJ: Rutgers University Press, 2018), 71.

41. Harris, "The Greatest City," 78.

42. Harris, "The Greatest City," 76.

43. Harris, "The Greatest City," 78.

44. Miranda and McCarter, *Hamilton: The Revolution*, 17.

45. Harris, "The Greatest City," 80.

46. Miranda and McCarter, *Hamilton: The Revolution*, 45.

47. Miranda and McCarter, *Hamilton: The Revolution*, 45.

48. Lyra D. Monteiro, "Race-Conscious Casting and the Erasure of the Black Past in *Hamilton*" in *Historians on Hamilton: How a Blockbuster Musical Is Restaging America's Past*, ed. Renee C. Romano and Claire Bond Potter (New Brunswick, NJ: Rutgers University Press, 2018), 64.

49. Miranda and McCarter, *Hamilton: The Revolution*, 152.

50. Michael Paulson, "As Broadway Returns, Shows Rethink and Restage Depictions of Race," *The New York Times*, October 23, 2021, accessed August 6, 2022, https://www.nytimes.com/2021/10/23/theater/broadway-race-depictions.html.

51. Paulson, "As Broadway Returns."

52. Miranda and McCarter, *Hamilton: The Revolution*, 161.

53. Monteiro, "Race-Conscious," 65; Harris, "The Greatest City," 85.

54. George Ip, "Fans of Aaron Burr Find Unlikely Ally In a 'New' Relative," *The Wall Street Journal*, October 5, 2005, accessed August 6, 2022, https://www.wsj.com/articles/SB112847391696860205.

55. Hannah Natanson, "Aaron Burr—Villain of 'Hamilton'—Had a Secret Family of Color, New Research Shows," *The Washington Post*, August 24, 2019, accessed August 6, 2022, https://www.washingtonpost.com/history/2019/08/24/aaron-burr-villain-hamilton-had-secret-family-color-new-research-shows/.

56. Monteiro, "Race-Conscious," 66.

57. Monteiro, "Race-Conscious," 58–70.

58. Monteiro, "Race-Conscious," 60.

59. Miranda and McCarter, *Hamilton: The Revolution*, 159.

60. Lyra D. Monteiro claims that the ethnicity of actors aligns with the predominant musical styles their characters sing, although this was primarily true of the original rather than subsequent casts (see Monteiro, "Race-Conscious"). The role of the fast-rapping Angelica Schuyler was created by Black women, Anika Noni Rose, Renée Elise Goldsberry, and Emmy Raver-Lampman (in the first US tour). Hamilton's wife, Eliza Schuyler Hamilton, sings more traditional Broadway songs and was played by a woman of color who was not of African descent: Ana Nogueira (Workshop) is Brazilian, Philipa Soo (Off- and On-Broadway) is Chinese American, Solea Pfeiffer (first US tour) identifies as "mixed," Arianna Afsar (Chicago) is Bangladeshi American, Shoba Narayan (second US tour) is South Asian American, Julia K. Harriman (Puerto Rico/San Francisco) is biracial with Asian heritage, and Victoria Ann Scovens (San Francisco) lists her ethnicities as ethnically ambiguous, multiracial.

61. Miranda and McCarter, *Hamilton: The Revolution*, 49.

62. Miranda and McCarter, *Hamilton: The Revolution*, 49.

63. Miranda and McCarter, *Hamilton: The Revolution*, 57.

64. Miranda and McCarter, *Hamilton: The Revolution*, 23.

65. Miranda and McCarter, *Hamilton: The Revolution*, 72.

66. Miranda and McCarter, *Hamilton: The Revolution*, 26.

67. Miranda and McCarter, *Hamilton: The Revolution*, 26–27. See also Catherine Allgor, "'Remember . . . I'm Your Man': Masculinity, Marriage, and Gender in *Hamilton*," in *Historians on Hamilton: How a Blockbuster Musical Is Restaging America's Past*, ed.

Renee C. Romano and Claire Bond Potter (New Brunswick, NJ: Rutgers University Press, 2018), 94–118.

68. Miranda and McCarter, *Hamilton: The Revolution*, 70.

69. Miranda and McCarter, *Hamilton: The Revolution*, 70.

70. Ron Chernow, *Alexander Hamilton* (New York: Penguin Books, 2004), 95.

71. Hamilton to Laurens, quoted in Chernow, *Alexander Hamilton*, 123.

72. Chernow, *Alexander Hamilton*, 124.

73. Elaine Atwell, "Alexander Hamilton Was Probably Queer," *The Dart*, last modified January 30, 2017, accessed August 6, 2022, https://www.thedart.co/2017/01/30/alexander-hamilton-was-probably-queer/. For a more balanced discussion of Hamilton's sexuality, see Caroline V. Hamilton, "The Erotic Charisma of Alexander Hamilton," particularly the section "Too Pretty to be Straight? Hamilton as Gay Icon." *Journal of American Studies* 45, no. 1 (February 2011): 1–19. Available on *Cambridge Core* at https://www.cambridge.org/core/journals/journal-of-american-studies/article/erotic-charisma-of-alexander-hamilton/BC911E604C376A4F3CCBFB6F3731B3A0/core-reader.

74. Chernow, *Alexander Hamilton*, 95.

75. Chernow, *Alexander Hamilton*, 95.

76. Chernow, *Alexander Hamilton*, 133.

77. Miranda and McCarter, *Hamilton: The Revolution*, 70.

78. Miranda and McCarter, *Hamilton: The Revolution*, 70; Chernow, *Alexander Hamilton*, 95.

79. Miranda and McCarter, *Hamilton: The Revolution*, 44.

80. Miranda and McCarter, *Hamilton: The Revolution*, 44.

81. Miranda and McCarter, *Hamilton: The Revolution*, 43.

82. Miranda and McCarter, *Hamilton: The Revolution*, 43.

83. Miranda and McCarter, *Hamilton: The Revolution*, 43.

84. Miranda and McCarter, *Hamilton: The Revolution*, 44.

85. Allgor, " 'Remember . . . ,' " 94–118.

86. The lyrics and a version of Cabinet Battle #3 are available at https://genius.com/Lin-manuel-miranda-cabinet-battle-3-lyrics. Miranda claimed that "it was tough to justify keeping that rap battle in the show, because none of them did enough" and it is not correct "to say Hamilton was the anti-slavery crusader." Chris Hayes, "Billboard Cover: 'Hamilton' Creator Lin-Manuel Miranda, Questlove, and Black Thought on the Runaway Broadway Hit, Its Political Relevance and Super-Fan Barack Obama," *Billboard*, July 30, 2015, accessed August 6, 2022, https://www.billboard. com/articles/news/magazine-feature/6648455/hamilton-lin-manuel-miranda-questlove-black-thought-the-roots-chris-hayes-interview.

87. See the original comic at Neda Ulaby, "The 'Bechdel Rule,' Defining Pop-Culture Character" (initially heard on *All Things Considered*), NPR, last modified September 2, 2008, accessed August 6, 2022, https://www.npr.org/templates/story/story.php?storyId=94202522?storyId=94202522.

88. Mele and Healy, " 'Hamilton' Had."

89. Miranda and McCarter, *Hamilton: The Revolution*, 16.

90. Paulson and Gelles, "'Hamilton' Inc."; Eliza Berman, "*Hamilton* Nation: It Conquered Broadway. Next Stop, The World," *Time*, October 10, 2016, 51-54; Harry Cheadle, "It's Time to Tear Down the 'Hamilton' Parody Industrial Complex," *Vice*, July 4, 2016, accessed August 6, 2022, https://www.vice.com/en_us/article/vdqgqd/trump-hamilton-jokes-are-obvious.

91. For a summary of *Hamilton*'s social media performances, see Claire Bond Potter, "'Safe in the Nation We've Made': Staging *Hamilton* on Social Media," in *Historians on Hamilton: How a Blockbuster Musical Is Restaging America's Past*, ed. Renee C. Romano and Claire Bond Potter (New Brunswick, NJ: Rutgers University Press, 2018), 324–350.

92. Jesse Lee, "Poetry, Music and Spoken Word," *The White House: President Barack Obama* (blog), entry posted May 12, 2009, accessed August 6, 2022, https://obamawhitehouse.archives.gov/blog/2009/05/12/poetry-music-and-spoken-word. See also "Lin-Manuel Miranda Performs at the White House Poetry Jam: (8 of 8)," video, YouTube, posted by The Obama White House, November 2, 2009, accessed August 6, 2022, https://www.youtube.com/watch?v=WNFf7nMIGnE.

93. Romano and Potter, "Introduction," 4–5. See also "Alexander Hamilton," audio, 03:56, YouTube, posted by Usnavi, April 20, 2017, accessed August 6, 2022, https://www.youtube.com/watch?v=VhinPd5RRJw&list=PL-krihKw82nf_RrmGLyUxINL6jLxButQi.

94. Potter, "'Safe in the Nation," 326.

95. Potter, "'Safe in the Nation," 326.

96. Potter, "'Safe in the Nation," 326.

97. Potter claims, "To be perceived as truly authentic, the social media celebrity has to enjoy, and feed off of, the connection to fans, and Miranda clearly does. His tweets and video posts are remarkable for their playfulness, intentionality, humor, and sweetness" (Potter, "Safe in the Nation," 327). While Miranda quite likely does enjoy connecting with fans, his social media personality is still a cultivated performance.

98. Forrest Wickman, "The Show Is Nonstop: Ham4Ham, the joyous, free sidewalk performances outside *Hamilton* that are stoking the passions of a new generation of theater lovers," *Slate*, November 24, 2015, accessed August 6, 2022, https://slate.com/culture/2015/11/ham4ham-lin-manuel-miranda-and-the-cast-of-hamilton-reward-ticket-lottery-entrants-with-free-shows.html.

99. See "#Ham4Ham Complete (?) Chronological July 2015–2016," video playlist, YouTube, posted by Jane, February 4, 2022, accessed August 7, 2022, https://www.youtube.com/playlist?list=PLb1ayNIj3f8o2-ZVuklNfYxrGPwkKBzjs. See also "Lin-Manuel Miranda, How He Met Jonathan," video, YouTube, posted by Luv saengie, July 25, 2015, https://www.youtube.com/watch?v=8aha37ONzL4&list=PLb1ayNIj3f8o2-ZVuklNfYxrGPwkKBzjs&index=1.

100. The #Ham4Ham performances are available on a YouTube playlist titled #Ham4Ham Complete (?) Chronological July 2015–2016, see "#Ham4Ham Complete," video playlist. Last updated February 4, 2022 with 101,609 views as of September 1, 2022. Unless otherwise noted, all #Ham4Ham performances I discuss are available on this site.

101. Howard Sherman, "The Generous Audience Engagement of Lin-Manuel Miranda," Howard Sherman, last modified August 5, 2015, accessed August 7, 2022, http://hesherman.com/2015/08/05/the-generous-audience-engagement-of-lin-manuel-miranda/.

102. "HAMILTON Ham4Ham 12/9/15 with Billy Porter," video, YouTube, posted by Howard Sherman, December 9, 2015, accessed August 6, 2022, https://www.yout ube.com/watch?v=0W48v1iiMVo&list=PLb1ayNIj3f8o2-ZVuklNfYxrGPwkKB zjs&index=91.

103. "#Ham4Ham 8/26/15," video, YouTube, posted by Gnoeyk, August 26, 2015, accessed August 6, 2022, https://www.youtube.com/watch?v=duhIIx3WEuY&list= PLb1ayNIj3f8o2-ZVuklNfYxrGPwkKBzjs&index=41.

104. Trevor Boffone, "Ham4Ham: Taking Hamilton to the Streets," editorial, *HowlRound Theatre Commons*, last modified March 18, 2016, accessed August 7, 2022, https://howlround.com/ham4ham. Boffone considers #Ham4Ham in the context of Latinx street performance that "originated from a place of social protest" and promotes an "aesthetics of accessibility" (see Boffone, "Ham4Ham: Taking," editorial, *HowlRound Theatre Commons*). It is worth footnoting that street performance does not have a consistent political orientation and can be used to protest structural racism and support #Black Lives Matter or promote antisemitism and white supremacy in the manner of the National Socialist movement.

105. Miranda and McCarter, *Hamilton: The Revolution*, 161–162.

106. See "#Ham4Ham Complete," video playlist. See also "HAMILTON Ham4Ham 7/27/15 with Lin-Manuel Miranda & Thayne Jasperson," video, YouTube, posted by Howard Sherman, July 28, 2015, accessed August 6, 2022, https://www.yout ube.com/watch?v=LcMuuNLsOt4&list=PLb1ayNIj3f8o2-ZVuklNfYxrGPwkKB zjs&index=16.

107. Allgor, "'Remember . . . ,'" 98.

108. "Sister Kings Ham4Ham," video, YouTube, posted by Oge Agulué, October 24, 2015, accessed August 6, 2022, https://www.youtube.com/watch?v=TX2fuGIRY5Q&list= PLb1ayNIj3f8o2-ZVuklNfYxrGPwkKBzjs&index=70.

109. Anne Koenig found, "there was greater concern, compared to females being agentic or dominant, that (a) elementary-aged boys should not be communal, (b) adolescent boys and young adult men should not be communal or weak, and (c) adult men should not be weak." See Anne M. Koenig, "Comparing Prescriptive and Descriptive Gender Stereotypes About Children, Adults, and the Elderly," *Frontiers in Psychology* 9, no. 1086 (June 26, 2018), accessed August 7, 2022, https://doi.org/10.3389/fpsyg.2018.01086.

110. Karen Rought, "'Hamilton's' first digital Ham4Ham show features legendary Alan Menken," *Hypable*, last modified January 17, 2016, accessed August 6, 2022, https://www.hypable.com/hamilton-digital-ham4ham-alan-menken/.

111. Adam Holmes, "Disney Has Shut Down Production on *The Little Mermaid* Remake and More Movies," *Cinemablend*, last modified March 13, 2020, accessed August 6, 2022, https://www.cinemablend.com/news/2492566/disney-has-shut-down-pro duction-on-the-little-mermaid-remake-and-more-movies.

112. Nadine Matthews, "Is #NotMyAriel Just Another Russian Troll of Black Twitter?" *Shadow and Act*, last modified July 12, 2019, accessed August 6, 2022, https://shado wandact.com/is-notmyariel-just-another-russian-troll-of-black-twitter.

113. Matthews, "Is #NotMyAriel Just Another Russian Troll."

114. Jon Swaine, "Twitter Admits Far More Russian Bots Posted on Election Than It Had Disclosed," *The Guardian*, January 19, 2018, accessed August 6, 2022, https://www. theguardian.com/technology/2018/jan/19/twitter-admits-far-more-russian-bots-posted-on-election-than-it-had-disclosed.

115. A "gofundme" campaign was begun to pay Disney to recast Ariel with Sophia Lillis, but nobody donated, and the campaign was discontinued. See Brooke Newman, "The White Nostalgia Fueling the 'Little Mermaid' Backlash," *The Washington Post*, July 9, 2019, accessed August 6, 2022, https://www.washingtonpost.com/outlook/2019/07/09/white-nostalgia-fueling-little-mermaid-backlash/.

116. Gerald D. Higginbotham, Zhanpeng Zheng, and Yalda T. Uhls, "Beyond Checking a Box: A Lack of Authentically Inclusive Representation Has Costs at the Box Office," *The Center for Scholars & Storytellers*, UCLA, 2020, accessed August 6, 2022, https://static1.squarespace.com/static/5c0da585da02bc56793a0b31/t/615502460261b977556933bd/1632961103708/CSS+AIR+Final+Research+Report.pdf.

117. "World of Belonging," The Walt Disney Company, website, accessed August 6, 2022, https://impact.disney.com/diversity-inclusion/.

118. Newman, "The White Nostalgia."

119. Hope Wabuke points to the trend in "Disney's Disembodied Black Characters," *Los Angeles Review of Books*, March 23, 2021, accessed September, 12, 2022, https://lareviewofbooks.org/article/disneys-disembodied-black-characters/.   Wabuke writes, "To date, *The Lion King* is the highest grossing traditionally animated Disney movie of all time. But back in 1994, Disney couldn't imagine that this success could be repeated by making *more* Black stories, perhaps even with *people*, rather than animals."

Part IV

1. Stuart Miller, "The Theater Talkback: Why They're Popular, and Why Playwrights Aren't Always Pleased," *The Los Angeles Times*, September 28, 2017, accessed August 9, 2022, https://www.latimes.com/entertainment/arts/la-ca-cm-theater-talkback-20170928-htmlstory.html. As Miller points out, many in the theatrical community disagree with Mamet; Andrew Leynse, Artistic Director of the off-Broadway company Primary Stages, described Mamet's fine as "a very extreme reaction," arguing, "We need to expand and diversify our audiences, and talkbacks are a useful way to engage audiences and deepen their experience." See Miller, "The Theater Talkback."

2. Caroline Heim claims that the Actor's Playhouse in New York introduced talkbacks weekly after performances of Arthur Miller's adaptation of Henrik Ibsen's *An Enemy of the People* in 1959. The number of talkbacks jumped precipitously and then

declined in the eighties with the rise of the Broadway musical but grew in popularity again in the early years of the twenty-first century. See notes 1 and 8 in Caroline Heim, "'Argue with Us!': Audience Co-creation through Post-Performance Discussions," *New Theatre Quarterly* 28, no. 2 (May 2012): 197. In Heim's earlier *Audience as Performer: The Changing Role of Theatre Audiences in the Twenty-First Century* (New York: Routledge, 2016), Vitalsource Ebook, she has a brief section on the "The Post-Show Discussion" in "Audience as Critic." Pagination is not available in the digital version of the book I used while libraries were closed for the COVID-19 pandemic. See Caroline Heim, "Audience as Critic," in *Audience as Performer: The Changing Role of Theatre Audiences in the Twenty-First Century* (New York: Routledge, 2016), Vitalsource Ebook.

3. Caroline Heim writes, "The darkening of the theatres combined with the enforcement of theatre etiquette strictures anesthetised demonstrative audience performance" in "The Auditorium Fades to Black," in "Theatre Etiquette (1880–2000)." See Caroline Heim, "Theatre Etiquette (1880–2000)," in *Audience as Performer: The Changing Role of Theatre Audiences in the Twenty-First Century* (New York: Routledge, 2016), Vitalsource Ebook.

4. See also Richard Butsch, *The Making of American Audiences: From Stage to Television, 1750–1990* (Cambridge: Cambridge University Press, 2000).

5. These are just two examples I have studied and discuss elsewhere. See Carrie J. Preston, *Learning to Kneel: Noh, Modernism, and Journeys in Teaching* (New York: Columbia University Press, 2016) and my "Introduction: Modernism and Dance" in *Modernist Cultures* 9, no. 1 (2014), 1–6.

6. Michael Mark Chemers, *Ghost Light: An Introductory Handbook for Dramaturgy* (Carbondale, IL: Southern Illinois University, 2010), 169.

7. Chemers, *Ghost Light*, 169.

8. Chemers, *Ghost Light*, 171.

9. Laurie Brooks, "Put a Little Boal in Your Talkback," *American Theatre* 22, no. 10 (December 2005): 59.

10. Heim describes her method of researching the audience in the "Introduction" to *Audience as Performer: The Changing Role of Theatre Audiences in the Twenty-First Century* (New York: Routledge, 2016), Vitalsource Ebook: "A small number of interviews with friends of friends were prearranged in the UK. Some additional interviews were undertaken after post-show discussions or after I delivered public lectures on theatre where I asked for volunteers who were regular theatre-goers, but not theatre professionals." Heim used recordings of twenty audience talkbacks to, as she writes, "provide additional audience comments" for her qualitative study of audience responses to mainstream theater. In a book that treats audiences as performers, it is striking that she does not analyze the talkbacks as performance events. See Caroline Heim, "Introduction," introduction to *Audience as Performer: The Changing Role of Theatre Audiences in the Twenty-First Century* (New York: Routledge, 2016), Vitalsource Ebook.

11. Heim, "The Post-Show Discussion" in "Audience as Critic." For a summary of the field known as audience research, see Kirsty Sedgman, "Audience Experience in an Anti-expert Age: A Survey of Theatre Audience Research," *Theatre Research*

International 42, no. 3 (2018): 307–322. For examples of qualitative studies of audiences, see Chris Megson and Janelle Reinelt's description of the "Theatre Spectatorship and Value Attribution," a project conducted by the British Theatre Consortium in "Performance, Experience, Transformation: What Do Spectators Value in Theatre?" *Journal of Contemporary Drama in English* 4, no. 1 (2016): 227–242. Ben Walmsley pointed out that talkbacks were valued by UK and Australian audiences and also keep audiences in the venue longer, which increases their chances of purchasing souvenirs. Ben Walmsley, "Why People Go to the Theatre: A Qualitative Study of Audience Motivation," *Journal of Customer Behaviour* 10, no. 4 (2011): 335–351.

12. See Bob Harlow, *The Road to Results: Effective Practices for Building Arts Audiences* (New York: The Wallace Foundation, 2014), 44. See also Heim, "Case Study—Steppenwolf Theater Company: Playing Critic in the Public Square" in "Audience as Critic."

13. Chemers, *Ghost Light*, 171.

14. Harlow, *The Road to Results*, 44.

15. "Free Virtual Arts Education Programs," Steppenwolf Theatre, accessed August 10, 2022, https://www.steppenwolf.org/education/virtual-workshops/.

16. Some scholarship and popular writing have also recommended designing a new format for the talkback. See Heim, " 'Argue with Us!,' " 189–197; Damon Krometis, "Dissonant Witnessing: The 'in' and 'above' of *Thou Proud Dream*," *Theatre Topics* 26, no. 3 (November 2016): 321–331; Laura Nessler, "Staging Truth to Invite Dialogue: Elements of Group Work in Documentary Theatre Talkbacks," *Social Work with Groups* 41, no. 1–2 (2018): 34–48; Laurie Brooks, "Put a Little Boal in Your Talkback," *American Theatre* 22, no. 10 (December 2005): 58–60; Anne Ellis, "The Art of Community Conversation," *Theatre Topics* 10, no. 2 (2000): 91–100.

17. Harvard University, "Act II at A.R.T.," A.R.T., accessed August 10, 2022, https://americanrepertorytheater.org/about-us/act-ii/.

18. Harvard University, "Act II at A.R.T.," A.R.T.

19. Harvard University, "Act II at A.R.T.," A.R.T.

Chapter 6

1. Harvard University, "Act II at A.R.T.," A.R.T.

2. Louise Kennedy, "Anna Deavere Smith ' 'Does Time' in the 'School-to-Prison Pipeline,' " WBUR, last modified August 25, 2016, accessed August 10, 2022, https://www.wbur.org/news/2016/08/25/anna-deavere-smith-notes-from-field.

3. Participants were asked to write these questions on white note cards, several of which were shared with me by audience members.

4. Harvard University, "Act II at A.R.T.," A.R.T.

5. Anna Deavere Smith, "About the Pipeline Project," Anna Deavere Smith Projects, accessed August 10, 2022, http://www.annadeaveresmith.org.

6. Anna Deavere Smith, *Notes from the Field* (New York: Anchor Books, 2019), xviii.

7. A.R.T. Educational Toolkit, *Notes from the Field: Doing Time in Education*, American Repertory Theatre, 2016, 15, accessed August 10, 2022, https://american-rep-assets. s3.amazonaws.com/wp-content/uploads/2019/10/27143248/Notes-Toolkit-Final. pdf; U.S. Department of Education Institute of Education Sciences: National Center for Education Statistics, *Racial/Ethnic Enrollment in Public Schools*, 2022, accessed August 10, 2022, https://nces.ed.gov/programs/coe/indicator_cge.asp.

8. "A.R.T. Educational," 7.

9. "A.R.T. Educational," 17.

10. In her "Production Notes," Smith wrote, "A nonspeaking helper is used in lieu of a stagehand. In the Second Stage Theater and American Repertory Theater productions, a twentysomething white male was the helper. As the helper is visible, and race is both significant and movable in this and other works of Ms. Smith, selection of the nonspeaking helper's presence should be an aesthetic and perhaps sociological consideration." Clearly the aesthetic and sociological considerations related to the "helper" are deeply connected to racial and gendered presence. Anna Deavere Smith, "Helper," "Production Notes" to *Notes from the Field* (New York: Anchor Books, 2019), xxiii.

11. Anna Deavere Smith, "Introduction," introduction to *Notes from the Field* (New York: Anchor Books, 2019), xvi.

12. Smith, "Introduction," introduction, xxii. The published text combines two stage productions and also incorporates elements of the 2018 HBO film, so it is somewhat different from the "Portraits" included in the A.R.T. production (see Smith, "Introduction," introduction, xviii). Sari Muhonen, Denise Dodsen, and Bryan Stevenson were not portrayed at A.R.T. Linda Wayman and Cheryl Hendrickson do not appear in the book. My summary of the play follows the "Order of Portraits."

13. Smith, "Introduction," introduction, xxii.

14. Smith, "Introduction," introduction, xv.

15. Smith, *Notes*, 7.

16. Smith, *Notes*, 49.

17. Smith, *Notes*, 48.

18. Jean Marbella, "Beginning of Freddie Gray's Life as Sad as Its End, Court Case Shows," *The Baltimore Sun*, April 23, 2015, accessed August 10, 2022, https://www.baltimore sun.com/ maryland/baltimore-city/bs-md-freddie-gray-lead-paint-20150423-story. html. Freddie Gray and his siblings had lead levels in their blood that were over seven times higher than what the Centers for Disease Control (CDC) indicates can cause brain damage (see Marbella, "Beginning of Freddie"). See also Michael Anft, "Freddie Gray: The Running Man," Bloomberg CityLab, last modified November 10, 2015, accessed August 10, 2022, https://www.bloomberg.com/ news/articles/2015-11-10/ the-baltimore-life-and-death-of-freddie-gray.

19. Marbella, "Beginning of Freddie"; Anft, "Freddie Gray."

20. Smith, *Notes*, 76.

21. Don Lemon Tonight, "Classmate of Arrested South Carolina Teen Speaks out," video, CNN, October 27, 2015, accessed August 10, 2022, https://www.cnn.com/videos/tv/ 2015/ 10/28/niya-kenny-interview-south-carolina-school-arrest-video-ctn.cnn.

22. Wltx, "No Criminal Charges to Be Filed in Student Dragging at Spring Valley," News19, last modified September 2, 2016, accessed August 10, 2022, https://www.wltx.com/ article/news/local/no-criminal-charges-to-be-filed-in-student-dragging-at-spring-valley/101-312983906.

23. Smith, *Notes*, 130.

24. Smith, *Notes*, 130.

25. Smith, *Notes*, 133.

26. Smith, *Notes*, 137.

27. Smith, *Notes*, 138.

28. For a discussion of Smith and American documentary theater, see Jules Odendahl-James, "A History of U.S. Documentary Theater in Three Stages," *American Theatre*, August 22, 2017. Accessed August 10, 2022. https://www.americantheatre.org/2017/08/22/a-history-of-u-s-documentary-theatre-in-three-stages.

29. Smith, "Introduction," introduction, xxi.

30. Smith, *Notes*, 1.

31. Smith, *Notes*, 10, 16.

32. Smith, *Notes*, 23.

33. Smith, *Notes*, 24.

34. Smith, *Notes*, 29.

35. Smith, *Notes*, 50, 138.

36. Smith, *Notes*, 130.

37. Smith, *Notes*, 82.

38. Smith, *Notes*, 82.

39. Smith, *Notes*, 82.

40. Smith, *Notes*, 84.

41. The conversation took place on August 28, 2016.

42. Elizabeth Cooper Davis, interview by the author, American Repertory Theater, Boston, MA, May 17, 2018.

43. Smith, *Notes*, 14.

44. See Samantha Mann, Sarah Ewens, Dominic Shaw, Aldert Vrij, Sharon Leal, and Jackie Hillman, "Lying Eyes: Why Liars Seek Deliberate Eye Contact," *Psychiatry, Psychology, and Law* 20, no. 3 (2013): 452–461; Samantha Mann, Aldert Vrij, Sharon Leal, Pär Anders Granhag, Lara Warmelink, and Dave Forrester, "Windows to the Soul? Deliberate Eye Contact as a Cue to Deceit," *Journal of Nonverbal Behavior* 36 (2012): 205–251; Jack Schafer, "How to Detect a Liar," *Psychology Today*. Last modified March 11, 2014. Accessed August 10, 2022. https://www.psychologytoday.com/us/blog/let-their-words-do-the-talking/201403/how-detect-liar.

45. Smith, *Notes*, 25.

46. Smith, *Notes*, 25.

47. Smith, *Notes*, 25.

48. Smith, *Notes*, 142.

49. Davis, interview by the author.

50. "Additional Information," in *Notes from the Field: Doing Time in Education* (New York: American Repertory Theatre, 2016).

51. Kerry Reid, "Talkback Backtalk: Up for a Post-Show Discussion? Four A.D.s Explain Why They Are—And You Just Might Be Too," *American Theatre*, September 25, 2018, accessed August 10, 2022, https://www.americantheatre.org/2018/09/25/talkback-backtalk/.

52. See the program: *Notes from the Field: Doing Time in Education* (New York: American Repertory Theatre, 2016).

53. Cy Ashley Webb, "Policy Pivots along 'School-to-Prison-Pipeline' with Anna Deavere Smith," StarkInsider, last modified July 21, 2015, accessed August 10, 2022, https://www.starkinsider.com/2015/07/anna-deavere-smith-notes-from-field-berkeley-rev iew.html.

54. See Webb, "Policy Pivots."

55. Cy Musiker, "Anna Deavere Smith Fights School-to-Prison Pipeline with New Play," KQED, last modified July 19, 2015, accessed August 10, 2022, https://www.kqed.org/news/10603541/anna-deaveare-smith-fights-the-school-to-prison-pipeline-with-theater.

56. See Musiker, "Anna Deavere Smith."

57. Musiker asked Smith whether she really believed art can make social change and reported that she "bristled a bit" at the question: "It's so obvious," she said, "that art is a form of expression that gets beyond the official language. That complicates things. It has the opportunity to really draw more people in, and particularly in a place in their heart, where they might just make an adjustment about how they think about things." See Musiker, "Anna Deavere Smith."

58. Patti Hartigan, "*Notes from the Field: Doing Time in Education*," in "The Week Ahead: Pop Music, Theater, Dance, Art, and More," *Boston Globe*, August 30, 2016, G.4, https://ezproxy.bu.edu/login?qurl=https%3A%2F%2Fwww.proquest.com%2Fnewspapers%2Fweek-ahead-pop-music-theater-dance-art-more%2Fdocview%2F1815161930%2Fse-2%3Faccountid%3D9676.

59. Hartigan, "*Notes from the Field*," in "The Week Ahead."

60. Patti Hartigan, "In 'Notes,' an education in injustice from Anna Deavere Smith," review of *Notes from the Field: Doing Time in Education*, American Repertory Theatre, Boston, MA, United States, *Boston Globe*, August 26, 2016, G.1, accessed August 10, 2022, https://www.bostonglobe.com/arts/theater-art/2016/08/26/notes-education-injustice-from-anna-deavere-smith/XkZjGj1S4bP5gHq6GTohzH/story.html.

61. Hartigan, "In 'Notes,'" review.

62. Jeremy D. Goodwin, "Class IN SESSION: With her interactive 'Notes from the Field' at the ART, Anna Deavere Smith explores the school-to-prison pipeline," *Boston Globe*, August 19, 2016, G.1, https://ezproxy.bu.edu/login?qurl=https%3A%2F%2Fwww.proquest.com%2Fnewspapers%2Fclass-session%2Fdocview%2F1812387356%2Fse-2%3Faccountid%3D9676.

63. Goodwin, "Class IN SESSION."

64. Goodwin, "Class IN SESSION."

65. A.R.T., "Notes from the Field Act II Facilitator Application," Jotform, accessed August 11, 2022, https://form.jotform.com/62037905835156. The deadline was August 5, 2016.

66. Davis, interview by the author.

67. The job description for the Act II Manager stated: "The ACT II manager is responsible for thinking about how to shape the audience experience in this 25-minute interlude in such a way that helps people connect what they are experiencing in the performance to their own lives, and to the possibility of being an instrument of change in their communities." See Pipeline Project, "Act II Manager for Anna Deavere Smiths' Pipeline Project and Play," JobRoller, last modified June 12, 2016, accessed August 11, 2022, https://gofetchjobs. com/jobroller/jobs/act-ii-manager-for-anna-deavere-smiths-pipeline-project-and-play/.

68. Davis, interview by the author.

69. Davis, interview by the author.

70. Davis, interview by the author.

71. Davis, interview by the author.

72. SK Kerastas, "Challenges with Radical Hospitality in Act II of Berkeley Rep's Production of *Notes from the Field, Doing Time in Education*—The California Chapter by Anna Deveare Smith," editorial, HowlRound Theatre Commons, last modified August 28, 2015, accessed August 11, 2022, https://howlround.com/challenges-radi cal-hospitality-act-ii-berkeley-reps-production-notes-field-doing-time-education.

73. Kerastas, "Challenges with Radical Hospitality."

74. Kerastas, "Challenges with Radical Hospitality."

75. Jacques Derrida and Anne Dufourmantelle, " 'Step of Hospitality / No Hospitality' [Pas d'hospitalité]," in *On Hospitality* (Stanford, CA: Stanford University Press, 2000), 77.

76. Derrida and Dufourmantelle, " 'Step of Hospitality," 77.

77. Kerastas, "Challenges with Radical Hospitality."

78. Kerastas, "Challenges with Radical Hospitality."

79. Kerastas, "Challenges with Radical Hospitality."

80. Kerastas, "Challenges with Radical Hospitality."

81. Davis, interview by the author.

82. Kerastas, "Challenges with Radical Hospitality."

83. Derrida and Dufourmantelle, " 'Step of Hospitality," 77.

84. Davis, interview by the author.

85. Davis, interview by the author.

86. See Kerastas, "Challenges with Radical Hospitality."

87. Davis, interview by the author.

88. Davis, interview by the author.

89. Davis, interview by the author. Robert Duffley, interview by the author, American Repertory Theater, Boston, MA, August 15, 2018.

90. Robert Duffley, interview by the author.

91. Robert Duffley, interview by the author.

92. Harvard University, "Witness Uganda Act III," A.R.T., accessed August 11, 2022, https://americanrepertorytheater.org/witness-uganda-act-iii/.

93. Many of these discussions are available at "In the Body of the World Act II Discussion Series." See Harvard University, "In the Body of the World Act II Discussion Series,"

A.R.T., accessed August 11, 2022, https://americanrepertorytheater.org/in-the-body-of-the-world-act-ii-discussion-series/.

94. *Notes from the Field: Doing Time in Education—The California* Chapter (July 11–August 2, 2015), website accessed March 16, 2019 but no longer available on Berkeley Rep's website: https://www.berkeleyrep.org/season/1415/9293.asp

95. Davis, interview by the author.

Chapter 7

1. Other dinner party plays include Neil Simon's *The Dinner Party* (2000), Edward Albee's *Who's Afraid of Virginia Woolf* (1962), Caryl Churchill's *Top Girls* (1982), Tracy Letts's *August: Osage County* (2007), George S. Kaufman and Edna Ferber's *Dinner at Eight* (1932), Oscar Wilde's *An Ideal Husband* (1895), *Table Manners*, the first play in Alan Ayckbourn's 1973 trilogy *The Norman Conquests*, George Bernard Shaw's, *You Never Can Tell* (1897), and many more.

2. Claudia Rankine, *The White Card: A Play* (Minneapolis: Graywolf Press, 2019), 19.

3. Rankine, *The White Card*, 61.

4. Rankine, *The White Card*, 88.

5. Rankine, *The White Card*, 74.

6. Rankine, *The White Card*, 76.

7. Rankine, *The White Card*, 80.

8. Rankine, *The White Card*, 9.

9. Rankine, *The White Card*, 11.

10. Rankine, *The White Card*, 13.

11. Rankine, *The White Card*, 67.

12. Rankine, *The White Card*, 69.

13. Rankine, *The White Card*, 81.

14. Rankine, *The White Card*, 85.

15. Rankine claims that she chose the names Charles and Charlotte before the 2015 massacre in Charleston, South Carolina, and the white nationalist rally in Charlottesville, Virginia, in 2017. See Patti Hartigan, "Claudia Rankine Wants Us to Talk—Really Talk—About Race, So She Wrote 'The White Card,'" *Boston Globe*, February 21, 2018, https://www.bostonglobe. comarts/theater/dance/2018/02/21/claudia-rankine-wants-talk-really-talk-about-race-she-   wrote-the-white-card/EudZwjKYmCnC4cbN6MjANN/story.html.

16. Rankine, *The White Card*, 81.

17. Rankine, *The White Card*, 80.

18. Randy Kennedy, "White Artist's Painting of Emmett Till at Whitney Biennial Draws Protests," *The New York Times*, March 21, 2017, accessed August 11, 2022, https://www.nytimes.com/2017/03/21/arts/design/painting-of-emmett-till-at-whitney-biennial-draws-protests.html.

19. Rankine, *The White Card*, 80, 76.

20. Rankine, *The White Card*, 76.

21. Rankine, *The White Card*, 80.

22. Rankine, *The White Card*, 54.

23. Rankine, *The White Card*, 54.

24. Rankine, *The White Card*, 81.

25. Rankine, *The White Card*, 81, 82.

26. Rankine, *The White Card*, 16. See Jessica Hamzelou, "How Pregnancy Could Affect an Elite Athlete Like Serena Williams," *New Scientist*. Last modified April 20, 2017. Accessed August 11, 2022. https://www.newscientist.com/article/2128439-how-pregnancy-could-affect-an-elite-athlete-like-serena-williams/. The article acknowledges that there is little evidence to support theories that pregnancy would be an asset in a sports competition, but it does give surprising space to "rumours of 'abortion doping' in the 1970's and 80's. The idea is that women were encouraged or even forced to become pregnant before competing, and later had abortions." See Hamzelou, "How Pregnancy Could Affect an Elite Athlete."

27. Rankine, *The White Card*, 16.

28. Rankine, *The White Card*, 16.

29. Rankine, *The White Card*, 16. This is a reference to the 2014 comments of Shamil Tarpischev on a Russian television show; the Women's Tennis Association responded with a fine of $25,000 and banned him for a year. Press Association, "Shamil Tarpsichev Forced to Apologise after Calling Williams Sisters 'Brothers,'" *The Guardian*, October 21, 2014, accessed August 11, 2022, https://www.theguardian.com/sport/2014/oct/21/shamil-tarpischev-forced-apology-williams-sisters-slur.

30. Claudia Rankine uses athletics, particularly the Williams sisters, to discuss white supremacy and patriarchy because, as she said in an interview about her 2014 book, *Citizen: An American Lyric*, sports are "trackable. You can look them up. You can replay . . . Serena was being condemned for having an anger that had no source." See "Claudia Rankine on Serena Williams at the 2015 L.A. Times Festival of Books," video, 02:52, YouTube, posted by PBS Books, December 23, 2015, accessed August 11, 2022, https://www.youtube.com/watch?v=sQaMat_BzyA. The story of Serena told in *Citizen* includes extremely poor officiating, media "finger-wagging" when Serena responded to bad calls with anger, but no finger-wagging when the Danish tennis player Caroline Wozniacki stuffed towels down her shirt and skirt to accentuate her bosom and rear end in mimicry of Serena. See Claudia Rankine, *Citizen: An American Lyric* (Minneapolis: Graywolf Press, 2014), 24–36.

31. In November 2016, Pamela Taylor, then director of the Clay County Development Corporation, posted on Facebook, "It will be refreshing to have a classy, beautiful, dignified First Lady in the White House. I'm tired of seeing a Ape in heels" [sic]. Clay County Mayor Beverly Whaling "liked" the post and commented, "Just made my day Pam." Whaling later resigned, and Taylor made headlines again in 2019 when she was found guilty of embezzling $18,000 in FEMA benefits and sentenced to ten months in prison, two months of home confinement, and a $10,000 fine. See Morgan Winsor, "Woman Who called Michelle Obama an 'Ape in Heels' Pleads Guilty to FEMA Fraud," ABC News, last modified February 18, 2019, accessed August 11, 2022, https://abcnews.go.com/US/woman-called-michelle-obama-ape-heels-pleads-gui

lty/story?id=61142401. For the sentencing, see Department of Justice U.S. Attorney's Office Southern District of West Virginia, "Clay County Woman Sentenced for FEMA Fraud," news release, May 30, 2019, accessed August 11, 2022, https://www. justice.gov/usao-sdwv/pr/clay-county-woman-sentenced-fema-fraud. See Rankine, *The White Card*, 17.

32. Rankine, *The White Card*, 17.
33. Rankine, *The White Card*, 17.
34. Rankine, *The White Card*, 15.
35. Rankine, *The White Card*, 31.
36. Rankine, *The White Card*, 31.
37. Rankine, *The White Card*, 31.
38. Rankine, *The White Card*, 27.
39. Rankine, *The White Card*, 37.
40. Rankine, *The White Card*, 26.
41. Rankine, *The White Card*, 26.
42. Rankine, *The White Card*, 28.
43. Rankine, *The White Card*, 28.
44. Rankine, *The White Card*, 25.
45. Rankine, *The White Card*, 21.
46. Rankine, *The White Card*, 38.
47. Rankine, *The White Card*, 45.
48. Executive Order 13769, "Protecting the Nation from Foreign Terrorist Entry into the United States," signed by Donald Trump on January 27, 2017, has been called the "Muslim ban" or "Muslim travel ban" because it barred people from seven majority-Muslim countries from entering the United States, halted refugee resettlement, and banned Syrian refugees. In September 2018, the Supreme Court allowed a revised version of the travel ban to be enforced.
49. Rankine, *The White Card*, 39–40.
50. Rankine, *The White Card*, 39.
51. Rankine, *The White Card*, 40.
52. U.S. Department of Justice, "Phasing Out Our Use of Private Prisons," The United States Department of Justice Archives, last modified August 18, 2016, accessed August 11, 2022, https://www.justice.gov/archives/opa/blog/phasing-out-our-use-private-prisons.
53. Brett C. Burkhardt, "Who Is in Private Prisons? Demographic Profiles of Prisoners and Workers in American Private Prisons," *International Journal of Law, Crime and Justice* 51 (2017): 31. Jill Filipovic details horrific prisoner abuse in private prisons. See Jill Filipovic, "America's Private Prison System Is a National Disgrace," *The Guardian*, June 13, 2013, accessed August 11, 2022, https://www.theguardian.com/commentisfree/2013/jun/13/aclu-lawsuit-east-mississippi-correctional-facility.
54. Christopher Petrella argues that health and age stipulations in private prison contracts serve as proxies for race to create racial disparities. See Christopher Petrella, "The Color of Corporate Corrections, Part II: Contractual Exemptions and the Overrepresentation of People of Color in Private Prisons," *Radical Criminology* 3 (2014): 81–100.

55. Burkhardt, "Who Is in Private Prisons?," 31.

56. The memo, dated August 18, 2016, is available in the Department of Justice Archives; see Memorandum, "Reducing Our Use of Private Prisons," August 18, 2016, accessed August 11, 2022, https://www.justice.gov/archives/opa/blog/phasing-out-our-use-private-prisons. See also Jon Swaine, Oliver Laughland, and Jana Kasperkevic, "US Justice Department Announced It Will End Use of Private Prisons," *The Guardian*, August 18, 2018, accessed August 11, 2022, https://www.theguardian.com/us-news/2016/aug/18/us-government-private-prisons-use-justice-department.

57. Lauren-Brooke Eisen, "Trump's First Year Has Been the Private Prison Industry's Best," *Salon*, last modified January 14, 2018, accessed August 11, 2022, https://www.salon.com/2018/01/14/trumps-first-year-has-been-the-private-prison-industrys-best/.

58. Huawa Ahmed, "How Private Prisons Are Profiting under the Trump Administration," Center for American Progress, last modified August 30, 2019, accessed August 11, 2022, https://www.americanprogress.org/issues/democracy/reports/2019/08/30/473966/private-prisons-profiting-trump-administration/.

59. Rankine, *The White Card*, 49.

60. Rankine, *The White Card*, 49.

61. Rankine, *The White Card*, 48.

62. Rankine, *The White Card*, 48.

63. Rankine, *The White Card*, 52.

64. Rankine, *The White Card*, 47.

65. Rankine, *The White Card*, 27.

66. Rankine, *The White Card*, 47.

67. Bill Marx, "Theater Review: Playing 'The White Card,'" review of *The White Card*, American Repertory Theater, Boston, MA, The Arts Fuse, last modified March 7, 2018, accessed August 11, 2022, https://artsfuse.org/168315/theater-review-playing-the-white-card/.

68. Marx, "Theater Review."

69. Winsor, "Woman Who Called Michelle."

70. *The White Card* by Claudia Rankine, ArtsEmerson promotional site, accessed August 11, 2020, but no longer available on ArtsEmerson's website, https://www.boston.com/event/artsemerson-the-white-card-6543952.

71. Davis, interview by the author.

72. Davis, interview by the author.

73. Davis, interview by the author.

74. Davis, interview by the author.

75. Davis, interview by the author.

76. See Ariel Baker-Gibbs, "Where Do We Look? Going to the Theater as a Deaf Person," editorial, HowlRound Theatre Commons, last modified April 6, 2014, accessed August 11, 2022, https://howlround.com/where-do-we-look-going-theater-deaf-person. "The standard for most theatres is to put the interpreters on the stairs leading down to the house floor at one end of the stage, and all the deaf theatregoers on that side of the theatre, which leads to a lot of missed action onstage regardless

of whether it's a proscenium or a thrust stage. . . . Since a lot of theatres sell the ASL seats at a discount, they choose the less popular seats to sell to deaf theatregoers, on less popular dates, such as the Sunday of Labor Day weekend." See Baker-Gibbs, "Where Do We Look?"

77. Christopher Robinson, interview by the author, Boston University, Boston, MA, April 18, 2018.
78. Robinson, interview by the author.
79. Robinson, interview by the author.
80. Robinson, interview by the author.
81. Robinson, interview by the author.
82. Robinson, interview by the author.
83. Marx, "Theater Review."
84. Marx, "Theater Review."
85. Marx, "Theater Review."
86. "Citizen Read," ArtsEmerson (January–March 2018), accessed August 11, 2020, but no longer available on ArtsEmerson's website, https://artsemerson.org/Online/default.asp?BOparam::WScontent::loadArticle::permalink=Citizen_Read&BOparam::WScontent::loadArticle::context_id=.
87. See "Citizen Speak: A Conversation with Claudia Rankine at ArtsEmerson, Boston—4 March 2018," video, 01:24:26, YouTube, posted by HowlRound Theatre Commons, March 4, 2018, accessed August 11, 2022, https://www.youtube.com/watch?v=EIoK1qd0QA8.
88. Davis, interview by the author.
89. Davis, interview by the author.
90. Davis, interview by the author.
91. Kevin Becerra et al., *Citizen Read Facilitation Guide*, ed. Brenna Nicely and Nicole Olusanya (2018), accessed August 11, 2020 but no longer available on ArtsEmerson's website, https://artsemerson.org/ArticleMedia/Files/CRFacilitatorGuide.pdf.
92. Davis, interview by the author.
93. Davis, interview by the author.
94. Robinson, interview by the author.
95. Robinson, interview by the author.
96. Matt Steven, "Starbucks C.E.O. Apologizes after Arrests of 2 Black Men," *The New York Times*, April 15, 2018, accessed August 11, 2022, https://www.nytimes.com/2018/04/15/us/starbucks-philadelphia-black-men-arrest.html.
97. Teo Armus, "White Woman 'Terminated' from Job after Calling Police on Black Birdwatcher Who Asked Her to Leash Her Dog, Company Says," *The Washington Post*, May 27, 2020, accessed August 11, 2022, https://www.washingtonpost.com/nation/2020/05/26/amy-cooper-central-park/.
98. Robinson, interview by the author.
99. Robinson, interview by the author.
100. Rankine, *The White Card*, 80.
101. Rankine, *The White Card*, 74.

Coda

1. Robinson, interview by the author.
2. Rankine, *The White Card*, 80.
3. Robinson, interview by the author.
4. Rankine, *The White Card*, 80.
5. American Association for Justice, "Ten Worst Insurance Companies in American: How They Raise Premiums, Deny Claims, and Refuse Insurance to Those Who Need It Most," accessed December 30, 2022, https://www.decof.com/documents/the-ten-worst-insurance-companies.pdf.

Bibliography

"Additional Information." In *Notes from the Field: Doing Time in Education*. New York: American Repertory Theatre, 2016.

Ahmed, Huawa. "How Private Prisons Are Profiting Under the Trump Administration." Center for American Progress. Last modified August 30, 2019. Accessed August 11, 2022. https://www.americanprogress.org/issues/democracy/reports/2019/08/30/473 966/private-prisons-profiting-trump-administration/.

Ahmed, Sara. *On Being Included: Racism and Diversity in Institutional Life*. Durham, NC: Duke University Press, 2012.

"Alexander Hamilton." Audio, 03:56. YouTube. Posted by Usnavi, April 20, 2017. Accessed August 6, 2022. https://www.youtube.com/watch?v=VhinPd5RRJw&list=PL-krih Kw82nf_RrmGLyUxINL6jLxButQi.

Allgor, Catherine. "'Remember . . . I'm Your Man': Masculinity, Marriage, and Gender in *Hamilton*." In *Historians on Hamilton: How a Blockbuster Musical Is Restaging America's Past*, edited by Renee C. Romano and Claire Bond Potter, 94–118. New Brunswick, NJ: Rutgers University Press, 2018.

Almukhtar, Sarah, Mercy Benzaquen, Damien Cave, Sahil Chinoy, Kenan Davis, Josh Keller, K. K. Rebecca Lai, Jasmine C. Lee, Rochelle Oliver, Haeyoun Park, and Destinée-Charisse Royal. "Black Lives Upended by Policing: The Raw Videos Sparking Outrage." *The New York Times*, July 30, 2015. Accessed June 18, 2022. https://www.nytimes.com/interactive/2017/08/19/us/police-videos-race.html.

American Association for Justice. "Ten Worst Insurance Companies in America: How They Raise Premiums, Deny Claims, and Refuse Insurance to Those Who Need It Most." Accessed December 30, 2022. https://www.decof.com/documents/the-ten-worst-insurance-companies.pdf.

Andrews, Travis M., Wesley Lowery, Michael E. Miller. "Outrage after Video Captures White Baton Rouge Police Officer Fatally Shooting a Black Man." *The Washington Post*, July 7, 2016.

Anft, Michael. "Freddie Gray: The Running Man." Bloomberg CityLab. Last modified November 10, 2015. Accessed August 10, 2022. https://www.bloomberg.com/news/articles/2015-11-10/the-baltimore-life-and-death-of-freddie-gray.

Angelou, Maya. *The Heart of a Woman*. New York: Random House, 1981.

Anonymous. "Happy Endings." *The Saturday Review*, December 21, 1861, 633–635.

Appel, Alfred. *Jazz Modernism: From Ellington and Armstrong to Matisse and Joyce*. New Haven, CT: Yale University Press, 2004.

Apuzzo, Matt, and Sharon LaFraniere. "13 Russians Indicted as Mueller Reveals Effort to Aid Trump Campaign." *The New York Times*, February 16, 2018. Accessed August 6, 2022. https://www.nytimes.com/2018/02/16/us/politics/russians-indicted-mueller-election-interference.html.

"A.R.T. Educational Toolkit." In *Notes from the Field: Doing Time in Education*. New York: American Repertory Theatre, 2016. Accessed December 24, 2022. https://www.yumpu.com/en/document/read/55894530/artists/3.

A.R.T. "Notes from the Field Act II Facilitator Application." Jotform. Accessed August 11, 2022. https://form.jotform.com/62037905835156.

Aslam, Salman. "Instagram by the Numbers: Stats, Demographics & Fun Facts." *Omnicore* (blog). Entry posted February 27, 2022. https://www.omnicoreagency.com/instagram-statistics/.

Atwell, Elaine. "Alexander Hamilton Was Probably Queer." The Dart. Last modified January 30, 2017. Accessed August 6, 2022. https://www.thedart.co/2017/01/30/alexan der-hamilton-was-probably-queer/.

Aucoin, Don. "A Revealing Mashup of the Present, Past in 'An Octoroon.'" *Boston Globe*, February 2, 2016. Accessed June 17, 2022. https://www.bostonglobe.com/arts/thea ter-dance/2016/02/02/revealing-mashup-present-and-past-octoroon/shVXIsOeWLi Rg51XBzEBnM/story.html.

Baker-Gibbs, Ariel. "Where Do We Look? Going to the Theater as a Deaf Person." Editorial. HowlRound Theatre Commons. Last modified April 6, 2014. Accessed August 11, 2022. https://howlround.com/where-do-we-look-going-theater-deaf-person.

Baldwin, James. "Everybody's Protest Novel." In *Notes of a Native Son*, by James Baldwin, 13–23. Boston, MA: Beacon Press, 1984. Previously published in *Notes of a Native Son*. Henry Holt, 1955.

Barrett, Felix. "Punchdrunk About." Punchdrunk. Accessed July 30, 2021. https://www.punchdrunk.com/about-us/.

Baugh, John. *Out of the Mouths of Slaves: African American Language and Educational Malpractice*. Austin: University of Texas Press, 1999.

Becerra, Kevin, Stacy Blake Beard, P. Carl, Robert Duffley, Ryan McKittrick, and James Montaño. *Citizen Read Facilitation Guide*. Edited by Brenna Nicely and Nicole Olusanya. 2018. Boston: ArtsEmerson. Accessed August 11, 2022. https://tickets.arts emerson.org/ArticleMedia/Files/CRFacilitatorGuide.pdf.

Berg, Manfred. *Popular Justice: A History of Lynching in America*. Lanham, MD: Rowman & Littlefield, 2011.

Berman, Eliza. "*Hamilton* Nation: It Conquered Broadway. Next Stop, The World." *Time*, October 10, 2016, 51–54.

Birger, Jon. "'Hamilton' Cast Lectures VP-Elect While Barring Immigrant Actors from Broadway Roles: Pence-Scolding Musical Star Needs a Lesson on AEA Immigrant Policy." *The Observer*, November 25, 2016. Accessed August 6, 2022, https://obser ver.com/2016/11/hamilton-cast-lectures-vp-elect-while-barring-immigrant-actors-from-broadway-roles/.

The Blacks: A Clown Show. Written by Jean Genet. Directed by Christopher McElroen. Classical Theatre of Harlem, New York. March 18, 2003.

Boffone, Trevor. "Ham4Ham: Taking Hamilton to the Streets." Editorial. HowlRound Theatre Commons. Last modified March 18, 2016. Accessed August 7, 2022. https://howlround.com/ham4ham#sthash.qKqZxiPy.dpuf.

Boston University Center for Antiracist Research. Accessed October 5, 2022. https://www.bu.edu/antiracism-center/.

Boucicault, Dion. "International Copyright." *The Musical World*, November 9, 1867, 758.

Boucicault, Dion. "The Octoroon. A Play, in Four Acts." In *Dicks' London Acting Edition of Standard English Plays and Comic Dramas*, 1–18. New York: De Witt House, 1859. Accessed June 17, 2022. https://archive.org/details/octoroonplayinfo00bouciala.

Boucicault, Dion. *Selected Plays of Dion Boucicault*. Compiled and edited by Andrew Parkin. Gerrads Cross, Buckinghamshire: Colin Smythe, 1987.

Boucicault, Dion. "Suum Cuique, The Octoroon." *The Athenaeum*, December 7, 1861, 764–765.

Boucicault, Dion. "To the Editor of the *Times*." *The Times* (London), November 20, 1861, 5.

Bowling Green State University Police Integrity Research Group. *On-Duty Shootings: Police Officers Charged with Murder or Manslaughter, 2005–2019*. By Philip M. Stinson, Sr. and Chloe A. Wentzlof. Research brief no. 9. 2019. Accessed June 18, 2022. https://www.bgsu.edu/content/dam/BGSU/health-and-human-services/document/Criminal-Justice-Program/policeintegritylostresearch/-9-On-Duty-Shootings-Police-Officers-Charged-with-Murder-or-Manslaughter.pdf.

Bradby, David, and Clare Finburgh. *Jean Genet*. New York: Routledge/Taylor & Francis, 2012.

Brantley, Ben. "Review: Theater as Sabotage in the Dazzling 'Fairview.'" *The New York Times*, June 17, 2018. Accessed July 7, 2022. https://www.nytimes.com/2018/06/17/theater/review-theater-as-sabotage-in-the-dazzling-fairview.html.

The Broadway League. *The Demographics of the Broadway Audience 2018–19*. New York: The Broadway League, 2019.

Brooks, Laurie. "Put a Little Boal in Your Talkback." *American Theatre* 22, no. 10 (December 2005): 58–60.

Brooks, Peter. *The Melodramatic Imagination: Balzac, Henry James, Melodrama, and the Mode of Excess*. New Haven, CT: Yale University Press, 1976.

Burkhardt, Brett C. "Who Is in Private Prisons? Demographic Profiles of Prisoners and Workers in American Private Prisons." *International Journal of Law, Crime and Justice* 51 (2017): 24–33.

Butler, Judith. *Gender Trouble: Feminism and the Subversion of Identity*. New York: Routledge, 1999.

Butler, Judith. "Imitation and Gender Insubordination." In *Literary Theory: An Anthology*, edited by Julie Rivkin and Michael Ryan, 722–730. Malden, MA: Blackwell, n.d.

Butsch, Richard. *The Making of American Audiences: From Stage to Television, 1750–1990*. Cambridge: Cambridge University Press, 2000.

C1Dramaturgs. "Melodramatic Poses in Silent Film." *An Octoroon: A Rehearsal and Production Blog of Company One Theatre* (blog). Entry posted January 22, 2016. Accessed September 19, 2016. https://octorooncl.wordpress.com/2016/01/22/melodramatic-poses-in-silent-film/.

C1Dramaturgs. "Tableaux." *An Octoroon: A Rehearsal and Production Blog of Company One Theatre* (blog). Entry posted January 14, 2016. Accessed September 19, 2016. https://octorooncl.wordpress.com/2016/01/14/tableaux/.

Catanese, Brandi Wilkins. *The Problem of the Color[blind]: Racial Transgression and the Politics of Black Performance*. Ann Arbor: University of Michigan Press, 2012.

Catanese, Brandi Wilkins. "Teaching *A Day of Absence* 'at [Your] Own Risk.'" *Theatre Topics* 19, no. 1 (2009): 29–38.

Catanese, Brandi Wilkins. "Transgressing Tradition: Suzan-Lori Parks and Black Performance (as) Theory." In Catanese, *The Problem of the Color[blind]: Racial Transgression and the Politics of Black Performance*, 112–142. Ann Arbor: University of Michigan Press, 2012.

Cave, Damien, and Rochelle Oliver. "The Raw Videos That Have Sparked Outrage over Police Treatment of Blacks." *The New York Times*, July 7, 2016. Accessed August 1, 2016. http://www.nytimes.com/interactive/2015/07/30/us/police-videos-race.html?r=0.

Chaudhuri, Una. "Close Encounters: My *Blacks* Story." *Hunter On-line Theater Review.* Accessed August 9, 2021. http://www.hotreview.org/articles/myblacksstory.htm.

Cheadle, Harry. "It's Time to Tear Down the 'Hamilton' Parody Industrial Complex." *Vice,* July 4, 2016. Accessed August 6, 2022. https://www.vice.com/en_us/article/vdqgqd/trump-hamilton-jokes-are-obvious.

Chemers, Michael Mark. *Ghost Light: An Introductory Handbook for Dramaturgy.* Carbondale, IL: Southern Illinois University, 2010.

Chernow, Ron. *Alexander Hamilton.* New York: Penguin Books, 2004.

Chiles, Katy L. "Blackened Irish and Brownfaced Amerindians: Constructions of American Whiteness in Dion Boucicault's *The Octoroon.*" *Nineteenth Century Theatre and Film* 31, no. 2 (2004): 28–50.

"Citizen Speak: A Conversation with Claudia Rankine at ArtsEmerson, Boston—4 March 2018." Video, 01:24:26. YouTube. Posted by HowlRound Theatre Commons, March 4, 2018. Accessed August 11, 2022. https://www.youtube.com/watch?v=EIoK1qd0QA8.

Clark, Emily. *The Strange History of the American Quadroon: Free Women of Color in the Revolutionary Atlantic World.* Chapel Hill: University of North Carolina Press, 2013.

"Claudia Rankine on Serena Williams at the 2015 L.A. Times Festival of Books." Video, 02:52. YouTube. Posted by PBS Books, December 23, 2015. Accessed August 11, 2022. https://www.youtube.com/watch?v=sQaMat_BzyA.

CNN Wire. "Pence: 'I Wasn't Offended' by Message of 'Hamilton' Cast." Fox 17: West Michigan. Last modified November 20, 2016. Accessed August 6, 2022. https://www.fox17online.com/2016/11/20/pence-i-wasnt-offended-by-message-of-hamilton-cast.

Cohen, Cathy J. "From Combahee to Black Lives Matter: Black Queer Politics, Yesterday, Today and Tomorrow." Lecture presented at The Seventh Annual Eve Kosofsky Sedgwick Memorial Lecture in Gender and Sexuality Studies, Boston University, October 25, 2016. Honoring Eve. Accessed February 5, 2017. https://www.bu.edu/honoringeve/cohen/.

Colman, Nancy. "Why We're Capitalizing Black." *The New York Times,* July 5, 2020. Accessed August 3, 2022. https://www.nytimes.com/2020/07/05/insider/capitalized-black.html.

Company One—Boston Theatre. "An Octoroon." An Octoroon at C1 Theatre. Accessed June 17, 2022. https://companyone.org/production/an-octoroon-play/.

Company One. Call for Applications. "C1 Street Team Program Director," August 4, 2015. Accessed March 17, 2016. https://companyone.org/wp.../05/C1-Street-Team-Program-Director.pdf.

Congress.gov. "Voices from the Days of Slavery: Freed People Tell Their Stories." Library of Congress. Accessed August 18, 2016. https://www.loc.gov/collections/voices-remembering-slavery/about-this-collection/.

Connon, Derek F. "Confused? You Will Be: Genet's *Les Nègres* and the Art of Upsetting the Audience." *French Studies* 50, no. 4 (1996): 425–438.

Cox, Gordon. "Air Raids, Ghosts and Escape Rooms: Inside New York's Immersive Theater Boom." *Variety,* July 27, 2017. Accessed August 9, 2021. http://variety.com/2017/legit/news/immersive-theater-off-broadway-1202506336/.

Cutler, James Elbert. *Lynch-Law: An Investigation into the History of Lynching in the United States.* New York: Negro Universities Press, 1969.

Dale, Alan. " 'Shuffle Along' Full of Pep and Real Melody." In *Reminiscing with Noble Sissle and Eubie Blake,* edited by Robert Kimball and William Bolcom. New York: Cooper Square Press, 1973. Previously published in *New York Journal-American.*

Daly, Rhian. "'Hamilton' Just Broke Another Record." NME. Last modified March 6, 2018. Accessed August 6, 2022. https://www.nme.com/news/hamilton-just-broke-another-record-2255970.

Das, Joanna Dee. "Choreographic Ghosts: Dance and the Revival of *Shuffle Along*." *Dance Research Journal* 51, no. 3 (2019): 84–96.

Davis, Elizabeth Cooper. Interview by the author. Cambridge, MA. May 17, 2018.

Deavere Smith, Anna. "About the Pipeline Project." Anna Deavere Smith Projects. Accessed August 10, 2022. http://www.annadeaveresmith.org.

Deerwester, Jayme. "Social Media Explodes over 'Hamilton'/Trump Duel." *USA Today*, November 19, 2016. Updated November 20, 2016. Accessed August 6, 2022. https://www.usatoday.com/story/life/theater/2016/11/19/social-media-explodes-over-hamilt ontrump-duel/94129798/.

Degen, John A. "How to End 'The Octoroon.'" *Educational Theatre Journal* 27, no. 2 (1975): 170–178.

De Gennaro, Mara. "What Remains of Jean Genet?" *The Yale Journal of Criticism* 16, no. 1 (2003): 190–209.

Department of Justice U.S. Attorney's Office Southern District of West Virginia. "Clay County Woman Sentenced for FEMA Fraud." News release. May 30, 2019. Accessed August 11, 2022. https://www.justice.gov/usao-sdwv/pr/clay-county-woman-senten ced-fema-fraud.

Derr, Holly L. "Branden Jacobs-Jenkins' An Octoroon." Editorial. HowlRound Theatre Commons. Last modified March 26, 2015. Accessed August 18, 2016. https://howlro und.com/branden-jacobs-jenkins-octoroon.

Derrida, Jacques, and Anne Dufourmantelle. "'Step of Hospitality / No Hospitality' [Pas d'hospitalité]." In *On Hospitality*, 75–155. Stanford, CA: Stanford University Press, 2000.

DiAngelo, Robin. *White Fragility: Why It's So Hard for White People to Talk About Racism*. Boston, MA: Beacon Press, 2018.

Dixon-Fyle, Sundiatu, Kevin Dolan, Vivan Hunt, and Sara Prince. *Diversity Wins: How Inclusion Matters*. May 19, 2020. Accessed August 6, 2022. https://www.mckin sey.com/featured-insights/diversity-and-inclusion/diversity-wins-how-inclusion-matters.

Don Lemon Tonight. "Classmate of Arrested South Carolina Teen Speaks Out." Video. CNN. October 27, 2015. Accessed August 10, 2022. https://www.cnn.com/videos/tv/2015/10/28/niya-kenny-interview-south-carolina-school-arrest-video-ctn.cnn.

Douglas, Frederick. "Gavitt's Original Ethiopian Serenaders." In *The Life and Writings of Frederick Douglass*, edited by Philip S. Foner, 141–142. Vol. 1. New York: International Publishers, 1950–75. Previously published in *The North Star*, June 29, 1849.

Douglas, Frederick. "The Hutchinson Family—Hunkerism." In *Uncle Tom's Cabin and American Culture*, edited by Stephan Railton. Charlottesville: The University of Virginia, 2005. Previously published in *The North Star*, October 27, 1848. Accessed August 4, 2022. http://utc.iath.virginia.edu/minstrel/miar03bt.html.

Drury, Jackie Sibblies. *Fairview: A Play*. New York: Theatre Communications Group, 2019.

Duffley, Robert. Interview by the author. American Repertory Theater, Boston, MA. August 15, 2018.

Dyer, Richard. *White: Essays on Race and Culture*. New York: Routledge, 1997.

Ehlers, Nadine. "'Black Is' and 'Black Ain't': Performative Revisions of Racial 'Crisis.'" *Culture, Theory & Critique* 47, no. 2 (2006): 149–163.

Ehlers, Nadine. "Passing Phantasms/Sanctioning Performatives: (Re)Reading White Masculinity in Rhinelander v. Rhinelander." *Studies in Law, Politics, and Society* 27 (2003): 63–91.

Eisen, Lauren-Brooke. "Trump's First Year Has Been the Private Prison Industry's Best." Salon. Last modified January 14, 2018. Accessed August 11, 2022. https://www.salon.com/2018/01/14/trumps-first-year-has-been-the-private-prison-industrys-best/.

Ekotto, Frieda. *Race and Sex across the French Atlantic: The Color of Black in Literary, Philosophical, and Theater Discourse.* Lanham, MD: Lexington Books, 2011.

Elam, Jr., Harry J. "Ritual Theory and Political Theatre: *Quinta Temporada* and *Slave Ship*." *Theatre Journal* 38, no. 4 (1986): 463–472.

Eligon, John. "Yearbook Pages at Northam's Medical School Recorded Both Memories and Prejudices." *The New York Times*, February 5, 2019. Accessed August 4, 2022. https://www.nytimes.com/2019/02/05/us/northam-yearbook.html?module=inline.

Ellis, Anne. "The Art of Community Conversation." *Theatre Topics* 10, no. 2 (2000): 91–100.

Erdman, Harley. "Caught in the 'Eye of the Eternal': Justice, Race, and the Camera, from 'The Octoroon' to Rodney King." *Theatre Journal* 45, no. 3 (1993): 333–348. https://doi.org/10.2307/3208358.

Feldman, Adam. "The Best Immersive Theater in New York Right Now." *Time Out*, March 30, 2022. Accessed June 1, 2022. https://www.timeout.com/newyork/theater/immersive-theater-in-nyc.

Feldman, Kate. "Lindsay Lohan Offers to Play Ariel in Lin-Manuel Miranda's 'Little Mermaid' Remake." *New York Daily News*, February 20, 2017. Accessed August 6, 2022. https://www.nydailynews.com/entertainment/movies/lindsay-lohan-offers-play-ariel-mermaid-remake-article-1.2977041.

Filipovic, Jill. "America's Private Prison System Is a National Disgrace." *The Guardian*, June 13, 2013. Accessed August 11, 2022. https://www.theguardian.com/commentisfree/2013/jun/13/aclu-lawsuit-east-mississippi-correctional-facility.

Fox 13 News. "Mike Pence on Being Booed at 'Hamilton' Showing: 'That's What Freedom Sounds Like.'" Fox 13: Salt Lake City. Last modified November 20, 2016. Accessed August 6, 2022. https://www.fox13now.com/2016/11/20/mike-pence-on-being-booed-at-hamilton-showing-thats-what-freedom-sounds-like/.

Freeman, Joanne B. " 'Can We Get Back to Politics? Please?': Hamilton's Missing Politics in *Hamilton*." In *Historians on Hamilton: How a Blockbuster Musical Is Restaging America's Past*, edited by Renee C. Romano and Claire Bond Potter, 42–57. New Brunswick, NJ: Rutgers University Press, 2018.

"Free Virtual Arts Education Programs." Steppenwolf Theatre. Accessed August 10, 2022. https://www.steppenwolf.org/education/virtual-workshops/.

Fuchs, Elinor. "Theater as Shopping." *Theater* 24, no. 1 (1993): 19–30.

Gans, Andrew. "The U.K. Evening Times Reports That 11-Year-Old Sam Angell, Who Had Successfully Auditioned to Play the Role of Boy Tarzan in the Upcoming Disney Musical *Tarzan*, May Not Be Permitted to Do So Because He Is Not an American Citizen." *Playbill*, October 14, 2005. Accessed August 6, 2022. http://www.playbill.com/article/report-actors-equity-blocks-angell-from-broadway-tarzan-com-128612.

Gardner, Amy, Kate Rabinowitz, and Harry Stevens. "How GOP-Backed Voting Measures Could Create Hurdles for Tens of Millions of Voters." *The Washington Post*, March 11, 2021. Accessed August 6, 2022. https://www.washingtonpost.com/politics/interactive/2021/voting-restrictions-republicans-states/.

Genet, Jean, and Bernard Frechtman. "A Note on Theatre." *Tulane Drama Review* 7, no. 3 (1963): 37–41.

Genet, Jean. *The Blacks: A Clown Show*. Translated by Bernard Frechtman. New York: Grove Press, 1960.

Genet, Jean. *The Declared Enemy: Texts and Interviews*. Edited by Albert Dichy. Translated by Jeff Fort. Stanford, CA: Stanford University Press, 2004.

Genet, Jean. "*Les Nègres: clownerie* [The Blacks: A Clown Show]." In *Théâtre complet*, edited by Michel Corvin and Albert Dichy, 471–569. Paris: Gallimard, 2002.

Genet, Jean. "Preface to *The Blacks*." Translated by Clare Finburgh. In Preface to *The Politics of Jean Genet's Late Theatre: Spaces of Revolution*, by Carl Lavery, 227–234. Manchester: Manchester University Press, 2010.

Genet, Jean. *Prisoner of Love*. Translated by Barbara Bray. Middletown, CT: Wesleyan University Press, 1992.

Genet, Jean. "Violence and Brutality." In *The Declared Enemy: Texts and Interviews*, 171–177. Stanford, CA: Stanford University Press, 2004.

Goodwin, Jeremy D. "Class IN SESSION: With Her Interactive 'Notes from the Field' at the ART, Anna Deavere Smith Explores the School-to-Prison Pipeline." *Boston Globe*, August 19, 2016, G.1.

Gray, Margaret. "Spotlight Shines Brighter on 'Appropriate' Playwright Branden Jacobs-Jenkins." *Los Angeles Times*, September 24, 2015.

Green, Jesse, and Salamishah Tillet. "'Fairview': Watching a Play in Black and White." *The New York Times*, August 7, 2019. Accessed July 7, 2022, https://www.nytimes.com/2019/08/07/theater/fairview-ending-debate.html.

Hamilton, Caroline V. "The Erotic Charisma of Alexander Hamilton." *Journal of American Studies* 45, no. 1 (February 2011): 1–19.

"HAMILTON Ham4Ham 7/27/15 with Lin-Manuel Miranda & Thayne Jasperson." Video. YouTube. Posted by Howard Sherman, July 28, 2015. Accessed August 6, 2022. https://www.youtube.com/watch?v=LcMuuNLsOt4&list=PLb1ayNIj3f8o2-ZVuklNfYxrGPwkKBzjs&index=16.

"HAMILTON Ham4Ham 12/9/15 with Billy Porter." Video. YouTube. Posted by Howard Sherman, December 9, 2015. Accessed August 6, 2022. https://www.youtube.com/watch?v=0W48v1iiMVo&list=PLb1ayNIj3f8o2-ZVuklNfYxrGPwkKBzjs&index=91.

Hamzelou, Jessica. "How Pregnancy Could Affect an Elite Athlete like Serena Williams: Williams Was 8 Weeks Pregnant at the Australian Open. Some Theories Suggest Early Pregnancy Boosts Athletic Performance, but There Isn't Much Evidence." New Scientist. Last modified April 20, 2017. Accessed August 11, 2022. https://www.newscientist.com/article/2128439-how-pregnancy-could-affect-an-elite-athlete-like-serena-williams/.

"#Ham4Ham Complete (?) Chronological July 2015–2016." Video Playlist. YouTube. Posted by Jane, February 4, 2022. Accessed August 7, 2022. https://www.youtube.com/playlist?list=PLb1ayNIj3f8o2-ZVuklNfYxrGPwkKBzjs.

"#Ham4Ham 8/26/15." Video. YouTube. Posted by Gnoeyk, August 26, 2015. Accessed August 6, 2022. https://www.youtube.com/watch?v=duhIIx3WEuY&list=PLb1ayNIj3f8o2-ZVuklNfYxrGPwkKBzjs&index=41.

Hansberry, Lorraine. *The Collected Last Plays: Les Blancs, The Drinking Gourd, What Use Are Flowers*. Edited by Robert Nemiroff. New York: New American Library, 1983.

Hansberry, Lorraine. "Genet, Mailer, and The New Paternalism." *The Village Voice*, June 1, 1961, 10, 14–15.

Hansberry, Lorraine. *Les Blancs: The Collected Last Plays of Lorraine Hansberry.* New York: Random House, 1972.

Harlow, Bob. *The Road to Results: Effective Practices for Building Arts Audiences.* New York: The Wallace Foundation, 2014.

Harmon, Amy. "BIPOC of POC? Equity or Equality? The Debate over Language on the Left." *The New York Times,* November 1, 2021. Accessed July 5, 2020. https://www.nyti mes.com/2021/11/01/us/terminology-language-politics.html.

Harvard University. "Act II at A.R.T." A.R.T. Accessed August 10, 2022. https://americanr epertorytheater.org/about-us/act-ii/.

Harvard University. "In the Body of the World Act II Discussion Series." A.R.T. Accessed August 11, 2022. https://americanrepertorytheater.org/in-the-body-of-the-world-act-ii-discussion-series/.

Harvard University. "Witness Uganda Act III." A.R.T. Accessed August 11, 2022. https://americanrepertorytheater.org/witness-uganda-act-iii/.

Harris, Leslie M. "The Greatest City in the World? Slavery in New York in the Age of Hamilton." In *Historians on Hamilton: How a Blockbuster Musical is Restaging America's Past,* edited by Renee C. Romano and Claire Bond Potter, 71–93. New Brunswick, NJ: Rutgers University Press, 2018.

Hartigan, Patti. "Claudia Rankine Wants Us to Talk—Really Talk—About Race, So She Wrote 'The White Card.'" *Boston Globe,* February 21, 2018. Accessed August 11, 2022. https://www.bostonglobe.com/arts/theater/dance/2018/02/21/claudia-rankine-wants-talk-really-talk-about-race-she-wrote-the-white-card/EudZwjKYmCnC4cb N6MjANN/story.html.

Hartigan, Patti. "In 'Notes,' an Education in Injustice from Anna Deavere Smith." Review of *Notes from the Field: Doing Time in Education,* American Repertory Theatre, Boston, MA. *Boston Globe,* August 26, 2016, G.1. Accessed August 10, 2022. https://www.bost onglobe.com/arts/theater-art/2016/08/26/notes-education-injustice-from-anna-deav ere-smith/XkZjGj1S4bP5gHq6GTohzH/story.html.

Hayes, Chris. "Billboard Cover: 'Hamilton' Creator Lin-Manuel Miranda, Questlove, and Black Thought on the Runaway Broadway Hit, Its Political Relevance and Super-Fan Barack Obama." *Billboard,* July 30, 2015. Accessed August 6, 2022. https://www.billbo ard.com/articles/news/magazine-feature/6648455/hamilton-lin-manuel-miranda-questlove-black-thought-the-roots-chris-hayes-interview.

Heim, Caroline. "'Argue with Us!': Audience Co-creation through Post-Performance Discussions. *New Theatre Quarterly* 28, no. 2 (May 2012): 189–197.

Heim, Caroline. "Audience as Critic." In *Audience as Performer: The Changing Role of Theatre Audiences in the Twenty-First Century.* New York: Routledge, 2016. Vitalsource Ebook.

Heim, Caroline. *Audience as Performer: The Changing Role of Theatre Audiences in the Twenty-First Century.* New York: Routledge, 2016. Vitalsource Ebook.

Heim, Caroline. "Introduction." In *Audience as Performer: The Changing Role of Theatre Audiences in the Twenty-First Century.* New York: Routledge, 2016. Vitalsource Ebook.

Heim, Caroline. "Theatre Etiquette (1880–2000)." In *Audience as Performer: The Changing Role of Theatre Audiences in the Twenty-First Century.* New York: Routledge, 2016. Vitalsource Ebook.

Herrera, Brian Eugenio. "Looking at *Hamilton* from Inside the Broadway Bubble." In *Historians on Hamilton: How a Blockbuster Musical is Restaging America's Past,* edited by Renee C. Romano and Claire Bond Potter, 222–248. New Brunswick, NJ: Rutgers University Press, 2018.

Hershberg, Marc. "Audra McDonald Stars in New Lawsuit." *Forbes*, November 14, 2016. Accessed August 3, 2022. https://www.forbes.com/sites/marchershberg/2016/11/14/audra-mcdonald-stars-in-new-lawsuit/?sh=31ab5e4354c2.

Higashida, Cheryl. "To Be(come) Young, Gay, and Black: Lorraine Hansberry's Existentialist Routes to Anticolonialism." *American Quarterly* 60, no. 4 (2008): 899–924.

Hinderliter, Beth, and Noelle Chaddock. "A Rejection of White Feminist Cisgender Allyship: Centering Intersectionality." In *Antagonizing White Feminism: Intersectionality's Critique of Women's Studies and the Academy*, edited by Noelle Chaddock and Beth Hinderliter, 137–145. Lanham, MD: Lexington Books, 2020.

Historic Tours of America. "Boston Tea Party Ships & Museum, December 16, 1773: A Revolutionary Experience." Boston Tea Party Ships & Museum: #1 Best Patriotic Attraction. Accessed June 1, 2022. https://www.bostonteapartyship.com.

Holland, Jesse J. "Blackface, Explained: Why Ralph Northam, Mark Herring and Others Darkening Their Faces Is Such a Big Deal." *USA Today*, February 6, 2019. Accessed August 4, 2022. https://www.usatoday.com/story/news/nation/2019/02/06/blackface-offensive-why-explaining-ralph-northam-mark-herring/2790475002/.

Holly, Derr L. "Branden Jacobs-Jenkins' An Octoroon." *HowlRound Theatre Commons*, March 26, 2015.

Holmes, Adam. "Disney Has Shut Down Production on The Little Mermaid Remake and More Movies." Cinemablend. Last modified March 13, 2020. Accessed August 6, 2022, https://www.cinemablend.com/news/2492566/disney-has-shut-down-production-on-the-little-mermaid-remake-and-more-movies.

Hutchinson, Bill. "Why Derek Chauvin's Sentencing Is a Rarity for the US Legal System." *ABC News*, June 25, 2021. Accessed June 18, 2022. https://abc7news.com/why-derek-chauvins-sentencing-will-be-rarity-for-the-us-legal-system/10831170/.

Ignatiev, Noel. *How the Irish Became White*. New York: Routledge, 1995.

"I'm Simply Filled with Jazz." Audio, 02:44. YouTube. Posted by Marco Dog, December 18, 2016. Accessed August 6, 2022. https://www.youtube.com/watch?v=C0kZleE4dh8 .

Instagram. "Instagram Today: 500 Million Windows to the World." June 21, 2016.

Ip, George. "Fans of Aaron Burr Find Unlikely Ally in a 'New' Relative." *The Wall Street Journal*, October 5, 2005. Accessed August 6, 2022. https://www.wsj.com/articles/SB112847391696860205.

Jackson, John L., Jr. *Harlemworld: Doing Race and Class in Contemporary America*. New York: Oxford University Press, 2001.

Jackson Jr., John L. "White Harlem: Toward the Performative Limits of Blackness." In *Harlemworld: Doing Race and Class in Contemporary America*, 159–190. New York: Oxford University Press, 2001.

Jacobs-Jenkins, Branden. *An Octoroon*. New York: Dramatists Play Service, 2015.

"Judy Garland & Gene Kelly - Ballin" the Jack." Video, 02:51. YouTube. Posted by Ohujapaksu, June 26, 2013. Accessed August 4, 2022. https://www.youtube.com/watch?v=xWryDF_y yH0.

Ibram X. Kendi. *How to Be an Antiracist*. New York: One World, 2019.

Kennedy, Louise. "Anna Deavere Smith 'Does Time' in the 'School-to-Prison Pipeline.'" WBUR. Last modified August 25, 2016. Accessed August 10, 2022. https://www.wbur.org/news/2016/08/25/anna-deavere-smith-notes-from-field.

Kennedy, Randy. "White Artist's Painting of Emmett Till at Whitney Biennial Draws Protests." *The New York Times*, March 21, 2017. Accessed August 11, 2022. https://www.nytimes.com/2017/03/21/arts/design/painting-of-emmett-till-at-whitney-biennial-draws-protests.html.

Kennard, Jr., James K. "Who Are Our National Poets?" *Knickerbocker* 26, no. 4 (1845): 331–41.

Kennelly, Brian Gordon. "*En dire trop sur les Noirs?* Contextualizing Genet's Preface to *Les Nègres.*" *Journal of Arts and Humanities* 3, no. 11 (2014): 51–66.

Kenny, Kevin. *The American Irish: A History.* New York: Routledge, 2016.

Kerastas, S. K. "Challenges with Radical Hospitality in Act II of Berkeley Rep's Production of *Notes from the Field, Doing Time in Education* The California Chapter by Anna Deveare Smith." Editorial. HowlRound Theatre Commons. Last modified August 28, 2015. Accessed August 11, 2022. https://howlround.com/challenges-radical-hospitality-act-ii-berkeley-reps-production-notes-field-doing-time-education.

Kimball, Robert, and William Bolcom. *Reminiscing with Noble Sissle and Eubie Blake.* New York: Cooper Square Press, 1973.

Koenig, Anne M. "Comparing Prescriptive and Descriptive Gender Stereotypes About Children, Adults, and the Elderly." *Frontiers in Psychology* 9, no. 1086 (June 26, 2018). Accessed August 7, 2022. https://doi.org/10.3389/fpsyg.2018.01086.

Kooy, Dana Van, and Jeffrey N. Cox. "Melodramatic Slaves." *Modern Drama* 55, no. 4 (2012): 459–475.

Krasner, David. *A Beautiful Pageant: African American Theatre, Drama, and Performance in the Harlem Renaissance, 1910–1927.* New York: Palgrave Macmillan, 2002.

Krometis, Damon. "The Dissonance of An Octoroon." Editorial. HowlRound Theatre Commons. Last modified April 17, 2016. Accessed April 18, 2016. https://howlround.com/dissonance-octoroon.

Krometis, Damon. "Dissonant Witnessing: The 'in' and 'above' of *Thou Proud Dream.*" *Theatre Topics* 26, no. 3 (November 2016): 321–331.

Law, Anna O. "Lies, Damned Lies, and Obama's Deportation Statistics." *The Washington Post*, April 21, 2014. Accessed August 6, 2022. https://www.washingtonpost.com/news/monkey-cage/wp/2014/04/21/lies-damned-lies-and-obamas-deportation-statistics/.

Lawrence, Jesse. "'Hamilton' Is Broadway's Most Expensive Show—Ever." The Daily Beast. Last modified May 3, 2016. Accessed August 3, 2022. https://www.thedailybeast.com/hamilton-is-broadways-most-expensive-showever?ref=scroll.

Lee, Jaeah, and A. J. Vicens. "Here Are 13 Killings by Police Captured on Video in the Past Year." *Mother Jones*, May 20, 2015. Accessed July 31, 2016. https://www.motherjones.com/politics/2015/05/police-shootings-caught-on-tape-video/.

Lee, Jesse. "Poetry, Music and Spoken Word." *The White House: President Barack Obama* (blog). Entry posted May 12, 2009. Accessed August 6, 2022. https://obamawhitehouse.archives.gov/blog/2009/05/12/poetry-music-and-spoken-word.

Levenson, Eric. "How Minneapolis Police First Described the Murder of George Floyd and What We Know Now." *CNN*, April 21, 2021. Accessed June 18, 2022. https://www.cnn.com/2021/04/21/us/minneapolis-police-george-floyd-death/index.html.

LighthouseImmersive. "Immersive Frida Kahlo: Her Life. Her Love. Her Art." Immersive Frida Kahlo Boston: The Immersive Art Experience. Accessed August 14, 2022. https://www.immersive-frida.com/boston/.

"Lin-Manuel Miranda, How He Met Jonathan." Video. YouTube. Posted by Luv saengie, July 25, 2015. Accessed August 6, 2022. https://www.youtube.com/watch?v=8aha37ONzL4&list=PLb1ayNIj3f8o2-ZVuklNfYxrGPwkKBzjs&index=1.

"Lin-Manuel Miranda Performs at the White House Poetry Jam: (8 of 8)." Video. YouTube. Posted by The Obama White House, November 2, 2009. Accessed August 6, 2022. https://www.youtube.com/watch?v=WNFf7nMIGnE.

Lott, Eric. *Love & Theft: Blackface Minstrelsy and the American Working Class*. New York: Oxford University Press, 1993.

Lyall, Sarah. "Starring Me! A Surreal Dive into Immersive Theater." Theater. *The New York Times*, January 7, 2016. Accessed May 16, 2016. https://www.nytimes.com/2016/01/08/theater/starring-me-a-surreal-dive-into-immersive-theater.html?partner=IFTTT.

Machon, Josephine. *Immersive Theatres: Intimacy and Immediacy in Contemporary Performance*. Basingstoke: Palgrave Macmillan, 2013.

Mailer, Norman. "Theatre: The Blacks (Cont.)." *The Village Voice*, May 18, 1961, 11, 14–15.

Mann, Samantha, Sarah Ewens, Dominic Shaw, Aldert Vrij, Sharon Leal, and Jackie Hillman. "Lying Eyes: Why Liars Seek Deliberate Eye Contact." *Psychiatry, Psychology, and Law* 20, no. 3 (2013): 452–461.

Mann, Samantha, Aldert Vrij, Sharon Leal, Pär Anders Granhag, Lara Warmelink, and Dave Forrester. "Windows to the Soul? Deliberate Eye Contact as a Cue to Deceit." *Journal of Nonverbal Behavior* 36 (2012): 205–251.

Marbella, Jean. "Beginning of Freddie Gray's Life as Sad as Its End, Court Case Shows." *The Baltimore Sun*, April 23, 2015. Accessed August 10, 2022. https://www.baltimoresun.com/maryland/baltimore-city/bs-md-freddie-gray-lead-paint-20150423-story.html.

Martin, Jonathan, and Alan Blinder. "Second Virginia Democrat Says He Wore Blackface, Throwing Party into Turmoil." *The New York Times*, February 6, 2019. Accessed March 19, 2019. https://www.nytimes.com/2019/02/06/us/politics/virginia-blackface-mark-herring.html?emc=edit_cn_20190207&emc=edit_cn_20190209&nl=politics&nl=politics&nlid=39002302amp&te=1&te=1.

Martin, Michel. "The Pulitzer-Winning Play 'Fairview' Is About Being Watched While Black." NPR. Last modified July 14, 2019. Accessed July 7, 2022. https://www.npr.org/2019/07/14/739057321/the-pulitzer-winning-play-fairview-is-about-being-watched-while-black.

Marx, Bill. "Theater Review: Playing 'The White Card.'" Review of *The White Card*, American Repertory Theater, Boston, MA. The Arts Fuse. Last modified March 7, 2018. Accessed August 11, 2022. https://artsfuse.org/168315/theater-review-playing-the-white-card/.

Matthews, Nadine. "Is #NotMyAriel Just Another Russian Troll of Black Twitter?" Shadow and Act. Last modified July 12, 2019. Accessed August 6, 2022. https://shadowandact.com/is-notmyariel-just-another-russian-troll-of-black-twitter.

McDonald, Soraya Nadia. "On Broadway: There Is No 'Hamilton' without 'Shuffle Along.'" The Undefeated. Last modified June 11, 2016. Accessed August 3, 2022. https://theundefeated.com/features/hamilton-shuffle-along-2016-tonys/.

McGlone, Peggy. "For Third Year in a Row, Trump's Budget Plan Eliminates Arts, Public TV and Library Funding." *The Washington Post*, March 18, 2019. Accessed August 6, 2022, https://www.washingtonpost.com/lifestyle/style/for-third-year-in-a-row-trumps-budget-plan-eliminates-arts-public-tv-and-library-funding/2019/03/18/e946db9a-49a2-11e9-9663-00ac73f49662_story.html.

McNulty, Charles. "How 'Shuffle Along' Director George C. Wolfe Brought Back the 1921 Show That Changed Broadway Forever." *The Los Angeles Times*, April 25, 2016. Accessed August 6, 2022. http://www.latimes.com/entertainment/arts/theater/la-et-cm-george-wolfe-20160425-column.html.

McWhorter, John. "Capitalizing 'Black' Isn't Wrong. But It Isn't That Helpful Either." *The New York Times*, March 4, 2022. Accessed August 3, 2022. https://www.nytimes.com/2022/03/04/opinion/capitalizing-black.html.

Megson, Chris, and Janelle Reinelt. "Performance, Experience, Transformation: What Do Spectators Value in Theatre?" *Journal of Contemporary Drama in English* 4, no. 1 (2016): 227–242.

Meisel, Martin. *Realizations: Narrative, Pictorial, and Theatrical Arts in Nineteenth-Century England*. Princeton, NJ: Princeton University Press, 1983.

Mele, Christopher, and Patrick Healy. "'Hamilton' Had Some Unscripted Lines for Pence. Trump Wasn't Happy." *The New York Times*, November 19, 2016. Accessed March 10, 2019. https://www.nytimes.com/2016/11/19/us/mike-pence-hamilton.html.

Memorandum. "Reducing Our Use of Private Prisons," August 18, 2016. Accessed August 11, 2022. https://www.justice.gov/archives/opa/blog/phasing-out-our-use-private-prisonss.

Merrill, Lisa. "'May She Read Liberty in Your Eyes?' Beecher, Boucicault and the Representation and Display of Antebellum Women's Racially Indeterminate Bodies." *Journal of Dramatic Theory and Criticism* 26, no. 2 (2012): 127–144.

Miller, Stuart. "The Theater Talkback: Why They're Popular, and Why Playwrights Aren't Always Pleased." *The Los Angeles Times*, September 28, 2017. Accessed August 9, 2022. https://www.latimes.com/entertainment/arts/la-ca-cm-theater-talkback-20170928-htmlstory.html.

Minor, Nancy McGown. "Facing the Reservation: The Fourth Crisis Point in Lipan History, 1852–60." In *Turning Adversity to Advantage: A History of the Lipan Apaches of Texas and Northern Mexico, 1700–1900*, 159–163. Lanham, MD: University Press of America, 2009,

Miranda, Lin-Manuel, and Jeremy McCarter. *Hamilton: The Revolution: Being the Complete Libretto of the Broadway Musical, with a True Account of Its Creation, and Concise Remarks on Hip-Hop, the Power of Stories, and the New America*. New York: Grand Central Publishing, 2016.

Mirón, Louis F., and Jonathon Xavier Inda. "Race as a Kind of Speech Act." *Cultural Studies: A Research Annual* 5 (2000): 85–107.

Monteiro, Lyra D. "Race-Conscious Casting and the Erasure of the Black Past in *Hamilton*." In *Historians on Hamilton: How a Blockbuster Musical Is Restaging America's Past*, edited by Renee C. Romano and Claire Bond Potter, 58–70. New Brunswick, NJ: Rutgers University Press, 2018.

Moriah, Kristin. "Shuffle and Repeat: A Review of George C. Wolfe's *Shuffle Along*." *American Quarterly* 69, no. 1 (March 2017): 177–186.

Morris-Reich, Amos. *Race and Photography: Racial Photography as Scientific Evidence, 1876–1980*. Chicago: University of Chicago Press, 2016.

Musiker, Cy. "Anna Deavere Smith Fights School-to-Prison Pipeline with New Play." KQED. Last modified July 19, 2015. Accessed August 10, 2022. https://www.kqed.org/news/10603541/anna-deaveare-smith-fights-the-school-to-prison-pipeline-with-theater.

Musser, Charles. "Why Did Negroes Love Al Jolson and *The Jazz Singer*?: Melodrama, Blackface and Cosmopolitan Theatrical Culture." *Film History: An International Journal* 23, no. 2 (2011): 196–222.

Natanson, Hannah. "Aaron Burr—Villain of 'Hamilton'—Had a Secret Family of Color, New Research Shows." *The Washington Post*, August 24, 2019. Accessed August 6, 2022.

https://www.washingtonpost.com/history/2019/08/24/aaron-burr-villain-hamilton-had-secret-family-color-new-research-shows/.

Nathan, George Jean. "The Lesson of Another Failure." In *Reminiscing with Noble Sissle and Eubie Blake*, by Robert Kimball and William Bolcom. New York: Cooper Square Press, 1973. Previously published in *New York Journal-American*, May 25, 1952.

National Endowment for the Arts. *A Decade of Arts Engagement: Findings from the Survey of Public Participation in the Arts, 2002–2012*. Research report no. 58. January 2015. Accessed August 10, 2022. https://www.arts.gov/sites/default/files/2012-sppa-feb2015.pdff.

National Endowment for the Arts. *U.S. Patterns of Arts Participation: A Full Report from the 2017 Survey of Public Participation in the Arts*. December 2019. Accessed August 10, 2022. https://www.arts.gov/impact/research/publications/us-patterns-arts-partic ipation-full-report-2017-survey-public-participation-arts.

"The Negro Writer in America: A Symposium." *Negro Digest*, June 1963, 54–63.

Neklason, Annika. "Blackface Was Never Harmless." *The Atlantic*, February 16, 2019. Accessed August 4, 2022. https://www.theatlantic.com/entertainment/archive/2019/ 02/legacy-blackface-ralph-northam-didnt-understand/582733/.

Nelson, Alfred L. Nelson L., Gilbert B. Cross, and Joseph Donohue, eds. "The Adelphi Theatre Calendar." The Adelphia Theatre Project: Graphics, Image for The Octoroon; or, Life in Louisiana. Accessed June 17, 2022. https://www.umass.edu/AdelphiThea treCalendar/img038f.htm.

Nessler, Laura. "Staging Truth to Invite Dialogue: Elements of Group Work in Documentary Theatre Talkbacks." *Social Work with Groups* 41, no. 1–2 (2018): 34–48.

Nevin, Robert P. "Stephen C. Foster and Negro Minstrelsy." *Atlantic Monthly* 20, no. 121 (1867): 608–616.

Newman, Brooke. "The White Nostalgia Fueling the 'Little Mermaid' Backlash." *The Washington Post*, July 9, 2019. Accessed August 6, 2022. https://www.washingtonpost. com/outlook/2019/07/09/white-nostalgia-fueling-little-mermaid-backlash/.

The New York Times. "Dion Boucicault Dead; Pneumonia Suddenly Ends a Wonderful Career. Career of the Most Conspicuous English Dramatist of the Nineteenth Century—His Plays." September 19, 1890, 5.

The New York Times. "The Octoroon." December 15, 1859, 4.

The New York Times. " 'Shuffle Along' Premiere: Negro Production Opens at Sixty Third Street." May 23, 1921, 20.

Notes from the Field: Doing Time in Education. New York: American Repertory Theatre, 2016.

Nowatzki, Robert. "Paddy Jumps Jim Crow: Irish-Americans and Blackface Minstrelsy." *Éire-Ireland* 41, no. 3&4 (2006): 162–184.

Nowatzki, Robert. *Representing African Americans in Transatlantic Abolitionism and Blackface Minstrelsy*. Baton Rouge: Louisiana State University, 2010.

NPR Staff. "Trump's 2016 Victory Speech, Annotated 1 Year Later." NPR. Last modified November 7, 2017. Accessed August 6, 2022. https://www.npr.org/2017/11/07/561597 910/trumps-2016-victory-speech-annotated-1-year-later.

An Octoroon. Directed by Summer L. Williams. Written by Branden Jacobs-Jenkins. Produced by Company One and ArtsEmerson. Paramount Center, Boston. January 29-February 27, 2016.

Odendahl-James, Jules. "A History of U.S. Documentary Theater in Three Stages." *American Theatre*, August 22, 2017. Accessed August 10, 2022. https://www.american theatre.org/2017/08/22/a-history-of-u-s-documentary-theatre-in-three-stages/.

Ogden, A. N. *Reports of Cases Argued and Determined in the Supreme Court of Louisiana, Vol. 14: For the Year 1859*. New Orleans: Office of the Price Current, 1860.

Ostrowski, Ramona. Interview by the author. Boston, MA. August 25, 2016.

Parkin, Andrew. "Introduction." Introduction to *Selected Plays of Dion Boucicault*, by Dion Boucicault, 7–22. Gerrards Cross, Buckinghamshire: Colin Smythe, 1987.

Paulson, Michael. "Decision to Close 'Shuffle Along' Is Debated Along Broadway." *The New York Times*, June 24, 2016. Accessed August 3, 2022. https://www.nytimes.com/2016/06/25/theater/decision-to-close-shuffle-along-is-debated-along-broadway.html.

Paulson, Michael. "'Hamilton Leads a Record-Breaking Holiday Week on Broadway." *The New York Times*, January 2, 2019. Accessed August 6, 2022, https://www.nytimes.com/2019/01/02/theater/broadway-grosses-hamilton-record.html.

Paulson, Michael. "'Hamilton' Producers Will Change Job Posting, but Not Commitment to Diverse Casting." *The New York Times*, March 30, 2016. Accessed August 6, 2022. https://www.nytimes.com/2016/03/31/arts/union-criticizes-hamilton-casting-call-seeking-nonwhite-actors.html.

Paulson, Michael. "'Shuffle Along' and Insurer Drop Pregnancy-Prompted Lawsuit." *The New York Times*, October 21, 2020. Accessed August 3, 2022. https://www.nytimes.com/2020/10/21/theater/shuffle-along-audra-mcdonald-insurer-pregnancy-lawsuit.htmll.

Paulson, Michael. "'Shuffle Along' Decides It Can't Go on Without Audra McDonald." *The New York Times*, June 23, 2016. Accessed August 3, 2022. https://www.nytimes.com/2016/06/24/theater/shuffle-along-decides-it-cant-go-on-without-audra-mcdonald.html.

Paulson, Michael, and David Gelles. "'Hamilton' Inc.: The Path to a Billion-Dollar Broadway Show." *The New York Times*, June 8, 2016. Accessed August 3, 2022. https://www.nytimes.com/2016/06/12/theater/hamilton-inc-the-path-to-a-billion-dollar-show.html.

"The Pence Agenda for the 107th Congress: A Guide to Renewing the American Dream." Mike Pence for Congress. Accessed August 6, 2022. http://web.archive.org/web/20010519165033fw_/http://cybertext.net/pence/issues.htmll.

Petrella, Christopher. "The Color of Corporate Corrections, Part II: Contractual Exemptions and the Overrepresentation of People of Color in Private Prisons." *Radical Criminology* 3 (2014): 81–100.

Pipeline Project. "Act II Manager for Anna Deavere Smiths' Pipeline Project and Play." JobRoller. Last modified June 12, 2016. Accessed August 11, 2022. https://gofetchjobs.com/jobroller/jobs/act-ii-manager-for-anna-deavere-smiths-pipeline-project-and-play/.

Potter, Claire Bond. "'Safe in the Nation We've Made': Staging *Hamilton* on Social Media." In *Historians on Hamilton: How a Blockbuster Musical is Restaging America's Past*, edited by Renee C. Romano and Claire Bond Potter, 324–350. New Brunswick, NJ: Rutgers University Press, 2018.

Press Association. "Shamil Tarpischev Forced to Apologise after Calling Williams Sisters 'Brothers.'" *The Guardian*, October 21, 2014. Accessed August 11, 2022. https://www.theguardian.com/sport/2014/oct/21/shamil-tarpischev-forced-apology-williams-sisters-slur.

Preston, Carrie J. *Modernism's Mythic Pose: Gender, Genre, Solo Performance*. New York: Oxford University Press, 2011.

"Princess's Theatre - Posters - Theatre posters, 1870–1900." National Library of Scotland. Accessed June 17, 2022. https://digital.nls.uk/theatre-posters-1870-1900/archive/74561470#?c=0&m=0&s=0&cv=2&xywh=-1243%2C-185%2C4985%2C3695.

Prokop, Andrew. "Trump Fanned a Conspiracy about Obama's Birthplace for Years. Now He Pretends Clinton Started It." Vox. Last modified September 16, 2016. Accessed September 16, 2019. https://www.vox.com/2016/9/16/12938066/donald-trump-obama-birth-certificate-birther.

Pugh, Meghan. *America Dancing: From the Cakewalk to the Moonwalk*. New Haven, CT: Yale University Press, 2015.

The Pulitzer Prizes—Columbia University. "The 2021 Pulitzer Prize Winner in Special Citations and Awards: Darnella Frazier." The Pulitzer Prizes. Accessed June 18, 2022. https://www.pulitzer.org/winners/darnella-frazier.

Punchdrunk Global. "Punchdrunk About." Punchdrunk International. Accessed July 30, 2021. https://www.punchdrunk.com/about-us/.

Rankine, Claudia. *Citizen: An American Lyric*. Minneapolis: Graywolf Press, 2014.

Rankine, Claudia. *The White Card: A Play in One Act*. Minneapolis: Graywolf Press, 2019.

Rao, Mallika. "'The Dutchman' Solves the Biggest Problem with Immersive Theater." The Huffington Post. Last modified November 27, 2013. Accessed May 16, 2016. https://www.huffpost.com/entry/dutchman-immersive-theater_n_4340779.

Reid, Kerry. "Talkback Backtalk: Up for a Post-Show Discussion? Four A.D.s Explain Why They Are—And You Just Might Be Too." *American Theatre*, September 25, 2018. Accessed August 10, 2022. https://www.americantheatre.org/2018/09/25/talkback-backtalk/.

Rickford, John R., and Russell J. Rickford. *Spoken Soul: The Story of Black English*. Hoboken, NJ: Wiley Press, 2000.

Riley, Charles A. *Free as Gods: How the Jazz Age Reinvented Modernism*. Lebanon, NH: University Press of New England, 2017.

Roach, Joseph. *Cities of the Dead: Circum-Atlantic Performance*. New York: Columbia University Press, 1996.

Robinson, Christopher. Interview by the author. Boston University, April 18, 2018.

Rodriguez, Matthew. "HIV Needs to Be Part of the Conversation When We Talk about Mike Pence and 'Hamilton.'" Mic. Last modified November 22, 2016. Accessed August 6, 2022. https://www.mic.com/articles/160080/hiv-needs-to-be-a-part-of-the-conversation-when-we-talk-about-mike-pence-and-hamilton.

Romano Renee C., and Claire Bond Potter. "Introduction: History Is Happening in Manhattan." Introduction to *Historians on Hamilton: How a Blockbuster Musical Is Restaging America's Past*, edited by Renee C. Romano and Claire Bond Potter, 1–14. New Brunswick, NJ: Rutgers University Press, 2018.

Rought, Karen. "'Hamilton's First Digital Ham4Ham Show Features Legendary Alan Menken." Hypable. Last modified January 17, 2016. Accessed August 6, 2022. https://www.hypable.com/hamilton-digital-ham4ham-alan-menken/.

Sandman, Jenny. "A *CurtainUp* Review, *The Blacks: A Clown Show*." Review of *The Blacks: A Clown Show*, Classical Theatre of Harlem, New York. The Internet Theater Magazine of Reviews, Features, Annotated Listings. Accessed August 9, 2021. http://www.curtainup.com/blacks.html.

Saravis, Marissa. "Shuffle Along Down to the Courthouse: Broadway Producers Argue Actor's Pregnancy is an Accident Worth $14 Million." *Fordham: Intellectual Property, Media & Entertainment Law Journal*, November 19, 2018. Accessed August 3, 2022.

http://www.fordhamiplj.org/2018/11/19/shuffle-along-down-to-the-courthouse-broadway-producers-argue-actors-pregnancy-is-an-accident-worth-14-million/.

Sartre, Jean-Paul. *Saint Genet: Actor and Martyr*. Translated by Bernard Frechtman. New York: Pantheon Books, 1963.

Savran, David. *Highbrow/Lowdown: Theater, Jazz, and the Making of the New Middle Class*. Ann Arbor: University of Michigan Press, 2009.

Schafer, Jack. "How to Detect a Liar." Psychology Today. Last modified March 11, 2014. Accessed August 10, 2022. https://www.psychologytoday.com/us/blog/let-their-words-do-the-talking/201403/how-detect-liar.

Sedgman, Kirsty. "Audience Experience in an Anti-Expert Age: A Survey of Theatre Audience Research." *Theatre Research International* 42, no. 3 (2018): 307–322.

Seymour, Lee. "Thanksgiving Breaks Many Broadway Records, 'Hamilton' Takes Highest Gross in History." *Forbes*, November 28, 2016. Accessed March 10, 2019. https://www.forbes.com/sites/leeseymour/2016/11/28/thanksgiving-breaks-all-broadway-records-hamilton-takes-highest-gross-in-history/?sh=480612995b2a.

Shadow and Act Staff. "About Us." Shadow and Act. Last modified April 13, 2011. Accessed August 6, 2022. https://shadowandact.com/about-us.

Sherman, Howard. "The Generous Audience Engagement of Lin-Manuel Miranda." Howard Sherman. Last modified August 5, 2015. Accessed August 7, 2022. http://hesherman.com/2015/08/05/the-generous-audience-engagement-of-lin-manuel-miranda/.

Shindle, Kate. " 'Hamilton' Casting Controversy Spotlights the Importance of Diversity." *Variety*, April 5, 2016. Accessed August 6, 2022. https://variety.com/2016/legit/opinion/hamilton-diversity-casting-actors-equity-guest-column-1201745244/.

Sissle, Noble, Eubie Blake, Flournoy E. Miller, and Aubrey Lyles. *Shuffle Along*. Edited by Lyn Schenbeck and Lawrence Schenbeck. Music of the United States of America; Recent Researches in American Music 29; 85. Middleton, WI: A-R Editions, 2018.

"Sister Kings Ham4Ham." Video. YouTube. Posted by Oge Agulué, October 24, 2015. Accessed August 6, 2022. https://www.youtube.com/watch?v=TX2fuGIRY5Q.

Smith, Anna Deavere. "Introduction." In *Notes from the Field*, xv–xx. New York: Anchor Books, 2019.

Smith, Anna Deavere. *Notes From the Field*. New York: Anchor Books, 2019.

Smith, Anthony. "Donald Trump's Star of David Hillary Clinton Meme Was Created by White Supremacists." Mic. Last modified July 3, 2016. Accessed September 16, 2019. https://www.mic.com/articles/147711/donald-trump-s-star-of-david-hillary-clinton-meme-was-created-by-white-supremacists.

Smith, Shawn Michelle. *Photography on the Color Line: W.E.B. Dubois, Race and Visual Culture*. Durham, NC: Duke University Press, 2004.

Soloski, Alexis. "Branden Jacobs-Jenkins Tries to Revive *The Octoroon*." *The Village Voice*, June 15, 2010. Accessed December 29, 2022. https://www.villagevoice.com/2010/06/15/branden-jacobs-jenkins-tries-to-revive-the-octoroon/.

"Sprig of Shillelagh; Untitled." MP3 audio, 02:55. *Irish Traditional Music Archive*. Posted by Peter Wyper, 2018. Accessed August 4, 2022. https://www.itma.ie/digital-library/sound/cid-232155.

Stearns, Jean, and Marshall Stearns. *Jazz Dance: The Story of American Vernacular Dance*. New York: Da Capo Press: 1968, 1994.

Steven, Matt. "Starbucks C.E.O. Apologizes After Arrests of 2 Black Men." *The New York Times*, April 15, 2018. Accessed August 11, 2022. https://www.nytimes.com/2018/04/15/us/starbucks-philadelphia-black-men-arrest.html.

Sturm, Susan. "Activating Systemic Change Toward Full Participation: The Pivotal Role of Mission-Driven Institutional Intermediaries." *Saint Louis Law Journal* 54 (2010): 1117–1137.

Sturm, Susan, Time Eatman, John Saltmarch, and Adam Bush. *Full Participation: Building the Architecture for Diversity and Community Engagement in Higher Education.* 2011. Accessed August 6, 2022. https://surface.syr.edu/cgi/viewcontent.cgi?article=1001&context=ia

Sullivan, John Jeremiah. "'Shuffle Along' and the Lost History of Black Performance in America." *The New York Times Magazine*, March 24, 2016. Accessed August 3, 2022. https://www.nytimes.com/2016/03/27/magazine/shuffle-along-and-the-painful-hist ory-of-black-performance-in-america.html.

Swaine, Jon, Oliver Laughland, and Jana Kasperkevic. "US Justice Department Announced It Will End Use of Private Prisons." *The Guardian*, August 18, 2018. Accessed August 11, 2022. https://www.theguardian.com/us-news/2016/aug/18/us-government-priv ate-prisons-use-justice-department.

Swaine, Jon. "Twitter Admits Far More Russian Bots Posted on Election Than It Had Disclosed." *The Guardian*, January 19, 2018. Accessed August 6, 2022. https://www. theguardian.com/technology/2018/jan/19/twitter-admits-far-more-russian-bots-pos ted-on-election-than-it-had-disclosed.

Thompson, David S. "Shuffling Roles: Alterations and Audiences in *Shuffle Along*." In *Theatre Symposium, Vol. 20: Gods and Groundlings*, 97–108. Tuscaloosa: University of Alabama Press, 2012.

Thrasher, Steven W. "Mike Pence Is Still to Blame for an HIV Outbreak in Indiana—but for new Reasons," *The Nation*, October 4, 2018. Accessed August 6, 2022. https://www. thenation.com/article/archive/mike-pence-is-still-to-blame-for-an-hiv-outbreak-in-indiana-but-for-new-reasons/.

Tran, Diep. "Jackie Sibblies Drury: Thinking and Feeling." *American Theatre*, May 29, 2019. Accessed July 7, 2022. https://www.americantheatre.org/2019/05/29/jackie-sibbl ies-drury-thinking-and-feeling/.

Trump, Donald (@realDonaldTrump). "Our wonderful future V.P. Mike Pence was ha-rassed last night at the theater by the cast of Hamilton, cameras blazing. This should not happen!" Twitter. November 19, 2016, 8:48 a.m.

Trump, Donald (@realDonaldTrump). "The Theater must always be a safe and special place. The cast of Hamilton was very rude last night to a very good man, Mike Pence. Apologize!" Twitter. November 19, 2016, 8:56 a.m.

Ulaby, Neda. "The 'Bechdel Rule,' Defining Pop-Culture Character." NPR. Last modified September 2, 2008. Accessed August 6, 2022. https://www.npr.org/templates/story/ story.php?storyId=94202522?storyId=94202522.

U.S. Department of Education Institute of Education Sciences: National Center for Education Statistics. *Racial/Ethnic Enrollment in Public Schools.* 2022. Accessed August 10, 2022. https://nces.ed.gov/programs/coe/indicator/cge#suggested-citation.

U.S. Department of Justice. "Phasing Out Our Use of Private Prisons." The United States Department of Justice Archives. Last modified August 18, 2016. Accessed August 11, 2022. https://www.justice.gov/archives/opa/blog/phasing-out-our-use-private-prisonss.

Valencia, Brian D. "Musical of the Month: Shuffle Along." *NYPL Blog*. Entry posted February 10, 2012. Accessed August 4, 2022. https://www.nypl.org/blog/2012/02/10/ musical-month-shuffle-along.

Village Voice Contributor. "Disgruntled Cast Member Issues Invite to P.S.122's Troubled Octoroon." *The Village Voice*, June 18, 2010. Accessed June 17, 2022. https://www.

Villagevoice.com/2010/06/18/disgruntled-cast-member-issues-invite-to-p-s-122s-troubled-octoroon/.

Walmsley, Ben. "Why People Go to the Theatre: A Qualitative Study of Audience Motivation." *Journal of Customer Behaviour* 10, no. 4 (2011): 335–351.

Waltz, Robert B., ed. "Old Black Joe." The Minnesota Heritage Songbook. Accessed August 6, 2022. https://mnheritagesongbook.net/the-songs/addition-song-without-recordings/old-black-joe/.

Wardle, Claire. "How Did News Organisations Handle the Philando Castile Facebook Live Video?" *First Draft*, August 6, 2016. Accessed June 25, 2018. https://medium.com/1st-draft/how-did-news-organisations-handle-the-philando-castile-facebook-live-video-549ff9a1da36.

Warner, Lacy. "An Octoroon: Reflections on a Play about Race, Performance, and the Performance of Race." *Brooklyn*, March 30, 2015. Accessed June 17, 2022. http://www.bkmag.Com/2015/03/30/an-octoroon-reflections-on-a-play-about-race-performance-and-the-performance-of-race/.

Webb, Cy Ashley. "Policy Pivots along 'School-to-Prison-Pipeline' with Anna Deavere Smith." StarkInsider. Last modified July 21, 2015. Accessed August 10, 2022. https://www.starkinsider.com/2015/07/anna-deavere-smith-notes-from-field-berkeley-review.html.

Weber, Bruce. "Race Peers Out of Masks." Review of *The Blacks: A Clown Show. The New York Times*, February 13, 2003. Accessed August 9, 2021. http://www.nytimes.com/2003/02/13/arts/theater/13CLOW.html .

"We See You, White American Theater." Statement—We See You W.A.T. Last modified June 8, 2020. Accessed July 20, 2022. https://www.weseeyouwat.com/statement.

White, Edmund. *Genet: A Biography*. New York: Knopf, 1993.

Wickman, Forrest. "The Show Is Nonstop: Ham4Ham, the Joyous, Free Sidewalk Performances outside *Hamilton* That Are Stoking the Passions of a New Generation of Theater Lovers." *Slate*, November 24, 2015. Accessed August 6, 2022. https://slate.com/culture/2015/11/ham4ham-lin-manuel-miranda-and-the-cast-of-hamilton-reward-ticket-lottery-entrants-with-free-shows.html.

Winsor, Morgan. "Woman Who Called Michelle Obama an 'Ape in Heels' Pleads Guilty to FEMA fraud." ABC News. Last modified February 18, 2019. Accessed August 11, 2022. https://abcnews.go.com/US/woman-called-michelle-obama-ape-heels-pleads-guilty/story?id=61142401.

Wischenbart, Rüdiger, and Layla Shahid Barrada. "Interview with Rüdiger Wischenbart and Layla Shahid Barrada." By Jean Genet. In *The Declared Enemy: Texts and Interviews*, by Jean Genet, 232–256. Stanford, CA: Stanford University Press, 2004.

Wltx. "No Criminal Charges to Be Filed in Student Dragging at Spring Valley." News19. Last modified September 2, 2016. Accessed August 10, 2022. https://www.wltx.com/article/news/local/no-criminal-charges-to-be-filed-in-student-dragging-at-spring-valley/101-312983906.

Wolfram, Walt, and Benjamin Torbert. "When Worlds Collide: The Linguistic Legacy of the African Slave Trade." PBS. Accessed August 18, 2016. https://www.pbs.org/speak/seatosea/americanvarieties/AAVE/worldscollide/#worlds.

Wolfram, Walt, and Erik R. Thomas. *The Development of African American English*. Malden, MA: Blackwell, 2002.

Wolfram, Walt. "The Sociolinguistic Construction of African American Language." In *The Oxford Handbook on African American Language*, edited by Sonja L. Lanehart, 338–352. Oxford: Oxford University Press, 2015.

Woll, Allen. *Black Musical Theatre from Coontown to Dreamgirls*. Baton Rouge: Louisiana State University Press: 1989.

Workneh, Lilly. "This Striking Image of a Black Man Hanging a Klansman Shows a Different Side of America's Racist History." Editorial. HuffPost. Last modified May 19, 2015. Accessed August 18, 2017. https://www.huffpost.com/entry/tyler-shields-lynching-photo_n_7310806.html.

Wright, Richard. *Native Son and How 'Bigger' Was Born*. New York: HarperCollins, 1993.

Yelp. "Best Interactive Theater in Boston, Massachusetts." Yelp. Accessed June 1, 2022. https://www.yelp.com/search?find_desc=interactive+theater&find_loc=Boston%2C+MA

Young, Harvey. *Embodying Black Experience: Stillness, Critical Memory, and the Black Body*. Ann Arbor: University of Michigan Press, 2010.

Young, Harvey. "Introduction: Black Plays." *Theatre Topics* 19, no. 1 (2009): xiii–xviii.

Young, Jean. "The Re-Objectification and Re-Commodification of Saartjie Baartman in Suzan-Lori Parks's *Venus*." *African American Review* 31, no. 4 (1997): 699–708.

Index

Printed in the USA/Agawam, MA
August 14, 2024

870976.006